Developmental Play Therapy in Clinical Social Work

Elizabeth M. Timberlake, D.S.W.
The Catholic University of America

Marika Moore Cutler, M.S.W.

Allyn and Bacon

Boston ▪ London ▪ Toronto ▪ Sydney ▪ Tokyo ▪ Singapore

Editor in Chief, Social Sciences: *Karen Hanson*
Editorial Assistant: *Alyssa Pratt*
Marketing Manager: *Jackie Aaron*
Editorial-Production Administrator: *Annette Joseph*
Editorial-Production Coordinator: *Holly Crawford*
Editorial-Production Service: *Modern Graphics*
Composition Buyer: *Linda Cox*
Electronic Composition and Art: *Modern Graphics*
Manufacturing Buyer: *Julie McNeill*
Cover Administrator: *Brian Gogolin*
Cover Designer: *Jenny Hart*

Between the time Website information is gathered and then published, it is not unusual for some sites to have closed. Also, the transcription of URLs can result in unintended typographical errors. The publisher would appreciate notification where these occur so that they may be corrected in subsequent editions. Thank you.

Library of Congress Cataloging-in-Publication Data
Timberlake, Elizabeth M.
    Developmental play therapy in clinical social work / Elizabeth M. Timberlake, Marika Moore Cutler.
        p. cm.
    Includes bibliographical references and index.
    ISBN 0-205-29749-8 (casebound)
    1. Child welfare. 2. Play therapy. 3. Psychiatric social work. 4. Social work with children. I. Cutler, Marika Moore. II. Title.

HV713.T54 2000
618.92'891653—dc21

00-041620

Printed in the United States of America
10 9 8 7 6 5 4 3 2 1   FLD   05 04 03 02 01 00

To the children and their families

CONTENTS

7 Child Interviews in Biopsychosocial Assessment and Planning   167

PART THREE   Alternative Model   193

8 Integrating Cognitive-Behavioral Theory with Play Therapy: An Alternative Model   195

PART FOUR   Clinical Application   215

9 Attachment Problems   217

PREFACE

In the world today, numerous children experience the pain of extraordinary external stress and great internal distress. Some are resilient and manage to cope with life's challenges. Others are more vulnerable and have difficulty dealing with a chaotic external world filled with family and neighborhood violence, school terrorism and hate crimes, drug and alcohol abuse, parental divorce and desertion, or poverty and homelessness. Still others, an estimated eight million (Estrada, 1997), are vulnerable to the marked internal distress associated with severe emotional and behavioral developmental disturbances and mental disorders. These children experience their internal worlds as full of pain and suffering, anxiety and rage, despair and hopelessness. Their parents experience distress at not knowing how to care for and help them.

Wherever and however these children manifest clinical symptoms and convey their pain, social workers are most often the frontline service professionals who see them. Yet to assess their problems and intervene successfully, their social workers must comprehend the symbolic language of childhood—play. They must know what children mean when they are trying to (1) convey that they are overwhelmed by stress and crying out for help; (2) reveal that they are developmentally compromised in their ability to cope with the inner mental world of self and imagination and the external world of relationships and reality; and (3) evidence their struggle with the interpersonal, cognitive, emotional, and behavioral challenges of mental disorders. All too often, however, professionals find children's play metaphors a confusing and mysterious language that complicates rather than facilitates the content and process of therapeutic communication. Therefore, *Developmental Play Therapy in Clinical Social Work* is directed to both experienced and novice social work clinicians who treat the increasingly disturbed children brought to their attention in mental health clinics, social service agencies, schools, health care settings, and private practice offices.

Drawing on classic and current materials and employing a psychodynamic developmental perspective, the authors have built a clinical social work model of developmental play therapy and concurrent parent work. This model reflects the biopsychosocial development of the child, developmental disturbances, and mental disorders, and the ways in which play in the context of the therapeutic alliance makes use of developmental processes to stimulate change and growth. The principles, processes, and techniques of such developmental play are drawn primarily from the works of psychodynamic clinical theorists (e.g., A. Freud, Erikson, Fraiberg, Fonagy, and Winnicott) and the primary authors' training and clinical social work practice experience with seriously disturbed children and their families. The book's focal psychodynamic developmental approach is supplemented by material depicting cognitive and social learning approaches to play therapy. These latter approaches draw on the work of selected cognitive and behavioral theorists and clinicians (e.g., Kendall and Knell).

Throughout, the authors demonstrate how theoretically framed models of therapy are modified in the real world of everyday practice to fit the presenting problems and treatment needs of elementary school–age children from different clinical populations, various multicultural backgrounds, and diverse socioeconomic circumstances. Illustrative case vignettes and longer case studies are interspersed liberally throughout the book to bring the conceptual framework alive and illuminate treatment concepts, principles, and process. Although the clinical material represents real therapy carried out by real clinical social workers, each case has been carefully disguised through factual changes, picture and story disguise, and process reconstruction, as necessary, to protect client confidentiality. The essence, heart, and soul of the therapy, however, have been faithfully maintained.

The clinical focus of the book is on the increasingly disturbed children referred to social workers today; specifically, those children evidencing serious behavioral, emotional, cognitive, and somatic manifestations of developmental disturbance and mental disorders. In the therapeutic narratives of the case examples, the authors pay attention to the difficult realities of clinical social work practice with very troubled children, as well as to the ideal prototypical world in which play therapy proceeds smoothly along a predictable path. Throughout, the authors convey the dynamic synergism and power of symbolic metaphor, play process, and therapeutic alliance in facilitating: exploration of difficulties in the child's real and make-believe worlds; coping with developmental disturbance, mental disorders, and external stressors; and problem-solving, behavior change, healing, and growth. The developmental play therapy work with the children is clearly set in the essential context of concurrent parent work and consultation with teachers and community service providers.

The first part of the book provides an overview of the focal model and the theoretical underpinnings of developmental play therapy in clinical social work. Attention is given to the therapeutic alliance and the developmental change process, play language and metaphor, treatment stages, and concurrent parent work. Part Two describes a conceptual framework for parent and child interviews in biopsychosocial assessment and treatment planning. Part Three presents cognitive and behavioral models of play therapy and concurrent parent and community work.

Part Four presents individualized application of theory to practice with attachment problems, learning and attention problems, anxiety disorders, and post-traumatic stress disorders. The final part of the book addresses issues of practice accountability and responsibility, with attention to assessing both therapeutic process and outcome.

ACKNOWLEDGMENTS

The authors are particularly indebted to Dr. Maria O'Neil McMahon, an experienced social work clinician and educator whose idea it was to write a social work book about play therapy. Unfortunately, her untimely illness and death precluded her collaboration in its evolution. We gratefully acknowledge the significant contribution of Martha W. Chescheir, Ph.D., who generously reviewed the conceptual framework for developmental play therapy and concurrent parent work. Her abiding assistance, thoughtful suggestions, and friendship are treasured. The authors thank E. James Anthony, M.D., for his helpful comments about development in general, and for his critique and supervision of the case in Chapter 11 in particular.

Developmental Play Therapy in Clinical Social Work would not be complete without the theoretical and case material of its contributing authors. We especially appreciate the contributions of Karen Block, Martha Chescheir, Barbara Early, Michaela Farber, Mary Owen, Christine Sabatino, and Jennifer Weaver. We would like to thank the following reviewers for their pointed and meaningful comments: Jerry Brandell, Wayne State University; I. Sue Jackson, Bloomsberg University; Gwynelle O'Neal, Rutgers University. Judy Fifer, our editor at Allyn and Bacon, has been most helpful in guiding us through the intricacies of the publication process.

We cherish the affection and devotion of the Timberlake, Moore, and Cutler families who supported our efforts in immeasurable ways. Locally, we especially thank Mia, Jillian, and Barry Cutler for their enduring support, consideration, and encouragement.

ABOUT THE AUTHORS

Authors

Elizabeth M. Timberlake, D.S.W., LCSW-Clinical, an Ordinary Professor of social work at The Catholic University of America, teaches clinical social work, model development and advanced clinical research for doctoral students, and advanced clinical practice with children and their families for masters students. A senior clinician, she has specialized in treating children and their parents and worked with them in family service agencies, mental health centers, school settings, and private practice. Her extensive research and scholarship have focused on children's coping and adaptation in the face of various life stressors and mental illness, treatment process and outcome, and improving clinical practice and services for children and youth.

Marika Moore Cutler, M.S.W., LCSW-Clinical, is an experienced clinical social work practitioner specializing in play therapy with children and adolescents who have complex emotional and mental disorders. She has taught social work graduate students at The Catholic University of America, is on the faculty of the Washington School of Psychiatry, and has been a frequent lecturer on child development and clinical work with children and their families. She has practiced at Children's National Medical Center, was Director of Clinical Resources at Chestnut Lodge Hospital, and maintains a private practice in Chevy Chase, Maryland.

Contributing Authors

Karen Block, M.S.W., LCSW, is a clinical social worker at the Regional Institute for Children and Adolescents in Prince Georges County, Maryland.

Martha Wilson Chescheir, Ph.D., LCSW-Clinical, is a former Associate Professor of social work at The Catholic University of America, Smith College, and the Washington School of Psychiatry. She is currently a clinical faculty member at the Institute for Clinical Social Work of Washington, DC. A senior clinician, she has specialized in both child and adult work and maintains a private practice. Her extensive research and scholarship have focused on psychodynamic-theory development in social work and clinical issues in social work practice.

Barbara Peo Early, D.S.W., LCSW, is an Associate Professor of social work at The Catholic University of America. She chairs the MSW program and has taught clinical social work theory and practice with children and adolescents; family and children's services as a context of social work practice; family preservation; and cognitive and behavioral theories and social functioning. She has practiced for many years as a school social worker, clinical social worker, consultant, and researcher in multidisciplinary settings. Her research and scholarship have focused on child/adolescent treatment, family preservation, school social work consultation, and spirituality in clinical practice. She has earned a certificate in child and adolescent psychotherapy from the Post-Graduate Training Program of the Washington School of Psychiatry.

Michaela Zajicek Farber, D.S.W., LCSW-Clinical, is a Faculty Research Associate at the National Research Center for Child and Family Services and a lecturer at The Catholic University of America. She has taught research and context of practice with children and families. She has practiced social work with children and adults with physically challenging conditions and mental illness. Her scholarship focuses on children's services.

Mary C. Owen, M.S.W., LCSW, is an adjunct faculty member in social work at The Catholic University of America. She has taught clinical social work theory and practice with children and adolescents, human growth and development, and psychopathology. She maintains a private practice specializing in attachment issues. She has practiced extensively as a school social worker, child and family therapist, clinical social work supervisor, and clinical director of a restrictive day school setting for seriously disturbed children and adolescents. Her scholarship focuses on clinical social work with children and adolescents.

Christine Anlauf Sabatino, D.S.W., LICSW, LCSW-Clinical, is an Associate Professor of social work at The Catholic University of America. She has taught generalist social work theory and practice, human behavior, and cultural diversity. Her research and scholarship have focused on school social work practice, consultation, and research; homeless children; and social work personnel issues. She has extensive practice as a school social worker, consultant, group-home social worker, and clinical social worker, as well as program director and clinical supervisor of a private school counseling program.

Jennifer Weaver, M.S.W., LCSW, is a Registered Play Therapist and treats children and their families at the College Park (Maryland) Youth and Family Services Agency.

PART ONE

Overview

1 Developmental Play Therapy in Clinical Social Work

A babysitter from the local university service arrived at the Smith residence at 6:30 p.m. to care for Johnnie, age five, while his mother was to attend a neighborhood community meeting. Mrs. Smith showed the sitter the following items on the coffee table in the living room: a video on *Animals in Africa*, a board game for children ages eight through twelve, and three exercise books for children to learn their alphabet and numbers. She directed the sitter as to the priority in which the items were to be used with Johnnie. The sitter replied, "Thanks, Mrs. Smith, but if it's okay with you, maybe Johnnie and I will just play." Mrs. Smith looked shocked and very disapproving as she said, "Play? Why play?"

Why play? Isn't play a waste of time? Shouldn't every effort be made to provide children with meaningful learning opportunities whenever they have free time? In addressing these questions, numerous authors have stated that spontaneous, unstructured play is a necessity for children's growth and development and, therefore, is important in and of itself (Axline, 1947; Erikson, 1977; Fraiberg, 1954b; Nickerson, 1973, 1983; Solnit, 1987). Indeed, play serves many functions. It provides opportunities for physical activity, joyful entertainment, intellectual challenge, and social interaction (Allen and Brown, 1993; Bruner, Jolly, and Sylva, 1976; Ellis, 1973). In their play, children find ways to enjoy their interests and talents, express their feelings, and practice growing up. They experience their own identities, develop a sense of self and other, rehearse social roles, and strive to understand their real world lives in the fantasy worlds they create. In the process, children engage their internal resources, strengths, and potential; that is, they tap into their forward developmental thrust, increase their capacity for self-direction, and engage their motivation to achieve personal competency. They also find ways to confront problems, act out real or imagined dangers, and work through conflicts. In other words, spontaneous play serves as a constructive mode of expression, communication, social connection, and problem-solving.

Is there value in directing a child's play time? Yes, sometimes; especially when structured or directed play contributes to children's interpersonal skills, psychosocial coping, and social adaptation. For example, structured activities such as board games, paint by numbers, musical instruments, and sports contain directions and restrictions that teach children how to follow rules, persevere, and socialize.

Many children, however, are so fully engaged in directed activities in school, after school, and on weekends that there is little time or opportunity for free play. Under such circumstances, the very rules and restrictions essential to structured play not only inhibit spontaneous expression of thoughts, feelings, and hopes, but also block the possibility of expressing and working through concerns or fears. With little free-play opportunity for responding to their own internal affective worlds or the personal impact of ordinary life experiences, many children have even fewer options available for addressing the larger fears, conflicts, and traumas associated with extraordinary life events or chronic family circumstances. Over time, this pattern of containment may itself become an additional stressor and elevate a child's level of internal distress. The distress, in turn, may interact with biopsychosocial developmental risk and protective factors, and escalate into serious behavioral, emotional, cognitive, or somatic symptoms that serve as dysfunctional modes of release.

Thus, in answer to Mrs. Smith's question in the opening scenario, the babysitter might have responded, "Mrs. Smith, last semester we learned in our human behavior course that play is fundamental for the healthy development of children. It really is not only desirable, but also a basic necessity."

Play in Growth and Development

Sociocultural Influences on Play

Although play activity satisfies the needs and desires of all human beings, this universal medium takes on various expectations, forms, and constraints in different cultures (Sutton-Smith, 1979, 1986). Through culture-specific play, children learn about the history, traditions, and values associated with their cultural identities. They also learn the role expectations and goals held by the cultural community for children, adults, and families. In addition, children use play to try on and rehearse many of the ideas, values, behaviors, and consequences associated with expected child and adult roles.

In that it establishes the values, norms, and behavioral expectations surrounding play at different ages, culture contextualizes play within children's social heritage and life space. Consider, for example, how family lifestyle and socioeconomic status, family-value traditions and religious practices, gender roles and expectations, and childrearing beliefs and practices influence what play materials are made available to children, which materials children choose, and what children do with the materials selected.

Cultural norms or expectations also influence the degree of parental involvement in their children's play. The type of play valued and the extent of a child's imaginative play are highly correlated with parental tolerance for and modeling of creative activities (Singer and Singer, 1990). For example, in cultures where individual achievement is valued, parents may strongly encourage children to succeed in competitive games or creative endeavors. In cultures where family or community is emphasized, children may be encouraged to play by the rules and participate in traditional games (Johnson-Powell and Yamamoto, 1997; Kluckhohn and Strodtbeck, 1961; Whiting and Whiting with Longabaugh, 1975). Sociocultural play variations are also apparent in the activity and noise level tolerated, expression of pain and joy permitted, family secrets and openness allowed, interpersonal style encouraged, and degree of politeness expected.

In brief, culture establishes ecological parameters for many of the life opportunities and choices that are available, accessible, and acceptable to children and their families. In so doing, culture influences a particular child's identity by giving contextual meaning to subjective experience and life narrative, patterns to interpersonal relationships, structure to speech and behavior, and form to play and family activities. Cultural factors, in turn, interact with risk and protective factors in influencing children's capability, biopsychosocial developmental level, and life experiences, thereby yielding culture-specific variations in the form, function, and expression of play.

Development and Play in the Early Years

Throughout childhood, there are identifiable play activities, behaviors, and processes expected of children according to their culture, biological capability, biopsychosocial developmental level of functioning, chronological age, and, at times, gender. Biological influences on play capability may include factors such as genetic predisposition, in utero exposure to drugs/alcohol and malnutrition, environmental insult such as lead and smoke poisoning, major physical illness or accidental injury, and age-related maturational changes such as motor-muscular development and puberty. Age-related maturational changes, age-normed expectational influences, and gender impact on psychosocial development and play, however, are best considered in concert with the whole child-in-social situation; that is, children in the context of their family and community relationships, sociocultural backgrounds, and life experiences.

Infants (Newborn to One Year).   Newborns are pushed forth into the world by their own instinctual reflexes and by the outer nurturance of their caregivers' responses. While children are born with adaptive mechanisms for calling their mothers to them, it is the responsiveness of an empathic, psychologically attuned mother who stimulates growth and facilitates development of a sense of self. In turn, the early availability and engagement of mother, in concert with the child's unique temperament, lays the foundation for children's later interpersonal experiences. In Winnicott's (1945, 1965a) terminology, an infant's experiences of being held, nursed, touched, soothed, and kept warm by a *good enough* mother constitute the holding environment for development. In the good enough environment, the psychologically attuned mother (or other primary caregiver) understands the child's needs and desires, likes and dislikes. In addition to nurture and protection, she initiates contact and provides stimulation, all important aspects of mother/child interaction and play. If the infant becomes overstimulated in this earliest play, the attuned mother catches it and helps the baby relax. A playful cooing exchange may then ensue. In this to-and-fro process, the infant's responses cue and train caregiving adults to individualize and tailor their responses to that infant's unique temperament, needs, and interests (Stern, 1995).

Initially, infant play is characterized by an intense visual gaze upon mother's face and involves various sensory-motor activities such as kicking and arm-waving. The nature of the play revolves around the social contact evoked through mutual or reciprocal gazing, touching, smiling, and vocalizing. Initially, the early smile is an instinctive reaction to satisfaction. In that it elicits an exciting response from others, the three-month smile is considered the first psychic organizer of the social relationship (Spitz and Wolff, 1946).

By the sixth month, babies know and prefer their mother's face to all others, a competency that may well account for the intense separation anxiety of eight-month-olds. Between the seventh and twelfth months, their developing sensory, motor, and cognitive abilities promote a growing awareness of the difference between self and others, and the difference between inner and outer experiences. Their behavior is becoming goal-oriented, intentional, and based on particular beliefs about the caregiver. Through the visual perceptual experience of mutual gazing, for example, infants learn about pleasurable emotions in another. They smile at mother and she returns the smile; or mother looks at her infant who, in turn, smiles back. In learning that smiling leads to shared satisfaction, infants are developing the capacity to understand the mind of another. In learning that hunger leads to satiation, infants are learning how the contents of the mind, a thought for example, direct a certain course of action (Baron-Cohen, 1995). To elaborate, increased physiological tension is produced when hunger occurs. The tension leads to the wishful thought for food. This, in turn, influences the child's desire to be fed, held, soothed, and comforted. In this iterative interactive process, the infant gains the experience of a nurturing caregiver, and develops mental representations of mother as loving and self as lovable. The collection of these good and—for that matter—bad images is important to the development of the self in interaction with others.

During the six to twelve months age period, babies are able to imitate the behavior of others. Their play is characterized by pushing and pulling things that can be manipulated, touching and patting toys and other objects, and playing pat-a-cake and peek-a-boo. They have preferences for certain toys, understand when the toys are out of sight, and, by twelve months, will search for them. As infants begin to recognize significant others, a central preoccupation in their play revolves around their concern with presence and absence, with separation and loss. Initially, when an object disappears from view, infants believe that it no longer exists, thus giving rise to the separation anxiety characteristic of this age. Eventually, through repeated games such as peek-a-boo and other reassuring hide-and-seek experiences, infants learn that objects may be hidden but still extant (Fraiberg, 1959; McCall, 1979). About this time, their growing cognitive abilities become apparent in their play and social interaction. Overall, this first year of life is the period of developing sensorimotor intelligence (Piaget, 1952) and establishing basic trust in their providers (Erikson, 1950, 1959).

Toddlers (One to Three Years).   Children's love affair with the world begins during their second year of life as they become aware of themselves and how their actions influence others (Greenacre, 1959). They are interested in every aspect of themselves, their bodily functions, and their physical environment, as well as in the responses they elicit from others. As junior toddlers practice walking and talking, they are learning to be relatively autonomous. At this time, there is a renegotiation of their relationship with mother, who beams excitedly at every step. In turn, toddlers delight in getting up, moving away, and then returning to mother. Shortly thereafter, the mother/child relationship negotiations begin to be organized around bowel functions. Now, everyone is excited about the bathroom and bodily productions that land in the toilet. Concomitantly, toddlers are introduced to parental and societal limitations and expectations of conformity to certain norms. Curiosity about their physical environment is apparent as they rush to put a finger in an electrical outlet or place a shape into a form board. Delight in feeding themselves fingerfoods is reflected in their play as they pretend to feed dolls, pets, or siblings. Fearless exploration may land them in a kitchen cabinet playing with pots and pans or in a recycle bin pulling out bottles, while mother washes dishes or stacks them in the dishwasher. Through such play, toddlers nurture themselves, test out boundaries, and explore the complexities of objects. At about this time, they also begin to initiate parallel play with peers.

During this developmental period, the toddler's capacity for symbolization unfolds in concert with the acquisition of language. Within one year, the fifty-word vocabulary of eighteen-month-olds expands exponentially (Lewis, 1982). In addition, they connect language with actions and mental images in a way that now represents a social relationship. For example, they are able to picture in their minds that a certain person brings comfort, a particular word represents this person, and a gesture may evoke some response from this person. This ability to form mental representations and engage in symbolization permits linkages of ideas, gives meaning to communication, and is exemplified in toddlers' language and play. Besides facilitating creative and imaginative play, this ability enables toddlers to engage in problem-solving through repetition and other efforts at mastery. Clearly, this growing capacity for symbolic thought and mental representation is the landmark achievement of the second year.

In seeking developmental precursors of the two-year-old's capacity for representational thought, Winnicott (1953) turned to the transitional phenomenon in preverbal early play. He described how infants latch onto special objects, such as a specific baby blanket or particular stuffed animal, for purposes of self-soothing. Whether the special object is a blanket or teddy bear, the infant imbues it with qualities of self and mother, and uses it as a transitional substitute in mother's absence. During the early years of life, this special transitional object is called upon in times of stress, loneliness, or separation. In later years, substitute objects may serve this same function. Winnicott (1953) thought that the ability to give special meaning to such objects was the first truly creative act and laid the ground-work for symbolic and imaginative play to develop.

For the first time, triadic representations become apparent as toddlers point to something and know that mother knows what is meant. For example, a child points toward the cupboard containing cookies and both mother and child know exactly what the child wants.

> The shared attention of mother and child as they point together is based on their mutual representation of each other's intentions. Insofar as children can imagine what another thinks and apply this knowledge socially, they can be said to have a theory of mind (Yates, 1996, p. 152).

Thus, toddlerhood ushers in the mental state of pretend, where children under-stand that they and others make-believe in play. This capacity for pretending is crucial in further developing a theory of mind, in which children learn to imagine and predict the meaning of their own and others' beliefs, desires, and thoughts accurately—and also how these beliefs, desires, and thoughts relate to subsequent behavior and actions (Wellman, 1992).

Play blossoms in the second year of life. At this time, the relationship with mother changes yet again and a new need appears. One- to two-year-olds bring toys and objects to mother and drop them in her lap. They clearly want attention given to their objects and are very sensitive to mother's approval or disapproval. In short order, however, they usually want their objects back. In related play, children take a ball, then push it away; or give something up but then must have it returned. Two-year-olds also become fond of auditory pull toys with strings attached. While toddling around with a pull toy, there is no visual contact but the child hears it. This play symbolizes what is occurring when mother leaves the room but remains symbolically present and available to the child who can still hear her. Thus, these to-and-fro play patterns recapitulate the toddler's on-going developmental struggle to achieve autonomy in relation to mother.

The hallmark of two- to three-year-old behavior is the effort to find auton-omy; to be the power, the controlling other. Senior toddlers are primitive and impulsive. They are fascinated with flushing toilets, collecting and hoarding ob-jects, and banging kitchen utensils. They are known to be simplistic, crude, ag-gressive, and negative. They hold in with tenacity and let go with a vengeance. Through parental prohibitions and admonitions, demands for toilet-training, and expectations that they take care of themselves and their own toys, senior toddlers learn what is and is not allowed. At this age, they are caught between a wish for regression to the joys and pleasures of mother/infant symbiosis and a drive for progression and autonomy. In between these two yearnings lies a monumental developmental crisis, wherein one day they are clingy and cranky and the next day, the exact opposite (Mahler, Pine, and Bergman, 1975). In other words, two-to three-year-olds are discovering their own way, their own sense of self, and the presence of other people. Not surprisingly, the developmental movement from dyadic toward triadic relationships is reflected in their play, which gradually loses its parallel nature, becomes increasingly reciprocal with special people, and eventually widens toward the more cooperative play style of preschoolers.

Preschoolers (Three to Five Years).   With the development of cognition, preschoolers begin to find ways of moving thoughts and actions into a new reality, even though the facility for magical thinking continues to flourish. Significant adults welcome the opportunity to bring children to a developmental level where they convey their thoughts and imaginings in words. Preschoolers, however, still relish the protection of fantasy and play. Using their newly found cognitive abilities, children extend their world of make-believe and imaginary friends. In their play with both tangible things and people, they frequently personify or transform these real objects into imaginary creatures that represent their projected developmental issues, tasks, and conflicts. At this age, fantasy comes into its own and is more important now than at any other time of life. Preschoolers often wish to hold onto the magic and resist letting go of the projections and power reflected in their play.

By age three, youngsters are able to figure things out by thinking and using pretend play. Made-up stories become a way of solving problems. Wishing or thinking something makes it so. Fairy tales captivate their minds as girls imagine themselves to be princesses with ball gowns and glass slippers, and boys imagine themselves to be heroes with big swords and vanquished enemies. Between three and five, youngsters become increasingly aware of how much bigger and more powerful adults are than children in the real-life world. As a consequence, they frequently identify with big and powerful pretend creatures in their make-believe worlds.

Preschoolers enjoy their own bodies, wonder about others, and constantly ask why bodies are the way they are. Erotic gratifications are achieved through visual arousal that brings considerable pleasure in looking, showing, and competing. They note body differences and usually express shock upon first observing genital differences. The observation that something appears to be missing from girls leads to concern that perhaps something was taken away or cut off. Such perceptions or fears of castration are often apparent in the themes and content of their play. These are the days of "Show and Tell." At this time, youngsters are trying to master body integrity and wholeness, and are utterly convinced that their bodies literally can be taken apart and changed. For example, an adult pretends to remove a child's nose and the child searches repeatedly for it in the adult's hands. Not surprisingly, these youngsters adore toys that change from one thing to another and endlessly play with transformers, wherein one moment the toy is a rocket ship and the next a robot.

In addition to their observation of body differences and involvement in imaginative role play, three- to four-year-olds begin to imitate adult roles, engage in more reality-oriented play, and demonstrate more self-generated activity initiatives (Erikson, 1959, 1977). They quickly discern gender role differences and distinguish between valued and devalued gender roles (Bloom, 1984). Although limited in their perceptions of actual adult roles, five-year-olds have been de-scribed as being in the golden age of sociodrama and make-believe play (Singer and Singer, 1990).

Another theme frequently found in their dreams, wishes, and stories is the desire to marry the parent of the opposite sex; that is, the family drama. During this period, a boy's libidinal and aggressive energy remains invested with his mother and does not shift to his father until he begins to strive for male identi-fication and gender consolidation at age six and seven. By contrast, three- to five-year-old girls undergo a marked transformation in the mother/daughter rela-tionship (Chodorow, 1978; Gilligan, 1982; Miller, 1991). As they experience an upsurge of aggressive and retaliatory feelings toward their mother, they withdraw emotionally and invest their libidinal energy in their father. Not surprisingly, preschoolers' imaginative play often involves monsters, goblins, or superhumans who engage in annihilation or destruction of others. Such fantasies are usually accompanied by heightened feelings of fear, guilt, love, and aggression.

From their earlier parental identifications, six-year-olds begin the task of acquiring a positive identification with the parent of the same sex—the parent who previously had been seen as a rival or competitor (Fraiberg, 1959). For girls, however, the earlier relational shift may not be completely worked through before the social pressure of the reality-oriented elementary school years swings their emotional and interpersonal investment and gender-identification issues back once again to their mother (Miller, 1991).

Development and Play in the Elementary School Years

With the resolution of preschool developmental issues, six-year-olds have devel-oped a sense of how both their minds and the minds of others work (Mayes and Cohen, 1994). They have formulated internal mental representations of their object worlds that are in line with their subjective experiences (Sandler and Rosenblatt, 1962). This constructed representational world lays the foundation for the acquired *theory of mind,* through which children anticipate and interpret motives, thoughts, actions, and feelings (Wellman, 1992).

Between the ages of six and eight, children begin to relinquish the fun, magic, and fantasy of the earlier years in exchange for the more reality-oriented demands of learning and socialization. They strive to please their parents and teachers, and are now able to delay immediate gratification. As they become more compliant and more socially appropriate in their play with peers, their aggression becomes increasingly muted. By the age of eleven or twelve, school-age children have usually accomplished the basic developmental task of learning that there is a difference between work and play. They have consolidated their social identity as that of a child industriously engaged in child's work.

Same-Sex Peer Play.   Between the ages of six and seven, children experience social pressure to relinquish sexual desire and aggression directed toward parents. Interest in genitals and the family drama is pushed out of sight and repression becomes the host to all other defenses. A sublimated interest in bodily functions, autonomy, and power is seen in children's fascination with taboo words, primitive jokes, collections, hobbies, compulsive rules, and games. Developing internal prohibitions and evolving idealizations of gender role models redirect energies and identification toward persons of the same sex. There is a new interest in learning from the same-sex parent. As a consequence of this developmental shift, expressions of tender love between girls and boys are usually few and far between. Overall, developmental issues at this time for both boys and girls revolve around deepening their capacity for peer relationships, increasing their social competence, and building their capability in differentiating relationships (Surrey, 1991).

Prohibition, Expectation, and Fair Play. The child's ideal self grows out of both the child's wish to be lovable and the parental introjects of prohibition acquired earlier. The internal self-regulatory system that manages the child's developing conscience and ego ideal takes form as the superego. For example, eighteen-month-olds learn not to bite people. Toddlers struggle mightily to conform to the demands of toilet training. Preschoolers grapple with their desires for sexuality and feelings of grandiosity; that is, their desires to masturbate, marry the opposite sex parent, and rule the world.

Development of the superego begins from an external position of shame. The initial stance is "I don't or do wish to do something because I *am punished.*" This belief that the thought and the action are bad gives way to anticipation, to "I don't or do wish to do something because I *will be punished.*" Next, the child begins to develop an internal sense of guilt and the stance becomes "I don't do something because it will *make me feel bad.*" Finally, the child's stance shifts to the internal moral position, "I don't do something because *it isn't a good thing to do*" (Noshpitz, 1993). When this internal voice of authority is realized, the superego is operational and capable of regulating the self by (1) connecting children with their culture, (2) making moral demands, and (3) carrying the signals of anxiety and guilt that influence behavior and regulate the feeling of well-being.

The three prohibitive functions of the internal self-regulatory system that comprise the conscience act in concert or in sequence, and include warning and forbidding, inhibition or the blocking of a wish from taking action form, and punishment (Noshpitz and King, 1991). The punishment takes the form of mental torture for wrongdoing and is carried out in the presence of enormous internal pain.

The aspect of the internal self-regulatory system that manages the expectational wishes about behavior and accomplishments takes form as the ego ideal. The driving functions of the "self I would like to be" (Sandler, Holder, and Meers, 1963) derive from parental expectations of the child and from the child's own yearnings and expectations. If the wished-for self or ego ideal is set too high, the child chases the impossible dream, feels inadequate or insufficient, and is thrown off balance. If set too low, there is little to strive for and hope may convert to hopelessness. Generally, the measure of a child's happiness and self-esteem is contained in healthy tension between the conscience, the ego ideal, and where the child is in real life; that is, in the child's realistic capacity to work toward the ideal achievement (Jacobson, 1964).

This developing internal self-regulatory system of conscience and ego ideal is reflected in children's play and adaptation to the elementary-school environment's demands for achievement and civility. At this age, children become fascinated with and highly value rules and regulations in all of their activities. Early on, their values and ethics are governed by the Old Testament adage of "an eye for an eye, a tooth for a tooth," an ethic exemplified in the classic, "She called me a bad name first so it's okay to call her one back." Gradually, however, an evolving sense of fair play becomes apparent in their play activities, peer relationships, school activities, and various competitions. Indeed, development of a doctrine of fairness is one of the major achievements of the elementary-school-age child (Noshpitz and King, 1991).

Cognition and Play.   At around six to seven years, children experience a shift or transmutation from preoperational thinking to the less self-centered level of concrete operations. Preoperational thinking is characterized by the ability to deal with simple relations between representations of things present and not present in their immediate environment. Concrete operational thinking, by contrast, involves children's ability to deal systematically with the logic and complexities of actual representations of concrete objects and events inside and outside of their experience (Piaget, 1952, 1969). At the same time, they are shifting from the pleasure principle to the reality principle as their psychic-life organizer. Their primary process fantasies and impulses have become less useful in problem-solving and find more sublimated expression in their play, dreams, and creative productions. Comprehension that knowledge can now be shared through the relationship between two people motivates children to use their growing cognitive capabilities and further develop their logical thinking skills. Operational symbols and logical thought are increasingly the means of solving the everyday problems-in-living experienced by the child. Because the focus is how things work in the here and now, secondary process thinking quickly outdistances the primary process problem-solving of the earlier years (Freud, 1933).

The social and emotional consequences of this developmental leap forward are seen in the emergence of concern for others and the reduction in personal grandiosity. The growing cognitive and empathic ability to think about and imagine the feelings of others is crucial for the child's successful entrance into the wider social and cultural world. This is an exciting moment as children become logical thinkers for the first time.

Imaginative and Competitive Play.   Although cooperative in nature, children's play during the school years becomes increasingly productive and competitive. The physical landscape inspires hours of fun and goal-directed effort. The wall of an old building, for example, becomes a graffiti artist's canvas, a handball player's backboard, or the anchor for a makeshift basketball hoop. The beach architect creates a crenelated sand castle and thrives on admiring glances from beach strollers. The artist transforms the kitchen into a museum full of colorful productions. The playwright turns the basement into a stage set for dramatic theatrical events. For children and their parents, these goal-directed accomplishments yield tremendous joy and satisfaction.

Game-playing gains added momentum through verbal gusto, intellectual pursuit, and physical passion. Children's folklore incorporates secret languages, jump-rope rhymes, jokes, tongue twisters, and riddles. Board, card, and computer games challenge mental mastery and yield enthusiastic wins or agonizing losses. Organized team sports such as soccer, basketball, and Little League facilitate increased motor-muscular activity and stimulate peer cooperation and competition. The sports of karate, gymnastics, skating, and swimming provide for more individualized skill development and achievement. As a whole, these game-playing activities reflect the developmental shift to body/mind development, coordination, and mastery.

Grandiose, narcissistic fantasies and daydreams become important in the elementary-school years as children begin to transfer their emotional involvement to the world outside the family. Girls turn to idealized prototypes, such as Barbie dolls, and boys to superhero figures, such as the Hulk and Ninjas, in the pretend hours devoted to make-believe beauty, sexuality, power, and fame. Fantasies blossom as a sublimatory mechanism for imagining themselves as competent and successful. In their daydreams, the delayed learner becomes a scholar; the shy child, outgoing; the socially isolated child, popular; and the clumsy child, a great athlete (Noshpitz and King, 1991). Family romance fantasies intricately weave together imagined dramas of different, more glorified parents (Freud, 1908). One youngster described how she would look out her bedroom window and long for her "real" parents to rescue her. Other children confide their inner thoughts, wishes, and fantasies to an imaginary friend who neither castigates nor criticizes. Although present, masturbatory fantasies are usually displaced onto play activities. Taken together, these imaginings are indicative of the intrapsychic distancing and de-idealization of parents as ten- to twelve-year-olds transfer their emotional investment from the family to the outside world of peers, teachers, and communities in preparation for their move into adolescence.

Social Identity and Play.   By age eleven or twelve, children's internalized self-regulatory systems become more apparent in their characteristic ways of knowing, being, and behaving at home, in the classroom, on the playground, and in the neighborhood (Ellis, 1979). Teachers replace parents as the overvalued authority figure. Expanded gender identity is consolidated as the business of what boys and girls do is reflected in their increasingly differentiated play and social relationships. A more accurate body image makes children of this age vulnerable to the opinions and ridicule of their peers. New identifications with peers develop in concert with individual friendships and group play. Play activities combine the intrigue of rules with the challenge of peer competition and wish to win. Losing is often experienced as quite distressful. Motoric and intellectual competency becomes increasingly important, with youngsters devoting hours to a particular sport, musical instrument, or collection, and coming to view their accomplishments in these arenas as extensions of themselves. School plays an especially vital and well-loved role in intellectual and interpersonal accomplishments.

The continuum of children's perception of themselves and their social environment at this age ranges from sensing enormous academic and social pressure to succeed to a growing awareness of their own increasing competence. While elementary-school–age children may reach extraordinary levels of achievement, the competition itself yields even more excitement for them than the outcome. As they compete and learn in school and in the community, these children develop a sense of self, direction, and social identity.

Internal hormonal changes commence between nine and ten for girls and between eleven and twelve for boys (Noshpitz and King, 1991). The underpinnings of puberty bring on an unsettling extension in behavioral changes and emotional reactions. Youngsters' sense of uncertainty and anxiety about their potential for change is reflected in their increased emotionality.

At this time, boys are playing keenly competitive and complex games in larger groups and strut their physical prowess in an effort to manage their increasing sexual impulses. Same-sex peer play becomes more defensive as boys begin to prepare themselves for the social pressures of adolescence by both teasing and avoiding girls. Within the peer culture, boys' roles become more entrenched as they choose leaders, scapegoats, and helpers. The secret gangs and exclusive clubs have well-defined rules and rituals for membership, and may even include the hazing threat of having to kiss a girl.

Because girls undergo hormonal changes earlier, it is not surprising that they develop and behave differently during the later elementary-school years. Girls' sense of self is "becoming organized around their ability to make and maintain affiliation and relationships" (Miller, 1976, p. 83). Initially, there is more of a bossiness and intrusiveness with girls' peer relationships than with boys'. Secrecy takes on a life of its own with long telephone conversations, gossip, and cliques. Girlfriends and peer relationships are all important. By fifth and sixth grade, girls usually come up with various coping mechanisms to deal with their developmental changes. Through denial, for example, they pretend that nothing is happening. There can be considerable exaggeration as they whisper about their friends. Stories about who is wearing a bra are formidable. Some girls are quite matter of fact and take their maturational changes during these years in stride; others experience great distress.

In sum, the growth of cognition, perception of self and reality, social skills, gender identity, and peer identity come together to form the whole of the social identity and self-concept of the school-age child. This intricate work represents the organization of self and is the critical psychological formation during this period.

A Particular Child's Development and Play

For a particular child, biopsychosocial influences on development and play may occur as expected within an age-appropriate and culturally sanctioned time frame or unexpectedly at less appropriate times. These influences may be experienced as ordinary and desirable or extraordinary and stressful. When the impact of stressful influences on development is highly negative, play content and process are likely to reveal (1) delay or disruption in biopsychosocial growth and development, (2) regression to earlier developmental levels in response to stressful and overwhelming life experiences, or (3) repetitive play organized around the stressor and deprivation in the capacity for imaginative play. However, to assess the unique implications of a particular child's play pattern under stress and distress, clinical social workers must learn about that child's biopsychosocial history, current life situation, and ways of coping, and then be able to juxtapose this knowledge against a general understanding of the following:

- child development
- patterns of risk and resilience and styles of coping and adaptation
- developmental variations in the nature, type, and content of play
- cultural, gender, and age diversity in play patterns
- therapeutic play principles, processes, and procedures
- the play materials available

Biopsychosocial Functioning

Healthy Children

Whatever the developmental stage, healthy children have a dynamic generative response to life. They evidence a capacity to play joyfully and creatively and to form supportive relationships with peers and adults. They are constantly involved in an active state of being and in ongoing developmental progression. They convey pleasure in their own activity, excitement about learning, respect for themselves and others, and an expectation that others will like them.

In addition, healthy children have multiple personal and social resources for meeting developmental challenges and coping with life experiences and stressors. Their personal resources include the following:

- biological, cognitive, emotional, and social strengths
- ability to perceive and process cognitive and affective information accurately
- values and morals that are developmentally and socioculturally appropriate
- resilience in coping and adaptation

Their social environmental resources and protective factors include the following:

- families whose nurturance, protection, and stimulation is empathically attuned to the child's particular needs
- significant persons in their schools, neighborhoods, churches, and communities who offer support, guidance, and role-modeling
- peer friendships and activities
- cultural and faith-based group memberships and support
- an adequate level of economic subsistence

Child Clients

Developmental and Environmental Crises and Dysfunction.   Although presented in stages, the developmental sequences and organizational patterns that reflect the growth, maturation, and development of children do not unfold in linear fashion. For many children, there are times when genetic endowment, biological factors, family forces, and various cultural and environmental influences combine with developmental tasks and processes to create developmental crises, and either stall forward progression or trigger regressive episodes of transient psychosocial dysfunction. There are also times when children are overwhelmed by the stress and distress associated with environmental crises such as death, divorce, disaster, or relocation. Often family supports, other social protective factors, and their own personal protective factors, resilience, and coping strengths (Anthony and Cohler, 1987; Fraser, 1997) enable these children to deal with the developmental or environmental crisis, and to make the forward leap required for continued growth. In other instances, brief clinical social work intervention facilitates child and family management and resolution of the crisis, reestablishes family equilibrium, and restores psychosocial functioning and developmental progression.

Chronic Environmental Stress and Dysfunction.   Other children are exposed to multiple chronic environmental stressors such as poverty and homelessness, family and neighborhood violence, drug and alcohol abuse, neglect and desertion. Some resilient children are able to mobilize the personal and social resources to cope fairly well with such toxic social circumstances. More vulnerable children, however, are less able to cope, evidence psychosocial dysfunction, and need professional help in modifying their destructive life environments. They also need help in learning to cope with the residual effects of such extraordinary environmental challenges. In these instances, social workers in child protective services, family wraparound services, educational and employment services, schools, hospitals, and mental health clinics are often called upon to combine resources and services in order to address the multiple subsistence, caring, social support, developmental, and mental health needs of these children and their families.

Major Mental Illness and Developmental Dysfunction.   From 7.5 to 8 million children evidence serious behavioral, emotional, cognitive, and somatic manifestations of psychosocial dysfunction, and meet the *Diagnostic and Statistical Manual IV* (American Psychiatric Association, 1994) criteria for the various disorders of childhood as well as for disorders not necessarily developing solely in childhood (e.g., anxiety, mood, and conduct disorders) (Estrada, 1997; Institute of Medicine, 1989). Frequently, these children are diagnosed with comorbid as well as primary conditions. For some of them, exposure to toxic social environments compounds the mental illness. Often, their psychosocial histories reveal an abundance of mental health risk factors with few protective factors available to balance the life equation.

In their day-to-day lives, the actions, affect, and thoughts of these children are usually considered undesirable by adults, become the foci of negative attention, and trigger further self-defeating psychosocial dysfunction. They seem to have lost their social, psychological, and developmental equilibrium and are unable to live up to the expectations of the significant adults in their lives. Indeed, their capacity to develop progressively seems to have been damaged. Co-occurring with the various mental disorders, such developmental dysfunction takes the form of either (1) developmental disruptions, in which children's mental processes of emotion, imagination, curiosity, and cognition either diminish significantly or cease to operate; or (2) developmental distortions evidenced through intrapsychic or interpersonal mental conflict. Although sometimes co-occurring, developmental disruptions and developmental distortions more often are experienced sequentially in the lives and therapeutic work of the children.

Developmental Disruptions in Mental Processes. Ordinarily, children use mental processes of imagination and cognition to solve problems or cope. They are expected to be curious, motivated to learn, and socially engaged. By contrast, children with developmental disruptions in their mental processes have one or more of the processes of emotion, imagination, curiosity, and cognition constricted, defensively inhibited, and unavailable as appropriate resources for coping. That is, the process has simply shut down, not only relative to the distressful situation, but also in its entirety (Fonagy, Edgecumbe, Kennedy, and Target, 1993). Thought, for instance, becomes no longer available for use in the service of developmental task mastery or problem-solving. That is to say, if thinking about an event such as abuse, rejection, or abandonment is too painful, then thinking becomes too dangerous and is excluded from mental activity even in school. Or, children may attempt to make sense out of their experience but become flooded with anxiety that, in turn, compromises the essential way they behave and relate to others. Thus, children with developmental disruptions in mental processes often experience both their internal affective and real interactive worlds with a great deal of pain and suffering, anxiety and rage, despair and vulnerability. Their feelings are experienced as fragmented, chaotic, confusing, and overwhelming.

Without access to one or more of the basic building blocks of the mind (i.e., emotion, imagination, curiosity, and cognition), children's mental structure develops inappropriately and inaccurately. When this happens, much of children's psychosocial functioning, including their day-to-day affective and interactive experience, retains the presymbolic representational characteristics and behavioral enactment level of mental organization in the earlier developmental years. When younger than three years old, for example, children are unable to think about and respond behaviorally to things, persons, and ideas not present in their immediate experience. Similarly, youngsters with disrupted processes of the mind have difficulty with the core mental abilities that organize, connect, and regulate emotions, ideas, and behaviors. They also have difficulty with those core mental abilities that symbolize or represent conceptual thinking about their internal and external worlds. That is, children experiencing these developmental disruptions display deficits in their ability to form accurate mental images, construct appropriate feeling states, and develop fantasies from their presymbolic states. They are unable to abstract from their experiences and develop ideas for critical reflection and cognitive understanding. Unable to make sense of their lives, these youngsters feel vulnerable to outside forces and react behaviorally to their own experiences. They appear confused and overwhelmed by their strong feelings of anxiety, rage, and despair. Their perceptions and mental representations of the part that they and others play in creating and maintaining their own psychosocial dysfunction are inaccurate. As a consequence, they frequently project angry feelings and blame onto their siblings, peers, parents, and teachers, and demonstrate little or no comprehension of their own responsibility for distressing social situations.

When this occurs, the children's personal models of their own internal and external worlds become characterized by faulty mental processes, such as distorted logic and magical thought, in which fantasy blurs reality. They appear tentative in comprehending, acknowledging, and verbalizing their actual feelings about the real world. Together, these deficits in mental processes compromise the essential way these children behave and relate to others. These deficits form part of the presenting clinical symptom picture in many severe mental illnesses.

In seeking to clarify clinicians' understanding of children experiencing disrupted processes of the mind, Anna Freud noted that such

> disturbance is not due so much to internal conflicts as to a mixture of early neglect and damage, lost opportunities for development, unavailable permanent objects, and all sorts of adverse environmental influences (as reported in Sandler, Kennedy, and Tyson, 1980, p. 256).

Therefore, for these children, developmental play therapy needs to provide opportunities for (1) assessing developmental disruptions in mental processes to understand whether and how the mind of this particular child is activating his or her thoughts, feelings, intentions, motivations, and behaviors; and (2) providing an optimal psychosocial environment that stimulates and recharges these disrupted processes of the mind and also facilitates subsequent development. As illustrated by the following case, this corrective developmental experience in therapy usually operates at an experiential, reflective, behavioral level.

Theory of mind informs us that by age three, children know that their thoughts and wishes occur inside their heads and cannot be seen by others. This

Molly, A Vignette of Developmental Disruption

Molly, a ten-year-old child, presented in treatment with limited autonomous ego functions, gender-identity confusion, impaired reality testing, and a psychosocial history of maternal depression during which Molly was unable to elicit empathic responses from mother. Molly's mental processes had shut down. She presented with limited attention span, concrete thinking, and no curiosity about the world. She experienced her internal and external worlds as empty. Her cognition, judgment, and communication skills were seriously impaired, especially in the emotional context. The first epistemic mental state of pretend was not present the way it is in normal eighteen- to twenty-four-month-old children. Rather, Molly thought this pretense was real. Psychological testing ruled out psychotic processes.

One day before her summer vacation, she came in saying, "Wee . . . I don't have to come here. I won't miss you. Not one bit. I don't like you. It's torture. You eat me. You are my thoughts. You control my thoughts. I saw you on TV telling the world about how I want to be a boy. I wish I were a boy . . . then my life would be different. I'd be smart. I know. I'll be a boy from here up [points to her waist] and a girl from here down. You stay right here in the office until I come back. When I come back, you can eat me up for lunch. That way, I'll be dead." Here we have a fragmentation of self in which self and object boundary fusion yielded both total dependency and vulnerability. In a way, Molly tried to be separate but yearned to be fused.

Our work revolved around affective mirroring. No matter how crazy it seemed, I would say things like, "It feels safe for you not to have feelings. You speak of torture, so of course you don't want to come here." I attempted to give her a safe parameter around self because she experienced us as one. We worked on boundaries . . . that it might seem as if I could read her mind but that actually we were separate. "See, you are sitting in one chair and I am in another. Even though it feels like we're one, we're really separate." In response to her scary feelings that I could eat her thoughts, I commented, "Is it less scary for you to eat my thoughts?" and "This is an important feeling. There may be different feelings, but sometimes the scary feeling is the most important one." I reflected her discomfort by mirroring the affect so she could feel safe.

Molly's defenses were impoverished and the affects overwhelming. She employed a very primitive isolation of affect that seemed like a thought disorder. Her theory of mind was, "They expect me to be crazy, so I'll be crazy." Once in a while, I would be gently mocking, "Boy, you see me as having quite an appetite!"

Over four years of treatment, Molly was able to see herself as separate. The rekindling of the earliest developmental issues gave way to more autonomy while she was growing in her understanding that there is safety in relationship. The gender-identity problems were, in part, worked through during play with transformers, GI Joe, Barbie, and Ken. Hours were devoted to the latency fantasy of the Hulk who changes but changes back. I put a stop to father's nudity as well as his bathing of his daughter. I explained how firm boundaries must be enforced . . . that father and daughter needed to be separate and that he would have to find other ways of closeness with her.

case is an example of a youngster with developmental disruptions in her mental processes and an inability to form an integrated representation of herself. Developmental play therapy was used to recharge her mental processes through experiencing, reflecting, problem-solving, and transference rather than through interpretation of her defenses or conflicts. During intervention, it was clear that Molly alternately shifted between acting out her developmental issues behaviorally and representing her disrupted mental processes symbolically within the play metaphor.

Developmental Distortions Associated with Conflicts of the Mind.   Children's intrapsychic conflict distorts their developmental processes and may have far-reaching consequences in their external social worlds. Interpersonally, for instance, they may cling to both teachers and adults, thereby limiting their acceptance into the peer culture. Or they may be exquisitely sensitive to the slightest affront and misinterpret social nuances. Tom, for example, could walk into a room and know right away that his peers did not want him there. He would get this idea by seeing someone's facial expression and then misinterpreting and distorting it. His self-experience was that no one wanted him there. In time, this developmental distortion became his mental representation. It is important to note, however, that he was not entirely misinformed, because he actually evoked from his peers what he was thinking that they were thinking about him.

The internal struggles associated with intrapsychic conflict may be expressed through clinical symptoms such as phobias, inhibition, and anxiety. These children suffer mightily and, usually, silently. Conflicted children often display a tentative or indefinite quality in their school work and social interactions. Frequently, their mental representation of self and others becomes distorted. These symptoms are readily apparent in their social world with parents, teachers, and peers.

Whether intrapsychic conflict takes the form of distorted mental representations or agonizing inhibition, these conflicted children often reveal repetitive and constricted patterns of thinking, feeling, behaving, and relating. The representational content of the repetitive patterns suggests preoccupation with developmental themes organized around Bowlby's schema of attachment/loss (1969, 1973a, 1973b, 1980); Mahler's phases of separation/individuation (Mahler, Pine, and Bergman, 1975); and Erikson's epigenetic stages of trust/mistrust, autonomy/shame, initiative/guilt, or industry/inferiority (1950).

Therefore, clinical social work intervention provides opportunities for working through developmental distortions that take the form of unresolved intrapsychic mental conflicts and engaging in problem-solving. As illustrated in the following case, these internal conflicts of the mind are readily apparent in play therapy, both in terms of the content of the play and the nature of the transference. During intervention, child clients alternately shift between acting out behaviorally and representing the mental conflicts symbolically within the play metaphor. Sometimes, they grapple with internal demands of conscience in opposition to the stimulating influence of their sexual or aggressive impulses.

Jenny, A Vignette of Developmental Distortion

Jenny, age eight, was referred to the clinical social worker by her parents for low self-esteem and sadness. She readily came to therapy with three bears represented through drawings and verbalizations. They symbolized her internal world. Jenny said, "Poor Rachel bear is so sick, I think she may be dying. Her mother, Mrs. Bramblebrook, flew in from Conscience Land to take care of her but Rachel wanted to be left alone. She's too sick to do anything. Rachel bear is right here," as she pointed to the right side of her head. "I think Mrs. Bramblebrook bear is in the middle," she added. "Rachel bear caught the measles from Karim bear who wants her to die. He is so evil. Now remember, Karim is bad so he stays in the left side of my head." As treatment progressed, Rachel bear began to get stronger and Mrs. Bramblebrook bear said, "You should never give up on someone who is getting better." Eventually, Jenny as Rachel bear noted that her only problem now was that Karim bear said his job was to make her unhappy by doing evil things to her. During the termination phase, Mrs. Bramblebrook bear told Rachel bear, "I might have to leave you because you aren't in trouble anymore. There are lots of little bears in Conscience Land who need help growing up. After all, I've taken care of you for three years now." Rachel bear replied, "I'll miss you a lot, but I've learned how to manage evil Karim bear when he tries to get me into trouble." Jenny's regulatory system had indeed been internalized.

The sense of self languishes. The intervention operates at reflective and interpretive levels.

In this vignette illustrating processes of developmental distortion, Jenny—through Karim bear—demonstrated how the superego makes moral demands and punishes. The superego, as seen through Mrs. Bramblebrook bear, was also supportive and fair. The therapeutic task was to strengthen Jenny's intrapsychic structure through Rachel bear, thereby helping her become more realistic in her demands on herself. After three years of treatment, Jenny turned to the world of her peers with enthusiasm and to the demands of learning with eagerness.

Intervention.   Social workers, as the frontline service professionals in social agencies and clinics, are most often in a position to treat these vulnerable children. Whatever the practice setting and however the transient or more marked biopsychosocial dysfunction is manifest, successful assessment and intervention with these children and their parents first requires an understanding of children in their sociocultural and developmental contexts and then an ability to communicate professionally with them in the language of childhood—play.

Apart from children experiencing developmental and environmental crises, brief clinical intervention is rarely enough with the children seen by social workers today. When they are referred for mental health services, intensive treatment and concurrent parent intervention are usually indicated. Yet, according to the National

Alliance for the Mentally Ill, only one fifth of those needing mental health services actually receive them (Estrada, 1997).

Play and Therapy

Social Work and the Play Therapy Tradition

A rich professional tradition undergirds the play therapy and parent treatment models used in clinical social work practice today. For example, use of psychosocial histories in client case formulations dates back to Mary Richmond's (1917) direct case-based approach to social work practice. The use of play materials as treatment tools to facilitate growth and development traces back to the group work approaches of Jane Addams (1938). The family-centered approach to direct practice with individuals grows out of Florence Hollis's (1939) depiction of family casework method. The life model approach to clients' developmental growth traces back to Genevieve Oxley (1971).

Although key principles from these classic publications are clearly applicable to social work practice with children and their parents, it is important to note that these early authors did not write directly about specialized practice with children. Rather, it remained for Gordon Hamilton and Selma Fraiberg to take up that task in the late 1940s and early 1950s. Hamilton (1947) codified existing social work practice with children as a psychodynamic child guidance approach, in which child and parent were treated separately but concurrently by a multidisciplinary team of psychiatrist and social worker. Fraiberg (1951, 1954a) incorporated psychoanalytic principles into a social work practice model combining psychodynamic social casework with parents and play therapy with children.

Since that time, various social workers have continued to document developments in books about child treatment, play therapy, and parent work (Chethik, 1989; Lieberman, 1979; Mishne, 1983; Timberlake, 1978a; Webb, 1991, 1994, 1996). However, as with other fields of social work practice, clinical models of theory and practice with children and parents have evolved primarily through the profession's oral tradition, in which knowledge is developed and shared by means of supervisory case review rather than by means of an experimental research tradition.

Value and Purpose of Play in Therapy

Earlier Therapeutic Models.   It is difficult to identify the value of play in therapy without addressing the specific purposes for which the play is to be used. For Erikson (1950), play serves as an experiential laboratory in which children learn to cope with their developmental concerns and their social environments. Emphasizing play's cognitive value, Piaget (1969) depicts play as a mental digesting process that enables children to understand experiences and situations; White (1966) defines it as an opportunity for developing problem-solving skills.

Fraiberg (1954b), on the other hand, addresses the psychodynamic and communicative values of play in therapy and notes its usefulness as (1) the symbolic medium within which child clients express and work through their intrapsychic conflicts and psychosocial concerns, and (2) the ground from which the social worker develops interpretive comments linking the content and process themes of the play metaphor with the child's conflicts and concerns. Schaefer (1980) elaborates on values related to the affective qualities, expressive nature, and re-educative potential of play therapy:

> . . . it releases tensions and pent-up emotions; it allows for compensation in fantasy for loss, hurts, and failures; it facilitates self-discovery of more adaptive behaviors; it promotes awareness of conflicts revealed only symbolically or through displacement; and it offers the opportunity to reeducate children to alternate behaviors through role-playing or storytelling. (p. 95)

More recently, Webb succinctly addressed the value of play activity in helping children "express and work through their emotional conflicts in a helping relationship with a therapist, who interacts with the children through the metaphoric language of play" (1994, p. 3).

Developmental Play Therapy Model. Developmental play therapy is a dynamic child treatment model that integrates theoretical concepts and principles from psychodynamic, psychosocial, life model, and cognitive developmental traditions. This model uses play media, symbolic metaphor, and the therapeutic alliance to:

- stimulate children's mental, physical, and verbal expression of developmental disruptions and inhibited mental processes, distorted intrapsychic developmental conflicts, cognitive distortions, and biopsychosocial concerns
- provide opportunities for experiencing a corrective psychosocial environment that stimulates and recharges mental processes and development
- provide opportunities for working through unresolved developmental conflicts
- engage in problem-solving that strengthens children's ability to understand and cope with their developmental concerns, life experiences, and psychosocial environments.

Thus, developmental play therapy represents an accelerated process of growth, learning, and change that restores children to age-appropriate maturational levels and healthy biopsychosocial functioning.

In aligning the growth processes of play and the processes of biopsychosocial development to restore children to their age-appropriate maturational level, developmental play therapy uses play in a way that:

. . . is pretend, another way of using the mind and body, in an indirect approach to seeking an adaptive, defensive, skill-acquiring, and creative expression. It is a mode of coping with conflicts, developmental demands, deprivation, loss, and yearnings through the life cycle. What makes play unique is the coordination of mental and physical activities that convey to both the actor and the observer the characteristics of suspended reality, the use of illusions and fantasies, and their dramatization (Solnit, 1987, p. 214).

When used in this manner, developmental play therapy involves exploring situations and relationships, testing other options, and pretending that alternative vignettes could be real. In so doing, this therapeutic intervention expands children's sense of their own abilities and empowers them to become as active in sharing their stories, meeting their developmental needs, and influencing their psychosocial environments as they can tolerate.

Biopsychosocial assessment in the developmental play therapy model gathers information from a variety of sources (e.g., child, parent, teacher, and pediatrician, among others) to create a multidimensional data base about the whole child-in-environment. In this model, assessment considers the multiple ecological dimensions of the child's community and family environments with their interpersonal processes and conditions. It is grounded in the various epigenetic phases of cognitive, biological, emotional, and social development. By taking into account these developmental spheres that organize children's intrapsychic and interpersonal worlds, the data base of this model facilitates in-depth analysis and the creation of a comprehensive assessment and intervention plan.

Clinical social workers use the developmental play therapy model together with concurrent parent work in short-term, intermediate, and long-term treatment that addresses the problems-in-living and biopsychosocial dysfunction associated with the following:

1. *Environmental and developmental crises.* In these instances, developmental play therapy may be used to address the short-term therapeutic goal of mobilizing children's strengths, resilience, problem-solving abilities, and coping resources to facilitate their handling of the stressors, resolving the developmental crisis, and restoring psychosocial functioning. Concurrent parent work mobilizes the parents' strengths, resilience, and ability to nurture and protect their children.

2. *Chronic multiple environmental stresses.* After family wraparound services or child protective services stabilize a child's living situation—either within or apart from chronic multiproblem chaos and deprivation—developmental play therapy may be used first to address the short-term therapeutic goal of mobilizing the child's ability to cope with the current environmental challenges and changes. Subsequently, developmental play therapy may be used to address long-term therapeutic goals of either (1) recharging disrupted mental and developmental processes shut down by developmental inhibition or compromise in the face of overwhelming stress and a chaotic internal affective world; or (2) working through unresolved internal and interpersonal conflicts associated with intrapsychic conflicts and distorted mental representations.

3. *Major mental illness and developmental dysfunction.* In these instances, developmental play therapy may be used to address (1) the short-term therapeutic goal of focused symptomatic improvement or temporary symptom remission; (2) the intermediate goals of mobilizing strengths and resources, handling daily problems-in-living, and facilitating interpersonal relationships; or (3) the long-term goals associated with resolving developmental issues connected with developmental disruptions in mental processes and developmental distortions associated with conflicts of the mind. The long-term therapeutic task with the former is to reestablish the operational functioning of children's mental processes of emotion, imagination, curiosity, and cognition—processes that have been defensively inhibited for various reasons (Fonagy, Edgecumbe, Kennedy, and Target, 1993). The long-term therapeutic task with the latter is to address distorted dynamic mental representations, thereby resolving children's internal conflicts and their handling of interpersonal conflicts (Fonagy and Target, 1996; Fraiberg, 1954b).

In developmental play therapy, the growth process is evidenced and may be assessed along multiple lines of change over the course of the treatment sessions as children

- progress in the development and use of the therapeutic alliance
- progress in choice of play object, use of symbolic metaphor, and movement through the stages of developmental play—solitary, parallel, cooperative, imaginative, and competitive
- demonstrate movement along the maturational lines and developmental stages inherent in human growth and development

Behavioral and Cognitive Play Therapy Models. Sometimes, however, developmental play therapy is not the treatment model of choice. When the issue is limiting out-of-control behavior to retain and better maintain children in their own environment, a behavioral or cognitive framework may be useful. From a social-learning-theory perspective (Bandura, 1977), play therapy becomes a tool for building the relationship necessary to carry out the reinforcement contingencies and desensitization programs designed to alter children's behavior so that it is more age-appropriate. The goal of behavioral play therapy is to identify and gain control over whatever shapes, maintains, eliminates, or changes undesirable behavior.

When framed in cognitive theory (Piaget, 1952, 1969), play therapy rests on an educational rationale and uses principles of reframing and rational thinking to accompany the play activity (Barth, 1986; Bruner, 1966). The goals of cognitive play therapy are directed toward "issues of control, mastery, and responsibility for one's behavioral change" (Knell, 1996, p. 44).

At times, behavioral and cognitive play therapies are used as distinct models of play therapy and concurrent parent work. In selected instances, they may be used as adjunctive approaches to supplement psychodynamically oriented developmental play therapy.

Conclusion

This overview of the role and diverse meanings of play in the everyday lives of children of various ages and cultures sets the stage for understanding developmental play therapy and a subsequent in-depth look at its various dimensions. In so doing, this discussion underlines the reasons why clinical social workers who treat children evidencing serious psychosocial difficulty and, in many instances, having primary and comorbid diagnoses of mental illness need to be knowledgeable about children's developmental processes and play. This discussion also lays the groundwork for the subsequent in-depth look at concurrent parent work relative to developmental play therapy with their children.

2 Therapeutic Alliance and Developmental Change Process

In therapy, child clients express themselves and relate to their clinical social workers through play, verbalization, and enactment (Sandler, 1980). In turn, their clinical social workers employ the same communicative media to develop an alliance toward growth and change. In that this therapeutic alliance is the vehicle for developmental play therapy's accelerated growth process, it is best explored and understood as both a construct and a process. Exploration of the alliance as a construct yields an understanding of its multidimensional nature—of its value-based goals, general relational conditions, and the clinical attachment bond formed through the elements of a real attachment relationship and a working alliance. Exploration of the alliance as process puts the goals, conditions, and elements together in a dynamic pattern and then reveals how play within a relational holding environment becomes a medium of expression and communication that makes use of symbolic and transferential means to create a shared clinical narrative. However, to restore children to age-appropriate maturational levels and healthy psychosocial functioning, an additional dynamic process must be integrated into the therapeutic alliance—that of purposive developmental growth and change.

Therapeutic Alliance as Construct

Background

Although descriptions and prescriptions for professional use of self in working toward change in client functioning have varied over time, the professional relationship has been an explicitly valued component of social work intervention since the days of Mary Richmond (1917). Indeed, by mid-century, Felix Biestek (1957), Helen Harris Perlman (1957), and Bernece Simon (1960), respectively, had written of the professional relationship as the soul and essence, the heart, and the keystone of social work intervention. Today, social work theorists continue to refine and clarify the central nature and role of the professional relationship in promoting change within various practice models (Applegate and Bonovitz, 1995; Edward and Sanville, 1996; Meyer, 1993; Saari, 1986). In a parallel development, clinical researchers from allied professional fields have identified a positive therapeutic alliance as necessary for positive clinical outcomes (Gaston, 1990;

Lambert, Shapiro, and Bergin, 1986) and have found that the nature of the thera-peutic alliance is the best predictor of outcome (Horvath and Symonds, 1991; Lambert, Shapiro, and Bergin, 1986; Safran, Crocker, McMain, and Murray, 1990). Currently, there is almost universal acceptance of the professional relationship, or therapeutic alliance, as necessary for client change and successful intervention outcome.

Definition.   In developmental play therapy, the therapeutic alliance is defined as the purposive affective and relational connectedness that occurs between clin-ical social workers and their child clients as they work together toward problem resolution, age-appropriate maturation, and healthy psychosocial functioning. This professional therapeutic connectedness consists of three interrelated concep-tual elements: value-based treatment goals, general relational conditions, and mutual clinical attachment bonds that evolve over the course of therapy.

Value-based Goals.   On the one hand, the nature of the therapeutic alliance in developmental play therapy is purposive, goal-directed, and designed to meet the needs and aspirations of a particular child and family. On the other hand, the established purpose and goals reflect societal framing, culture-specific nuances, and professional limits. That is, the goals and outcomes are broadly framed by society's assumptions about psychopathology, health and well-being, and the behavioral and psychosocial functioning patterns deemed both age and gender appropriate. They are further influenced by culture-specific beliefs, attitudes, norms, mores, and nuanced expressions about pathology, well-being, and desir-able behavior for boys and girls of certain ages (Johnson-Powell and Yamamoto, 1997).

The purpose and goals of the therapeutic alliance are also clearly located within the bounds of the values, ethics, and intervention models of the social work profession. That is, the goals, means, and outcomes considered desirable for a particular child and family are also framed within and limited by social work's value base and ethical imperatives. As noted in the recently updated *Code of Ethics* (NASW, 1996), for example, social workers are cognizant of the dignity and worth of each human being, recognize the central importance of relationships between and among persons engaged in the helping process, and seek to "pro-mote, restore, maintain, and enhance the well-being of individuals, families . . ." (p. 6). In this context, it is important to note that the therapeutic alliance is a professional relationship that exists only within the specific clinical situation. It has no value or place apart from its contribution to established therapeutic goals and desired outcomes.

General Relational Conditions.   In developmental play therapy, the clinician purposefully strives to establish the underlying relational conditions for all clinical practice models, thereby facilitating the therapeutic interchange. According to Rogers (1951), these facilitative conditions include congruence, empathy, and un-conditional positive regard. Strupp's (1960) larger listing includes basic personal and professional characteristics of respect, interest, understanding, tact, maturity, and belief in one's ability to help. Collated from various sources, Compton and Galloway's (1994) listing of facilitating conditions essential for all professional relationships includes concern for other (unconditional affirmation), commitment and obligation, acceptance and expectation, authority and power, and genuineness and congruence. Although perhaps useful as idealized behavioral checklists about general relational conditions, these listings of static personal and professional characteristics fail to consider that the clinical social work relationship is dyadic, interactive, and the result of dynamic collaborative work on problems and conflicts presented by a particular client.

By contrast, Biestek's (1957) classic analysis of the casework relationship identifies the core facilitative conditions for a purposive professional interchange as incorporating the basic values of the social work profession, the common human needs (Towle, 1945) of persons with problems in psychosocial functioning, and the dynamic dyadic nature of the change process. His depiction of the professional relationship provides principles for establishing the safety and security essential for client problem solving, development, and change. These principles clearly locate the responsibility for creating and maintaining an appropriate therapeutic alliance with the clinical social worker:

- *Purposive expression of feelings:* recognizing the client's need to express feelings freely
- *Controlled emotional involvement:* being sensitive to the client's feelings, understanding their meaning, and making purposeful, appropriate use of the clinician's emotions in response to the client's feelings
- *Acceptance:* recognizing the innate dignity, ultimate destiny, human equality, basic rights, and needs of the client
- *Individualization:* recognizing and understanding each client's unique qualities and the differential use of principles and methods in assisting each toward a better adjustment
- *Nonjudgmental attitude:* having the conviction that the treatment function precludes assigning client responsibility for causation of the problems or needs
- *Client self-determination:* supporting the right of the individual to make his or her own choices and decisions
- *Confidentiality:* preserving secret information concerning the client that is disclosed in the professional relationship (Biestek, 1957, p. 60)

Evolving Clinical Attachment Bond

The therapeutic alliance develops within the shared contextual space between the clinical social worker and child client and forms the core of the dyadic professional relationship. As they co-construct the interpersonal and intrapersonal clinical narrative, a mutual attachment bond develops and evolves. This evolving bond reflects a composite of the whole range of real relationships and professional working alliance elements that both child and clinician bring to the treatment process.

At times during developmental play therapy, for example, children relate easily; are relatively conversational and open in their play; and readily explore their feelings, tensions, and conflicts. They clearly convey their problems and developmental issues through narrative content, symbolic metaphorical themes, and clinical process. At other times, however, the nature of the therapeutic alliance is distorted by child clients' and/or clinical social workers' idiosyncratic constructions of reality. Children may bring alliance distortions and processes that consist of symbolic and transferential playing out of their various past and current relationships and experiences, as well as their very real dependence on their parents (Fraiberg, 1951). Clinicians bring alliance distortions that consist of the various countertransference elements associated with their own past and present relational experiences. Many theorists suggest that, although these attachment elements are interdependent, distinguishing among them is essential in understanding the therapeutic process of a particular client (Gaston, 1990, 1991; Gelso and Carter, 1985; Greenberg and Horvath, 1991; Greenson, 1965).

Real Attachment Relationship.   The reality-based elements of the clinical attachment bond are based on the child's experience of the clinician's personal characteristics, professional style, and clinical competence, as well as the goodness of fit between their actual and anticipated experiences in developmental play therapy. Ideally, the child and clinician mutually value each other and the work in which they are engaged. From this value base, the child client acknowledges the clinical social worker in the helping role and the play therapy sessions as a place for suspending habitual coping and adaptation, and working toward developmental, psychosocial, and behavioral change. At times, however, three types of distortion in the real attachment relationship may be transferred into a treatment session and become challenges for understanding and work.

1. *Learned Cognitions.*   Children learn ways of perceiving and thinking in their families and cultures that become part of their current feelings, behaviors, and ways of relating to others. As part of children's psychosocial functioning, these learned cognitions not only become part of the communication patterns in developmental play therapy, but also influence the therapeutic alliance and clinical outcome. Thus, when different from those of their therapist or the mainstream culture, it is the clinician's responsibility to assess, understand, and work with the child's learned cognitions from the perspective of the child's own familial and cultural context. When dysfunctional distortions are apparent in the child's learned cognitions, narrative theme processing or cognitive reframing may become a part of the play therapy intervention.

2. *Current Preoccupations.*   Sometimes children are preoccupied with reality-oriented, age-appropriate interpersonal relationship issues that impact on their psychosocial functioning and clinical attachment bond. These preoccupations manifest themselves as displacements from current relationships onto the therapeutic-alliance and change-process themes. For example, a child consumed by rage at being grounded for a school-behavior problem may displace the anger onto the clinical social worker and act out in the session. In such instances, emotional catharsis may be useful in draining away sufficient affect so that the child and clinician can process the emotion and experience within the play narrative. Usually, the impact of such experiences on treatment is transient and short-lived. Sometimes, however, child clients may be preoccupied with extremely pathological, life-threatening situations. In situations of chronic and severe abuse/neglect, for example, removal from the home may be indicated for the child's safety. Similarly, circumstances of acute violence and drug use also may trigger child protective service arrangements. Once the living situation is stabilized and safe, growth through developmental play therapy can begin.

3. *Characteristic Behavioral Patterns.* From a psychodynamically oriented developmental perspective, children's characteristic behavior patterns are viewed as residuals of earlier object relationships and defensive/adaptive patterns (Sandler, Kennedy, and Tyson, 1975). From a cognitive/behavioral perspective, child behavior patterns are considered part of social learning and conditioning (Barth, 1986). As children grow older, however, both residual object-relationship patterns and learned-behavior patterns can spread indiscriminantly to current interpersonal relationships and become entrenched habitual ways of behaving in all current social situations, whether appropriate or not. Whenever such patterns appear in the therapeutic alliance, they become grist for the mill.

Working Alliance Elements.   In the working alliance, the clinical social worker builds on the bonding begun through the real relationship but shifts its nature more toward the therapeutic task at hand. That is, the therapist recognizes, accepts, and clarifies child clients' needs, feelings, and attitudes as expressed through play or verbally. Thereby, the working alliance provides them with an opportunity to learn about self-in-social situation and develop life-coping skills (Chethik, 1989; Fraiberg, 1954b; Lieberman, 1979). In the working alliance, the specific therapeutic goal and the child's readiness to work toward that goal determine how and when the clinician combines particular intervention techniques with particular relational and motivational qualities. Indeed, it is the purposiveness of the alliance that taps into a child's strengths and motivations, encourages choice of play tools, and facilitates use of the therapeutic process for problem solving, corrective emotional experiences, working through, and psychosocial development. Although the symbolic behavior and associated feelings triggered by the therapeutic alliance are accepted without restraint, the clinical social worker sets appropriate limits on destructive acting-out behavior that may harm the child or therapist. This limit-setting is done to address a particular underlying issue directly or rechannel destructive impulses toward self and other into symbolic expression for therapeutic work.

Within the working alliance, the clinician's therapeutic action may range along a continuum from nondirective to more directive intervention according to the overall context of the child's needs, treatment goals, theoretical and time framework of the practice model, and phase of therapy. In the more nondirective working alliance of longer-term developmental play therapy, the clinical social worker leaves responsibility and direction to the child but influences the purposiveness of the work through focused responsivity (Axline, 1947; Chethik, 1989; Fraiberg, 1951, 1954b; A. Freud, 1946; Hamilton, 1947; Moustakas, 1953). In the more directive working alliance of time-limited developmental play therapy or cognitive-behavioral play therapy, the clinical social worker assumes more active responsibility for motivating and guiding the child (Barth, 1986; Dennison, 1989; Webb, 1991). Despite their differences, these polar-opposite alliance forms—at least as used in clinical social work practice—view the child as a full participant in the process and as a unique individual to be treated with respect. The more nondirective approach, however, acknowledges the co-constructed nature of the relationship, the importance of the fit between the particular child and therapist, and the interpersonal experiencing of both participants in the process.

In establishing a working alliance, the clinical social worker serves as a nurturing, stimulating, and protecting agent who gratifies children's therapeutic needs through offering the professional self and play materials. Within realistic limitations, the clinician listens, offers support, and accepts expressions of affect and need. Although no explicit demands are made, the clinician conveys the hope and expectation that growth and change are possible. As treatment progresses, the clinician continues to follow the child's feelings, thoughts, and play expressions, but moves to help children explore different aspects of their intrapsychic and interpersonal worlds, as well as the shared experience of working together. Gradually, as the working alliance evolves, the child client increasingly understands and accepts the responsibility of investing in the work of developmental play therapy. The presence of an accepting and hopeful ally increases his or her sense of security, provides the basis for trust, and opens up the shared relational space in which to discover meaning together. As child clients become aware of their own needs, their internal capacity to engage and use the working alliance grows.

Over time, children increasingly express emotionalized attitudes and conflicts through the play process. The clinician follows their lead and reflects back the narrative in a supportive, yet appropriately stimulating manner, remaining within the metaphor in order to help children better understand self-in-situation. By means of an individualized working alliance, opportunity and contextual space are created for child clients to (1) express and master their feelings and concerns about their life experiences and problems; (2) re-experience, rework, and remediate developmental disruptions in earlier phases of psychosocial development; and (3) rework developmental distortions that interfere with coping and adaptation. Thus, the total person of the child client is gradually brought to full responsiveness through key elements of the working alliance: acceptance, expectation, support, and stimulation (Perlman, 1957, 1979). Although child clients attain and value the more mature levels of behavior gained, it is important to remember that the therapeutic play process moves backward and forward. At times, there is temporary regression to earlier gratifications for developmental remediation. At other times, there is progression through restorative developmental growth toward new satisfactions and more mature levels of behavior. Two clinical relational processes in the working alliance—transference and countertransference—are critical elements in this to-and-fro movement.

Transference Elements.   Early psychoanalytic theorists debated whether children in play therapy experienced a strong dependent attachment (A. Freud, 1946) or the transference neurosis considered an essential part of psychoanalytically oriented psychotherapy (Klein, 1950). Transference neurosis "is a very special intensification of the transference involving an externalization of a major pathogenic internal conflict onto the therapist, so that the conflict is felt by the patient to be between himself and the therapist" (Sandler, Kennedy, and Tyson, 1980, p. 82). Anna Freud (1946) informs us that the distinguishing feature of transference in children is that the internal conflict is based on present and real, rather than past and fantasized, relationships with parents.

More recently, major proponents of these two schools of thought have agreed that development of transference is possible when child clients have developed the capacity to retain a memory of human interactions and form a dynamic mental representation of an object (Chused, 1988; Fraiberg, 1966). Indeed, Chused elaborates:

> After a child has developed sufficient capacity to retain a memory of human interactions and to form an internal mental representation of an object, he has the capacity for transference, to "misperceive" an interaction with one person so that it "feels" the same as with another. And when he has sufficient structural development to sustain intersystemic conflicts and the ego capacity to tolerate (even minimally and only transiently) conflicted feelings, impulses, and fantasies, he can develop a transference neurosis (1988, p. 234).

Developmental play therapy follows this latter line of psychodynamic thinking and defines transference as "the way in which the child's view of and relations with childhood objects are expressed in current perceptions, thoughts, fantasies, feelings, attitudes, and behavior" in relation to the clinical social worker (Sandler, Kennedy, and Tyson, 1975, p. 412). How the child revives these object expressions, brings them into the therapeutic alliance, and concentrates them on the person of the therapist is catalyzed by the nature of the service setting, theoretical model of intervention, play materials, and use of the professional self. More specifically, the therapist provides the facilitative conditions and sets the tone for the working alliance within which the child's issues are revived, freely expressed, and addressed as part of corrective psychosocial growth experiences or working through. As transference issues intensify within the therapeutic alliance, their manifestations elsewhere usually diminish. In this way, the transference elements of the working alliance become tools in assessing and remediating the developmental origins of problems and conflicts.

By contrast, the cognitive/behavioral tradition that supplements psychodynamically oriented developmental play therapy downplays the role of the child's past in the working alliance and focuses primarily on the present professional relationship. In this tradition, the working alliance is used in conjunction with social reward and limit-setting to strengthen children's motivation for change and willingness to adhere to problem solving, cognitive reframing, and practicing to achieve the desired change.

Countertransference Elements. Within the experiential gestalt of a child or parent, clinical social workers' countertransference reactions in a particular therapeutic situation stem from the effects of their own unconscious processes on their clinical understanding and technique with that particular client. No clinician is immune. Each brings their own mental processes, past history, and current life situation to the therapy sessions. In a session, affective and behavioral reactivity associated with unconscious phenomena may be triggered by assorted factors such as the child's or parent's reality, intrapsychic or interpersonal worlds, or transference (Littner, 1969). For example, an out-of-control child may elicit an affective reaction whereby the clinician either is immobilized by feelings (e.g., anger or anxiety) or brings mediating defenses into play to handle the feelings. In turn, these responses may translate into manifest behavioral reactions that take the form of hostile or punitive confrontation, helpless avoidance of the behavior and associated affect, or emotional withdrawal from relational connectedness in the shared interpersonal space.

Because such reactions block effective listening, comprehension, and responsiveness, the clinical social worker strives to manage the countertransference so that it does not interfere with the therapeutic process. Indeed, by maintaining continual observation and alert awareness of their own feelings, thoughts, and behavior while with a child or parent, clinicians are able to use themselves as tools in understanding and facilitating the therapeutic process (Chethik, 1989; Geddes and Pajik, 1990; Grayer and Sax, 1986).

Therapeutic Alliance as Process

As process, the shared relational space of the therapeutic alliance may be depicted as a holding environment in which clinicians figuratively contain their child clients to allow the child's innate growth and developmental processes to once again take hold (Chescheir, 1985; Winnicott, 1965a). In this safe interpersonal context, children's issues and conflicts emerge, are shared, and are explored. The experiential togetherness of the interactive therapeutic narrative permits the child and clinician to discover and create unique subjective meaning from the child's chaotic intrapsychic and interpersonal worlds. As part of this long-term process of working together, the child's transference and the clinician's countertransference influence the nature of the therapeutic alliance, and enter the clinical process narrative in somewhat circular iterations to yield developmental growth and change.

Transference Process

In developmental play therapy, children experience the freedom to bring their conflicts, symptoms, and anxiety into the transference or relational playground (Freud, 1914; Sanville, 1991). They are able to explore their worlds with the excitement and challenges facing youngsters who climb to the top of a slide for the first time and view their environment from a new perspective. Perhaps they are fearful as they attempt gymnastics atop the jungle gym. Perhaps they get stuck in between the two jump ropes of double dutch. Or they may stumble and fall. Just as there are multiple play activities occurring on the playground, so there are many affects experienced in the transference with the clinician. As the caregiver sits on the park bench watching while ready to intervene, so the therapist remains both distant and close (Anthony, 1986a), available to help the child develop self-awareness and ego mastery by making full use of symbolization, fantasy, and play within the context of the transference.

As the clinician and child set the stage for the mutual give and take of their relationship, the play scenario initially takes place in the present, with the full participation and observation of both the child and therapist. In time, the child begins to transfer experiences, affects, and modes of relating into the treatment with the unconscious expectation that these elements and processes will be replicated in the therapeutic alliance. The therapeutic playground permits freedom of relational movement and expression of the transference. For example, inhibited children relax their internal controls and dare to change; aggressive children risk taming their impulses. What was once solitary or parallel play becomes increasingly more interactive and thus more developmentally appropriate.

The four types of transference delineated at the Anna Freud Center correspond to some degree with the broader dimensions of the therapeutic-alliance construct discussed previously: "habitual ways of relating, of current relationships, of past experiences and transference neurosis." (Sandler, Kennedy, and Tyson, 1980, p. 78). A child's habitual way of relating, or characteristic behavior pattern in real relationships, is characterized by the sameness with which a child relates to whole groups of people. For example, an adopted child may view teachers, peers, and other persons as the original biological parent who abandoned him. Such a child begins all relationships, including the one with the clinical social worker, in a mistrustful way, and may actually invite rejection through actions that hold others at a distance. In this way, the child transfers a past relationship to real current relationships in the same repetitive way. This type of suspicious/distancing transference is often seen in the alliance that is formed during the early stages of treatment.

The major characteristic of the transference of past experiences is that it seems to emerge in the therapeutic narrative from repressed material and then

Case Example: Clarence's Habitual Ways of Relating

Clarence was eight years old when his adoptive parents brought him to treatment following a particularly aggressive outburst toward his parents, siblings, and peers on a family vacation. He was fearful and angry as his mother forced him to leave the hotel restaurant. Two weeks later, the child felt he was being forced into therapy, so he refused to enter the treatment room. Undaunted, the clinical social worker started working with Clarence in the hallway. Clarence responded with several aggressive outbursts, verbal attacks, and repeated testing as he tried to force his therapist to reject and abandon him. This same habitual mode of relating also was seen in his first three sessions with a tutor who was likewise castigated. The tutor characterized Clarence as the most uncooperative student she had ever seen and threatened to quit. The therapist, however, understood what was triggering the aggression.

is displaced onto the clinician. Such transference becomes apparent when a child regresses to an earlier developmental level in a session. For example, one omnipotent youngster wished to rule the world at the ripe age of nine years. He succeeded in ruling at home through demands that his every need be met. He was boisterous, manipulative, and cunning when his impulsive behaviors resulted in immediate intervention. During his first year of treatment, he was solicitous of the clinical social worker and attempted to take care of her every imagined need. He was overly controlled, too pleasing, pseudo-mature, and well-mannered beyond his years. In this way, he was manipulating the treatment to avoid dealing with his conflicts and defenses. In time, the clinician became increasingly alert to the pitfalls of the positive transference and resistance wherein this child did not express negative affect. Finally, he regressed to demands for control and power within the transference and was met with understanding and interpretation. Not surprisingly, his behavior at this point began to change at home and school.

When children relax their control of impulses in the treatment setting, transference phenomena become more obvious and may present as regressive behaviors, aggressive enactments, or primitive play. Even outside of treatment, the clinician takes on special meaning to the child. For example, one youngster had a special doll named after her therapist, who was initially touched by such a gesture. Then she found out that the child punctured the doll with pins and needles. Another girl made plaster of paris faces of the therapist, sat on them, and then froze them. A boy spent two hours designing a Valentine's Day card that said, "Thank you for helping me with my problems."

Sometimes, there are indeed heated moments during the transference when children enact primitive impulses and aggression through hitting, kicking, or biting the clinician. Other times, positive feelings may be enacted through attempts to kiss, hug, or sit on the therapist's lap. Whatever the expression of the multiple affects present within a single session, the clinical social worker attends to both the immediate real-world meaning and the transferential meanings, and responds within the metaphor according to clues from the unfolding clinical narrative.

Countertransference Process

It is generally acknowledged that child work is more likely to give rise to countertransference reactions than work with adults (Anthony, 1964). The intensity of the play together with the regressive pull and progressive push enacted within each treatment session stimulates emotional reactions and responses to a particular child or the child's parents and teachers (Anthony, 1986b; A. Freud, 1965). Yet, the rough and tumble of developmental play therapy calls for a flexible holding environment where clinical social workers tolerate, understand, and contain their own ambivalent feelings of love and hate, which stem from their past interpersonal relationships with their own primary caregivers and intrude into the current therapeutic alliance (Winnicott, 1949).

Technically speaking, countertransference refers to a therapist's unconscious mental processes that result in reflexive reactions to clinical material produced by a child. Although an unconscious dynamic, countertransference may serve as a clue to children's internal conflicts and the way they are perceived by others. Clinicians remain ever attuned to their affective reactions and responses, when treating children. For example, they note their own visceral responses such as a stiffened body posture or visual signs of exasperation, responses that children are likely to notice. They may also note that working with particular groups of children—for instance, those who are severely depressed or passive-aggressive—may bring on similar feelings and responses. Some common reactions that demand scrutiny are anger, rescue fantasies, over-identification with a child, overindulgence, or boredom, to name but a few. Once their own affective response is identified and sorted out, the clinician uses it to guide intervention with both child and parents. Thus, countertransference serves as a laboratory where the clinical social worker develops and utilizes professional and personal knowledge, self-observation, and self-awareness to facilitate client growth and change.

In addition to countertransference reactions with negative communications by children, clinicians may face countertransference difficulties when faced with strong affectively charged behavioral styles such as the aggressive child, the suicidal child, or the withholding child. In these instances, verbal communication is deemphasized and communication through the metaphor, gestures, affective facial expression, and posture provide more access to the child's mental life. Without understanding and using nonverbal communication with these children, negative countertransference reactions may be manifest in annoyance, dread, boredom, sleepiness, lateness, or missing and canceling sessions.

Purposive Developmental Change Process

According to Erikson (1977), play activity represents children's attempts to use the processes of make-believe to clarify, understand, and master their personal circumstances in the world around them. Building on this base, play therapy in clinical social work assumes that child clients (1) have the ability to form and use a therapeutic alliance; (2) have the ability to use play metaphor and the behavioral,

Case Example: Angel or Devil?

Eleven-year-old Ana Maria was caught in the conflict between the good and bad parts of herself with which she had struggled her entire life. At school, she was the angel, while at home she was the devil. During the initial phases of the transference, she clearly enacted the role of the devil. Through play, verbalization, and enactment, she cruelly punished her clinical social worker much the same way she punished her mother and brother at home. She would tear down people, dollhouses, the therapist, and all kinds of play materials. In public, she falsely accused her parents of child abuse. In treatment, she threatened to accuse her therapist of child abuse. Gradually, Ana Maria was able to build a therapeutic relationship with her clinical social worker through her actions, play, verbalizations, and silences. Her temper outbursts of "I hate you" gradually gave way to "I hate my mother," then to "I hate myself," and finally to "There are things I hate to do." Over time, she started to build up the dollhouse, her mental representations of self and others, and her relationship with her clinical social worker.

For some time, the therapist was convinced that she was dealing with a negative maternal transference. When Ana Maria was away for summer vacation, the clinical social worker was greatly relieved and found herself dreading her return. Upon further reflection, the therapist realized that while in reality, it was no fun to be hit or hated in the treatment setting, she had in actuality lost her objectivity and empathy for Ana Maria's inner struggles. The countertransference problem stemmed from the clinical social worker's desire to be liked and tendency to withdraw from meaningful relationships when she was not. Clearly, this withdrawal must have had an impact on the treatment of Ana Maria, a sensitive youngster who may well have sensed her therapist's hostility. Through consultation with her supervisor and self-observation based on her own therapy, the therapist was able to analyze her feelings, thus commencing a much improved treatment for this child.

Therapeutic change occurred when the transference became a playground where Ana Maria had more freedom to explore her resistances, ambivalence, and strong affect. By the end of treatment, her mental health and psychosocial functioning had been restored to the normal developmental pathway of a child her age. While there had been considerable transference and countertransference phenomena both in and out of treatment, her need for the therapist diminished as she sought new, meaningful object relationships. Ana Maria eventually was able to give up her "good enough" clinical social worker and the teddy bear that this therapist had symbolized.

---

affective, and cognitive strengths to communicate their concerns about themselves and their social, psychological, and physical environments through play and talk; (3) have varying levels of awareness of their problems and conflicts; (4) have the ability to resolve intrapersonal and interpersonal problems and conflicts, mature, and develop; and (5) are able to comprehend at some level that mature behavior is more satisfying than immature behavior.

In psychodynamically oriented developmental play therapy, children use play's projective element to create and structure their internal and external representational worlds so that the make-believe content, symbolic metaphors, and thematic processes within the play reflect their life experiences and problems, their inner feelings invested in these experiences, and their hopes and wishes for mastery over forces beyond their capacity in the real world. In building their make-believe worlds, children select play materials with form and thematic content familiar to their sociocultural and economic life situation, manageable at their biopsychosocial developmental level, and representative of their own unique configural reality. Thus, their context-specific play metaphors and thematic representations of psychosocial developmental processes serve as projections of their inner life space and represent a displaced expression of their personal internal worlds, feelings, and characteristic personality processes. In Lowenfeld's words:

> Play serves [as] the bridge between the child's consciousness and his emotional experiences, and so fulfills the role that conversation, introspection, philosophy, and religion have for the adult. Play represents to the child the externalized expression of his emotional life and, in this aspect, serves for the child the function taken by art in adult life (1935, p. 32).

Play Process

In clinical social work, the narrative metaphor found in play forms an intermediate language, neither truly nonverbal nor truly verbal. Its use is based on three assumptions: (1) that children referred for clinical social work treatment fear reprisals and rejection, and are seldom ready to confront problems and developmental conflicts directly; (2) that these children are able to reconstruct, project, and communicate their problems-in-living, interpersonal issues, and intrapersonal issues (i.e., disrupted and distorted mental processes, intrapsychic mental conflicts) in narrative metaphor form; and (3) that child clients are able to work toward resolution of these concerns within the narrative metaphor.

As with other social work models, play therapy begins where the child client is. To understand a child's narrative construction of the problem(s), the clinician takes note of not only the common elements that are shared by other children of similar age, gender, and cultural background, but also the unique elements that are significantly associated with the developmental issues and conflictual themes running through this particular child's life history and current psychosocial situation. Initially, the clinician comments descriptively on the observable behavior of the actors in the play narrative (*The little boy doll is sitting in the corner.*). The child client may elaborate (*He is all alone.*). The clinician consistently labels and comments on the actions and feelings of the actors (*Maybe the boy doll is scared.*). The child may agree and elaborate or may correct the clinician (*No, he's sad.*). The clinician's response reflects a desire to know more with an indirect question (*Oh? Wonder why?*) rather than a more direct question (*What happened? Why is he sad?*). In so doing, the clinical social worker is following the principle that reflective comments and indirect questions are more likely to elicit elaboration and open up the play activity and conversation; direct questions are more likely to structure too much and close down the narrative metaphor. With this and other treatment principles, however, it is critical to keep in mind that not all principles are equally applicable to all children and that there is likely to be an appropriate time for the polar opposite response.

In exploring the thoughts, feelings, and actions of the narrative characters in the play activity, the clinician slowly moves beyond reflecting back the child's comments and feelings to a gradual exploration of possible connections and causes. Drawing on background knowledge of the child, the clinician reflects the feelings and explores what triggered the feelings within the context of the narrative (*Sad? Perhaps the boy doll is sad because the mama doll has gone away.*). The child's behavioral and affective cues, together with the knowledge that this child was in foster care, suggested to the clinical social worker tentative reasons for the feeling of sadness and for the wishes accompanying the feeling. Although always accepting feelings expressed either metaphorically or directly, the clinical social worker may need to set limits on the child's behavioral responses and expressions of these feelings outside the play metaphor and verbalization. Assessment and understanding of how this particular child may act on his feelings undergirds the interpretations and anticipatory guidance (*I know the boy doll is sad and wishes he could run away to his mother doll. Wonder who he can talk to about this?*). A later interpretive generalization at the end of this play session would be more universal and focused on external reality outside the metaphor (*While we can understand and help boys with their feelings, we can't let them hurt themselves.*); thus, reminding the child client of the safety rules that are part of the treatment contract. Following the child's cues and depending on the treatment stage, the clinician might make a tentative move from comments within the symbolic metaphor of the play world to more direct comments about the reality situation of this child (*Maybe you have even felt that way?*). Such an interpretive connection, however, is made only when the child conveys a readiness and ability to deal directly with reality factors.

In the responsive therapeutic tradition, the child conveys the thematic narrative through the play process and the clinician responds to the meaning in the play language and symbolic metaphor that the child is using. Staying within the metaphor, the clinician comments on the underlying themes and process as the narrative unfolds. By interpreting within the process and metaphor, the clinician maintains the safe environment and avoids premature anxiety-provoking confrontation with reality. Such verbal responsiveness within the play narrative facilitates the child's efforts to grasp actual and psychic reality—to bring issues from the internal affective world into external expression through symbolic metaphor. Within this interactional therapeutic play process, children experience a corrective psychosocial environment and work through inner conflicts, resistances, and frustrations. In this way, they move toward problem resolution and developmental growth.

To understand and process children's metaphorical expression of clinical themes in treatment, the clinical social worker constantly confronts a series of silent questions that push beyond the overt information provided by the substantive play content, narrative themes, and working/playing behavioral style:

Silent Questions about the Child

- What is the child expressing at this time? What is the underlying clinical process of the narrative theme?
- Is this play typical for this child's age; representative of earlier developmental levels; or reflective of serious behavioral, emotional, cognitive, or somatic manifestations of psychosocial dysfunction?
- Is this play typical for this child's culture?
- Is the child communicating about a particular issue, conflict, or problem area?
- Is this play different from this child's usual play?
- What does this play convey about the working alliance bond? The transference?
- Where are we in the therapeutic change process?

Silent Questions for the Professional Self

- Should I passively follow or actively enter the play? Observe or comment? Reflect or interpret?
- Should I accept the behavior or set supportive limits?
- Am I following the underlying clinical process of the narrative theme and engaging the therapeutic-change process?
- What is this child triggering in my personal self? What countertransference? Why?

By definition, developmental play therapy represents an accelerated process of problem solving, growth, and change that restores children to their age-appropriate maturational levels, but are problem solving, developmental maturation, and change actually occurring? Thus, the clinician also confronts silent questions about change:

Silent Questions about Change

- Is problem solving occurring? In what areas? How? Why?
- Are the presenting problems changing? Which ones? How? Why?
- Are new symptoms developing in or out of the sessions? What? How? Why?
- Is developmental maturation becoming apparent in or out of the sessions? In what areas? How? Why?
- Is developmental regression apparent in or out of the sessions? In what areas? How? Why?

Developmental Process Themes as Maturation

An overarching treatment goal in developmental play therapy is to restart arrested psychosocial developmental processes and enable children to achieve age-appropriate development through thematic representation in the clinical narrative. The developmental issues are either re-experienced correctively or worked through experientially in the therapy (Allen, 1942; Fraiberg, 1954b, 1966; A. Freud, 1970; Greenacre, 1959). In such restorative play therapy, the clinical social worker creates a good-enough environment (Winnicott, 1965a) for the children to tackle unaccomplished growth tasks, thereby achieving their potential in each psychosocial developmental stage (Erikson, 1950; Mahler, Pine, and Bergman, 1975). Such a good-enough environment is created through careful assessment of developmental lacunae and strengths, sensitive attunement to progressive and regressive developmental forces, and empathic responsiveness to nuanced clinical exchanges as a child's representational developmental levels shift back and forth in the treatment process. As in the following vignette, the clinical foci, or units of attention, in restorative play are the multiple psychosocial-developmental-process themes underlying the play content; specifically, trust/safety, attachment/loss, and separation/individuation.

As illustrated in this case vignette, the process themes underlying the play content in restorative play therapy reflect different developmental tasks and stages and require diverse developmentally responsive therapeutic intervention techniques. The following process themes of trust and safety, attachment and loss, self/other differentiation and autonomy, gender and sexuality, and reality and industry represent common developmental deficits and treatment objectives that often appear in developmental play therapy.

Trust and Safety Theme.   When working on developmental tasks in the early psychosocial stage of trust versus mistrust (Erikson, 1950), child clients seek to recapture a sense of the ideal safety and satisfactions of infancy. They convey the trust and safety process theme through sensory-tactile exploration of their physical and social surroundings. Checking out both old and new environments helps them cope with fears of the unknown and also satisfies their curiosity about how safe they are. Indeed, the most concrete means of facilitating a primitive sense of security with a new child client is to permit free exploration of the office or playroom setting.

Case Example: Multiple Developmental Process Themes

After she refused to leave home to attend school for four months, ten-year-old Malika was brought to the Community Mental Health Center. Her school phobia seemed to be associated with separation anxiety triggered by her mother's surgery one year after divorce. Her vulnerability to separation and loss was associated with her family's frequent moves during her preschool years and being left with her maternal grandparents for several months at a time. During the early sessions, Malika's play included building fortresses and guarding doll families to stop them from leaving, keep them safe, and prevent spies from getting inside to steal secrets. In response to the play metaphor that she was not allowed to intrude into family business, the clinical social worker made observational comments, such as "The family was scared of people going away so they built forts to keep them safely inside," and "The forts helped them hide away and keep their secrets safe." From forts, wars, and new weapons to protect the family and guard the secrets, Malika shifted to play content about adults having to go out in the world to work and being afraid to leave their family behind. The clinician responded to these separation process themes with comments such as "It's scary to leave home to go to work," "Everybody worries about what will happen to their families when they go away," and "Wonder what might happen?" Although the separation process theme continued, Malika's play content shifted to drawing roads and incorporating the clinician into the play. Comments within the metaphor included "We're going out on the road together," and "Rough road we're driving on. It's scary." At about the fifth session and in response to comments that "Ending our time together each week is hard," Malika began to handle the separation at the end of appointments by putting toys back in the play bag and saying, "This puts the world back like it really is until next week."

Gradually, the process themes shifted to include separation/individuation, as evidenced by play content that broke things apart and put them back together again. After several weeks of this play, Malika broke play-doh into three parts and verbalized, "Just like my family." The clinical social worker simply reflected back, "Just like your family broke apart." Malika continued to work the play-doh and shift back and forth from play process to reality as she alternately talked about the three play-doh blobs separating and going their way and her parents' divorce. Her repetitive verbalization was "But baby blob owns the big blobs and if she doesn't let go and go out, they can't leave." The clinician variously commented at different points, "It hurts when blobs go away," "Baby blob feels responsible for keeping the family together but she can't do it. She isn't the grownup," "Baby blob is hurt and scared about what will happen to her," and "Baby blob worries whether she is big enough to be okay." Somewhat later, Malika added a rocket to the play and blasted it into space with the three blobs of play-doh on it. At blast off, the blob pilot fell off; the other two blobs "were scared but learning to fly." Malika then commented "And baby blob grew up and flew." In the next few appointments, Malika talked directly about her father, her own hurt and confusion about his departure, and her fears about her mother's surgery. After five months, she was no longer clinging to her mother and was attending school regularly, but continued to deal with separation/individuation themes. These themes were apparent in her doll play and storytelling with characters who practiced coming and going, holding on and letting go. Gradually, Malika's play conveyed more of a sense of object constancy. She no longer expressed fears that the characters might vanish or that the clinician might forget her appointments. Gradually, adventure play and mastery themes became apparent in her play.

At twelve months, her content and process themes began to include magic cures and the magician who made people feel better. She used this magic "fix-it" motif throughout the termination process. In the final appointment, Malika broke open a new can of play-doh, then sealed it back up and carefully filled in the cracks. In response to the comment that Malika still wanted to put the play-doh blobs back together in their house, Malika agreed, but added, "I guess treatment can open you up and fix your problems but can't put your family back together again—like Humpty Dumpty, huh?" The clinical social worker agreed that treatment could help people understand, could fix feelings, but couldn't fix wishes. With this, Malika sighed and announced that she wasn't scared any more and was ready to say goodbye.

In trust and safety play, the child relates to the clinician as a nurturing and protective caregiver. The narrative process theme revolves around gratification of infantile needs. In expressing this theme, children usually assume both symbolic roles in the parent/child role set. That is, the child is simultaneously both the symbolic caregiver who feeds and the symbolic infant (doll, pet) who is fed and generally cared for. For example, child clients play mother to doll babies—rocking, feeding, cleaning, putting to bed, and then beginning the process all over again. At times, the doll baby is reprimanded and punished for assorted transgressions. This play activity is alternately nurturing and being nurtured, comforting and being comforted, punishing and rewarding, providing safety and encouraging exploration. In summary, the process themes of the earliest developmental play as witnessed in therapy are characterized by rhythmic, repetitive expressions of nurturance and protection as children seek to develop trust in a good-enough environment (Winnicott, 1965a).

Attachment and Loss Theme.   When working on developmental tasks concerned with attachment, object constancy, separation, and loss (Bowlby, 1969, 1988; Mahler, Pine, and Bergman, 1975), child clients often attempt to turn passive experiencing of loss and abandonment into active doing to counteract feelings of helplessness in the face of abandonment. To work through their fears and process the attachment/loss motif, children often set up games and stories in which they actively control the players' comings and goings. Characterized by an insatiable repetitive style, this type of play is organized around two players—usually mother and child—engaged in ritualized plots of leaving/returning and caring for/being cared for. Peek-a-boo and hide-and-seek are exemplars of this theme.

Self/Other Differentiation and Autonomy Theme.   When working on developmental tasks of self/other differentiation (Mahler, Pine, and Bergman, 1975) and autonomy (Erikson, 1950), child clients seek to understand self in relation to both their physical and social environments. Initially, simple toys or other play tools are used in a rigid and obsessional style with little variation. The play pattern is neat and carefully controlled. Feelings are hidden. In response, the therapeutic relationship rapidly shifts back and forth from nurturance, acceptance, and permissiveness to protectiveness, stimulation, and expectation. Gradually, children perceive that the clinician understands their need for physical outlets but protects them from hurt. Freedom of action is allowed within safe limits. As children release built-up tension, they become open to new experiences and reasoning, and begin to search for the controls and behavioral limits of their choice. Thus, the process of easing internal constrictions and oppositional defenses and substituting prescriptions for voluntary self-control begins on a physical level. With the release of these constrictions and defenses, child clients acquire a less fearful concept of reality and begin to trust first the clinician, next their peers, and then other adults.

In brief, the therapeutic theme of this developmental play phase is differentiating self from others and establishing autonomy versus shame and doubt

(Erikson, 1950). The theme often appears to be "an eye for an eye" as children struggle to gain their heartfelt desires, obtain their fair share of previously limited nurturance supplies, and become autonomous.

Gender and Sexuality Theme. When working on developmental tasks in the psychosocial stage of initiative versus guilt (Erikson, 1950), children continue to explore the social world in relation to self, but focus more on gender identity and sexuality themes. They enact adult roles through doll and puppet play, fantasy, and storytelling. They assume impressive gender roles (masculine and feminine) with no thought as to age or power differences between self, parents, and other adults. The core of their fantasies revolves around being big enough to do what grownups do.

The plots reflect children's fluidity, creativity, endless change, and intense feelings. The process is unpredictable. The activity deals with gender identity and relationships, and also conveys complex social content with several persons in various roles. To support their play within this developmental stage, children select toys that enable them to be as big as grownups and to have the future now. At other times, they attempt to cope through monster fantasies. Whether human or animal, their monsters represent mysterious figures who are powerful and secretive. Sometimes the monsters are frightening. Sometimes they are powerful protectors who seek to revenge or rescue a helpless being. Although children are increasingly becoming a social self in this developmental stage, their actual play style at various times may be solitary, parallel, or interactional.

In restorative play reflecting this developmental theme, children's emotional and social deficits also must be understood in relation to the frustrations and deficits of earlier psychosocial stages. The clinician observes and works with children's conflicts, developmental lacunae, need for play activities that reflect regression (actual and in the service of intrapersonal growth), and both representational and imaginative projections. The beginnings of new growth processes are apparent through the play activities and narrative thematic process. In turn, these activities and processes become the means through which children mobilize further psychosocial development.

Reality and Industry Theme. When working on developmental tasks in the psychosocial stage of industry versus inferiority (Erikson, 1950), children use reality to disengage from unfulfillable fantasies. In addition, they begin to identify with adults and their work and productivity. As they use tools to master materials and construct miniature objects, their representational activity imitates that of adults. As children work on play objects, they are usually critical of self, not satisfied with their achievements, and especially vulnerable to the wishful fantasy of going back and starting all over again to do it perfectly. Possessions and collections become extensions of self. Making and collecting objects gives increasing satisfaction as they regularly add to their collections, reorganize them, care for them, and anxiously repair broken parts while mourning over the very personal hurt of the break. As child clients outgrow particular collections, they move on to others that are often increasingly sophisticated. Once the meaning of a particular sublimation and object transformation becomes clear in therapy, the clinician responds to the feelings and defenses that underly each collecting activity.

Fantasies tend to be modified and displaced. Rules, regulations, and organized games become increasingly important. Early-childhood fears, fantasies, and rivalries become transformed through sublimation into secret groups, hobbies and collections, sports, and games of chance. For example, fantasies begin to find expression in both positive and negative reality figures, such as robbers, addicts, hijackers, kidnappers, sports figures, models, singers, and actors/actresses. Fantasies also find expression in television, movie, and book characters. Play content often revolves around a loyal group of peers playing together by means of strict rules. By emphasizing control and conformity to standards, the external world of reality offers safety against the internal affective world of fantasy, which at times may be overwhelming to a child.

In brief, the developmental process theme of this transitional play phase in therapy is transforming fantasy into reality and achieving perfection in play activities through repetitive practice. By beginning over and over again, children deny the possibility of failure and the passage of time.

Symbolic Reframing as Reflective of Goal Accomplishment

Another treatment goal in developmental play therapy is to facilitate resolution of problems and conflicts and restore psychosocial functioning through symbolic reframing and problem solving (Hamilton, 1947; Lieberman, 1979; Mishne, 1983; Robinson, 1936). To understand the metaphor language and thematic content in play, clinical social workers first enter the world of childhood and draw on professional literature and traditional practice wisdom to familiarize themselves with the generic concepts, meanings, and values of play materials. From this vantage point, they then attend to how particular child clients translate generic human and animal figures into personally meaningful, context-specific metaphors that symbolically reframe their problems and conflicts for therapeutic work. Similarly, they note how children make toys, games, and other play materials personally meaningful by translating them into context-specific, representational, make-believe activity.

As these generic play materials take on specific symbolic meanings through play, child clients' reframing represents a displaced expression of their intrapersonal and interpersonal struggles in their internal affective and real worlds. To sort out the uniquely constructed and context-specific representations of a particular child, clinicians draw on their knowledge of this child as obtained from the social case history, biopsychosocial assessment, and observations over time. As seen in the following case example, they note and respond indirectly within the play metaphor to the observable content and process of the play, the associated feelings, and the possible meanings derived from their general knowledge and specific understanding of this particular child.

Case Example: Symbolic Reframing of Problems and Conflicts

Eight-year-old Tom was placed in foster care by court order as ungovernable, improperly supervised at home, and a chronic runaway. He refused to talk at all about his father. According to his mother and foster mother, Tom did not know that his father was in jail. The therapy sessions were usually conducted in the backyard or basement of his foster home, due to the reality of transportation and childcare problems. In one of their early sessions, Tom and the clinical social worker caught a grasshopper. Together, they fixed a cage for the grasshopper and discussed how to feed and care for it. The clinician then shifted the discussion and action from providing nurturance and protection to the feeling level—wondering how the grasshopper felt all locked up, how the grasshopper family felt without him, and what might happen to him. Tom quickly projected himself into the grasshopper's predicament and began to deal with the clinical social worker's "I wonder how ___" comments. Initially, Tom/grasshopper responded in terms of himself in foster care, although he did not openly spell this out. In her collaborative conference with the foster mother, the clinician alerted her to Tom's current identification with the grasshopper. Together, they worked out strategies for the foster mother to handle this identification, the nurturance and protection issues that might be raised, the feelings related to separation and loss, and the acting out that might be triggered.

In the following session, Tom announced that they had to name the grasshopper. Last week, he had thought about calling him Tommy, but Tommy didn't seem to fit any more. After going through the pros and cons of several names, Tom was able to talk about the grasshopper's feeling of not belonging anywhere and not knowing who he was. In the next session, Tom said, "Those were little-boy problems the grasshopper had before. He can manage those. Now, he's got grownup problems, so let's call him J.D." (These are his father's initials.) This time Tom/J.D./grasshopper responded to the clinical social worker's same "I wonder how _____" in terms of imprisonment, aggression, and runaway issues. For many weeks, they worked with variations on this theme through telling stories and drawing pictures about the grasshopper. Finally, Tom was able to say, "I made my Dad go to jail. He spanked me and I got mad and told him the cops would put him in jail for beating me—and they did." (The reality was that on several occasions his father had beaten Tom severely, broken multiple bones, and caused internal bleeding.) Needless to say, Tom continued to work on these issues for some months before he was ready to be reunited with his mother. During this period of Tom's foster placement, she was simultaneously working on her own personal and parenting issues with her social worker.

Along with each child's personally framed metaphor, the clinical social worker and child use the behavioral, affective, and cognitive dimensions of play therapy to process the problems and conflicts and restore psychosocial functioning. The behavioral dimension is used to focus the play activity on the problems and conflicts at hand, clarify the differences between play and play therapy, and improve the child's ability to communicate with the clinician. While communicating through play may include direct verbalization as an integral part of the process, the main method of communicating is indirectly through the metaphor.

Their communication most often begins with and is related to the play action and thematic process. The affective dimension of the play process refers to steps taken by the child and clinical social worker to provide a growth-inducing or corrective psychosocial experience for the child. In this sense, the play represents the externalized expression of the child's feeling state, problem solving, and emotional growth. Again, the clinician acknowledges these feelings within the metaphor. The cognitive dimension refers to those actions taken by the clinician to facilitate children's understanding of self—their perceptions and thoughts about the feelings, relationships, behavior, and influencing events associated with the problems and conflicts of concern.

Within this overarching therapeutic goal of facilitating resolution of problems and conflicts and restoring psychosocial functioning, four therapeutic objectives are frequently addressed: binding anxiety, establishing behavioral limits, coping with situational stress, and changing self-defeating behavior patterns.

Binding Anxiety.   Some child clients are unable to express themselves due to immobilizing anxiety. They remain silent, change the subject, cry, or stutter. Sometimes the clinician is able to give the child something to do or something to hold onto that binds or reduces the level of anxiety. In this sense, throwing a ball or working on a picture puzzle become play activities used to enable children to proceed with their concerns. Similarly, a teddy bear may serve as a transitional object between the world of home and the world of play therapy. Most of the time, the clinician responds indirectly to the symbolic metaphor in the play *(The teddy bear looks worried.),* less often with direct statements in response to the child's feelings illustrated by the play *(You seem worried today.).* A third technique is for the clinical social worker to enter the child's play and assume a role within the make-believe in order to reenact and rework events in the child's own life. When enacting a departure from what actually happened, the clinician may present children with alternative reenactments, help them grapple with these alternatives, encourage them to experiment with new ways of coping, and enable them to explore the rigidity of their coping responses in differing situations (Burns, 1970). These and similar techniques in the context of the therapeutic alliance help a child client recognize the kinds of feelings being expressed indirectly through their behavior and develop means for handling them. In their use of activity and toys or other belongings to bind anxiety, children convey their differing levels of awareness of the problem, current coping capacity, and the amount of directness that they can tolerate in confronting and dealing with their problems and ways of coping and adaptation.

Establishing Behavioral Limits.   Children's need to have their defenses supported and their acting out controlled rather than promoted appears frequently. Although accepting of the symbolic representation of all feelings, the clinician does not accept all behaviors. A few simple rules about protecting the child client, the therapist, and the premises from undue harm are usually sufficient to anchor play therapy in safe reality. As absolute limits within sessions, children are not allowed to attack the social worker, hurt self, or engage in dangerous activity. These limitations are established for the child's benefit and guard against children frightening themselves with their out-of-control behavior or developing guilt about harmful or destructive behavior. Such protective limits build a sense of security in the working alliance and the playroom as safe therapeutic holding environments (Winnicott, 1971). Limits on behavioral actions and activities are always stated in a firm, friendly manner. Unenforceable limits are to be avoided.

Routine clinical limits revolve around toys and time, and usually become treatment issues as children test the firmness of boundaries. For example, willful destruction of irreplaceable play material is not allowed; destruction of play-doh or building-block creations is. Toys are not to be taken from the playroom. Similarly, with a preestablished time limit (usually fifty minutes), leaving early or extending the time become boundary issues to be handled within the therapeutic process according to individual need. In most instances, the last few minutes become clean-up time, serve to bring closure to the therapeutic work, and provide a bridge back to the world of reality.

In general, the principle of as few limits as possible serves the clinical social worker and child client well. Occasionally, however, the therapeutic need arises for other limits to be set for reasons of ethics, law, social acceptability, or clinical appropriateness.

Coping with Situational Stress.   Basically, healthy children freely play out their tensions, fears, and conflicts. In the process, they learn to cope with changes in their physical and social environments. For example, all children sooner or later are faced with new family situations (e.g., birth, move), life transitions (e.g., school entry, promotion, graduation), major community events (e.g., fire, flood, hurricane, riot, racism, bombing), or family crises (e.g., illness, accident, unemployment, divorce, death). They often perceive the resulting life changes as threatening and stressful. In such situations, play may serve to diminish their anxiety and restore a sense of mastery and balance.

However, if they become overwhelmed by the stress, they may show confusion, high anxiety, strong hostility, or uncontrollable aggression. Crisis intervention may serve these distressed children well. In these instances, developmental play therapy may take the form of brief situational play activity and be combined with age-appropriate experiential and cognitive techniques; transitional objects also may be useful. Basically, this supportive growth-producing relationship provides these children with an opportunity to express and come to terms with their feelings about the event and its associated changes. It diminishes their anxiety and facilitates resolution of their concerns before the psychosocial dysfunction becomes chronic and the maladaptive coping style entrenched.

Availability of specific play materials is less important here than consideration of the child's needs and ability to project conflictual content and engage in functional process. The skilled clinician easily picks up clues from play action, metaphors, themes, and the narrative process with a child client. Through such attuned work, vulnerable children achieve more satisfying ways of coping with their current life situations, and also learn coping skills transferable to other areas of life and later stressful situations.

Changing Self-defeating Behavior Patterns.   Many children enter play therapy because of all-pervasive and self-defeating behavior patterns variously described as aggressive, demanding, self-destructive, seductive, and underachieving, to name a few. While at first glance these descriptors seem to reflect an accurate picture, it is quickly apparent that they are simply behavioral labels and do not depict children's intrapersonal and interpersonal worlds.

Because children's style of playing is reflective of their daily task performance and general coping at home, in school, and with peers, dysfunctional behavior patterns soon become apparent in play therapy. While their behavior clearly shows the what and how of their thinking and feeling, it does not necessarily convey why they think and feel in a particular way about a particular person or thing. Therefore, too quick a focus on surface behaviors and feelings in play therapy may truncate the symbolic reframing and processual development of the underlying core problem. The why is answered as the metaphors and process themes develop. In time, the clinician and child begin to learn about and grapple with how the child feels and thinks about his or her intrapersonal and interpersonal self in his or her miniature representational and real worlds.

Initially, children begin to understand and learn different ways of handling self within the play process in their representational world. Later, the clinician enables children to draw parallels at home, at school, and on the playground. By working with their cognitive understanding, affective development, and behavioral expression as a whole, the clinical social worker enables them to make and act on connections between their real and representational worlds. Only in this way does lasting change come about.

Conclusion

It is clear that the elements and processes of the co-created therapeutic alliance undergird the development and evolution of the clinical narrative and metaphors through which problems, issues, and conflicts are explored and maturational processes take hold. While the clinical social worker bears professional responsibility for the therapeutic alliance and clinical narrative, developmental play therapy follows Taft's (1933) view that children have the inner strength and capacity to direct their own lives and change their behavior constructively. Therefore, in this treatment model, children are given the freedom to choose to play or not play, to grow and mature or not.

3 Play Objects and Symbolic Metaphor: Tools in Developmental Change

Play materials serve as the basic language, tools, and techniques by which child clients and clinical social workers communicate symbolically and directly about whatever has brought the child into therapy and whatever the child needs to work on over the course of treatment. The play materials are selected and made available purposively to represent children's developmental needs, allow a range of choices, and have functional and symbolic flexibility for purposes of projective expression and communication of the clinical narrative. For example, children may use these materials to nurture and feed, make messes, build and construct, draw, tell stories, and play games in the service of problem solving, behavior change, conflict resolution, and reparative development. Given the budgetary and space constraints of most practice settings, however, the materials actually available are likely to be limited to what fits in a contained space, such as an office file drawer or a social worker's knapsack.

Because therapeutic play does not take place in a vacuum, attention in this chapter is first devoted to creating a safe environmental context for the action. Next, the focus shifts to an overview of the widest possible array of projective materials that could be used to communicate ideas and feelings about the developmental disturbances, conflictual issues, behavioral challenges, and clinical process themes that occur in clinical work. In this chapter, presentation of these materials is organized around six major developmental action themes in play therapy: (1) nurturing and feeding; (2) making a mess using various materials; (3) constructing and building; (4) drawing; (5) storytelling with words and representational toys; and (6) playing games. In conclusion, this broad ideal array is condensed into a realistic set of projective materials that form a basic play knapsack for clinical social workers.

Creating a Play Environment

Physical Environment

While the preferable location for therapeutic play is probably a separate playroom, the reality of space constraints in service settings generally means creative use of a designated place within the clinician's office, an empty classroom, or the child's home. Whatever the treatment space, it ideally will have an easily cleanable floor covering, a pleasant but not too stimulating color scheme, minimal furniture, and a sense of orderliness and safety. The latter is essential because many child clients experience their personal worlds as chaotic, overwhelming, or frightening. If possible, there should be a child-sized table, two chairs, both open and closed storage space for the play materials, and either a sink with running water or a modest-sized plastic container and towel. If the treatment space is in the clinical social worker's office, breakable furnishings should be kept to a minimum. Personal belongings (especially family pictures and mementos) should be avoided in order not to confound the treatment alliance. Clear physical boundaries and an atmosphere of safety provide a facilitating physical environment that serves as a backdrop conducive to the creation of the good-enough psychosocial environment needed for play therapy (Applegate and Bonovitz, 1995; Milos and Reiss, 1982; Oaklander, 1988; Winnicott, 1965a, 1971) .

Psychosocial Environment

To create a psychosocial environment with a sense of safety and security, the clinician ordinarily clarifies what will and will not be done together, and also spells out the cardinal limits of play therapy during the initial or early sessions. Spelling out what is expected of children in their designated play therapy space and specially allocated time prepares the child for responsible use of self and the therapeutic environment in the service of developmental growth and change. Ideally, these environmental safety, protection, and clean-up limits represent the highest level of reality expected of child clients.

Protective limits include a light explanation that children are not allowed to hurt themselves or the therapist, wantonly destroy the treatment environment or play tools, leave the playroom a mess, and extend the therapy session beyond the allotted time. As always with general principles, there are exceptions to the rule of when and how to introduce and enforce them. To stimulate expressive play with inhibited children or children who want to please, for example, the clinician usually elects to wait until the therapeutic alliance is formed and then sets limits only as the need arises. To avoid power struggles with oppositional children, the limits are usually established initially but not enforced in an authoritarian manner. With all children, limits are worked and reworked according to the ways in which developmental needs and conflicts play out within the play therapy process.

At some point within the clinical process, a few child clients will test their therapists' authority by attempting to hurt them or destroy the play materials and office furnishings. At these times, clinicians must be quick to react in nonthreatening ways and provide alternative scenarios. For example, the child who rushes to destroy the dollhouse may be told, "You really want to wreck the dollhouse. Let's talk about it instead." If the child proceeds to wreck the dollhouse anyway, the clinician reflects the feeling, "You are angry that I asked you not to destroy the dollhouse." The child may then say something like, "Shut up, stupid," or "You're really pissed off." In turn, the calm response is, "Hey, I think you're really pissed off. Let's fix this house together." Usually, the child will comply.

When a child tries to hit, kick, scratch, or bite, a stern emphatic tone exclaiming, "STOP! You may NOT hurt me!" may work. Often, the child will withdraw. Then, the clinician reflects the anger underlying the behavior, as well as that provoked by such an authoritative statement. For example, a youngster in treatment because of severe acting-out behavior at home pushed her adoptive parents to the limit. One day, her mother yelled, "Something must be done about you!" The message the child heard was her mother's desire to get rid of her. In treatment, she reenacted her fears of abandonment by breaking play materials. After reflecting back this child's angry feelings, her clinical social worker simply added, "You know, I'll be here for you and together we'll get through this." The child responded, "No! You'll get rid of me." After a few minutes of silence, she continued, "My mother wants to get rid of me." This incident served as a turning point in the therapy, and her usual resistance gave way to acceptance and understanding of interpretations.

Transitional Space

The rule of cooperative cleanup and pickup in the last few minutes of each session transitions a child from the therapeutic play world back to the real world outside the office. Child clients, however, love to test their therapists by not cleaning up. For example, one encopretic boy refused to help put away the materials. He would throw fifty-two cards around the room and march out the door. The expectation was that the therapist would clean up in the same way that he insisted his mother flush the toilet to clean up after his infrequent bowel movements. Until the underlying conflict of autonomy and control could be interpreted and understood, the clinical social worker permitted him to leave without cleaning up. While she did not clean up in his presence, she did reserve time for cleanup prior to the next child. Thus, in this and other instances, refusal to clean up, indeed, becomes a symbolic metaphor to be addressed at later, more clinically appropriate times.

Developmental Action Themes in Play Therapy

Nurturing and Feeding

Because food, nurturing, and feeding play such a prominent part in early child development and, indeed, throughout life, it is not surprising to find these themes and metaphors present in the clinical narrative. Food *per se* is endowed with complex beliefs, values, symbolic meanings, and emotional connotations of home and hearth, caring and warmth. Additionally, food and feeding are intermixed with nurturing throughout individual and familial life experiences in both the real and intrapersonal worlds of children and adults. Thus, in both life and therapy, it is often difficult to differentiate the physiological, psychological, and social aspects of food, nurturing, and feeding.

Therapist-provided Food and Imagery.   When therapists make food available or introduce real and imaginary food and feeding situations into developmental play therapy, they are presenting themselves either as need-satisfying, nurturing parents (Haworth and Keller, 1964; Lloyd, 1978; Litoff, 1959) or as parents concerned with rewarding positive actions and corrective socialization (Erikson, 1950; Lloyd, 1978). In the first scenario, early relational deprivations (not enough or poorly timed feeding) or power struggles (too much, forced, poorly timed feeding) may be reworked through use of real but preferably symbolic food that reawakens developmental disruptions or distortions in food intake (A. Freud, 1963) and stimulates projection of these child disturbances into the transference elements of the therapeutic alliance. As part of reworking these early relationships, the clinician responds with good-enough nurturant mothering to the child's psychosocial developmental needs and conflicts along the normal epigenetic developmental line of food intake:

- being nursed at breast or bottle either by clock or on demand
- weaning from breast or bottle, mother or infant initiated
- transitioning from being fed to self-feeding
- fading equation of food = mother
- moving toward self-determination and rational attitudes toward food (A. Freud, 1963)

Sometimes approaching this scenario through symbolic realization is sufficient. In other instances, children are so emotionally deprived that actual realization (in the form of candy, cookies, popcorn, or liquid snacks) may become useful.

In the second scenario, food and feeding are more tied into resocialization and behavior-correction treatment approaches. Here, food is used purposively and meaningfully to reeducate a child about acceptable ways of being and behaving. In this instance, the clinician is assuming more of an authority image than a nurturing one, and is employing food as control and reward in an educational, reconditioning process. While such behavior-management approaches (alternately termed "M & M treatment") make liberal use of food as positive reinforcement, they may also introduce derivative rewards equated with nurture and love in the form of special privileges (e.g., videogames, toys, television, activities) at home.

Child-introduced Themes.   Children introduce food, feeding, and nurturing themes in various play activities within the clinical narrative. They and their imaginary characters may evidence the voracious and uncontrolled food intake of the emotionally starved child or the aggressive rejection of food characteristic of the oppositional or withholding child. In terms of affect, children's food themes may incorporate feelings of love, rejection, danger, suspicion, guilt, shame, or aggression, to name a few. In their play, they may lovingly bottle-feed doll babies and small animals, serve themselves and the clinician make-believe tea and cake, or bring their own snack for whenever they feel the need for self-soothing. Conversely, child clients and their characters also may introduce narratives in which food is thrown, mangled, or otherwise repudiated. Additional themes may reflect angry, punitive withholding of food and starvation themes. Thus, food and feeding issues in developmental play therapy may reflect both real and representational worlds, ranging from total dependence on the provider for food to food intake regulated more on the basis of the child's own needs and appetites (A. Freud, 1963; Lloyd, 1978). For homeless children and children living in families below the poverty line, food themes are likely to represent real physical deprivation as well as emotional issues.

Making a Mess

Beginning clinical social workers often ask, "Why bother with sand, water, clay, and finger paints? They make such a mess!" That is precisely the reason for bothering. Messing around with these elementary materials allows child clients to give form to feelings and concerns for which they have no words. Indeed, it is the experiencing and symbolic expression in the work with these basic materials that enables the treatment process to go forward.

As part of mastering the social-adjustment tasks associated with control of bodily functions (i.e., oral, urethral, anal), most infants discover the tactile stimulation inherent in both the products of their bodies and the food put into their bodies. These things are experienced as warm/cold, dry/wet, and solid/liquid by infants and toddlers who happily splash, smear, and throw them. Eventually, the toddler learns to substitute water, sand, and clay as play objects and engages in an endless variety of play patterns. Squirting water and throwing sand, for example, may become either techniques of aggression or defensive techniques against the aggressive acts of others.

At the same time they are exploring their bodies and their environments, preschoolers are the recipients of adult efforts to curb their messy explorations. In some instances, young children are prematurely deprived of the growth-promoting activities of particular psychosocial developmental stages by their life circumstances or by their parents and caregivers. At other times, older children find themselves in overwhelming or traumatic life situations that precipitate regression to earlier psychosocial developmental stages and also trigger earlier conflicts and developmental tasks. When this has happened, child clients often seek symbolic substitutes for the traumatic event and the original developmental activities. They then use these symbolic substitutes in play therapy in proportion to the degree of environmental stress and developmental deprivation experienced.

Water Play.   In water play, for example, there is symbolic substitution of a clear neutral medium for the earlier oral and tactile exploration of body products. Water's primitive nonthreatening liquid nature allows children to regress in the play process; recapture the psychosocial developmental prerogatives of infancy and toddlerhood; and gain control over this symbolic substitute through messing, splashing, and manipulating it at will. To explore and mess, however, child clients often need advance permission and reassurance from the clinician that water play is okay at this special time and place and with these special materials.

Water play equipment is simple: a modest-sized sink or plastic container to hold water, a small container of liquid soap, a sponge to soak and squeeze, plastic bottles and cups to fill and empty, plastic utensils to beat and stir, and disposable straws to blow water bubbles (Caplan and Caplan, 1973). This equipment lends itself to various experimental activities and makes no skill or achievement demands on its users.

Water play is appropriate for any chronological-age child at any level of psychosocial development or with any developmental disturbance. For example, an older child whose behavior and developmental activities are reminiscent of eighteen-month-olds will simply splash and mess. Wiping up the mess provides as much fun and satisfaction for this child as splashing and spilling. By contrast, the older child whose behaviors and developmental activities are reminiscent of five-year-olds is ready for form and purpose in water play. Mopping floors and washing windows in imitation of adults takes the place of free-play splashing. The satisfaction for this child derives from both task accomplishment and the opportunity to identify with adult role models. Repetitive water play can soothe

The Peace Treaty

When Matthew was five years old, he was referred to the clinical social worker for aggressive behavior that included hitting his infant brother, kicking playmates, and temper tantrums. His parents and teacher described impulsivity and low frustration tolerance. He wet his bed and had "accidents" at school. During the biopsychosocial assessment, Matthew explained that he could not stop hitting and kicking: "I tell my brain to don't make me do it." He displayed magical thinking and was quite convinced that when he wished something, it would happen. The therapist offered various materials during the play. Matthew threw and kicked them around the room. His primitive drawings were like the scribbling of a two-year-old. Because he was unable to engage in interactive play, water was introduced as a medium to help Matthew gain control while making a mess. In the initial phase, he splashed the therapist much the way he would splash his younger brother in the bathtub. Over time, he took pleasure in establishing order out of chaos with battleships in the sink. The war that took place over a six-month period resulted in a peace treaty among combatants and, concomitantly, a change in his behavior at home and school.

explosive children, serve as an acceptable outlet for expression of aggression, and free constricted children to become involved in new activities (Allan and Lawton-Speert, 1993; Hartley, Frank, and Goldenson, 1964; Par, 1990). A note of caution is indicated with groups of children, however, as interactive water play tends to be stimulating and promotes splashing, chasing, and noisy behavior that may quickly escalate out of control.

Regardless of developmental disturbance, water can be useful as part of clean-up time at the end of each play therapy session. By conveying that it is time to finish the task at hand, water helps bring child clients back to the reality of everyday life before they leave the playroom.

Sand Play.   Although likely to be available only in exceptionally well-furbished playrooms, sand is a basic nonthreatening material that provides tactile stimulation and opportunity for unstructured activity. This play medium requires a modest-sized sand tray, an easily cleaned floor covering, sieves, molds, cups, bowls, utensils, and small plastic human and animal figures. This relatively clean material is useful with children who avoid getting dirty, expressing affect, and playing freely. A modern-day substitution of a box of styrofoam packing bits provides an alternative world children can control when they need to mess around in trial-and-error activity until their own play themes are established. For example, they may need to engage in repetitive play in which pouring, measuring, and filling are part of the exploration and reworking of earlier psychosocial development and adjustment tasks. They may use human and animal figures to play out familiar stories, conflictual developmental themes, or traumatic experiences in the safe environmental context of the sand tray or packing box (Allen and Berry, 1987; Caplan and Caplan, 1973). Children may bury their own secrets and fears as well as family secrets (Carey, 1990). They may seek to uncover treasures as metaphors

To Fly

Ten-year-old Alejandro wanted to become an astronaut. However, the prognosis for his particularly virulent form of muscular dystrophy was an early death. Alejandro was already utterly dependent on his parents for his basic needs of eating, toileting, and bathing. Although his arm movements were quite impaired, he was still able to move his hands and use a wheelchair for mobility. His neurologist referred him to the clinical social worker because of the verbal abuse he inflicted upon his family. So that Alejandro could experience tactile stimulation and control a tiny part of his environment, the clinician placed a portable sand tray on the arms of the wheelchair. Together, they built a space station where he could go to move freely, walk, run, and float unencumbered by gravity and reality. This make-believe activity led to a discussion of burial grounds on other planets where children with muscular dystrophy could go and where "Their spirits live on into eternity flying happily ever after."

representative of their own assets and strengths that they and their clinical social workers are seeking to discover in therapy. They may also build make-believe worlds where they establish their own version of reality, or they may build and destroy painful conflictual worlds.

Working with Clay. Sometime between the ages of two and four, children discover a new texture and form: mixed water/sand and water/dirt. They discover that clay not only has some of these same mixed properties, but also the definite advantages of being pliable to the slightest touch, maintaining desired shapes, and allowing constant change and reworking without destroying the play medium. Because working with this primitive material requires minimal cognitive sophistication, clay or the sanitized play-doh substitute are suitable for use with a wide range of children.

Mastering the multiple dimensions and meanings of clay requires both hands. In using clay for working out their own problems and conflicts, children should be allowed to manipulate and create freely. In so doing, they usually progress from the motor exercise of kneading and diffuse play to the more structured activity involved in transforming clay into molded forms representing real or imaginary objects. The meanings that youngsters attach to these objects in turn stimulate further fantasy projections. In working through developmental disturbances, for example, child clients can project developmental disruptions and distortions onto and create stories around clay objects. In this manner, clay facilitates bringing developmental disturbances, fantasies, conflicts, and problems to conscious levels where they become accessible to therapeutic work (Woltmann, 1964). Thus, the value of the clay work is that children surface some of their treatment issues in a form that is not only safe (Tait and Depta, 1994), but also visible, acceptable, available for discussion, and accessible to experimentation and change.

With clay, a child's fantasies usually center around anal content, socialization issues of public and private body activities, and autonomy issues. Some children, however, also use clay for issues related to initiative and industry. If children have not mastered the industry versus inferiority developmental tasks (Erikson, 1950), they may constantly pretend to build something but will rarely succeed in completing the task. Such child clients often waste clay material by using prodi-

Battling the Monster

Pete, age ten, was school-phobic. In the mornings, he awakened in tears and panic, complained of stomachaches and headaches, and obstinately refused to leave home to attend school. In therapy, Pete created a story in which monster clay figures tried to get into the dollhouse and a clay boy successfully kept them outside. After several sessions, Pete accepted a clay adult into the house to help him do battle. Thus, the therapeutic alliance was facilitated through combining clay creations with storytelling.

gious amounts, mishandling it, and being unrealistic in applying their energies to it. They seem unable to select and organize materials appropriately in their play. They have difficulty judging capacity in relation to ideas. Thus, completion of representational clay creations within the context of the therapeutic relationship gives these child clients a sense of mastery and accomplishment, aligns the clinical social worker with the forces of growth and maturation, and has major impact on their psychosocial development.

Finger Painting.   Often described as socially sanctioned playing with body products, finger painting serves as a medium of self-expression; a manifestation of children's psychosocial developmental capacities; and a form of projective play that provides insight into children's wishes, fantasies, fears, and conflicts. The soft substance and bright colors of the paints provide visual, tactile, and kinesthetic sensations as child clients actively smear with their hands, design symbols, create projective pictures with their fingers, and verbalize their associations (Arlow and Kadis, 1976). Because they can wipe out their productions and create anew, children are not discouraged by inadequate pictures or inhibited by fears of failure. In this way, the therapeutic process provides the freedom to both create and destroy without actually being destructive.

As a diagnostic tool, several aspects of finger painting have projective significance: the color, texture, symbolism, and balance of the painting; the neatness, motion, and technique of the painter; and the child client's feelings and thoughts while painting and upon completion of the product (Arlow and Kadis, 1976; Hartley and Goldenson, 1963). In terms of behavioral style, aggressive and impulse-ridden children often plunge immediately into the paints with both hands. Children who have difficulty with limits in other situations, as well as in play therapy, often smear the paints off the paper. With these children, the clinical social worker creates a safe structured environment for self-expression within pre-established limits and clearly demarcated boundaries. By contrast, the inhibited child client may use one fingertip cautiously dipped in the paint and may seem fearful of covering the entire paper. The clinician encourages such overly controlled children to express their feelings within the clear safe boundaries provided by the paper.

In terms of symbolism, darker colors such as brown or black may suggest hostility or depression; red, feelings of anger and being overwhelmed. Brighter colors of blue, yellow, and green often convey a more cheerful attitude. As always, the meanings of color to a particular child are clarified by the child's thoughts and comments, as well as the child's psychosocial history and assessment. Individual meanings are part of the child's autobiographical narrative, and are best understood in the context of a particular painting and the child's clinical issues over the course of the therapy (Timberlake, 1978a).

In using finger painting, the clinical social worker observes how the child applies self to the task, the rate and rhythm of the work, the colors selected, and the style and flow of the lines drawn. In addition to observing impulses and inhibitions during painting, the clinician encourages the child client to verbalize

The Imaginary Friend

Kazume was an inhibited, shy, anxious six-year-old who lacked the spontaneity and imagination of most youngsters of her age and culture. During the biopsychosocial assessment, she became mute, refusing to respond to projective questions and refusing to draw. Instead, she hid under the clinical social worker's desk. Responding developmentally, the clinical social worker played peek-a-boo, a game that brought Kazume to her feet. Then, she introduced a soft stuffed animal. Kazume returned to her crouched position under the desk. In the next session, the clinician brought out huge pieces of paper and finger paints. Kazume's face lit up as she dabbled her fingers in the messy paints. Upon completion of her masterpiece, she exclaimed, "Look, this is Weigong!" The therapist replied, "Yes, I see. A fine-looking fellow." Kazume then related stories of Weigong going with her to school, comforting her when she awoke from bad dreams, and listening as she told him everything. In fact, he was right here in the office. After Kazume introduced her therapist to imaginary Weigong, he became quite helpful in her treatment.

about the created product and express feelings about the process. As the child tells the story of the completed painting, the clinician comments descriptively on what is observed in the painting and on the affect conveyed by the painting. The clinician also may comment, "I wonder if this painting reminds you of anything." The correlation between the observable content of the product and the child client's verbalized fantasy provides one way of assessing the current psychosocial functioning and state of the child, thereby evaluating treatment progress—or the lack thereof.

Constructing

Manipulating materials and fitting them together satisfies children's universal desire to give form to their thoughts and feelings, build creations, and master their environment. Completing a Lego car, block tower construction, model plane, or picture puzzle conveys a child client's ability to work and persevere at a task, thereby gaining self-esteem through mastery of these materials.

In contrast to model-building kits, Legos, blocks, and puzzles are designed to be joined together, broken apart, and used anew. Thus, child clients can safely build, destroy, and repair these creations again and again. As they project their fears, anger, and other feelings onto their small constructions over which they have full control, children remove much of the power and scariness from their feelings. Thus, with free-play building materials, children can feel safe in playing out their fears of internal and external destruction, of destroying and being destroyed, of losing and being lost. Through this repetitive process, child clients are able to gain make-believe control over things in their environment that ordinarily dwarf and distress them (Caplan and Caplan, 1973; Urban, 1990).

The Racetrack

Yitzhak, age ten, came to see the clinical social worker because "I do everything wrong and nobody likes me." Yitzhak chose to build cars with Lego blocks and spent many hours with his therapist building, comparing, and racing cars. The building process, the creations themselves, the comparisons, and the competitive racing to see whose car would win—all became part of the therapeutic work related to acceptance and self-concept issues.

Drawing

For children, drawing is usually an enjoyable art activity in which paper and pen (or pencil, crayon, and magic marker) are used to create shapes and symbols, explore the connectedness of parts to the whole, and give visible form to feelings and ideas. Most children draw symbolic pictures that replace words, but still convey meaning and affect within the therapeutic relationship (Burns, 1970; LeVieux, 1994; Nickerson, 1973, 1983). Thus, drawing can be a purposive and fairly direct representational method for understanding the conflicts and issues that trouble a child client (DiLeo, 1970; Kramer, 1971; Loewald, 1987). For example, a child may select astronauts to symbolize conquering the unknown or fleeing a difficult situation, soldier or knight figures to represent conflict and aggression or rescue efforts (Reeves and Boyett, 1983).

While each drawing is individually configured and unique in meaning, common pictorial symbols and metaphors of human figures and animals, place and weather, and toys and games usually convey fairly general meanings—*albeit* at times with wide variance from one culture to another (Oster and Gould, 1987). For example, alligators and other big mouth animals may be used to reflect nurturant needs or oral aggression; dogs and other cuddly animals, companionship and transitional objects; or birds, flight and freedom. Caves may hide and protect or, conversely, trap. Mountains may be attainments, obstacles, or something else entirely. Rain may reflect crying or be cleansing. Snow seems cold, the sun warm. How then, with these and the myriads of other possible meanings, does the clinical social worker figure out what a particular child has in mind? In part, the answer lies in asking the child directly (Timberlake, 1978a; Webb, 1991). In addition, the representational ways in which individual children condense multiple metaphors, details, and memories into one picture and their action style in doing so provide indirect clues to the more individualized meaning in their drawings. To make educated decisions about which of these polar opposite or nuanced generic meanings most accurately represents a nonverbal child's intended meaning, clinicians draw on their understanding of this child gained during psychosocial assessment and other interviews, comment on the observable, and await the child's own nonverbal or verbal confirmation that the observation is accurate or not.

The Birds and the Bees

Althea G., age eight, was referred to the mental health clinic by her pediatrician for failure to attend school, fear of leaving home, anxiety about failing to perform adequately, nightmares, and morning nausea unrelated to physical illness. Her symptoms had worsened over the last two years. Two years ago, her maternal grandmother died. Her sister also entered school about this time. Biopsychosocial assessment revealed Mrs. G.'s depression, Mr. and Mrs. G.'s marital conflict, and Althea's school-phobic anxiety. Mrs. G. entered treatment for depression. Mr. and Mrs. G. were seen together biweekly for marital counseling and parental guidance work. Althea began play therapy and immediately expressed her concerns and issues through drawing. In her first drawing (Figure 3.1), Althea expressed her fears and anxiety about therapy by drawing herself in a window placed between two empty windows and guarded by a witch. She drew borders on her early pictures to contain her anxiety and avoid spillover. The remaining figures illustrate the ongoing metaphors and process themes throughout her year of treatment. Figure 3.2 is representative of early drawings of her feared school—a dark building that has bars on the door and windows and is located in a dreary environment. Figure 3.3 picks up on her concerns and fears about leaving her parents and conveys a sense of self caught between two parent teepees and roasted over fiery feelings.

Figures 3.4, 3.5, and 3.7 pick up a recurring sexual theme of the birds and bees. This theme surfaced as the clinical social worker began dealing with the parents' marital problems and working with them to move Althea out of the marital bed and back to her own room. This six-month-long theme slowly shifted as Althea became increasingly comfortable with her parents' realignment in their couple and parental roles. In Figure 3.7, for example, the bees are loudly communicating.

Figure 3.6 (about two thirds of the way through treatment and in the midst of the recurring birds and bees sexual narrative) is a graphic representation of Althea's reaction to the clinical social worker's vacation—the wicked witch flies away leaving the scared ghost to deal with the

FIGURE 3.1 Child and Witch

FIGURE 3.2 Feared School

FIGURE 3.3 Roasted between Two Teepees

fearful house alone. Figures 3.8 and 3.9 represent Althea's self-portraits at termination, presenting quite a marked contrast to her initial portrayal of self and a definite lessening of the heavily constricted boundaries surrounding her earlier pictures.

FIGURE 3.4   Birds and Bees Number 1

FIGURE 3.5   Birds and Bees Number 2

FIGURE 3.6   Witch Goes on Vacation

FIGURE 3.7   Birds and Bees Number 3

FIGURE 3.8   Althea at School

FIGURE 3.9   Althea's Self-portrait

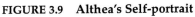

Therapeutic use of drawing is based on the assumption that child clients project their perceptions, feelings, conflicts, and developmental disturbances into their pictures. A note of caution is in order, however, as children's drawings are also influenced by (1) techniques and symbols taught in school; (2) symbols and metaphors familiar in their familial and cultural environments (Sutton-Smith, 1986); (3) psychosocial developmental stage, visual perceptual ability, and motor-muscular coordination; and (4) availability of particular drawing tools, colors, and paper.

The symbolic representations in their drawings offer child clients a sense of control over the external and internal forces depicted. The process of drawing provides opportunity for them to relive their experiences in an active role, even though the original role may have been passive or overwhelming. While integrative and healing properties are present in this creative process, it is important to note that the cathartic effect alone is not sufficient for lasting change (Barlow, Landreth, and Strother, 1985). For change to occur, the clinical social worker

Fat, Dumb, and Stupid

Pubescent at age eleven, Melinda used drawing to express conflicts she faced as a result of her parents' divorce, body image, and cognitive distortions. She assured the clinical social worker that she could speak freely to anyone but the therapist about her problems. She was enraged at her father for abandoning her and her mother lest she abandon her too. These affects were readily available during the sessions in which Melinda used virtually any technique to get thrown out of the office for good. Sometimes, she locked herself in the therapist's office as a way of expressing her extreme ambivalence. At other times, Melinda used drawing to calm herself. The therapist enjoyed these cooling-off periods and leaps of developmental gain from acting out to the more self-soothing and expressive technique of drawing. During a particularly emotionally charged time of negative transference, Melinda drew a series of pictures of herself and the therapist. The first few depicted a formless and faceless Melinda and a rather small insignificant therapist who had arms, legs, and hair but no face or ears. Three weeks later, the therapist emerged with eyes, a nose, and a smile. Melinda emerged as a fully formed fourteen-year-old dressed in a sexually seductive bikini top, mini-skirt, and high-heeled boots. Just before she left the office, she pointed to a book about obesity and said, "This is my problem." When she returned the following week, Melinda drew the clinical social worker in a motorized wheelchair, physically incapacitated after gaining a few thousand pounds. Interestingly, she dressed the therapist in the exact same attire as her earlier drawing of herself. Most striking were the very large eyes and ears. Perhaps Melinda realized and acknowledged that the clinician could hear her problems and see her pain. Then, again, maybe not, because this drawing was immediately followed by one of the therapist blown to smithereens. Melinda's parting words that day were, "You are fat, dumb, and stupid!"—a clear projection of her own felt inadequacies.

searches for the additional clues about children's conflicts, problems, and distortions of reality that are found in the drawings and related narratives. By following the child's therapeutic process, the clinician is able to encourage further exploration and comprehension, not only of the content being expressed in a picture or picture series, but also of the underlying developmental and conflictual themes. For example, child clients provide the key to their own unique symbolic logic, mental processes, and core conflictual themes through their picture content, distortions and emphases, inclusions and omissions, drawing style, and accompanying narrative. In using this play activity, it is easy to see that the clinician may either work within the metaphor and interpret only in terms of the picture itself or encourage verbalized self-observation, autobiographical narrative, reflection, and insight as part of the therapeutic process. Thus, through their drawings, children are helped to observe, interpret, and communicate their understanding of themselves and their world, their attitudes and affects, their issues and conflicts, their strengths and vulnerabilities.

Storytelling

As children grow and develop, they listen to, tell, draw, and play out fairy tales, folktales, bedtime stories, make-believe narratives, action adventure stories, and television plots (Burton, 1986; Franzke, 1989; Shanahan and Morgan, 1989). On the one hand, these stories entertain; on the other, their narrative themes contain experiential, cognitive, and affective dimensions that provide children with the opportunity to explore, re-experience, and confront psychosocial developmental disruptions and distortions, problems-in-living, and traumatic experiences indirectly (Bettelheim, 1950, 1977; Early, 1993; Fraiberg, 1954b, 1954c, 1959; Gardner, 1971), as well as the opportunity to work through issues of normal growth and development.

With Words.   Verbal storytelling, when used as a technique in its own right, ranges from responses to the child client's spontaneous traditional stories and original make-believe narratives to the clinical social worker's structured introduction of fairy tales, books, television plots, and projective tests. Whether traditional or creative, children's spontaneous stories tend to be autobiographical narratives expressed within the story metaphor (Brandell, 1984, 1985).

Storytelling fosters imaginative thought and establishes symbolic situations that children are likely to relate to and imitate. Indeed, according to Costantino and Malgady (1996), human identity develops as a result of narrative or story construction in real life. For years, sociocultural rules and customs, family and group standards of morality, and the achievements of real-life heroes and heroines were the subjects of folk narratives and storytelling. The metaphorical language used in folk and fairy tales has an affective dimension that transforms words into readily grasped visual images useful in enhancing psychosocial functioning.

The Charmer

Stanley made every effort to please the clinical social worker by bringing her gifts, regaling her with laughter about his school activities, and engaging in dramatic story-telling. The major problem was that his inflated self-esteem resulted in bullying and manipulative behavior with his peers and siblings. He seemed utterly convinced that he was popular and strongly denied any problems with friends. By the age of nine, he became a gang leader with his latency-age friends. He admired older boys and wanted to be a rock star so that everyone would fawn all over him. He felt entitled to devalue his playmates and act in manipulative, cruel, and destructive ways. While he charmed the adults in his world, Stanley needed considerable help in building socially appropriate interpersonal skills with his peers. His parents worked closely with the therapist and kept her informed about his teacher's complaints. Stanley himself would infrequently inform her of the idiots at school whom he would kick in the butt and scream obscenities at. One day when he was building the world's tallest house and being uncharacteristically quiet, the therapist said, "Let's play a game. You guess what I'm thinking and I'll guess what you're thinking." This idea fell on deaf ears. She then decided to use a displaced format and said, "I'll tell you what. I'm going to start and end a story and you fill in the middle." He liked this idea as it tapped into his flair for the dramatic. "Once there was this kid who thought he was really cool. He thought he had a lot of friends. Actually, the kids were afraid of him because he was a bully." The end of the story is, "He apologized." Stanley rose to the occasion. "When the kid was little, no one liked him, so he started watching older kids. They were cool, good dressers. Sometimes they were mean. Man, they had respect, so he started acting like them. Sure enough, people started doing what he ordered them to do. Only the problem was that he got caught tying a kid to a tree on the playground. The teacher was mad, so he apologized. The End." This was one of many short stories that, over time, introduced the concepts of remorse, mutuality, and humility, and served as content for further therapeutic work. The addition of a social skills group proved to be an excellent adjunct to his individual therapy.

Bettelheim (1977) and Early (1993), for example, used fairy tale and myth in their work with severely dysfunctional children.

Culturally sensitive use of storytelling may involve bringing cultural elements directly into the story narrative or adapting narratives so that the story is culturally congruent for a particular child. For example, many child clients live between two cultures, their home-based culture and the various Anglo-American and other cultures with which they come in contact in the United States. Stories are helpful in that the narrative can retain the basic cultural values of the child's racial/ethnic cultural group, but also incorporate new elements from other cultures as necessary to make the narrative contemporary and representative for the child. In this way, stories can help children bridge the gap between their heritage and prevailing American values, thereby facilitating the process of transcultural coping and adaptation.

Latino folktales, or *cuentos,* provide another example. These stories contain culturally familiar characters and model values and behaviors with which Latin American children can identify. By grafting themes of psychosocial functioning in the United States into the narrative plot, the clinical social worker integrates the old with the unfamiliar. Thus, behavioral and emotional adaptation in two cultures is depicted as constructive in working with problems of psychosocial dysfunction and transcultural adaptation (Costantino, Malgady, and Rogler, 1986). Imitative actions may result long before internalization occurs.

In selecting stories for structured intervention, the clinician chooses narratives with plots related to the child's life experiences (e.g., illness, death, abuse, sibling rivalry), culture, and developmental needs (e.g., trust, autonomy, initiative and creativity, industry). As stimuli, these stories provide opportunity for projective identification with fantasy characters, as well as opportunity for learning about feelings, ways of coping, and problem solving (Peirce and Edwards, 1988). In selecting stories, it is important to keep in mind the child's reading skills, verbal abilities, and developmental capacities, as well as the following questions: Are there significant persons in the story with whom the child client can identify? What is the overall context of the story? What are the typical and the extraordinary responses to the story? When structured storytelling is used in this planned manner, the preconscious thoughts and feelings of child clients are brought in varying degrees into the child's awareness through the processes of condensation, symbolization, displacement, and projection. In interpreting structured stories, however, the clinical social worker always keeps in mind the degree of awareness that the child actually possesses.

In structured mutual storytelling, a specialized technique formalized by Gardner (1971, 1976), the child is asked to tell a story. The clinician next repeats the story incorporating more adaptive ways of functioning. Then the child tells his or her second version, and so on. Through this ongoing mutual telling of the same story, the child is exposed to alternative ways of behaving and problem solving.

Through Doll Play.   Because childhood play depends on visual elements, it is not surprising that child clients often act out their autobiographical narratives with dolls. This added spatial and action dimension converts the verbal narrative into a miniature model life situation in which the past may be relived, the present revisited, and the future anticipated and at times rehearsed for better coping with known events. The projective rationale is based on the premise that doll play reflects family constellations, thereby capturing children's experiences and attitudes toward parental figures, siblings, and significant others in the interpersonal environment. Although, of necessity, the clinical social worker engages the content and drama of the play narrative with the child, the focal unit of attention and responsive work is the underlying thematic process because it is that process that addresses critical projections and core issues. For example, child clients frequently use large baby dolls to convey underlying process themes of nurture and protection, caring for and being cared for. Often, they will pick up, cuddle, and feed

The Orphanage

Kristen's dollhouse became an orphanage where Mrs. Flanigan terrorized children. The children, in turn, would throw her down the stairs, carve out her heart, or hang her. This eight-year-old adopted child loved the doll play in which she could safely kill off her biological parents by turning passive into active. Many children and potential adoptive parents passed through the halls of Mrs. Flanigan's orphanage, where children were sold to the highest bidder. Girls fetched $20,000 while boys brought $25,000 because they were better. This orphanage scenario endured for about six months. Then the action shifted to a mansion that Kristen shared with four adopted brothers. In reality, only one brother was spared either a learning, behavioral, or emotional disorder. In play, this brother became the object of her disgust. He too was tossed down the stairs. "I hate you," she screamed repeatedly. The parent dolls were rarely at home because they travelled the world over. One time the mother doll came home and entered the house. The Kristen doll yelled, "Get out! I hate you. You're not my real mother. You'll never be my real mother." Although the treatment action within the metaphor remained heated and fast-moving for a prolonged period, Kristen's behavior improved as her anger and aggressive feelings were channeled and drained off in the play sessions, and as her clinical social worker helped her begin to manage her feelings within play scenarios.

the baby doll as they develop a story with a different content theme. Their actions with the doll, however, clearly reflect the underlying theme of the treatment session—the child's own emotional neediness.

The most commonly used materials in doll play include an unroofed, one-story dollhouse; appropriate but minimal furniture; and bendable miniature doll figures representing grandparents, two sets of parent figures, and children (boy, girl, baby). In multicultural service centers, it is helpful to have doll sets representative of the African American, Asian American, Hispanic, and Caucasian families served. Alternatively, a child may need to create a different physical environment in which to share the story. In these instances, the house may become either a hospital (Garot, 1986) or a school.

When buying doll-play materials, the clinician selects basic dolls, dollhouse, and furnishings with few complex moving parts so the child can concentrate on the feelings and ideas to be expressed in the play. In furnishing the dollhouse, it is important to remember that the various rooms often are used to represent conflicts of the various psychosocial stages of development (Kuhli, 1983). For example, the kitchen and dining room may represent oral and trust/mistrust themes; the bathroom, anal, autonomy/shame, and doubt themes; and the bedroom, oedipal rivalry and initiative/guilt themes (Erikson, 1977; Kuhli, 1983).

Child clients are encouraged to select among the available materials for the dolls and furnishings needed to cast a story with the desired characters and create the environmental context for the play scenarios (Knell, 1996; Klem, 1992). Generally, the story or narrative contains common developmental themes such as nurturance and trust, autonomy and protection, anxiety and initiative, and inferiority and industry (Erikson, 1950, 1977). Doll-play dramas also may include real-life scenarios and conflictual themes dealing with power and aggression, attack and destruction, and separation and loss, as well as abandonment and other assorted fears (Gil, 1991; West, 1983). A seriously disturbed child client is often preoccupied with variations on one theme (Knell and Moore, 1990); a healthier child is more likely to complete one theme and move on to another.

With Puppets. If child clients are able to tolerate a greater degree of closeness to reality, they may act out stories with human figure-puppets. Their value as a diagnostic and treatment tool lies in the child's activity and involvement with this projective medium while maintaining behind-the-scenes anonymity. The basic premise underlying therapeutic use of puppets is that children can identify with the puppets and project their own unacceptable feelings, ideas, pain, and conflicts onto them (Bromfield, 1995). Puppets provide a means for testing reality, expressing needs symbolically, and relieving the pressure of anxiety (Carter, 1987; Machler, 1965). Because the puppet does the talking, the child is able to express feelings without guilt or anxiety. Thus, the worst wishes can be acted out and bad happenings can be turned into desired happenings within the play metaphor.

Puppet play can be used with one child or groups of children in structured or unstructured form. Puppet shows may be performed by the child client, the clinical social worker, or both—from prepared scripts or spontaneously. Structured

Annie Finds Her Voice

A few weeks before kindergarten, Annie was referred to the clinical social worker because of regressive behaviors including baby talk, crawling, thumb-sucking, and temper tantrums. The therapist evaluated this child and her family, and began treating Annie twice a week and her parents weekly. During the first two months of treatment, her only verbalizations were "Me, Annie" and "Me want Mommie." (Her mother stayed in the adjoining waiting room.) During this phase, Annie hid, lying down in the corner of the office. Occasionally, she slept. Finally, the therapist commented, "It seems you are going on strike. When people go on strike, they are usually angry about something. Sometimes kids are worried or sad." Shortly thereafter, Annie looked up from the floor and announced, "Me draw." She retrieved some drawing materials, returned to her corner, and compulsively drew stick figures of mice, which she gave to her mother. A few weeks later, she noticed the puppets Mickey and Minnie Mouse in a nearby corner. Once set into play, Annie had Minnie comment to social worker Mickey, "I like to be a baby." Mickey replied that he understood this feeling because baby mice stay with their mommies all day long. Minnie responded, "And they don't go to school." During this stage, Minnie found her voice in therapy, and Annie began using spontaneous speech at home to express her feelings and thoughts. Her baby talk decreased and her temper tantrums ceased. In therapy, she progressed from parallel play to interactive play with a family of dolls.

plays are usually written around age-appropriate, universal-experience themes with clear symbolic representation. For example, a policeman puppet may represent the authority function of a father. A witch puppet may represent a bad mother or, depending on the nature of the therapeutic alliance at a particular point in time, a bad clinician. Animal puppets provide more abstractness, symbolism, and fantasy with which to disguise the core conflict (Burch, 1980). Alligators, for example, may represent oral aggression or counteraggressive defenses. A skunk may represent the encopretic child's denial of her own odor. Again, the special meaning for a particular child depends on that child's projections, preferences, life experiences, and culture.

As the clinician and child take turns with the puppets (the same or different characters), the interaction provides a means of bringing out more clearly the problems and conflicts contained in the child client's fantasy and a means of interpreting within the metaphor of the play. Additional safety is offered in that the child and clinician put all the make-believe together again, and transition from the metaphor back to reality before the end of the therapy session. In this way, the reality of the outside world is differentiated from the fantasy expressions of the play therapy world.

With Animals and Pets.   Animals, whether live creatures or stuffed toys, often symbolize human issues, thereby possibly playing an important role in providing emotional support and maintaining emotional stability during treatment (George, 1988). Developmentally, for example, small furry animals such as the familiar teddy bear or Disney mice serve as transitional objects that provide comfort and aid in separation. In a similar vein, the Peter Rabbit story portrays the theme of separation and family reunification.

In autonomy play, by contrast, child clients use animals in a role reversal to shift from being small and insignificant to strong and powerful. In this play, the child client becomes the powerful controller (trainer, parent) of a fierce or strong animal (lion, horse) who obeys without question. Children also may use reaction formation in their identification with animals such as deer to allay anxiety about aggressive and sexual wishes.

In addition, animals enable relationships with living or representational objects without the threat of a human relationship. At times, a pet may be a child client's only remaining contact with reality. As part of diagnostic assessment, children may play out their family situation, feelings, and ways of reacting through stories about their actual or wished-for pets and animals. Animals supply the need for warmth, cuddling, and companionship. Animals also provide a child with an opportunity to feel in control of a situation. Repetitious play with animals as story characters gradually allows a child to come to terms with a painful conflict or reality situation.

Playing Games

Basically, children's games consist of any play activity with a competitive challenge against a task or opponent, specified goals and rules, and defined beginning and ending points. Game structure may be established through printed instructions on boxed and computerized games or through teaching or coaching across generations, as in sports games. Additionally, games may be newly created by participants. Because the life space (Lewin, 1964) of games occurs entirely within the experience of the players, children often think of games as real and use them as miniature social situations in which to release aggressive feelings, come to terms with significant persons, and try out more adaptive coping behaviors (Piaget, 1976). By repeating behavioral actions and events over and over in game play, children acquire a sense of power and control as they lose, cheat, strategize to recoup losses, and win (Coleman, 1976; Eifermann, 1987). Indeed, it is both the repetitive quality and the internally experienced social situation that make games useful intervention tools in play therapy (Terr, 1991a).

As a play therapy tool, however, the nature of game play changes. The inherent competitiveness usually gives rise to earlier developmental issues of control and sets the stage for a negative transference. Yet the goal in game use is to facilitate development of a constructive therapeutic alliance, involve child clients in productive communication and problem solving, and effect specified treatment goals. Thus, the clinical social worker needs to focus on the therapeutic alliance issues, and also use the basic structure and values of the game to initiate play activity and stimulate communication. The content communication in game play usually centers around the doing action. The process communication, by contrast, centers around how the game is played and, thereby, around the conflictual themes in the therapeutic alliance that emerge during play. Thus, on the one hand, the gaming process can become a key dynamic in moving treatment forward; on the other, it can retard progress or be the instrument of treatment resistance if not properly handled. For example, child clients may use games with clear boundaries and rules such as card games in a successful or unsuccessful effort to control angry feelings and impulsive behavior. In the process communication, the clinician remains attentive to the behavioral and verbal interchanges about the interaction rules in this miniature social situation, responds within the metaphor to the symbolic meanings conveyed, and watches that the child's feelings do not escalate out of control.

Slap Jack

Toward the end of the session in which she had been told that her clinical social worker was leaving, ten-year-old Beth suddenly asked to play "Slap Jack" and played the card game with a vengeance. Soon Beth commented, "It's okay to hit Jacks but not grownups." Her clinician agreed, adding that she understood why Beth felt like hitting grownups; that hitting Jacks was a good thing to do until Beth was ready to talk about her feelings. Before Beth left the office, however, she threw the cards in the social worker's face, splitting her lip open. Showing no remorse, Beth blithely left on schedule.

Red Light

Sean, age six, is best described as a negative two-year-old in that he resisted attempts to set limits. When Sean was first introduced to "Red Light," he was frequently caught and given penalties for cheating. As he tested the consistency of the rules and found them stable, Sean became somewhat less oppositional and moved into other play media to express his fears of dinosaurs and monsters. Whenever he felt overwhelmed, Sean would switch back to "Red Light" for safety. When his clinical social worker interpreted this to Sean, he yelled "Shut up!," but then continued the "Red Light" game in earnest.

More specifically, child clients actively seek to come to terms with the social and physical environment of the game. Thus, in a personal way, they recreate their identity within the game. In so doing, the children pave the way for their clinical social workers to begin confronting various problematic interpersonal issues, such as (1) the child's need to please and gain approval, (2) resistances, (3) power struggles—the need to control versus the need to be controlled, (4) cheating, (5) the child's difficulty in developing and maintaining a relationship, and (6) competitive style. To encourage the children to act and react within this circumscribed social space, clinicians verbally reflect on the child's thoughts, feelings, and actions within the metaphor of game play and established therapeutic goals. For example, games that emphasize playing within rules can be useful in helping children come to terms with authority. As they follow the child's process communication, clinicians offer support, protection, clarification, information, interpretation, differentiation, and synthesis. They set limits, stimulate interaction, note trouble spots in the gaming interaction, and help the child client find alternative ways of addressing the problem.

The characteristic behaviors and attitudes projected into game play by children provide clues to the nature of their problems in psychosocial functioning and suggest theoretical models that might inform the clinical social worker's use of games in play therapy with a particular child (Nickerson and O'Laughlin, 1983). From an intrapsychic model, for example, conflicts and relationship difficulties are addressed by following the child client's process communication and working within the play metaphor of the game. In this approach, the game situation becomes the play medium through which the therapeutic alliance is established, developmental needs are met, and conflicts are resolved. Whatever the theoretical model, problems occur if participants become so focused on game outcome that they lose sight of the treatment process and their core reason for being together. Additional problems occur if the fun element is overemphasized to the point that games become bribes in establishing a positive relationship.

The outside world firmly supports the structure and rules of game play and frowns on rule-changing, cheating, and inability to accept formalized, ritualized game structure (Loomis, 1964). In using games as treatment tools, however, it is essential to remember that game-playing behavior conveys intrapsychic and interpersonal problems and conflicts that child clients have difficulty putting into words. For example, child clients are conveying their underlying developmental issues and conflicts when they change the rules or cheat in an effort to lose because they fear winning or, conversely, to win by cheating because winning on their own does not seem possible. When considered as a symptom, cheating behavior may represent extreme intolerance of losing (anxiety), an incapacity to work in order to increase skill level (reality distortion), poor self-concept, or a helpless feeling of inherent inability or lack of control. Additionally, some children equate losing with total helplessness and winning with the reverse—omnipotence. Thus, gaming behaviors such as cheating and rule-changing must be viewed in terms of (1) the child's developmental stage, culture, and particular problem; (2) the significance, symbolism, and communicative message; and (3) developmental and relational issues within the therapeutic alliance.

Children with learning problems may cheat during organized games to compensate for their failures in academic subjects. For them, therapy games facilitate work on a destructive mode of functioning—the inability to lose games and/or cheating. In a sense, this behavioral cheating pattern appears to be associated with attempts to achieve a compromise between efforts at real competition and unresolved wishes for omnipotent control (Meeks, 1970). Because cheating or rule-changing involves strong emotions, the clinician must understand its meaning before attempting to intervene. Premature confrontation may result in a child feeling mistreated and superficially conforming. Responding nonverbally and verbally, the clinician may generalize the cheating occurrences in games to real life situations and say, for instance, "Things don't always happen the way we want them to happen." More often, however, the clinical social worker works within the metaphor of the game to reflect on the affect, spell out the unexpressed wish, identify the self-defeating role of cheating, and reflect on the consequences. Because the eventual goal to be achieved through therapy is to increase children's acceptance of their actual capacities and limitations, the therapeutic relationship is empathic, nurturing, and firmly protective in encouraging belief in self. By clarifying the futility of cheating, the clinician is working to make this behavior alien to self rather than allowing it to remain syntonic.

The Play Knapsack

While the broad array of experiential play materials presented here can be useful in the ideal playroom, it is important to note that all too often many of the fancy toys found in play rooms serve more to alleviate the clinical social worker's anxiety about what to do next with a child client than they do to meet the child's therapeutic needs. In the reality of today's movable office space and few playrooms, an abbreviated array of materials is usually more feasible.

In selecting materials for a play knapsack, it is useful to select tools representative of the six major developmental action themes. Choices might include the following:

- Nurturing and feeding: small baby doll, bottle, small blanket
- Making a mess: two cans of play doh, cup for water, sponge
- Constructing: Legos, tiny empty boxes, string, sandwich bags, blunted scissors, paste, paper, plastic hammer, pipe cleaners
- Drawing: paper, crayons, pencils, magic markers
- Storytelling: two bendable miniature doll families (multicultural), a big mouth puppet, a cuddly animal puppet, farm animals, soldiers, knights, matchbox cars and trucks
- Playing games: deck of cards, checker set, small soft ball

Conclusion

Play materials are a child client's natural medium for self-expression, experimentation, and learning. In play therapy, these materials provide the miniature situational opportunities and stimulate the metaphors through which children confront and work through pressing problems, developmental issues and conflicts, and life conditions. More specifically, play materials facilitate development of the therapeutic alliance, affective expression, and communication. They also provide opportunity to ventilate and put concerns into perspective. That children have varying levels of awareness of their issues, conflicts, and patterns of coping is apparent in their choices and uses of play tools to develop therapeutic content and process. As a general principle, children who play out their clinical issues with inanimate objects tend to be less aware of their conflicts and feelings than those who use animate objects. Of course, this principle holds only if the child has a choice of play materials and a choice of how the play materials are to be used.

4 Developmental Change Process across Treatment Stages

As noted previously, it is the problems, needs, and strengths of the child and the carefully formulated treatment goals that determine how the clinician purposively integrates play experiences, verbalizations, and the professional relationship with the elements and techniques of therapeutic change in order to create the optimal dynamic process for accelerating that child's development. In turn, these purposive combinations ebb and flow to create changing process themes and patterns at different times in the treatment. When this pattern flow is viewed over the course of developmental play therapy, five stages of intervention become apparent: Biopsychosocial Assessment, Creation of Therapeutic Alliance, Identification of Narrative Themes, Developmental Growth and Change, and Termination. Although these stages are conceptualized as sequential, it is with the understanding that there is some merging of boundaries and recycling of stages in actual clinical social work practice.

Therapeutic Change

Elements of Change

The following five dynamic elements of change are found in each stage of developmental play therapy:

> **Goals.** Goals specific to each stage of treatment focus and direct the therapeutic effort. These within-treatment goals delimit boundaries and transition points between stages and represent the desired result or outcome for a particular stage. Thus, they provide a means for assessing progression from one stage to the next over the course of treatment.

> **Procedures.** While many therapeutic procedures are used throughout treatment, their type, frequency, and clustering vary with the goals to be achieved in a particular stage. Procedures include the therapeutic alliance, play tools, and techniques used to frame corrective-growth experiences and the verbal narrative. Procedures combine with other elements to comprise the dynamic interactions and transactions of the therapeutic process. The

essential questions in selecting procedures are always which ones are most useful at which time? With which clients? Why?

Content Themes. Substantive content themes tend to vary from case to case depending on the focal problem, life circumstances, culture, and developmental history of the particular child. On the one hand, these themes represent the overt subject matter of children's play activities and verbal narratives. On the other, they convey meaning associated with symbolic metaphor and their substantive narrative carries the underlying process narrative.

Process Themes. Process themes comprise a systematic series of thoughts and actions directed toward some end. They usually underlie content themes and incorporate dynamic issues of therapeutic alliance, resistance, and progress. Thus, the symbolic meanings of process themes reflect the form and content of the therapeutic flow and the barriers or blocks that inhibit change. These real and distorted relational patterns, symbolic metaphors, and problem-solving configurations facilitate understanding of each child, his/her biopsychosocial dysfunction, and the dynamic processes of change.

Evaluation. Evaluation to determine the value or worth of the developmental play therapy intervention is both formative process and summative outcome. In the former, the degree and type of treatment progress are examined within individual therapy sessions and at transition periods along the way from one stage to the next. In the latter, by contrast, the focus is the changes that are securely in place when treatment ends. These end-point outcomes provide the means for assessing the benefits and effectiveness of play therapy for a particular child.

Techniques of Change

In conducting developmental play therapy, certain experiential and verbal techniques become operative in the corrective experiences and verbal narratives that forward the work of accelerating growth. The ordering of these techniques is not meant to convey any particular sequencing in their use throughout treatment.

In Framing Growth Experiences. In providing corrective-growth experiences, the purpose is to create a therapeutic holding environment that supports a child's strengths, mediates dysfunction, and allows a child's own developmental processes to restart or shift directions, as the case may be. The degree, timing, presentation, and style of working with each of the following experiential techniques varies in accordance with the developmental strengths and needs of each child, as does the packaging of these multiple experiential and verbal techniques into a therapeutic whole.

Accepting and Being With. To confront the growth and change tasks that lie ahead in developmental play therapy, children need to be in the presence of a clinician who fully accepts them as they are. Such unconditional acceptance involves more than the clinician's living, breathing presence; the clinician also must convey a willingness to lend the professional self to the child in order to help meet his or her needs. This requires both an affective giving of self to the child, and receiving and containing the child by the professional self. The contextual surround is one of warmth, liking, and respect for the child. Such initial accepting and being with deepens through proximity and engagement in treatment sessions. As clinician and child become increasingly connected in time, space, and action, they co-create a meaningful emotional connectedness.

Structuring and Limiting.   An orderly structure for treatment sessions includes consistent working routines about the content and process of sessions; basic behavioral safety rules; and the time, place, and length of sessions. Structuring conveys a concern for the comfort and safety of both child and clinician, establishes the clinician's authority and expertise, and minimizes the possibility of unpleasant surprises. By creating a sense of security for the child, structural containment enhances the therapeutic alliance, strengthens the child's own controls, and frees energy for intrapersonal and interpersonal work.

In structuring, the external controls apply to a child's behavior. The goal is to redirect the feelings from action expression to verbal or symbolic expression in the play narrative. Such verbal and symbolic release represents a rechanneling of destructive impulses into socially acceptable outlets. As the external authority figure, the clinician uses controls to define the boundaries of the therapeutic alliance, tie the alliance to reality limitations, and convey permission to work freely and expressively within the therapeutic structure. In the process of testing the external structure, the child learns that all wishes and feelings are permissible, but not all actions. In other words, a child may feel all feelings, but may not act as he or she pleases. A child may verbalize all wishes, but wishing does not make something happen or mean it is okay to carry out the wish.

When a child's behavioral actions trigger the need for structure, the clinician ordinarily:

- acknowledges the feelings and wishes
- facilitates their expression in words or play
- conveys clear limits on particular actions
- highlights alternate channels for expressing the feelings and wishes
- enables the child to express resentful feelings about the controls invoked

Sometimes when a child is out of control, the limits need to be calmly but emphatically stated first and the feelings dealt with as soon as feasible.

Another component of session structure is the transition from the waiting room into the session room, and the reverse at session's end. These transitions reflect the time of first and last awareness of the work together and comprise integral aspects of each session. The various ritual activities and verbalizations children create to focus their awareness and handle these transitions provide further information about their developmental level.

Supporting and Nurturing.   Both intrapersonal and interpersonal development require supportive and nurturing growth experiences. However, for nurturance to be growth-producing, it must be proffered in doses calibrated to the particular developmental needs of a child, not just in sweeping amounts. Nor is support to be offered indiscriminantly to assuage emotional pain without first ascertaining what the pain is related to and what it means in the overall scheme of things. When offering nurture and support, it is important that clinicians convey that their symbolic and actual interpersonal nurturing supplies for meeting this child's psychosocial developmental needs are unlimited.

Conveying Expectation and Hope.   Client hope and expectation are key enabling elements in producing and maintaining growth and change. Yet, when they enter treatment, many children convey a sense of powerlessness and hopelessness about their circumstances. To counter these feelings, the clinician creates a thera-peutic climate that conveys hopefulness about the future and an expectation that change is possible with developmental play therapy. Such an experiential climate is growth-inducing, in that it enhances children's belief in the treatment process, mobilizes their expectations of improvement, and supports their strengths and innate capacity for change.

Stimulating.   As the impetus for growth and development, optimal parent/child interventions provide stimulation along with acceptance, expectation, and sup-port. In treatment, children's developmental disruptions and distortions necessi-tate stimulation that is developmentally appropriate and that varies by developmental area. That is, children's uneven cognitive and psychosocial devel-opmental levels complicate the task of stimulating development, because the therapist must provide experiences to accelerate growth in the least developed areas while maintaining the forward thrust in other areas. Thus, the general rule-of-thumb is that providing stimulation at and slightly beyond a child's varying developmental levels will facilitate mastery and encourage tackling more advanced challenges.

In Framing the Verbal Narrative.   The impact of verbal comments, reflections, and interpretations is modulated by the narrative context and manner in which they are expressed. The narrative context may involve the following:

> **Context of the Play Metaphor.**   The verbalization is offered by a character or object in the play narrative and may reflect the meaning and feeling behind the behavioral action or thinking of other characters or objects, as well as alternative problem-solving strategies.
>
> **Context of Possible Shared Commonalities.**   At times, the children's verbal references in the session to a third person or play theme depict a parallel with their history and life experiences and appear representative of their feelings. In these instances, the clinician loosely connects the narrative to the child by commenting, "Maybe you've felt this way," "Maybe you've

thought about this," or "Maybe this has happened to you." Although the clinician has highlighted the commonality, the connection is tentative and general. This allows children to maintain a distance from the content if it is too threatening and anxiety-provoking.

Context of Therapeutic Alliance. Sometimes it is necessary to clarify or reveal the needs and motives underlying a child's actions in relation to the therapist. For example, a child may project feelings about abandonment and loss experiences onto the therapeutic alliance to the point of refusing to engage in treatment. The clinician does not initially interpret the abandonment issue, but does address the therapeutic relationship and might comment, "You're afraid to trust me. I think it is important for you to know I'm here for you." Such a comment is likely to defuse the situation and open up the connection. Needless to say, however, this abandonment theme will be worked and reworked over the course of treatment. A word of caution is in order about abandonment and loss issues. In a child's eyes and mind, therapeutic abandonment is likely to include missed appointments (illness and vacation, whether therapist's or child's) and changed appointment times and days (for whatever reasons), as well as the possibility of change in employment or a move to a new location by the family or therapist.

Eliciting Information. In the assessment stage, the primary focus is eliciting information. Here, questions structure session content. As treatment progresses, information tends to be revealed more indirectly in the child's verbal and play narratives. At times, however, it is necessary to elicit information about particular life events or experiences with which the child is grappling. In collecting information, the rule-of-thumb is that questions pressure a child and often have the effect of closing down discussion. Statements, by contrast, may elicit further elaboration. Consider, for example, the difference in the question "What happened to the girl?" and the statement "I'm not sure I understand what happened." A few clarifying questions amidst the statements convey the therapist's interest in really knowing the details about something and understanding the child's point of view.

Reflecting on the Observable. The clinician comments or reflects on what she or he observes happening in the play narrative in general, with a particular character, or with the child in a session.

- "The soldier is hitting him really hard."
- "The puppy is hiding up in the corner."
- "The baby drank three bottles."
- "You haven't taken off your coat today."

Reflecting on Accompanying Feelings. The clinician adds an affective component to the earlier observations to help children identify and process their internal experiences. Affective reflection also teaches children that feelings are part of treatment and that all feelings may be shared in therapy.

- "The soldier seems really mad."
- "The puppy seems really scared."
- "The baby seems really hungry."
- "Maybe your coat keeps you safe and warm?"

Reflecting on Repetitive Patterns and Themes.   When a child is responsive to the affective reflection, the clinician moves on to identify and reveal repetitive behavioral, cognitive, and affective patterns and sequences in the play sessions. This highlighting underlines the consistency of behavioral actions and reactions over time, and provides an opportunity to explore their context and meanings.

- "The play children are almost always hungry."
- "The play children are almost always fighting."
- "The play mom almost always seems so sad."

Conveying Dynamic Interpretations.   Building on the previous work, dynamic interpretations connect the feelings and behavioral patterns identified earlier and explore their dynamics first in single sessions, then across sessions, and later in the real world. In this way, children become aware of and work through the dynamic process and motivations that undergird their behavior.

The desired goal is for children to be able to reflect on their own and others' feeling states, so the child will understand that certain feelings or thoughts result in certain actions. That is, the clinician links the affect experienced by the sad play mom in the preceding example to the action of staying in bed all day. Similarly, a connection is made between the play child feeling mad and the fighting that results.

- "The play mom is so sad that she stays in bed all day."
- "The play child is so mad that he starts fights."

Next an interpretation is made about the individual child's own feeling and action.

- "Sometimes, I think you are so bossy because you want to be noticed by the other kids. Only the problem is that most kids don't like to be bossed."
- "I bet when your mom stays in bed all day you feel like she doesn't care."

Or, there might be an interpretation about how the child may have two conflicting feelings about the same person.

- "It is hard to be angry when you love your mom so much."

Thus, through observation, reflection, and interpretation, child clients feel understood. Their feelings are contained within a holding environment in which they become more hopeful and feel safe enough to risk change.

Treatment Stages in Developmental Play Therapy

Practice experience reveals that children in treatment seem to move through similar sequences of development and change, sequences in which they become involved in the following:

- a collaborative therapeutic relationship
- magnifying their awareness of dysfunctional developmental issues and coping patterns
- giving them up and testing out new ones
- consolidating their changes
- working to maintain their new patterns of psychosocial functioning, and then
- terminating

When framed within the five treatment stages, such sequencing plus the elements, techniques, and processes of therapeutic change yield dynamic meanings and clarify the contextual reality of therapeutic progression. When these organizing ideas and concepts are broken apart into smaller units, particular treatment phenomena become more visible and understandable, as seen in Table 4.1.

Stage I: Biopsychosocial Assessment

Basically, the first stage of intervention is a time when data are collected, analyzed, and integrated into case statement formulations about focal problems, contributing pathogenic developmental processes, family context, and cultural surround; diagnoses of salient features of the problems and covarying symptoms; and intervention plans. Thus, the two stage-specific goals for Stage I involve (1) completing the biopsychosocial assessment, case formulation, diagnosis, and treatment recommendations; and (2) developing a collaborative, mutually agreed upon (by family, child, and clinician) intervention plan and treatment contract that will enable the child to achieve the overall therapy goal of functioning more optimally in the real world.

However prepared for the initial interview(s) by their parents, children usually wonder what will happen to them in this new place. At some level, they may understand that this new person will help them with the difficulties and problems experienced in trying to cope with the world in which they live. They usually comprehend that their parents think they need to be changed and that this stranger will change them. Yet, the fact that they too come along conveys an expectation that they will have something to say about what happens to them.

TABLE 4.1 Stages of Developmental Play Therapy

	Stage I Biopsychosocial Assessment	Stage II Creation of Therapeutic Alliance	Stage III Identification of Narrative Themes	Stage IV Developmental Growth and Change	Stage V Termination
Goals	■ Assessment ■ Case formulation ■ Diagnosis ■ Treatment recommendations	■ Trust, credibility ■ Alliance beginning ■ Motivation	■ Identify cognitive, affective, behavioral patterns that will lead to change ■ Self-reflection and discovery	■ Self-understanding ■ Self-reflection and regulation ■ Developmental change ■ Consolidation	■ Separate with time to maintain change ■ Process loss, separation ■ Rapprochement
Techniques	■ Observation ■ Engagement ■ Inquiry ■ Collect, analyze data ■ Projective techniques through play	■ Engagement ■ Exploration ■ Convey empathy ■ Characterize roles ■ Reflection, support ■ Affirmation ■ Choice of play objects	■ Exploration ■ Development of play narrative ■ Magnify awareness ■ Work in the metaphor ■ Inquiry ■ Affective mirroring ■ Mastery ■ Convey dynamic interpretations	■ Containment ■ Exploration of insight ■ Reflect social support for change ■ Work within metaphor ■ Interpret affective responses ■ Cognitive development ■ Mirroring/modeling	■ Reworking ■ Gain family support for termination ■ Mastery work increases as metaphor decreases ■ Symbolic reframing to reflect goal accomplishment ■ Mutual agreement to terminate
Content Themes	■ Facts, thoughts re: presenting problem ■ Underlying feelings ■ History ■ Activity ■ Intervention planning ■ Ground rules	■ Presenting problem ■ Affective expression surfaces ■ Distrust ■ Treatment clarification	■ Identify kinds of play ■ Present alternatives ■ Clarify problems ■ Reflect on interpersonal style ■ Intrapsychic conflict arises	■ Capacity for insight ■ Mutuality ■ Interactive style of play ■ Responsibility/awareness ■ Exploring new coping skills	■ Tries new patterns alone ■ Fear failure, relapse ■ Mourning loss of relationship

	Stage I Biopsychosocial Assessment	Stage II Creation of Therapeutic Alliance	Stage III Identification of Narrative Themes	Stage IV Developmental Growth and Change	Stage V Termination
Change Process Process Themes	■ Blaming, guilt ■ Hopes, fears	■ Trust ■ Control, autonomy	■ Center around self ■ Boundary issues present	■ Maturation ■ Autonomy ■ Reality, industry	■ Separation/individuation ■ Ambivalence, autonomy ■ Attachment, loss
Resistances	■ Fear of knowing ■ Control issues ■ Relationship problems	■ To trust, change, ground rules, and self-observation	■ To limits ■ To therapeutic process ■ To play content	■ To change itself ■ To client limitations ■ Therapeutic impasse	■ Symptom recurrence ■ Regression ■ Negotiation
Therapeutic Alliance *Real relationship*	■ Ambivalence	■ Alliance	■ Attachment	■ Closeness	■ Separation, loss
Working alliance	■ Capability, expertise ■ Trust	■ Establish alliance ■ Build trust ■ Encourage self-observation	■ Transference reactions as products of previous intervention, events, or current work	■ Understands, practices new relational, behavioral, cognitive patterns in, out of therapy ■ Self-awareness	■ Interpersonal attempts to hold on ■ Negotiation
Transference	■ Initial response to therapist ■ Object relatedness ■ Trust/mistrust	■ Alliance distortions surface	■ Key interpersonal and intrapsychic patterns surface ■ Distortions ■ Affective expression of interactive patterns	■ Reactions subside ■ Fears of loss/separation	■ Interpersonal attempts to hold on, push away ■ Rapprochement
Evaluation	■ Establish prognosis ■ Ascertain expected outcomes	■ Achieve trust ■ Alliance-forming ■ Assess motivation	■ Patterns to be changed identified, magnified	■ Old patterns given up ■ New patterns consolidated ■ Problem resolution	■ Problem resolution

Against this backdrop of newness and uncertainty, it is not surprising that the experience of being assessed awakens strong feelings and a need for protection against the frightening power of this stranger. Consider, for example, the child who walked into the office for the first time and blurted out, "I didn't get into trouble. . .honest, I didn't do nothing." The clinical social worker simply reflected his worry by saying, "Wow! You were thinking you might get into trouble." Then he drew a picture of himself when he was happy and erased it. In its place emerged a picture of when he is invisible. That's when he feels small, when everybody steps on him, especially his older sister who squishes him into the floor. That way, no one can see him and his mom will leave him.

Prepared to fight or flee, this child and others are usually surprised to find a person interested in and accepting of them as they are. They find themselves interacting with a somewhat reasonable stranger who understands their need to be anxious and scared in this unknown situation and who does not try to take away their feelings with premature reassurance. Further, this stranger conveys the novel idea that, "This is your time and place where we can figure out together what is going on. We'll do this by talking some, doing some things together, and playing some." Thus, the clinician sets the tone for the semi-structured biopsychosocial assessment and, in the process, takes care not to replicate the child's other interpersonal relationships that may or may not be so accepting.

During the assessment period, the clinical social worker is purposively collecting and analyzing data to clarify the child's current developmental level with the objective of being able to provide the optimal growth environment in developmental play therapy. With both family and child, the clinician explores the present and past, the positive and the negative in the child's interpersonal relationships and life history. The clinician takes note of the content and form of whatever the child does and says, because these contributions convey the child's feelings about the immediate circumstances of being assessed, as well as children's efforts to cope with their life situation in general. For whatever the child does and says is already being influenced by the presence of the clinical social worker with him or her in the strange new room. For example, the play drama superimposed on the available toys and materials conveys meaningful clues about the nature of the developmental distortions and tangled inner world in which the child is entwined. Common content issues and process themes that comprise patterns of play provide clues about myths, reality, coping, and adaptation.

As part of data collection, clinicians find themselves asking informational questions about the child and the child's life, and structuring their participation together in selected activities. That is, for part of the interview, the therapist leads and the child follows. Because most children are used to answering adults' questions and working on assigned tasks, these activities do not seem too foreign and out of the ordinary. In the less-structured portion of the interview, however, the clinician is careful to reverse course; to convey that searching for understanding and trying to problem solve are a two-way responsibility. During these portions, the clinician follows the child's lead actively and responsively.

Not surprisingly, children in this initial stage are also gathering and analyzing data as they explore and evaluate the world of developmental play therapy and seek to discover and identify their part in it. They ask themselves, "Who does this world belong to? Where do I fit?" In response to this theme, the clinician replies, "How would you like this world to be?" While a child's questions may be partially answered, these requests are always used to further the clinician's understanding of the child, the focal problem, and the dynamics. Prior to the contract agreement, the therapeutic dilemma and cautionary warning for clinicians is not to promise a child more than they can deliver. For at this first stage, there is no assurance of continuance and ongoing treatment until parents and clinician reach agreement on the intervention plan and contract.

Stage II: Creation of Therapeutic Alliance

As noted in Chapter 2, the therapeutic alliance sets the stage for developmental play therapy's accelerated growth process over the course of treatment. In the first stage of assessment, the child and clinician have become acquainted. Thus, the primary goal for this second stage of treatment is to establish facilitative relational conditions for growth and development. The intent is to develop a strong, basically trusting working alliance that will provide relational acceptance, expectation, support, and stimulation (Perlman, 1957); enable the child to grow in understanding and handling self-in-situation; and withstand the positive and negative vicissitudes of growth and change. While initially tentative, this purposive relational connectedness continually evolves as child and clinician make use of corrective experiential activities and verbalizations in their work. The desired treatment outcomes become self-reflection and regulation, problem-resolution, age-appropriate developmental maturation, better coping, and healthier biopsychosocial functioning.

At times, these early stages seem to overlap as the clinician continues to clarify his or her role and gleans further information about why the children think they are coming, how they feel about this, and what they fear and hope will happen. In building the therapeutic alliance, the intent is to help the child move beyond the initial surface reaction to the clinician, toward hope and belief that the clinician can really help and toward a willingness to be influenced. The little boy who was both invisible and small started looking to the clinical social worker for help in staying out of trouble. Now he confides that he doesn't like to get in trouble all the time, it's just that he hates this certain kid who is trying to get rid of him. It was still someone else's fault, but the theme of rejection has begun to emerge. He wonders if the clinician will get rid of him too, and is relieved to find that it was okay for trust and competence issues to pervade the content and process themes of the early shared playroom experiences. In this stage, the focus is on (1) introducing the child to play as a purposive, meaningful method of expression and communication; and (2) creating a real working partnership in the here and now, with minimal attention to working on specific events or past issues.

In their early work with their child clients, clinicians empathize with their circumstances, accept any expression of need and emotion, and convey respect for the children's problem-solving ability and recuperative developmental powers. Limits are set as necessary to ground the work in the world of reality and maintain safety. From this supportive and protective stance, clinicians hold the children in a caring, nondemanding relationship, establish rapport, and create a safe interpersonal context for trusting, sharing, and exploring. Even though it may seem that nothing is occurring early on, the children are absorbing significant corrective experiences and bringing forth meaningful material.

In Stage II, clinicians work to deepen their commitment to being with the child and really hearing the child's perceptions, thoughts, feelings, and underlying meanings. In the process, intuitive clinical attunement to the child's rhythms and ways of being sharpens. As this happens, the clinician increasingly follows the child's leads, works within the child's symbolic metaphors, moves away from the semistructured data collection of assessment, and more and more turns responsibility for the therapeutic agenda over to the child. The underlying message is simply, "I'm here with you to support and serve you as you struggle to be and grow. I trust in your potential to change."

Throughout, the clinician supports the child's capacity to cope with and move affectively into the reality of this new growth-inducing relationship. As the child is increasingly drawn into the therapeutic alliance, the focus remains on the relational experience, how the child uses the relationship rather than the content of the experience. Initially, the child's emotional expressions in therapy are likely to be magnified, undifferentiated, easily evoked, and not particularly tied in to everyday realities and relationships. With increased feelings of security and comfort, the nature of the feelings expressed begins to shift toward the negative, but the feelings are still not clearly focused on particular emotional experiences, issues, or persons. Often at this time, there remains a sense of underlying fear of being deserted by the clinician, of being able to destroy this vital new therapeutic relationship that is becoming too important—too strong—too overwhelming.

In time, the child increasingly comprehends the relevance of the work of developmental play therapy, develops energy for change, and readily invests in changing; that is, in the ideal. For many children experiencing severe developmental disruptions and distortions, the process is much slower and more tentative. In any event, the process of creating a vital therapeutic alliance usually feels slow for the therapist.

Stage III: Identification of Narrative Themes

As the supportive alliance increases trust and attachment, children become more aware of their intrapersonal and interpersonal needs and their feelings about themselves and others. In response to this increased awareness, the stage-specific goal shifts to the particular developmental processes that underlie the symptoms and behavior problematic for this child. The focus is on surfacing these internal processes, channeling their expression through symbolic means and narrative themes, and generating responsive treatment strategies to process and work these metaphorical themes and bring about change.

Transference Reactions.   The negativity and testing noted toward the end of Stage II often carries over to be reworked as a narrative theme in Stage III. Such reactions periodically surface as the clinician works to keep the therapy grounded in the real world, while facilitating children's awareness of their responsibility in carrying out this work. At this time, the children are rebelling against the clinician's therapeutic intrusions into their usual patterns of being, doing, and interacting. They are struggling to maintain their old, somewhat comfortable equilibrium against the unknown and uncomfortable forces of development and change. The ways children attempt to manipulate and subvert the basic structures and limits of developmental play therapy provide clues as to how they handle stress and their maladaptive coping patterns in other interpersonal situations. During this period, it is important not to take for granted that a child can identify which feelings and issues have pushed him or her out of control. In their testing, they are trying to press their therapist into replicating their more usual interpersonal relationships, thereby maintaining the interpersonal and intrapersonal status quo. Thus, this period becomes a time for clarification of expectations, rules, and roles as the clinician refuses to get caught in replicating their old relationship patterns, and quietly and repeatedly conveys, "I'm different. I will be here with you and work with you whether you are angry or not." As therapeutic safety structures, limits and controls apply to behavior, not to verbal and play outlets for expressing emotions. In offering security, limits define the boundaries of the relationship in this stage and anchor the work within the therapeutic task at hand.

Surfacing Narrative Themes.   Play therapy narratives facilitate identification of problems, conflicts, developmental themes, and intrapersonal resistances. Often, they reflect family life and home situations as well. As child and clinician move forward during this third stage, they find that the therapeutic alliance has solidified and anxieties about it have diminished. In the play therapy narrative, the child begins to mirror, respond to, and work through needed changes. Repetition has begun to facilitate some degree of internalization of the therapeutic messages that the clinical social worker continues to reiterate in many forms within the metaphor. Changes occur in the play process themes and characters as child clients incorporate the clinician's messages and begin to express narratives that try out various solutions, alternatives, and options. In brief, the narrative of Stage III suggests that child clients recognize their problems, are working to develop alternative coping skills and resolve interpersonal problems, and are beginning to mature developmentally.

By the end of this stage, narratives change slightly as child clients begin to incorporate the play therapy experiences and new learning into the narratives. At this point, the narratives may convey hope and belief that change is occurring.

While the therapeutic alliance is grounded in the rational aspects of the working relationship where children understand they can trust the clinician, the transference represents more illogical and regressive factors. It can be used defensively as resistance. While the transference certainly reflects the child's overall feeling about the clinical social worker, the heart of the work has to do with the child's unrealistic expectations and unmet needs. This is the stage when things really heat up with all kinds of obstacles, storms, and battles. The child's expressions are met with containment by the clinician. In this stage, the clinical social worker focuses on relationship themes by bringing into awareness the child's affective reactions and the reasons for them. The therapist learns firsthand how the child interacts with others, especially his mother. Through the transference, clinicians offer security and trust as they accept the children. Over time, the children feel secure in their efforts to change and in trusting others to provide support for these efforts.

Patterning of Play Themes.   Whatever the play content theme, various patterns of activity are readily apparent within Stage III. At the healthier end of the continuum, child clients relate freely to the clinical social worker and are conversational, direct, spontaneous, and open. They play equally well alone or with the therapist in exploring feelings, tensions, and conflicts. Thematic process of their play activity clearly conveys developmental issues and concerns. Positive and negative feelings about others are freely expressed.

At the less healthy end of the continuum, by contrast, child clients appear uncomfortable relating to the clinical social worker and often want to be told what to do. They may relate aggressively through demands and questions or seek to manipulate. Their play activity may be intense and repetitive. Thematic content may appear diffuse and hard to follow. Feelings about others may split into all positives or all negatives. When viewed as a whole, variations in their play patterns may reveal different clusters of psychosocial behaviors and a patterning of play themes and activities into the following:

Anxious Play.   Anxious play tends to be either inhibited or scattered. Very anxious child clients are fearful of making mistakes, strive to please, and frequently ask, "Am I doing it right?" They view the world as overwhelming.

Hyperactive Play.   Hyperactive play begins as purposeless and scattered but picks up a quality of excitement that builds to excess until child clients are out of control. Usually these children are unaware that they are losing control and have little realization of the possible destructive consequences of their actions.

Aggressive Play.   Aggressive play conveys a powerful and pervasive impulse to destroy extensively. It is purposive and destructive in intent.

Oppositional Play.   Oppositional play conveys resistance, testing of limits, stubbornness, and negativism. The oppositional child client usually alternates between excluding or seeking to control the clinical social worker.

Obsessive Play.   Obsessive play is characterized by excessive rigidity, neatness, avoidance of feelings, and reluctance to express fantasy. It is constrained and repetitive.

Narcissistic Play.   Narcissistic play contains a self-centered element and conveys a play-acting quality designed for the benefit of observers. Narcissistic child clients comprehend only their own feelings of the moment and have difficulty understanding the viewpoint and feelings of others. These children easily feel threatened and overwhelmed, and quickly act on perceived threats.

Depressed Play.   Depressed play centers on themes of loss and grief, and repeats the precipitant over and over. Affective thematic components include hopelessness, loss and retrieval, being unwanted, self-destruction, and death. Sometimes child clients' depressed affect takes the form of emotional distance; other times, a higher level of activity to mask the depression.

Compromised Play.   In compromised play, child clients act as if they were much younger than their chronological ages. This pattern of play may be triggered by many factors. For example, environmental factors (e.g., poverty, cramped physical space, lack of opportunity or exposure) may influence play activity to such a degree that it resembles behavior produced by emotional conflict. Cultural factors may trigger gender-specific and culture-specific play patterns in which children's play differs markedly from that of the dominant culture. Neurological factors also impact on play activity and level of sophistication. Some child clients, however, have never progressed beyond the psychosocial stage of development reflected in the play. For others, the play reflects regression to earlier levels of psychosocial development. It is, however, important to remember that all children are likely to revert temporarily to an earlier developmental level when given an opportunity to do so in play.

In relation to these patterns, the clinician notes and works within them to minimize treatment disruption, increase awareness, and open the child to the ongoing therapeutic work.

Working Through Conscious Conflicts.   When a child client blocks in discussing certain things verbally, the clinician notes play situations and patterns in which the child fills in the details of the conflicts. In these situations, repetitive themes convey basic concerns and the level of conscious awareness of those conflicts and concerns.

As a general principle in working with conscious conflicts, a child client who plays out issues with inanimate objects tends to be less aware of the conflicts than a child who uses stuffed animals, dolls, or puppets. A child who incorporates doll figures into the play therapy process tends to be more aware of the feelings and thoughts associated with the clinical issue than children who use play tools that are less clearly representative of persons. Of course, this principle holds only if the child client has a choice of play materials and a choice of how these play materials are used in problem solving and working through.

Handling Unconscious Conflicts.   Repetition compulsion in which a child continuously reenacts painful experiences verbally or actively suggests that the child is probably not aware of the developmental issues and conflicts, and needs assistance in handling the unconscious material and relieving the accompanying tension. This cathartic use of play deals with symbolic material of strong significance to the child client who is arranging and rearranging variations of the original overwhelming theme. By projecting past unresolved experiences into manageable dimensions in their play, these children are actively trying to master a conflict by meeting it repeatedly and of their own accord. By reliving the past, these children are reworking leftover affects that may be interfering with their current psychosocial functioning.

The clinical social worker, however, must be aware of how much release in play at a given time a particular child client can tolerate without panic; that is, the amount and kind of participation and interpretation in which to engage the child. Indeed, a clinical social worker must be prepared to (1) make contact with the child's unconscious; (2) manage the ambivalence; (3) participate in the guilt released; (4) probe no deeper into the unconscious than is necessary for therapeutic growth; and (5) foster reconstruction that is true to the child's basic self, with the necessary clinical adjustment and change achieved through therapeutic integration.

In summary, clinical social workers work within a play situation in which child clients can act out feelings and conflicts to relieve tension. They permit children to fill in the details of the play activity. They participate verbally and nonverbally in a manner that helps children work out feelings. They interpret only through activity geared to the metaphor and process of the play. When the clinical social worker's responses follow substance rather than process, the child client's play is likely to become diffuse and lose focus. Or the child may change the play focus or stop play all together. In these instances, the child is likely to distance self from the therapist and may exclude the therapist from the play.

Stage IV: Developmental Growth and Change

By Stage IV, the techniques, media, and relational framework of developmental play therapy have taken shape within the context of the child's developmental levels and clinical issues. In the process, the child has begun to accumulate corrective growth experiences that are beginning to compensate for and remediate earlier developmental disruptions and distortions. Through responsively mirroring healthy parent/child transactions, the corrective experiential work together with verbal reflections and interpretations has enabled the child to give up some of the old ways of meeting need and to begin to try out alternatives. This relinquishing of old patterns and testing of new ones of being, relating, feeling, and acting forms the goals and dominates the scene in Stage IV.

Self-Understanding.   This is the stage when both the clinical social worker and the child take some satisfaction in the child's internal growth and external accomplishments. There is a definite feeling of optimism as transference reactions subside and the child views the clinician as a helping person in his or her own right, not solely as an extension of the child. It is a time of consolidation and self-understanding. Children clearly demonstrate the necessity of feeling understood before they dare to understand the contents of their mind or how it works. In response to their newly discovered insights, children are able to master new challenges. At first, the mastery efforts are tried out in the therapy session, then in the real world. Their new efforts at being and being with others engender sustaining and powerfully rewarding social support from significant persons in their lives.

Self-Regulation.   Impulse control is made stronger as the clinical social worker supports and reinforces children's efforts to connect what is going on in their minds with what they do. They learn that their actions lead to a continuum of responses and reactions within and from others. Through anticipation, they can predict what others may feel or do. Thus, they gain a sense of appropriate control. Now, they have the upper edge in knowing how to respond to people in their social world. In Stage IV, specific patterns of troublesome behaviors are explored and feelings worked through. Sometimes this is accomplished through reframing their usual expectations and modeling different scenarios through play and verbalizations. The play takes on a different feel and there may be a sudden burst of creativity, definitely a moment to be watched for. For example, the warring soldiers now decide they need a fort that is built in imaginative collaboration with the clinical social worker. There is more depth in the narrative in that the soldiers evidence distinct personalities and feelings. The play is no longer all about winning and losing. Distancing maneuvers are relinquished in favor of closeness. The child's style of relating has changed and retaliation is no longer a fear. Instead, the child now evidences control of impulses and the ability to slow down and stop before feelings and behavior escalate out of control.

A clinical example that comes to mind is that of a nine-year-old girl who was being treated because of extreme emotional neglect and severe maternal deprivation. All of this was compounded by poverty. The home and its many occupants were unkempt and filthy. Marybelle defensively inhibited memory and reasoning as a way to escape her agonizing circumstances. For two years, the therapist had worked mightily to help her understand her own mind through affective mirroring, something her mother had not been able to provide. One day, she bounced into the office attired in a beautiful dress from Goodwill that was ripped. The play narrative established in Stage III continued in the dollhouse where the children were forced to sweep and clean the house. The parents were going to jail for life for being mean to the children. After about twenty minutes, she asked the therapist if she could make a beautiful necklace to go with her beautiful dress. As she was doing this on the floor, she looked up and asked, "How do you know what makes me happy?" The clinician responded, "I can tell." "How?" she asked. The clinical social worker began, "Well, I know you pretty well." Marybelle interrupted, "But, how do you know?" "I can tell by the look in your eye—the smile on your face. I know from you what makes your mind happy." She said, "the way a mother is supposed to know. I love you." She ran out of the office to show her mother the necklace. Mother was curled up in a fetal position asleep on the waiting room couch. Marybelle woke her up. Mother did not respond and went back to sleep. Marybelle sadly came back into the office. A discussion then ensued about what makes her happy and sad—making a necklace with her therapist or trying to get any reaction from her mother. She was able to understand that, even though her mother was tired and sleepy, she still could have acknowledged Marybelle's happy feelings. Certainly, Marybelle was sad, but this time she didn't have to kick the walls or furniture. She was developing the capacity for both self-understanding and self-regulation to control her aggressive impulses. She could succeed in individuation with her own unique identity and characteristics separate from her mother.

Developmental Change.   Developmental change is the cornerstone of Stage IV. The incremental changes of prior stages are solidified through practice, repetition, and working through. Finally, accurate mental representations of the self and other permit the child to engage in new social interactions. Perceptions have changed. Memory is used in the service of understanding. Language is more expressive. Thinking is rational. Imagination blossoms. Defenses are becoming more mature and age-appropriate. The key to the growing self-knowledge is the children's increased ability to understand their own affective states. They can now integrate their representational worlds and use them effectively. The behavioral manifestations of distress are replaced by a more realistic sense of self. They take back the projections because now they understand the roles they played in their own difficulties. The clinical social worker feels this true developmental leap forward with the restoration of children's mental processes. While they were once tentative, the children now feel safe to proactively explore. The children have alternative means for problem solving in both their internal and real social worlds. They can now process negative affect through new competencies like verbalization and coping skills that are growth-promoting.

One youngster projected his inadequacies onto his younger "terrible, horrible, stupid, retarded sister," whose beauty and intelligence resulted in her being the apple of her parents' eyes. Joshua also displaced his aggression stemming from his academic and emotional difficulties onto his classmates, whom he tortured through his actions and words. He was restless, inattentive, and out of control during class. According to his teacher, Joshua's attitude was exemplified by remarks such as, "I don't have to listen to you." He spaces out. On the playground, he wants to be boss. If the other kids don't go along, Joshua thinks the world is unfair. He has been known to throw chairs, yell, and scream. The teacher thought he was "an aggressive personality" when, in fact, Joshua's behaviors were more reminiscent of a two-year-old.

Over time, Joshua's acting out in class ceased, because he had developed the capacity for self-observation as he tried to gain control of his own actions. However, he was put at a distinct disadvantage because he could not make out the social cues of others. Thus, he continued to respond inappropriately, albeit verbally instead of behaviorally. Joshua seemed to misperceive their intentions and would clash with the reality of what was really happening. In part, this misperception was due to his lacking insight, but it also had to do with his developmental lag in social relatedness. The clinical social worker finally came upon the idea of making a book together. Joshua cut out magazine pictures and told a story about what the person might be feeling based on the characters' facial expressions. Then, they incorporated what he might do or say in response. At first, the pictures were simply entitled, "He feels aggressive" or "She feels confused." One particularly intimidating picture of Genghis Khan was labeled, "He's angry and determined to do something." For the first time, he was able to identify and link a feeling to a subsequent action. There developed a range of possible reactions from killing or hitting to bargaining and compromise. The *Feeling Book* spurred this child into practicing his newfound ability to anticipate what others were thinking and feeling. As his capacity for self-reflection grew, he envisioned what other people might be feeling in order "to read their minds," thus giving him the advantage in knowing how to respond. Then he developed a repertoire of suitable responses that gratified him and satisfied others—a repertoire that endured over time as he returned to the pathway of normal development.

Consolidation.   Therapeutic change occurs throughout Stage IV because of children's growing freedom to explore their conflicts, ambivalence, and affective reactions. Through repetition and reciprocity within the play interaction and verbal exchange, youngsters are able to consolidate their gains. In the ideal, the crowning achievement is development of the capacity for insight. Conflicts no longer interfere with psychosocial functioning as the children go forth with competence. Their readiness to engage appropriately in new social interactions is confirmed by the outside opinion of parents and teachers. Behavior is now purposive and goal-directed. The clinical social worker senses a new mutuality within the therapy as the youngster is more interactive in play style. Verbalizations become more logical and meaningful. The youngsters become more creative and thoughtful in their endeavors. Natural development takes the place of the need for developmental play therapy. In turn, consolidation sets the stage for the clinical social worker, in consultation with the parents and then the child, to review the changes and progress and to discuss plans for termination.

Stage V: Termination

Ending is one of the universal goals of therapy. Indeed, terminating the purposive working together of the therapeutic alliance actually begins with the problem-exploration and goal-setting processes in the first session. At that time, the implicit expectation is that treatment ends when the goals are reached. In developmental play therapy, however, this final treatment stage involves much more than the event of stopping and is not a stage to be taken lightly. The intent is that the ending process be a significant culminating experience for the child, a desirable growth opportunity and not just one more loss situation in which the child feels rejected and abandoned. When handled well by all concerned, therapeutic termination assists children in knowing that they are ready to get on with living, dealing with feelings of separation and loss, and learning to say the inevitable goodbyes that will occur throughout their lives. Indeed, Littner writes:

> To the degree that he [child] cannot master these feelings and must repress them, the child will need to fend off close relationships, using the various techniques previously mentioned, and suffer the painful consequences of this self-imposed emotional isolation. He will keep bottled up within him an enormous desire for closeness, which he cannot allow himself to really satisfy (1956, p. 22).

In the ideal situation, readiness for termination is assessed in many ways, from symptom resolution to developmental gains. Conceptual criteria, however, tend to revolve around resolution of dysfunctional child development and have been phrased as follows:

- "held-up development proceeds again" (A. Freud, 1970, p. 243)
- "restoring the child to the path of normal development . . . and the child's developmentally appropriate adaptation in his life outside the treatment setting . . ." (Sandler, Kennedy, and Tyson, 1980, p. 241).

In developmental play therapy, indicators of readiness to terminate involve assessment of current strengths and weaknesses, areas of change, and areas still in need of change. Therefore, questions to be considered in assessment of termination readiness usually include the following:

1. To what degree has there been symptomatic improvement in problems, conflicts, and developmental dysfunction?
2. To what extent has there been improved coping, adaptation, and psychosocial functioning at home, at school, and with peers?
3. To what degree does this child evidence increased cognitive flexibility, problem solving, emotional spontaneity, object relatedness, and sense of pleasure?
4. Is there evidence of ongoing biopsychosocial developmental progression?
5. To what degree and in what areas has developmental dysfunction been remediated and/or rechanneled into more constructive developmental pathways?
6. Has an appropriate degree of congruence been achieved between the child's actual level of developmental task mastery and that expected for this child's age-related psychosocial developmental stage?

7. Given an average expectable environment and barring unforeseen trauma, to what extent is this child likely to integrate the work of developmental play therapy into his or her life and progress through subsequent developmental stages?

In addition to these questions, the clinical social worker searches for evidence of change in the therapeutic process—in the play content, verbalizations, narrative themes, and feeling tone. For example, there may be concerns about whether the child is addressing issues that appear less directly relevant to treatment. Sometimes, the child begins evidencing new behavioral firsts in the sessions. Sometimes, parents begin to cancel appointments. While cancelations can certainly represent resistance, they also can be signs of readiness to terminate.

Termination Process. In terminating, children most often follow sequential processes for dealing with their anxiety about the coming autonomy and their grief about the pending loss of their therapist.

Defensive Reactions. When termination is initially broached, many children simply ignore it and refuse to face what it will mean to lose the importance of a meaningful therapeutic alliance. Others may convey easy acceptance of stopping and, indeed, may indicate a willingness to stop immediately. Still others may deny the potential impact of ending and respond initially with little emotion or concern.

Sometimes there is depression that ushers in a sense of sadness that may range from mild to very severe. At this time, children are addressing their attachment to the clinician and their feelings of pending loss. Ambivalence is prevalent. Again, the clinician interprets and places the feelings of depression in the termination context and usually shares his or her own mixed feelings of sadness over the loss and gladness over the work achieved together. Comments might convey:

- "Jean wants to take something of mine home with her to help with her feelings of being sad and all alone."
- "You know, I'm glad for Dack because he worked hard to understand and get rid of his troubles. But, I'm also sad because I'll miss him."
- "Elian remembers how angry and scared he used to be all the time. He has grown up and wants to leave, but is scared of getting like that again."

At this phase, it is often helpful to review what it was like when the child first came for treatment, how the child has grown to date, and what the child thinks it will be like when treatment ends.

Regression. When children begin to convey angry feelings and demonstrate aggressive play, it is likely that they have faced, or at least heard, that termination is pending and are blaming the clinician for precipitously abandoning them. In playing out this theme, it is important that children be allowed to own, struggle with, and try to master their feelings to see if they can handle them autonomously. In this phase of termination, they often try to master separation and loss by actively causing rejection to occur. For example, a child may take things from the office or playroom, break or destroy objects, hit and kick, or split objects or persons into all good and all bad. The clinician's task is to acknowledge this affect and behavior in the context of the therapeutic tasks of the anger phase of ending; interpret the affect and behavior to the child; and facilitate the child's expressions of anger, fear, and frustration. Comments might convey:

- "I think Jack wants to make me angry at him so he won't have to feel bad about his angry feelings at me for ending."
- "I think maybe you're trying to start a fight and make me angry. Sometimes children do this so they don't have to feel bad about their own angry feelings or miss the person they're leaving."
- "I think you're trying to order me around so you can take charge of your worries about saying goodbye."
- "Maybe you want to take a little bit of me and the office home with you to make leaving easier."

Negotiation.   In the negotiation phase, the child tries consciously and unconsciously to extend the treatment. When pleading for additional sessions fails to work, there may be a resurgence of old symptoms or the emergence of new affective and behavioral problems. This phase corresponds to the child's more open acknowledgment of anxiety about the impending separation and represents efforts to avoid the pain of loss. The clinician's task is to place the old and new concerns in their termination context, interpret them, and remain firm about the ending time. Usually, these symptom flare-ups respond readily to interpretation and subside easily. Comments might convey the following or similar messages:

- "Perhaps you're worried about not seeing me and wondering what will happen if you need help?"
- "I think you feel two ways about leaving. The grownup part of you feels ready to stop. The little boy part remembers how unhappy you used to be and is kind of scared to stop."

Rapprochement.   In progressing through these termination phases, the child has reviewed the work and progress of treatment and has dealt with the important feelings associated with loss of the therapeutic alliance. As clinician and child have reviewed their progress together and the changes made, the special nature of their relationship becomes increasingly apparent to both. Their mutual delight in the progress achieved is also openly shared. Both acknowledge the importance of this relationship and that, though they will stop seeing each other, their memories of their work together will remain in their hearts and minds. With some children, making and exchanging a gift or a graduation ritual may be helpful in symbolizing that the relationship in its present form has ended and the transition to therapeutic independence has begun.

Premature Termination.   Although termination ideally occurs upon completion of treatment goals, there are times when it is premature. Sometimes the reasons are family-related and may involve resistance to the treatment process, a change of schools and the necessity of transferring to a new school social worker, or a move out of the area. Sometimes the reasons are clinician-related such as moving, changing jobs, or completing an internship. That the clinician is leaving does not preclude the importance of terminating with a child and family. Sometimes premature terminations involve transfer to another clinician; sometimes not.

Premature termination of developmental play therapy is a separation that children have great difficulty understanding. With reason, they feel rejected, abandoned, and sad over the loss of their therapist and the incompleteness of their work together. As with timely termination, earlier experiences related to separation and loss are reawakened and must be handled in the termination process. Especially with premature termination, it is important to remember that the actual event of termination must occur before children can fully work through their ambivalent feelings and move beyond the anticipatory grief process. In transfer situations, children use the early sessions to detach from their departed clinician and attach to their new one.

Premature termination and transfer often trigger reactions in the therapist as well. For example, as the clinician's narcissistic needs and feelings of grandiosity come into play, so may feelings of "No one can help this child like I can." Therapists usually feel guilty when ending a child's treatment for their own reasons and worry about the impact on a child, especially those who have already experienced multiple losses in their young lives. There is sadness for clinicians in ending with clients in whom their energy and emotional investment has been great and the investment return of client development and change incomplete. Thus, it is important that these and other termination-related feelings be surfaced and addressed by clinical social workers so that neither they nor their clients are burdened by them.

The End Game

Freud is reputed to have compared therapy to a chess match and referred to termination as the end game. The case of Letitia was an unusually challenging match, in which she tried symbolically and literally to checkmate her clinical social worker. In the reality of the chess games that were played, the child would not permit her king to be checkmated. Instead, she would turn him over to forfeit the game.

In good time, termination was agreed upon by all concerned. Her mother's anxiety surfaced as that time approached and she told her daughter that she wanted her to stay in therapy. This response had been provoked by the teacher's ambivalence. The clinical social worker had expected the parents' and Letitia's anxiety, but wondered about the school. Maybe the termination idea was premature?

Letitia sauntered into the office with her old frown and exploded with anger and tears. She cried for about twenty minutes, expressing her feeling that the clinician couldn't help her, never had. She hated her. While Letitia was certainly regressing in some ways, now she could talk about it. She exclaimed, "Look, I've got to learn how to manage on my own. Maybe I needed you once, but I don't need you now. I promise I know what to do. I know how I feel. I'm okay." The clinician surprised Letitia by agreeing that Letitia was okay. Together, they traced the enormous progress she had made under very difficult circumstances. They agreed that it was mother's idea to continue the therapy.

The clinician told Letitia about the contents of her mother's call. Apparently, the teacher thought Letitia seemed a bit worried in class and didn't wait to take her turn. Immediately, she started negotiating, "I promise, I'll wait for my turn. Don't force me to continue." The clinician reminded her that the two of them had agreed to stop in July and that's what they would do, unless together they decided to continue for just a little while, to go the extra mile. Letitia emphatically stated, "I don't want to go the extra mile. I've gone the extra mile. It's my mother who needs to go the extra mile, not me." The clinician agreed, "Your mom sounds a little worried about ending. You might even be a little worried about it yourself." She informed the clinician that she had been coming for a very long time and then recounted the various play objects she had enjoyed. This discussion led her to talk about the troubles she used to have, that in a way she had thought she was strange because of the temper tantrums, kicking, and hitting. Then she remembered that was because of her anger.

Letitia got out the chess set and played skillfully until she was about to be checkmated. A resurgence of frustration resulted in her quitting the game. Shortly thereafter, she calmed herself down, reassuring the clinician that she had learned a lot and that she was honestly okay. Again, the clinician agreed and got her calendar to schedule the last day of therapy some three months hence. Then Letitia announced that she might miss the clinical social worker and came up with the idea of coming monthly for six months thereafter just to check in. Relieved when the clinician agreed, Letitia left the office saying, "You're okay too. I'm sorry I'm so mean to you."

The ensuing three months were filled with a continuous reworking of her conflicts and developmental gains. Narrative themes resurfaced, but now her affective reactions were manageable. The last session, Letitia decided to play chess. She surrendered two out of three games but was able to tolerate the frustration. She had abandoned the normal rituals that used to accompany the chess matches. There was little verbalization in the last session. Letitia was now launched and ready to succeed in her own unique world separate from her therapist. The battle of wills that so dominated her therapy and the chessboard were relinquished in favor of a rapprochement with her therapist. The end game was complete. Letitia left victorious.

CHAPTER

5   Concurrent Parent Work

Many parents go through their daily childrearing routines well enough with few problems, many successes, and much joy and satisfaction. Some deal satisfactorily with their children until a crisis such as job loss, illness, or divorce disrupts their lives and their parenting. Others may deal well enough with some of their children but, for various reasons, find themselves unable to cope with a particular child. They often comment, "We thought our child would outgrow it—but it didn't happen that way." Sometimes that child simply has a set of needs that differ from the rest of the family. Other times, that child manifests developmental disturbances in his or her mental life and/or symptoms of a mental disorder. Whatever the case, the parents have decided that they need help.

When seeking help, parents usually expect to pinpoint the specific causes of and remedies for their child's problem and to have whatever is wrong fixed. Some parents expect to be involved in their child's treatment; others see no need to involve themselves. Yet, the underlying premises of developmental play therapy and concurrent parent work are that (1) parents are central figures in their children's lives; (2) parents' overall psychosocial functioning is one key to the quality of their parenting; (3) children's difficulties do not occur in an ecological vacuum; and (4) it is the parent/child relationship that will either facilitate or hinder the child's growth and change in therapy. Given the centrality of parents in their child's treatment, this chapter focuses on understanding parenthood, engaging parents, establishing goals and outcomes, and employing the major methodologies in concurrent parent work to achieve optimal parenting. The case of the Dobsons provides an individualized treatment model illustrating how the various methodological approaches are selectively combined to address the problems and meet the needs of the parents and children in one family.

Parenthood

For the most part, having a baby or adopting a child are relatively straightforward processes compared to rearing a child. Actually being a parent involves a rapid role shift from responsibility only for oneself to complete responsibility for the care of another. In addition to providing physical care, parental role responsibilities include (1) forming and maintaining a secure attachment with a child (Bowlby,

1988); (2) providing an average expectable environment (Hartmann, 1939) that is good enough (Winnicott, 1965b) to facilitate growth and maturation throughout the developmental course of childhood; and (3) negotiating the evolving demands of life and parenthood within the ever-changing context of the family and the ecology of childhood. These responsibilities are performed privately and publicly on a real-life stage amid varying scenarios, sets, and circumstances. Sometimes the supporting cast and resources for learning and performing the parental role are readily available and accessible, sometimes not. The role script is constantly evolving and incorporating expected and unexpected events, social situations, and multiple spheres of influence. The value sphere, for example, reflects familial and cultural traditions, faith-based beliefs and practices, current societal fashions, and individual ideals. The competence sphere includes the parenting knowledge, experience, and capabilities brought to the role. The personal sphere of influence includes personal preferences, interpersonal style, and intrapersonal maturity.

Within the personal sphere of influence, intrapersonal maturity takes the form of the parents' internal mental representations of self and other. These representational models have grown out of parents' own physical and emotional experiences in being parented—sometimes by their parents, sometimes by other caregivers, sometimes well—sometimes poorly. To meet their intrapersonal needs and maintain a sense of subjective well-being, parents create dynamic mental representations of parent self and child other. These reciprocal representations influence their ability to appraise, understand, and respond empathically to their child. It is the interactive and reflective mental processes in their sensitive attunement to their child's real and mental worlds that enable parents to connect affectively with their child, perceive that child as a distinct autonomous being, and inject coherence and regulation into the child's affective experience and development. If this capacity is reduced by parents' disturbed early mental representations, a child's affective experience and mental worlds become chaotic and without appropriate regulation (Fonagy, 1993).

Engagement at Intake

The clinical social worker's first contact with parents usually occurs during the intake process, a time of problem identification, history-taking, and assessment of whether and how the agency clinician or private practitioner may be able to help. The intense scrutiny of the historical and cultural context of problem development provides the initial opportunity to address parents' ambivalence, mobilize their problem-solving strengths, and facilitate their understanding of this particular child.

Assessing Parenting in Context

To establish goals for the concurrent parent work that accompanies developmental play therapy, the clinician must assess the parent-in-situation—the context in which the problem parenting behavior and affect occur; the consequences to the child; the resources of the parent, the child, and the social environment for the promotion of change; and finally, the effects that a change in parenting affect and behavior would have on the child, the parent, and the total family. Thus, as they initially talk with a parent by phone or in person, the clinical social worker keeps five key questions in mind:

1. What is the nature and significance of the problem as the parents see it? In what areas are the parents experiencing difficulty with this child?
2. Why are the parents seeking help now?
3. What has happened to strain the resiliencies and coping resources of the family and upset the psychosocial functioning and equilibrium of the family unit?
4. In what ways have the parents tried to solve the problem and cope?
5. What do the parents want the clinical social worker to do?

Forming part of the comprehensive biopsychosocial assessment (see Chapters 6 and 7), this information comes from interviews, observations, and knowledge of the parents' past history obtained from the parents, as well as reports by other persons who know the child or parent and any other source that can provide reliable and relevant information. In addition, the clinician explores how parents respond to their child's behaviors, distress, demands, and conflicts. The completed assessment reveals any parental factors that may have contributed to the child's presenting clinical picture, including issues and conflicts stemming from their own early-life experiences that have been displaced onto the parent/child relationship. It also reveals the particular stresses and demands placed on the parent by the needs of this particular child and by the family's sociocultural environment. The assessment includes the strengths and vulnerabilities of the child and parent and the resources available to them. It also may include parenting behaviors and affect that require attention and specific information about the child's needs and the parent/child relationship that would facilitate setting problem-solving priorities with the parents. And, finally, the process of thinking through and sharing their distress, concerns, and ideas about their child with an attentive clinician engages the parents as therapeutic allies and begins to mobilize their strengths and problem-solving processes.

Placing Concerns in Cultural Context

In clinical social work, parents are viewed as a direct source of information not only about the nature of their child's presenting problems, but also the meaning of their own and their child's life experiences, the family's cultural reality, and their personal interpretation of significant events in their own and their child's psychosocial histories (Boyd-Franklin, 1989; Johnson-Powell and Yamamoto, 1997). Therefore, the starting point for culturally relevant and personally meaningful engagement of parents in concurrent parent work is direct exploration of the personal and sociocultural reality of their concerns about their child and their expectations about therapy.

To accomplish this task, clinical social workers ground themselves as much as possible in a family's sociocultural world and create a therapeutic holding environment for child and parents, in which the cultural issues and themes relevant to understanding parent and child problems and relationships, strengths and resiliencies, world views, and backgrounds can emerge and be explored. For example, the presence of Caucasian, African American, Hispanic, and Asian doll families and multicultural food miniatures among the available play materials conveys permission and the expectation that children and their parents will address sociocultural and diversity issues drawn from their real worlds, as well as those created in their children's make-believe worlds. These representational toys and other visual materials, such as stuffed animals, pictures, and games, also may be used to stimulate exploration of developmental issues, themes, and needs that vary in importance to different families. While children use these materials in their therapeutic narrative, parents simply take in their presence visually and comprehend the implicit permission that their presence conveys. The presence of such stimuli may facilitate autobiographical narrative and family stories, myths, and rituals. In the early interviews with some parents, a clinical social worker may need to actively structure the interview and therapeutic environment with direct questions about sociocultural influences and issues. Such directness provides an explicit invitation to access and address the sociocultural themes and patterns of culturally reinforced behavior and illness that may hinder engagement and ongoing work, as well as those that represent strength and resiliency in familial problem solving, coping, and adaptation.

Seeking Help

For most parents, the decision to seek help for a child from a clinical social worker or other mental health professional is neither easy nor taken lightly. At the time they are making this decision, parents may feel anxious, guilty, or angry about their children's problematic behaviors, distressed by their own difficulty in managing day-to-day parent/child interactions, and overwhelmed by the ordinary and extraordinary problems of childrearing. They may experience themselves as out-of-sorts and out-of-sync with their children and as failures in their parental roles. They may feel uncertain about trusting an unknown authority with their child, fearful of change, and worried about upsetting the family *status quo*. At the same time, most want help and feel relieved that the first step in obtaining help has been taken. In light of these mixed feelings, it is not surprising that many parents are cautious and somewhat defensive as they seek help.

Parents express their ambivalence about seeking help in a variety of ways. They may push for an immediate appointment, then cancel. To present their child and themselves in the best light, they may minimize certain problems and deny others. They may present logical arguments and rationalizations that the problems stem from external causes, such as poor teachers or bad advice from experts. A parent may seek to shift responsibility for the child's problems within the family unit and project blame onto a spouse or other family members. Parents also may displace their distress and anger onto others, often the clinical social worker as the person in closest proximity when they are telling their story and sharing their distress. They may engage in magical thinking that the act of seeking help will somehow undo their child's problems and make everything better (Sandler with A. Freud, 1985; Weber and Timberlake, 1986).

Initially, parents seek help because they have identified their child as having a problem that they are unable to handle. Yet, at intake, they may not fully understand their child's difficulties and their own responsibilities in clarifying the presenting and underlying problems, providing relevant background information, problem solving, and generating needed resources. Thus, the clinical social worker's early tasks involve:

1. assessing and diagnosing the child's problem and the parental role (if any) in creating and maintaining the problem
2. clarifying and redefining the problem in terms the parents can understand, feel less helpless and hopeless about, and feel more empathic with their child about
3. educating parents about their child's problems and treatment needs within a holistic developmental context
4. engaging parents in an active collaborative alliance that clarifies the potential for effective action in terms of both the child's problems and the parents' difficulty with this child
5. redirecting parents toward a more balanced approach to parenting this particular child
6. referring the child and parent for appropriate additional services, if indicated

Establishing Goals and Outcomes

Good intervention in concurrent parent work is built collaboratively with a clear rationale for the major goals and outcomes selected for the purpose of improving parenting in each case. Five frequently used ones include the following:

1. *To increase parents' subjective emotional comfort.* High levels of stress, external or internal to the family, create great distress and are associated with psychosocial dysfunction. Alleviating stressors has positive ramifications for the entire family. In general, when anxiety or emotional tension is relieved, parents are able to handle their parenting role more effectively. The strengths, knowledge, and skills that were previously inhibited by overwhelming stress and affect become more readily available and accessible. If, however, the parent's problems are partly socioemotional and partly related to parenting deficiencies, reduction of emotional tension alone is likely to be insufficient.

2. *To decrease particular problematic parenting behaviors and restabilize family functioning.* When a limited set of troublesome parenting behaviors is decreased or a particular cognitive mindset reframed, parenting usually becomes more effective. However, if the underlying purpose that the targeted behaviors or the particular mindset serve in the family system is misunderstood, the parent/child situation may not improve or another problematic set of parenting behaviors may replace the original set.

3. *To improve parents' role-image.* Techniques for improving parents' perceptions of their own parenting role behavior assume that an improved role-image is sufficient to help them feel more adequate and perform more constructively. Role-image includes personal parenting goals, competence in parenting, and sense of adequacy or self-esteem in role performance.

4. *To increase parents' sensitivity and ability to meet their children's developmental needs.* When parents have missed out on being nurtured and protected in their own young lives, it is not likely that they will be able to nurture and protect their children. Meeting parents' needs for nurture and protection increases their ability to attend to their children's needs.

5. *To achieve limited insight about how past experiences influence present parenting.* When parents establish a connection between their current difficulties as a parent and their past history, this awareness—together with the satisfaction of understanding their own emotional experiences and parenting issues—serves as a beginning point for changing actual parenting behaviors.

The first three goals often may be accomplished through short-term concurrent parent work. The last two goals, however, are usually accomplished in long-term parent treatment, although beginning work in these areas may be started in short-term treatment.

Intervention

Methodological Approaches

The eight major methodological approaches to goal accomplishment in the concurrent parent work of developmental play therapy include supportive buffering between the parent and child, environmental modification, supportive educational guidance, supportive family work, parent mobilization and empowerment, focused problem solving, developmental parent work, and parent/child relationship work. The general rule-of-thumb for all eight approaches is to remain focused on the overarching purpose of improving parenting. Within this broad purpose, each approach varies in objectives and outcomes, theoretical framework, degree and type of parental involvement, time frame, degree of directness, and the methodological techniques employed. In actual clinical practice, it is rare that one approach is used alone and in pure form. More often, aspects of several approaches are selected and integrated into an eclectic intervention model, whose methodological structure, processes, and techniques are designed to operationalize case-specific goals and outcomes.

Eclectic models of concurrent parent work often begin with the tip of the iceberg. That is, they address practical parenting issues with information, educational guidance, and focused problem solving, and only later move into the more complex interpersonal and intrapersonal problems of parenthood as needed in a particular case. For example, discussion of their child's symptoms and development helps parents better comprehend the presenting problem, possible reasons why the difficulties arose in the first place, and why they became established and continue. These explanations, together with exploration of the practical aspects of day-to-day management, ideally help parents discover more constructive ways of relating to their child and dealing with the difficult behaviors. If necessary, parents are helped to make connections between present and past family circumstances and their children's psychosocial problems; that is, the impact that current stressors, such as marital conflict, alcoholism, illness, employment issues, and abuse/neglect, as well as past stressors originating in the parent's own history, have on this particular child. The parents and clinical social worker then collaboratively work to handle or remove the current stressors or at least to provide a buffer and limit the damage to the child. Removing current stressors involves resource mobilization and focused problem solving. When ghosts of the parents' past (Fraiberg, Shapiro, and Adelson, 1975) are intruding into the present, parents and clinician work toward limited parental insight into this intrusion and subsequent changes in parenting.

Supportive Buffering Between Parent and Child.   For those parents with severe psychiatric disorders, treatment by another mental health professional as clients or patients in their own right is indicated to deal with the mental illnesses that go well beyond the parental role. Along with individual treatment, however, concurrent parent work related to the pervasive and invasive effects of the illness on the parental role and on the biopsychosocial functioning of their children is usually also indicated. Often, the objective is simply to lessen the impact on the child by serving as a buffer between the parent's symptoms of mental illness and the child, and shifting responsibility for their parent off the child's shoulders. This buffering involves structuring parent/child interaction, engaging in direct work on management issues, mobilizing resources and social supports, educating parents about the impact of certain behaviors on the child, and educating the child about the form and origins of their parent's particular mental disorder.

For chronic multiproblem families with entrenched patterns of chaos and violence, pervasive and severe psychosocial dysfunction, or marked economic instability, family preservation and other wraparound family services may first be needed to meet basic living needs, shore up strengths, and stabilize family functioning. At times, out-of-home placement may be indicated to protect the child. Once these services are in place and the chaos has been tamed to some degree, reassessment may determine that parents and child could make use of individualized developmental play therapy and concurrent parent work.

Environmental Modification. The ultimate environmental modification in child work is out-of-home placement—foster care for the child in need of protection and nurture or residential treatment for the severely emotionally disturbed child whose mental illness requires a period of intensive milieu therapy in a residential treatment setting. The more usual environmental modification involves consultation work with school personnel in the child's mainstream educational setting or collaborative work with school personnel to achieve suitable placement in a special-education setting. The goal in this consultative and collaborative work is to help the school system provide educational experiences that will enable the child to learn academically and develop psychosocially.

Supportive Educational Guidance. Supportive educational guidance in concurrent parent work assumes that parents want to be good parents, but either lack the necessary knowledge and skills to support child development effectively or are blocked somehow in their ability to use what they know. The intent is to decrease stressors for both children and parents, enhance parental concern for and sensitivity to their child's emotional well-being, enhance the parent/child relationship, enable parents to think more clearly about their child's needs, improve behavioral management, and facilitate parental collaboration in addressing barriers to their child's development. This methodology mobilizes parents' strengths and adaptive capacities, enhances their ability to provide their child with both practical and emotional supports, and facilitates creation of a family environment that is more emotionally balanced and responsive to their child's needs. This approach makes developmental progress and improved psychosocial functioning of the child the major objectives in supportive educational guidance.

To accomplish these objectives, clinical social workers provide information about growth and development, practical help meeting children's needs, and assistance managing the day-to-day issues of childrearing and behavioral management. That is, clinicians identify with parents' circumstances and previous efforts at managing problems. They attend to the parents' adult issues primarily as related to the children's developmental needs. As noted previously, parental issues may include concerns and ambivalence about their child's therapy and their own engagement in concurrent parent work. They also may include parental differences in rearing and handling children, marital conflict that impacts on children, and individual life problems that interfere with the ability to parent (Chethik, 1989; Mishne, 1983; Timberlake and Truitt, 1981). The clinician seeks areas of parenting strength that can serve as a basis for creating new ways of being and doing.

By addressing conscious factors that influence parental-role performance with supportive and informational techniques, educational guidance relieves unrealistic and destructive pressures on the child and serves as a tool for cognitive reframing, problem solving, and skill acquisition. The intent is to help parents take a more middle-of-the-road approach to childrearing. The techniques used vary in degree of structure and directness, from sharing ideas that parents may wish to explore to offering direct advice about what to do under specific circumstances. The types of information that clinicians may make available to parents range from general knowledge of development and the maturing mental life of the child to more specific knowledge about a child's symptomatic behavior and intrapersonal dynamics. Universalization is often used to generalize the problem or proposed solution to other families and decrease parents' sense of isolation in their parenting efforts. Ventilation of negative feelings is useful in allowing parents to work together to help their child. Clarification of reasons for parents' internal stress may help them become aware of their own problems and be more available to their children.

When the issues of concern are counterproductive beliefs held by parents and family members, persuasive and cognitive reframing techniques may be combined with the more informational techniques to clarify misinformation or grant permission to use their own best judgment. When clarifying problematic parent/child interactions, the clinician highlights the interaction and provides information about the negative impact. Then the clinician offers advice about possible changes, provides explanations for the changes, and explores various alternatives with parents. When possible, the clinician uses parents' language to explain interactions and tries to formulate suggestions as expansions of existing parental tendencies. At these times, sensitivity to issues of cultural diversity and family values is especially critical.

Educational guidance teaches parents to attend to both the content of children's communication and the associated feelings. Parents also may learn about the needs and meanings that underlie children's behavior; for example, clinging and seeking attention as a need for sense of belonging and security, power struggles as autonomy issues. After learning to identify needs, parents learn strategies for meeting those needs and handling the behavior. They are taught nurturing strategies of accepting and identifying feelings, holding, and real and symbolic feeding, as well as guidance strategies involving consistent rules, clear values, and boundary enforcement. They are taught how to engage in companionable activities with their children that result in opportunities for sharing, imitation, and modeling. They are taught to convey that feelings are always acceptable, talking about feelings is permissible, and acting out feelings in destructive ways is not acceptable.

Behavioral management and punishment are usually key issues for parents. After exploring what has and has not worked, the clinician clarifies the purpose of punishment with parents: Does it prevent the child from repeating the behavior? Sometimes parents fail to understand that punishment is not an effective means of eliciting positive behavior. Role modeling, rewards, and encouragement are more helpful in encouraging constructive actions. In addition, the clinical social worker also teaches principles of using punishment sparingly, attending to child health and safety, being careful of the rights of others, and having the punishment fit the offense. When children are old enough, a frequent suggestion is allowing them to control their fate by selecting between two alternative ways of working off a punishment. In exploring support, reward, and punishment issues with parents, the aim is to help parents achieve a more balanced approach to behavior management.

Supportive Family Work. At times during developmental play therapy and concurrent parent work, it becomes apparent that selected aspects of family dysfunction involve all members of the immediate family and necessitate an interpersonal methodological approach with all concerned. This approach usually involves a relatively short period during which family sessions accompany the individual play sessions. Sometimes, the family approach addresses structural issues of boundaries, power, and alignments. Other times, the approach focuses strategically on the dynamic and behavioral sequences maintaining a particular problem, such as sibling rivalry, scapegoating, or manipulation. The goal in all such supportive work is to increase the family's ability to perform developmental holding functions for each member and provide the desired average expectable environment (Hartmann, 1939).

Parent Mobilization and Empowerment. A significant number of children experiencing a developmental disruption or mental disorder also have a chronic illness, genetic disorder, or physical disability. Their parents face the triple challenge of understanding the interactive impact of these conditions on their child, learning to care for their child more effectively, and renewing their sense of self-fulfillment in parenting and everyday life. In parent mobilization and empowerment methodology, the initial thrust is knowledge and skill development in order that the parent gain the expertise and tools essential for enacting their parental role and advocating for their child. The clinician addresses the parents' questions and provides information about the diagnosis, causes, treatment options available, potential risks, available resources, legal rights, and probable life course of the physiological condition. The clinician also clarifies the interplay of the physiologically based and developmentally/emotionally based conditions, and helps the parents gain a balanced understanding of the two and their impact on the child. Parents also need to know how the treatment proceeds, what they can expect, and what their responsibilities are in helping their child cope and adapt.

Equally important is that the parents learn how to access information, document the condition for medical follow-up and service eligibility, problem solve, and question professionals to clarify issues and concerns. They need to understand that professionals do not always have all of the answers and are not always right when they do provide answers. In turn, professionals need to understand that some shopping around for second and even third opinions is likely a sign of healthy concern for their child. At the point of fourth or fifth opinion, however, the equation changes and parents need to be helped to face the diagnosis and its implications for treatment and prognosis. As they learn to cope with the role pressures of having a child with a chronic illness, genetic disorder, or physical disability, parents may find self-help and parent support groups helpful in decreasing their sense of isolation and empowering them to advocate for the rights of their children.

As parents become more knowledgeable about their child's condition, they are able to empathize more with their child and explore how their child experiences his or her condition. They learn how to use available resources and experiences in ways that support the child's strengths and compensate to some degree for the vulnerabilities. They learn to note and deal with how others within and outside the family experience and react to their child. As parents become clearer about their child's needs and wishes, feel more competent in their parenting, and acquire a sense of control over their lives, they are able to be more active on their child's behalf.

Early on in seeking help, parents of children with physically challenging conditions need the tools for enacting the specialized aspects of their parental role (i.e., information, problem-solving skills, case-management skills, and service advocacy skills). In time, however, they also may need support and assistance in coping with the specific challenges of daily family routines, peer relationships, and school, as well as the general challenge of the never-ending role pressure experienced by parents of children with physically challenging conditions.

Most importantly, they may need support and assistance in looking at themselves in relation to their child. For example, what are their feelings and concerns at having a less than perfect child—anxious, depressed, angry, ashamed, guilty, isolated, or other? Are they overprotecting their child, keeping him or her out of mainstream situations, and truncating the normalization process? Are they exerting pressure for appropriate or impossible levels of achievement? Are they blaming social workers, physicians, and teachers for the child's condition (Seligman and Darling, 1989)?

In addition to the personal distress associated with the parental role, there also may be increased pressure on the marriage. Besides the childrearing pressures, there may be financial burdens and lack of time and energy for the spousal relationship or close friends. For the single parent especially, the sense of isolation may be very strong. Thus, often the parents need permission to pay attention to their own as well as their child's needs.

Focused Problem Solving.   An underlying assumption in focused problem-solving work is that parents have some comprehension of their child's difficulties or a particular parent/child conflict, but are overwhelmed and caught up in dysfunctional and downward spiraling parent/child interactions. Consequently, they are not free to use their strengths and resources. This approach focuses on the pressing psychosocial problems, present realities, and current needs of both child and parent. It concentrates the clinical social worker's and the parents' energy, attention, and activity narrowly on the parenting dimension of the adult life space and social ecology. Focused problem-solving work draws primarily on interpersonal and cognitive theories for collaborative intervention, which enables the parents to:

- select the focal psychosocial problem of attention and mobilize their strengths in relation to this problem
- express and cope with affective concerns associated with the focal problem
- begin to problem solve, explore precipitants, and formulate immediate goals and tasks

- learn alternative responses to problem behaviors
- comprehend and confront personal and community barriers to problem solving
- engage their strengths, resiliencies, and capacities in addressing the targeted problem, developing constructive alternatives, and adequate parenting for the child

In other words, focused problem-solving work empowers and mobilizes parents, enabling them to achieve specific self-selected parenting goals within clearly delineated service frames.

Developmental Parent Work.   Some parents are overwhelmed, hesitant, and dependent when they seek help for their child. They experience difficulty differentiating their own problems from their child's, and seem fearful of the responsibilities of childrearing. They have difficulty coping with the reality demands of day-to-day living and are easily overwhelmed by stressful life events. An infantile nature and a quality of affective impoverishment are often apparent in their lives. Their psychosocial histories often reveal deprived childhoods in which they received minimal nurture and protection from their own parents. Few have had a sustained relationship with someone they could trust or someone who offered help in handling their feelings and the demands of everyday life. Assessment of these parents reveals limited intrapersonal development and adaptive capacity, with few inner strengths and resources available for parenting or for exploring the source of their concerns about themselves and their children.

For these adults, the clinical social worker uses developmental parent work methodology and techniques to provide a corrective psychosocial experience. Specifically, the clinician provides a level of practical and emotional support sufficient to (1) meet some of the parent's unmet early developmental needs; (2) sustain an adequate level of psychosocial functioning in their present life circumstances; and (3) stabilize the family environment. The underlying assumption of developmental reparenting is that obstacles to adequate parenting may be mitigated by removing or minimizing some of the stressors of daily living, freeing parents' energies to move beyond their own needs and attend to their child's needs.

In this work, the clinician assumes the professional role of a nurturing and protective parent figure, models adequate parent/child interactions, and offers a consistent supportive therapeutic alliance. Clinicians make their presence known by caregiving activity that the parents will feel as activity designed to ease their load. Initially, these parents relate in a guarded and resistant manner. They are fearful of being hurt once again by engaging in another relationship that promises more than can be delivered. Thus, caution is in order with these parents and relational principles of availability, consistency, and empathy become critical in building trust and the dynamic mental representation of object constancy. Initially, the acceptance and support elements of the therapeutic alliance are maximized, the expectation and stimulation elements are minimized. In brief, the initial focus is meeting parents' unmet dependency needs.

Work with such parents, however, may elicit countertransference issues, especially when the clinical social worker offers massive doses of help yet is never able to satisfy the parents' needs and cravings. Feelings of inadequacy are fairly common in these circumstances. In addition, the clinician also may begin to feel swallowed whole, threatened by the lack of boundaries, and overwhelmed by parental efforts at merger. Often in these instances, a reminder of the developmental issues and tasks inherent in Mahler's (Mahler, Pine, and Bergman, 1975) separation/individuation phases and Erikson's (1950) trust/mistrust stage can be reassuring. That is, the real and symbolic nurture and protection in the corrective psychosocial experience provided by the clinical social worker is enabling the parents to rework some of their early deprivation through the transference elements of the therapeutic alliance.

Life, however, is not all nurture and protection, even in the early years. Thus, the key therapeutic issue is not that the parents are seeking to borrow the clinician's strength and resilience through merger of self with other; rather, the issue is at what point does the clinician begin to support and accept a little less and begin to inject more elements of expectation and stimulation into the therapeutic alliance. The intent is to move the parents forward developmentally into more autonomous functioning and exploration of the world.

During this portion of the corrective psychosocial experience, the clinical social worker is guided by Erikson's (1950) second stage of autonomy. Mindful of the developmental issues and tasks at the forefront during this period, the clinician slowly and carefully begins to set limits, clarify behavioral expectations, and establish clear boundaries between self and other. Together, clinician and parent also work to identify and mobilize the community resources needed by the parents and their children.

Parent/Child Relationship Work.   The crux of parenthood is the mutually reciprocating parent/child relationship. Within this relational context, the perceptions of parent and child are organized into dynamic mental representations that enable each to relate to the other in meaningful ways. These mutually reciprocal transactions of bonding and identification contain both interpersonal and intrapersonal elements. For example, when parents feed, guide, or play with their child, they integrate their mental representations of this actual child in the present reality with their mental representations of their inner child of the past, the wished-for ideal child, and the child of their future hopes and dreams. Thus, when parent and child interact, parents comprehend and react to their child's needs and affects not only in terms of the real child, but also how their own parents responded to their inner child of the past and how they view their child in relation to their wished-for ideal child and hoped-for future child.

When the mental representations of the real child and the symbolic children are congruent and when the caregiving for the inner child was sufficient, the parent/child relationship is likely to proceed with few glitches. When one or more of the representations are disparate, however, the representation of the real child is likely to take on some hidden meaning for the parent and be repetitively cast in the role of a person from the parent's past. It is this hidden or unconscious meaning that tends to foster parental hyper-reactivity to the child, difficulty in the parent/child relationship, and pathological sequelae that, over the years, may become internalized by the child. That is, there are likely to be childrearing difficulties not because of problems residing in the individual child, but because of the parents' conflicted issues and symbolic meanings that play out in their intense connectedness with their child. For example, these conflicts and problems may take the form of lack of boundaries and parent/child enmeshment, parental projection of conflicted parts of themselves onto their child and subsequent rejection of the child, or parental feelings about some traumatic event associated with and displaced onto their child.

Sometimes parents may project mental representations of their own early life and the associated affect onto their real child and then overidentify with this projected image. As a result, problems in interpersonal and emotional regulation develop. Thus, in these and multiple other ways, parents' internal lives and unfinished developmental tasks may impinge on their parenting role and be played out at various junctures in the parent/child relationship, especially if the parent begins to use the child to repair themselves. When this happens, psychosocial dysfunction appears in the parent/child interaction, the child's daily behavior, and the child's representational world.

The parent/child relationship constantly evolves in response to the child's unfolding developmental phases. The tasks of each phase may evoke the parents' own past issues and unresolved conflicts from that developmental phase. If parental resolution of maturational issues has been incomplete or pathological, the child's experiences are likely to intensify the parents' conflicts and may trigger inappropriate parent/child interactions. It is, however, important to note that childhood conflicts do not necessarily lead to pathological conditions or to parent/child relationship issues. However, when the parents' developmental lacunae do become apparent in their relationship with their child, parents experience a new opportunity to rework aspects of their own existing mental structure, disturbed mental processes, and conflicts (Benedek, 1959, 1970; Fisch, 1984; Fraiberg, Adelson, and Shapiro, 1975; Miller, 1981; Timberlake and Truitt, 1981).

Against this explanatory backdrop, the objectives in parent/child relationship work include helping parents (1) understand how their internal lives are impinging on their parenting role; (2) gain limited insight about the unconscious meaning their child has for them; (3) achieve increased differentiation between themselves and their child; and (4) achieve a new level of integration of unfinished developmental tasks that impinge on the parent/child relationship. In the initial phase of this work, supportive educational guidance may be used to identify the developmental issues of parents that are impinging on the parent/child relationship and impeding the child's growth and adaptation. As the clinical social worker begins to clarify the projected meaning of their child's specific symptoms and the displaced meaning of their child, parents often feel a combined sense of relief, guilt, and anxiety. They begin to see that in each critical period of development, children may stimulate a revival of their parents' related developmental conflicts and issues (Benedek, 1959).

As the therapeutic alliance strengthens, the clinician uses reflection to illuminate destructive comments and stimulate parental capacity for self-observation (*"You have said several times now about Serena, 'I feel so sad that you're going off to school and leaving me.'"*) and clarifying statements to highlight the child's needs (*"I understand your feelings but they reflect your needs. Your child needs you to attend to her feelings and reassure her that you're pleased and comfortable with her increased autonomy and readiness for the adventures of school."*) Then, if the parent is ready, the clinician shifts the focus back to the parents' earlier years with a connective statement underlining their needs and seeking the source (*"You have strong feelings about being left. Let's look at where they come from."*). This latter comment directs the parents toward their own underlying concerns and unresolved issues about separation and loss. As the parents begin to talk about their issues in this area, they begin to differentiate themselves from their child, become able to interact more freely with their child, and attend more readily to their child's issues.

In this methodological approach, exploration, uncovering, and modified interpretive work remain focused on the parent/child relationship, but attend to the parents' various developmental factors and mental processes as they impinge on their relations with their child. When that theme is repeatedly illuminated, parents begin to gain some perspective about what they are reliving through their child. At about this point, the momentum of parent/child relationship work often stimulates intense anxiety and resistance. When this happens, the clinician works supportively within the therapeutic alliance to help parents understand the nature of the therapeutic impasse in relation to what is occurring in the parent/child relationship (Chazan, 1995; Chethik, 1989; Fraiberg, 1954a, 1954b, 1961; Hamilton, 1947).

While the process of self-observation in parent/child relationship work is intense, the clinician limits transference regressions by continually reframing the boundaries of the work (*"Now, how does this material about the loss of your father when you were nine like Serena is now affect what is happening between the two of you?"*). Such comments move the parent away from the frightened, sad, inner child of the past that had surfaced while exploring the practical and emotional ramifications of their loss back to the present adult reality of parenting their child today. Such carefully delineated work meets the developmental needs of the children and helps parents comprehend that their inappropriate affect is not based in present reality but in earlier childhood experiences. Helping parents historically ground their earlier experiences re-places these experiences in their past context, strengthens parents' inner preparedness, moves these experiences away from the child in the present, and increases parents' ability to grow as the child develops (Chethik, 1989; Fraiberg, 1954b, 1961).

Treatment Issues in Concurrent Work

Confidentiality

In concurrent parent work, it is usual for parents and children to be treated by the same clinical social worker. Because the principle of confidentiality of client information is not absolute with children and their parents, it is critical to explain in advance what information may be shared, with whom, under what circumstances, why, and how. The clinician is expected to share information with parents that suggests danger to the child or others. The definition of danger and the question of degree, however, involve professional judgment and discretion. Even with advance preparation, sharing material from the child's individual sessions is likely to impair trust. When such a necessity arises, the clinician explores the matter first with the child. When telling parents is not optional, it is important not to convey that the child has a choice. Often, it is more helpful if the child can be supported in telling his or her parents in a conjoint session with the therapist. In this way, the therapist is immediately available to process the information with the parents and mediate as necessary. Conversely, it is often crucial to share information parents reveal about the child in order that the child understand the therapist knows what is going on in their real world as well as in their make-believe world. This sharing is, of course, done with the parents' awareness and understanding. Yet, this sharing too may impact the therapeutic alliance by increasing the child's mistrust and fear, unless there has been advance preparation.

Therapeutic Alliance

The therapeutic alliance formed by the parent and clinical social worker reflects the same wide range of real interpersonal attachment issues and intrapsychic working alliance elements found in the child/clinician therapeutic alliance. There are, however, critical differences associated with the parents' adult status. In contrast to the dependent child living with parents or other primary caregivers, the parent is expected to be autonomous and provide care for others. In addition, parents' mental development is expected to be fully capable of externalizing "major pathogenic internal conflict onto the therapist so that the conflict is felt by [the parent] to be between himself [or herself] and the therapist" (Sandler, Kennedy, and Tyson, 1980, p. 82). This pathogenic internal conflict is based on their mental representations of their past relationship with their own parents. Selected aspects of their internal conflicts are likely to be found in their connectedness with their child, as well as in their relationships with significant others, including the clinical social worker.

In concurrent parent work, parents share and explore their failures and successes as caregivers. In so doing, they usually find themselves reflecting on their earlier life experiences and their inner child of the past. For example, parents' earlier experiences with authority figures often come to the fore when they seek help. For the most part, though, the methodologies and techniques in concurrent parent work emphasize supportive guidance, include facilitative interventions, and address present parenting and childrearing issues. By focusing on the parent role, these treatment methods do not intensify the transference of the past to the present and the regression to earlier developmental levels usually found in insight-oriented psychotherapy with adults.

By contrast, the methodology in parent/child relationship work does intensify the transference of the past to the present, but only in terms of the implications of the past for troubling aspects of the parents' relationship with their child. This approach is essential when the parent/child relationship is disturbed by negative projections of parents' inner life space, and represents a displaced expression of their mental representations, internal affective world, and characteristic interpersonal processes. This methodology directs attention toward role-related self-observation and awareness, focuses on repetitive behavioral and affective patterns, and engages in limited interpretation of the past. In so doing, the therapeutic alliance is strengthened and transference of past experiences emerges in the clinical narrative from repressed material, is displaced onto the therapist, and leads to carefully limited regression within the session to an earlier developmental level.

Course of Concurrent Parent Work: Dobson Family by Martha Wilson Chescheir, Ph.D., LCSW-C

Stage I: Biopsychosocial Assessment

The Dobsons are a warm and closely knit African American family who have had real concerns about their ten-year-old daughter Denise ever since she was two years old. At that time, they realized she was not speaking normally and that her language development was delayed. As a consequence, she had extensive evaluations over a several-year period in which she was diagnosed variously as aphasic, autistic, and learning disabled. When Denise was three years old, one evaluator described her as "a very active child with dysphasia and mixed receptive and expressive problems who functioned intellectually in the mildly retarded range (IQ 60)." Over time and with special tutoring, her language skills improved rapidly. By the time she was in fourth grade, her intellectual potential was rated as slightly above average, but Denise was still showing signs of emotional difficulty with some schizoid-like or autistic features.

Presenting Problem.   The summer before Denise entered the fifth grade, Mr. and Mrs. D. brought her in for yet another evaluation. On this occasion, the parents were worried about her over-sensitivity and inability to make friends at school. In fact, she was often the brunt of teasing by other children who thought she was a little weird. Living at home with Denise was difficult because she balked and dawdled about doing everything and needed so much special attention. For example, she would spend hours getting dressed in the morning. Doing her homework at night had become a chore for the entire family. Her parents described Denise as a ten-year-old perfectionist and expressed the fear that she might never grow up and be able to take care of herself. According to her parents, she seemed incapable of accepting responsibility for herself. Denise's older sister never had problems like these. Fifteen-year-old Dora was bright, made friends easily, and was doing extremely well in school. Thus, the comparison between the two sisters created added complications for the parents.

The mental health clinic child psychiatrist who had done the most recent evaluation recommended counseling for the whole family and individual psychotherapy for Denise. He suggested the possibility of placement in a special school because of Denise's immaturity and the difficulty she had fitting in with her peers in a large public school setting. The case was referred to me following this psychiatric evaluation.

Psychiatric Evaluation: Reason for Referral. Denise, age ten, is a youngster who has shown disturbances from early life. It appears that early on she had severe emotional problems that were manifest in disturbances in language development. Now that language is present, she shows signs of dealing with emotion and social situations and some peculiar thinking. She is a very immature, tense youngster who has low frustration tolerance and spends much of her time absorbed in daydreams that interfere with her functioning in school and at home. She is reluctant to reveal the content of the daydreams and one wonders how bizarre some of the fantasies may be. Denise is very dependent on her family and quite isolated from peers. She is developing a severely schizoid manner and many compulsive traits. Although not overtly psychotic or schizophrenic, she shows a number of characteristics that are a milder version of what is sometimes seen in schizophrenic children. Because she is still very much in the latency stage of development, it seems most appropriate to consider her problem as a "withdrawn reaction to childhood." Without receiving treatment, she could develop into a schizoid personality or perhaps have more severe disturbance later on. Because Denise has never had mental health treatment, it seems most appropriate to refer the Dobsons for a combination of individual treatment for Denise and counseling for her family, and also to recommend looking into a special school placement.

Initial Evaluation: Family and Individual Sessions. The family arrived fifteen minutes late for our initial meeting and settled rather comfortably in my office. I noticed that Denise sat close to her father and across the room from her mother and older sister Dora. Denise is a tall, slender, African American ten-year-old. She is slender, wirey, and light complected like her father. Her eyes are set close together, giving her a strained, slightly odd appearance. She was tense and anxious, sat upright in her chair, and fidgeted throughout most of the initial family session. Mr. Dobson was the family spokesman and outlined the family's concerns in a quiet, matter-of-fact manner. By contrast, Mrs. Dobson could hardly contain her distress as she talked about how hard the family had tried to understand and help Denise over the years. She mentioned that Denise frequently complains about others being unfair and seems to have an unusual way of understanding social situations. For example, Denise remembers something that was done to her as if it happened just yesterday, when in fact the incident had occurred several months ago.

Dora voiced the family's exasperation with Denise's stubbornness, refusal to dress herself, and refusal to do her schoolwork. She explained how the family gets sucked into doing Denise's work for her. In this way, Denise keeps the whole family invested in her problems and up every night coaxing her to complete her work. Usually, she manages to get someone in the family to help her get dressed in the mornings. Most often, Dora ends up combing her hair, washing her face, or helping her get dressed so they won't be late for school. It became increasingly apparent that Denise's problems have kept the whole family over-involved. Denise seems young for her age and quite dependent and helpless. Dora, on the other hand, is unusually competent and patient for a fifteen-year-old girl. Mrs. D. is the emotional one and seemingly overprotective of Denise. At the same time, she tries hard to cover up her anger at Denise for causing so much trouble for everyone. Mr. D. remains slightly aloof and intellectual. He plays the role of placater, whose job it is to keep the peace among the complaining and fussy women.

There is an odd mechanical, almost sing-song quality about the way Denise relates to the others in her family. While she gave no definite evidence of a thought disorder, her thinking did seem a little odd. She spoke in a strained, high-pitched little voice but readily agreed that she does worry about many things, particularly when she hears her parents arguing or raising their voices. However, she couldn't seem to understand the difference between the pain of those kinds of feelings and concerns about Dora misplacing her library card. When the family session was over, her parents and Dora left the room so Denise and I could talk privately. Denise waved frantically after them much like a three-year-old might do.

After they left, Denise continued to talk about her fears when her parents go away and her worries that they may never come back. Then she mentioned some dreams about being left and told me that, even when she wakes up and knows that it is a dream, she still finds herself crying. Her first wish was to have a whole lot of brothers and sisters because then she would have more friends to help her with things. They would help her with homework, teach her to cook, fix her hair, and do other things. Her second wish was not to have any homework, and her third was that she would have her way all the time. She mentioned that her ambition is to become a cartoonist and then drew a picture of a mouse named Stuart Little. She explained that she liked the book *Stuart Little* because he is very small and helps people with problems. She can imagine him helping her with her homework, fixing the piano, or doing other useful things.

Denise readily acknowledged that she is very slow in doing most things like her homework or getting dressed because she spends a lot of time thinking about other things. However, she was unwilling to discuss what these daydreams were about. In response to the baby-bird fable, she said, "The bird flew to the mother's tree and then the mother had more eggs to hatch and the baby had lots of brothers and sisters and was happy."

My general impression after the Dobsons' initial visit was that the whole family revolved around Denise and her problems. They were all over-involved in their own ways, yet walking on eggs, fearful that they would do something wrong that might upset Denise or perhaps make her angry. In a way, Denise was in control of the entire household, but—at the same time—miserable.

The Dobsons seemed eager to begin treatment so I explained that, for starters, I wanted to see them separately until I had gotten to know Denise better. I also wanted to talk with Mr. and Mrs. D. on a biweekly basis. When they were all ready, we would schedule some family sessions for the entire family, including Dora. I suggested that they follow through with the school recommendation for updated psychological tests that could be especially helpful as we began our search for a more suitable school placement.

Summary of Psychological Testing.   At the request of her parents, Denise was referred for psychological tests by the principal at Jackson Elementary School. Her fourth-grade teachers and parents were concerned about how well Denise would get along next year in fifth grade because she was having serious interpersonal and learning problems.

Tests Administered

1. Wechsler Intelligence Scale for Children–Revised
   Verbal Score 102
   Performance Score ...106
   Full-Scale IQ 104
2. Wide-Range Achievement Test
   Reading........Grade equivalent 10.7
3. Bender–Gestalt
4. Draw-a-Person Test
5. Sentence-Completion Test
6. Rorschach
7. Informal Interview and Observations

Findings.   Denise and her parents were almost an hour late for their first appointment. The lateness plus how slowly Denise worked necessitated scheduling a second appointment. Denise attended a special program during kindergarten but has received no other special assistance from the school system. Currently, however, both the school and her parents report that Denise's relationship with other children is fraught with difficulties. She is often teased and harassed by the others, but does not complain because she wants to be accepted. She refuses to ask her parents to intercede on her behalf. Denise talked of feeling lonely and left out. Her parents mentioned that she sometimes laughs inappropriately and is often confused about what she is asked to do, especially when commanded to do something. These symptoms have been getting worse for the last three or four months. Denise's favorite pastime is drawing pictures of animal cartoons. Sometimes, she draws pictures of a family with only one child, but if anyone comments about that, she immediately adds a second child. Her parents also expressed concern because she is so easily distracted from her task and seems lost in her own world.

A review of Denise's school records revealed that during the last two years, her scholastic progress has declined. Many school papers identified her primary problem as failure to complete her work. She has begun to fail in many subjects.

Results of the psychological tests seem to confirm the observations and impressions of parents and teachers. Denise has the intellectual ability, but actual performance falls short of this. On the Wechsler, Denise earned a full scale IQ of 104, which places her intellectual functioning within the normal range. Although little scatter is apparent between her verbal and performance scores, deficiencies are noted in the subtests that measure reasoning, judgment, and understanding, and that require anticipatory skills in daily living and common sense in social situations and activities. Potential intellectual ability is estimated to be in the above-average range.

The Wide-Range Achievement Test found Denise to be working considerably above grade level in reading and on grade level in math. On the Bender–Gestalt, Denise earned a score appropriate to her age but exhibited some idiosyncratic behaviors, such as holding the cards very close to her, counting dots, and counting aloud. This examiner, however, thinks this behavior is due more to Denise's unique personality and behavior than to visual problems.

The drawing of a person that Denise completed was that of an age- and gender-appropriate prepubescent youngster, which suggests that sexual identification and its development are proceeding normally. The drawing, although artistically well executed, shows a girl with arms pressed close to her sides, with a stilted look and posture. This type of drawing has been found among children who have difficulty in interpersonal relations and are inflexible—both descriptions seeming characteristic of Denise.

Some of these findings were confirmed by Denise's responses on the Sentence-Completion Test. "What did she feel she needed most of all?" "Friends." A mother to Denise was a "female parent." In answer to the question, "I want to know _____," Denise replied, "Why God made the sun out of heat."

On the Rorschach, several of Denise's responses were normal popular ones such as "a bat" on Card Five. However, on those cards with color, Denise had difficulty integrating form and color. She usually handled this problem by describing the objects as a "rainbow, insect, crab, or monster." Problems in handling colors on the Rorschach usually have been associated with pathological personality disorder, and are suggestive of a similar process in this youngster.

As Denise has matured and overcome the language delay, some residual emotional difficulties remain that are becoming more pronounced in mid-latency. Many of Denise's problems are similar enough to those of autistic children to suggest a description of this youngster as having an "autistic shadow."

Stage II: Creation of Therapeutic Alliance

Concurrent Parent Work.   There were three tasks to consider in my early work with Mr. and Mrs. D.: (1) to get acquainted with them and understand something about their relationship to their children and as a couple; (2) to help them locate a new school for Denise and facilitate making that change; and (3) to obtain a developmental history, understand how Denise fits in with their expectations, and help them learn to accept realistically whatever Denise's limitations turned out to be.

Mr. D. is a tall, slender, light-skinned African American with a tidy mustache. He tends to be slightly obsessive, especially about dates, time, and place. However, his wife immediately began to brag about his artistic talents. He has been responsible for the church bulletins for a number of years, and is good at both overall design and little comical drawings of church activities. He is forty-one years old and a high-school graduate who works as an inventory specialist for a large firm. Mrs. D. is short, medium-dark complected, and rather stout with a pleasant, open face. Talking comes easily for her. She is much more forthcoming than her husband, who seems reserved and a little standoffish. Mrs. D. is 39 years old, completed the eleventh grade, and has always worked regularly at the post office. Mrs. D. and her older daughter resemble each other physically, Denise resembles her father.

Mrs. D. is the emotional one who talked freely about their long-standing concerns about Denise. It is hard for her to understand how she can have two daughters who are so opposite in every way. She met her husband in church shortly after they had moved into town from The South. Their life revolves around their children, work, and church. Both parents enjoy singing in the church choir and have been encouraging the girls to join the junior choir. Dora enjoys singing but Denise won't try out, even though the choir director would be glad to have her. Denise and Dora, however, take dancing lessons taught by a young woman at their church.

I inquired about their hopes for their children. They assured me that they had wanted to have several children but gave up that idea after Denise was born because she was such a difficult child from the very start. I wondered what some of the problems were. Mrs. D. explained that Denise wouldn't sleep and had terrible colic so she was always tired. She went on to say that "When Dora was a baby, we just packed her up and took her everywhere with us. She was a good eater and sleeper and easy to cuddle. This didn't happen with Denise, who was always fretting and crying. Then we discovered that Denise couldn't talk and that there was something really wrong with her. We have had serious problems ever since." Mr. D. tried to smooth things over by assuring his wife that they had done all they could, and were still trying to make things better for Denise and the rest of the family.

When I asked what was going on in their lives around the time of Denise's birth, Mrs. D. said, "I was pleased to be pregnant for the second time. It was alright for Denise to turn out to be another girl, but Mother predicted I would have a boy." Unfortunately, her mother had a massive stroke and died just a couple of months before Denise was born. "Having the first baby was fairly easy, but having Denise was hard from the very start because I was so tired from having to go to work and taking Dora to daycare. Denise wouldn't even eat right and what we gave her never agreed with her, no matter what we tried to do."

Her pregnancy with Denise was full term. While she retained a lot of fluids, she did not become toxemic. The water broke spontaneously but mid-forceps had to be used. Denise weighed 7 pounds 5 ounces, but the forcep marks made her look pretty awful. Mrs. D. had breast-fed her first baby successfully but, for some unknown reason, her milk just didn't seem to agree with Denise. She stopped trying to nurse her after the first three months. Nevertheless, Denise's developmental milestones were within the normal range except for her speech. She sat up at six months and walked at twelve months. She was three before she could use such words as "daddy," "hi," "mommy," and "baby" and three and a half before she could put words together. At preschool, Denise used to play by herself and often screamed out as though in agony. She often voluntarily bumped her knee or tried to hurt herself in other ways. After her screams, she would talk to herself saying "Shut your big mouth, Denny" or "Stop that noise, Denny."

We also discussed how to go about finding a school for Denise. The Dobsons had been given a list of five approved private schools that the Board of Education would pay for. Early on, we made arrangements for the Dobsons to visit them. Finding a school proved to be difficult because Denise's problems did not fit the usual categories of learning disabled or behavior disordered. She needed a school that provided individual attention, promoted socialization with the group, and encouraged her to emerge from her fantasy world. The school that we finally selected only partially met these requirements. The classes were open and un-structured. There were many more rowdy boys than girls. However, it was small and the teachers seemed knowledgeable and energetic.

Denise, who hadn't liked the idea of changing schools in the first place, was predictably balky and resistant. I encouraged the parents to be kind but insistent. Learning to handle herself around the more obstreporous boys proved to be a realistic life experience for Denise because these tough guys were full of anger and spoke their mind no matter what others thought. Both Denise and her parents complained about their rowdiness and poor manners. Denise's passive aggres-siveness was certainly noticed and discussed in their informal group meetings. In the long run, Denise and her parents seemed satisfied with the quality of care and hands-on treatment she received at the private school. She actually attended for two years and then was transferred back to public middle school.

As we worked together, the strain between this mother and daughter became more apparent. Mrs. D. was already overburdened when Denise was born, not having recovered from the loss of her own mother. When she spoke of Denise as a very young infant, I had the impression that the fit between mother and child never really flourished. Denise was like a weird little stranger to her: fretful, colicky, and demanding. As hard as she tried, Mrs. D. simply couldn't find a way to comfort her. As a consequence, Denise had some serious attachment problems.

Later, Mrs. D. talked about how much she blamed herself for Denise's problems because she stopped nursing her too soon. *(She must have had a hard time loving this strange little creature who just didn't fit her image of what a baby should be like. This lack of fit may very well have been the root of Mrs. D.'s need to alternately neglect and overprotect her child.)*

Social History and Discussion.   Mr. and Mrs. D. came from similar family backgrounds, as both have roots in the rural south and migrated north as young adults to seek employment. They met in the choir at the EMR Church and got along very well because they shared common values. While they may have been opposites temperamentally, they complemented each other well. Their daughter Dora was the first grandchild on both sides of the family. Shortly before Dora's birth, however, Mrs. D.'s father was killed in a tractor accident. As a consequence, Mrs. D.'s mother and younger twin sisters decided to sell the farm in Georgia and come to Washington, where they found an apartment just a few blocks down the street. This turned out to be a fortuitous move because Dora could be left off at grandmother's home each morning while her parents went to work.

Mr. D. grew up on the Mississippi River, where his father made a living as a cook on a river barge and his mother was employed as a domestic for a wealthy family in Natchez. He was their only child and sometimes when his father had to be away for several weeks at a time, he and his mother stayed over at the big house. Mr. D. often accompanied his mother to work and played with the other children in that family. He was a good student, and his teachers and the family in Natchez encouraged him in his studies. When he reached young adulthood, his parents reluctantly agreed that he should leave The South and seek further education and employment in a more prosperous urban area.

Having good jobs and finding a niche for themselves in their new community gave this young family a sense of accomplishment, and so they were pleased to discover that they were going to have a second child. Certainly, they had no reason to suspect everything would not turn out well. However, shortly before Denise was born, the beloved grandmother died from a massive stroke, leaving Mrs. D. grief-stricken and without adequate child care. Dora (age five years) was old enough to enter kindergarten, but without grandmother nearby, the parents had no safe dependable place to leave Denise. On top of that, Denise's birth was difficult because it was a forceps delivery that left a mean-looking scar down the side of her face, so she looked slightly damaged. She weighed 7 pounds, 5 ounces but her head seemed small and her eyes a little too close together, which gave her a rather odd appearance. To make matters worse, she was a fretful and colicky baby who demanded constant attention. A worker at the daycare center suggested that maybe mother's milk was disagreeing with Denise. That upset Mrs. D. so much that she stopped nursing when the baby was only three months old. In looking back over that difficult time, Mrs. D. now blames herself for giving up on Denise. Her guilt only increased the tension between mother and baby. The fit between the two was difficult from the beginning and seemed to have gotten things off to a bad start. This added to Denise's attachment problem and the family's need to overprotect her by not expecting her to learn to be self-sufficient.

Denise must have seemed like a little stranger to her mother because she was not the cuddly baby her sister Dora had been. Mrs. D. was in the throes of grieving the loss of her own mother and had little energy left over to cope with a colicky, tense, complaining infant. We cannot know for sure how many of Denise's problems were genetic in origin. The delayed speech may have had a genetic component. However, being left in a large daycare center and being a second child born to an overstressed mother probably complicated Denise's early years. It seems likely that she was left alone often and learned to entertain herself by developing a rich fantasy life.

A psychodynamic formulation would suggest that Denise had not yet reached the age of object constancy because, at age ten, she still clings to others and expects to be treated as a much younger child. Apparently, she was always a shy, inhibited, and withdrawn child who was narcissistically involved in a world of her own making. She may have seen others in her family as extensions of herself—only there to do her bidding—not as people in their own right. In this way, she got away with dominating the household and actually had no idea how to get along with others her own age. Instead, she found ways to direct her energies into solitary pursuits. There is reason to believe that Denise suffered from an overanxious attachment disorder. The relationship between mother and child, however, was difficult—one might say intensely ambivalent as expressed in inconsistent patterns of love/hate or pull/push.

This family has many strengths, but when faced with the death of grandparents and the difficulties surrounding Denise's birth, their coping skills were taxed to the limit. By the time they started treatment with me, they had seen many professionals, who had given them mixed messages about what was wrong with this child, and they were thoroughly disheartened and discouraged.

Goals. During this stage of my work with the parents, we developed some goals to use as markers for progress. The parents and I discussed them first and then shared them with Denise to increase her awareness of the main purpose of our work. The goals included:

1. locate an appropriate school for Denise
2. establish a working relationship with Denise and her parents
3. encourage age-appropriate behavior and activities
4. understand the nature of Denise's fantasy life and encourage more realistic ways of thinking and feeling
5. help her become more open and flexible in relationships with others

Child Work.   Transferring schools was hard for Denise. She visited the schools along with her parents and found something wrong with each of them. The school they finally selected was the one Denise had the fewest complaints about. As part of our regular routine, Denise and I spent a little time during each session talking about how things were going for her at school because she usually came with a litany of complaints about those "bad boys." Discussing these difficulties in some detail seemed to be useful in helping Denise handle some of the teasing she managed to bring on herself.

Because Mrs. D. did not drive, Mr. D. always brought Denise to my office. At first, he just sat in the waiting room, but as time went by, he would leave and come back to pick her up. My first impression of Denise was that she was much younger than her actual age (ten years) and that she was pretending to be a "good girl." As a result, she seemed stiff and prudish. Moreover, she insisted on a routine pattern of sameness that was repeated week after week. She began by drawing and meticulously coloring a series of mice people, one mouse per session—all girls—each wearing a different pants outfit depicting the days of the week. The pictures themselves were large, filling a whole sheet of poster-size newsprint paper. She wanted them set up side by side along the wall in my playroom. I wondered if she felt a little like one of these mouse girls—small like a mouse because of being the youngest in her family but large in the sense of importance. She didn't respond to my remark, just continued to create more large mouse girls, saying, "They are all in a show together where they sing songs and dance. They get along very well—never fight; everybody likes them and thinks they are 'real good'. All of their names begin with the letter 'D'—Dorothy, Dolly, Donna, Danielle, Deborah, Diane, and Della. They are like sisters so they are never lonely."

In this way, Denise took control of the sessions. Any suggestions or ideas that I might have about deviating from the routine were summarily dismissed. It was as if Denise could only feel safe when she took up all the space—reminiscent of the mouse girls taking up all the available space on the poster paper. In this case, she created the illusion that she was surrounded by friends. Midway into the session, she regularly excused herself to go to the bathroom where she stayed for an unusually long period—sometimes as long as five minutes. When she returned, she ignored me and just continued where she left off, focusing on her drawings. (*I often felt she wasn't even aware that I was in the room with her, and from time to time made a point of shifting in my seat or making mini-comments just to keep something going between us.*)

Then one day Denise announced that she was writing a book. I expressed a lot of interest in that and wondered if she would share some of it with me. She brightened, saying that she would bring the book next week. Writing and illustrating chapters in this book then became the focus of the next few months of our work. Her story was about an eight-year-old girl named Olivia who lived with her father and younger brother Harry. Denise explained in a matter-of-fact way that Olivia's mother was run over by a car and killed. When I asked how Olivia felt about not having a mother, Denise seemed startled as if she hadn't given that any thought. She simply replied that Olivia has lots of friends. She went on to give detailed accounts about the kinds of things they did together, like go to the movies, play card games, go to an amusement park, and form a secret society. Each chapter was illustrated with a picture of whatever activity was being featured that week.

Suddenly one day, the theme shifted. Olivia's father invited her to go to a restaurant with him. Soon after they arrived, Olivia found herself attracted to the tall, good looking Italian waiter named Romero. In fact, she developed an instant crush on him, because she was drawn to him "like a magnet." He was nice to her but pretended not to care. Moreover, Mario, the cook in the kitchen, helped Olivia think up four tricks to play on Romero in order to get his attention. When her father wasn't looking, Olivia would sneak back to the kitchen to talk with Mario, and together they played these tricks on Romero. In the kitchen episodes, conversations were very lively and arguments or fights flared up between the cook and the waiter. By contrast, in the main part of the restaurant, Olivia always behaved properly because her father questioned her about where she had gone and why she was away from the table so long. Finally, her brother Harry joined them at the table. After he observed what was going on, Harry whispered some advice to Olivia that she should make a career of becoming a sex maniac. The father, on the other hand, was oblivious to what was happening. He just scolded them about their table manners and not saying please and thank you.

Discussion. After working together, I began to gain a clearer understanding of what Denise's fantasy life was about and was generally encouraged. In the first place, Denise had a wonderful imagination. Because her life in the real world wasn't working for her, she created an imaginary world. Her pictures of the mouse girls were rigid and inflexible with arms straight down at their side—actually the same position as the draw-a-person figure Denise had done for the psychologist. Yet, she called these figures her friends and told us they were singing and dancing, so I felt Denise might loosen up and have some fun.

The novel Denise was writing followed a similar theme. The main character Olivia had many friends. These wish-fulfilling fantasies protected Denise from painful feelings of loneliness and isolation. During the second half of the story, the theme suddenly shifted with the invitation to go to the restaurant with her father. Now, men and boys enter the scene and the story takes a different twist. We are introduced to some lively and mischievous characters. I think it's quite possible that the model for these men came from some of her encounters with the delinquent boys she was learning to deal with at school. It was apparent that the men and boys introduced the element of suspense and excitement.

Over time, a therapeutic alliance gradually developed between us. At some level, Denise seemed to understand what we were doing and where we needed to go. In the beginning, I was pretty much ignored and only present as an appendage to her grandiosity. She would, however, allow me to enter her world from time to time as an admirer and observer. As time went on during the first year, an idealizing transference seemed to be emerging. *(From the countertransference perspective, I found myself both fascinated and bored with Denise; fascinated because of her imagination because I was always curious about where that would lead us. Most of the time, I was bored by being left out and tired of the repetitiveness of her thinking and behavior. Denise's obsessive-compulsive tendencies certainly interfered with her hu-manness and comfort level in relating to another person. Her politeness was a facade that I hoped would eventually give way to a little more authenticity.)*

Stage III: Identification of Narrative Themes

Several themes seemed to emerge during the middle phase of our work. The first had to do with Denise fitting into the new school because neither Denise nor her parents were entirely satisfied with the school selected. The issue was that some of the other students had difficulty with authority, and were often outspoken with their complaints and used a great deal of profanity, much to the Dobsons' disapproval. Even though I had planned to work with Denise and her parents separately in the beginning, I found it necessary to hold several family meetings to discuss this issue, and also to help the family consider different ways of handling Denise's stubbornness and procrastination when everyone was trying to get off in the mornings.

As it turned out, Denise became accustomed to the new school sooner than her parents because she became fascinated with what happened in the classroom when some of the rowdy boys acted up in class. At these times, group meetings were held to resolve issues and discuss the sources of conflict. Fortunately, Denise's teachers looked out for her and the group meetings helped her handle herself differently to avoid being scapegoated. As it turned out, some of the tough boys began talking to her so she felt more accepted.

The second theme had to do with parent guidance work. In this case, it meant encouraging the parents to talk about their disappointment in having a child with special needs and letting Mrs. Dobson discuss her overload of guilt and need to blame herself for not loving Denise in the same way she loved Dora. In the process, we discussed her sadness about losing her mother and the additional guilt for not being able to prevent her mother's stroke. Mrs. D. was also extremely frustrated with her twin sisters. They live close by but consistently refuse to help out with the girls because they work and are involved in their own social life (with men of whom the Dobsons disapprove). One day Mrs. D. remarked, "My sisters just rip and snort around and never give a thought to how they might be helpful. When I ask them for help, they're so mean about it that I've just stopped asking them for anything. That will teach them a lesson. Just wait until the next time they want to borrow money." I commented about how angry she must feel and how hard it must be for her to ask for help of any kind. Then I supported the Dobsons for having the courage to find professional help for Denise and wondered how difficult it was for them to work with me because I was a white woman. Mr. Dobson quickly assured me that both he and his wife had a lot of confidence in me. He thought perhaps this was because he had learned a lot from the white family his mother had worked for in Natchez. They had been particularly kind and generous to him as he was growing up. Mrs. D. echoed this sentiment by saying she had a lot of white teachers who were really good.

As the parents' trust in me grew, we began to notice signs of progress. Mr. D. started to take a greater interest in ways to make their home life easier. He paid close attention when we mentioned that Denise seemed to take after him and his side of the family. He was especially proud of Denise's talents as an artist and definitely encouraged her work. It was actually therapeutic for him to drive Denise to my office once a week because, without realizing it, he was carrying on age-appropriate conversations with her.

We frequently discussed Mrs. D.'s guilt about not having been the right kind of mother for Denise and concerns that she had about her own health; especially her high blood pressure and fear that the same thing might happen to her as happened to her mother. Then, of course, that conversation would lead into how Denise would ever learn to care for herself without them.

The crux of our work involved changing the family system so that Denise could no longer control them with her passive-aggressive helplessness, which played right into her parents' guilt for not really spending time with Denise. While we discussed what to do intellectually, it seemed almost impossible to put their thoughts into meaningful action until we decided to hold regular biweekly family meetings, along with individual work with Denise.

Discussion. At the end of the second school year, the decision was made to allow Denise to return to the regular public school because her neighborhood school was opening a special learning center for children who needed more individual attention. By this time, Denise had developed the semblance of a trusting relationship with me. I felt that it was time to concentrate more on the family interaction, and so we began to have some family sessions. These two changes created quite a shift in the work for all concerned.

Stage IV: Developmental Growth and Change

Family Work. Denise disliked the idea of returning to public school, saying that she did not want to be mainstreamed. She wanted to remain as a special student, but she wasn't given that choice by the school system. So, once again, we had to help her face an unwanted reality. However, very soon after the school year started, Denise began to talk enthusiastically about the wonderful guidance counselor at the new school—a young, beautiful African American whose name was Cherise Jones. I spoke with Ms. Jones on a number of occasions and felt she understood Denise quite well. She was setting aside private time to help Denise fit into the hurly-burly of the large school.

Meanwhile, at home, there was more open conflict. The sisters were quarreling more. Denise was becoming more aggressive and talking back to her parents. They found this behavior unacceptable. I tried to help the parents understand that Denise needed to assert herself more if they wanted her to learn to speak up and express her positive as well as her negative feelings.

We started holding meetings with the entire family on a biweekly basis. Everyone except Denise found the family meetings useful. It was hard for Denise to learn to share me with the other family members. She did not like the fact that Dora and her parents had numerous complaints about her, especially how she monopolizes the time in their one bathroom. Mr. and Mrs. D. also began to give Denise more responsibility around the house so she would do her share of the chores. During some of the family meetings, Denise simply tuned out. She would bury her head in a pillow or put her hands over her ears, even though I tried to encourage her to speak up about things she didn't like that others did.

In our individual sessions, Denise had mentioned several things that annoyed her. For example, she felt that grownups take advantage of their power and didn't give kids credit for having feelings. I was encouraged by these comments because part of the trouble in the beginning was that Denise denied ownership of her feeling life. Also, Denise disliked having her parents talk down to her and treat her like a much younger kid. They make her stay at home after school, so she just sits in front of the television and gets bored. She would like to ride a bicycle, but her mother won't even let her have one because it is too dangerous. Finally, with my help, Denise brought these issues up at a family meeting. The parents heard it as her growing need for independence, but were at a loss to know how to give her more freedom unless she could find acceptable friends whose parents invited her over after school. Her mother was too overprotective to consider a bicycle. She was afraid of Denise hurting herself and did not think the neighborhood was a safe enough place for a girl to be riding around alone. Denise mentioned some of these things to Ms. Jones, who helped her sign up to play a trumpet in the school band. The band practices took up a couple of afternoons a week. On another late afternoon, she and Dora took dance lessons at a local church within walking distance of the house. On still another afternoon, her father brought her to weekly appointments with me. This new plan worked fairly well.

At the end of the school year, the family sent me an invitation to the girls' dance recital. I was pleased to go because that way I would have a chance to see how Denise was getting along with her contemporaries. Denise actually performed well as a tap dancer, seemed to fit right into the group, and was not noticeably stiff or overly self-conscious.

Child Work.   This stage was marked by much resistance from Denise because she was reluctant to return to the large public middle school and was unhappy with me for insisting on the family meetings. One day during one of the individual sessions, she put her head down on the sofa and claimed to be sick. I was generally sympathetic, and we talked quietly about how she felt and where she hurt. The next session, she lay down on the sofa again, this time covering her head with the cushion. I sat near her for a while. Then, after she refused to respond to my comments, I told her that I was feeling left out and that I wished she would talk about what was troubling her. Silence. Then I ventured the thought that she might be angry at me, and I wondered what that was about. More silence. Then I said it was possible that she got real angry at me during the family meetings because I listened to what others in the family had to say and couldn't always be on her side. She sort of nodded but crunched further down in the sofa. Finally, I insisted that she sit up and that if we couldn't talk about it, we could at least do something together. She began walking around, excluding me. Clearly provoked, she stopped to finger a book on my shelf called *Feelings* and then knocked over a black doll. At that point, I suggested that maybe people had disappointed her lately. She had mentioned in our previous session that her counselor Cherise Jones was away on a trip. I suggested that she might be mad at me because I'm not Ms. Jones. "No," she denied. Then I went on to wonder if she might find it easier to talk to Ms. Jones because she was black and wondered if she could be missing that connection. Because I was white and older, maybe Denise thought of me as being more on her parents' side. She didn't answer but picked up the book she was writing and tried to do a repair job on her picture of Olivia and Romero, muttering about her mother trying to make her into a slave. I asked if she could say more about that but she simply started writing furiously. Then she asked for an eraser, which I found and handed to her. She seemed to be fixing up a few words. When I inquired about what she was writing, she put her arm over the paper, so I said, "Guess you're not ready to share that yet?" She nodded. As she left at the end of the session, she asked if she could still have some candy from the candy jar. I said sure and she stuffed her pockets with candy. I had never seen her do this before.

(This was a difficult time for me as well as Denise, because she adopted the pattern of coming into my office, collapsing onto the sofa, covering her head, and playing as if she were asleep. She simply refused to have anything to do with me. This put me in a bind because I worried that her parents were wasting their hard-earned money. I was stuck and at my wits end to figure out what to do. At first, I tried to find different ways to invite Denise to come out of her shell.)

The summer between sixth and seventh grades was the worst but, in the long run, the most productive. Denise was taking some art classes. Other than that, she mostly slept or sat in front of the television. Her sister, on the other hand, had graduated from high school, gotten a job, and was looking forward to college in the fall.

Denise, now twelve, adopted the pattern of only answering my questions, which she did in a slightly provocative manner. She never initiated any activity and refused to play any games or participate in any way. I tried to insist that we needed to find some common ground—some new way to spend time together. We tried jigsaw puzzles and board games. Finally, I suggested that we learn to crochet together, saying that I had never learned to do it and that it might be fun. So I brought yarn and crochet needles and, with some assistance from Denise, tried to decipher the directions. At the end of the hour, Denise said she was going to take hers home, which she did even though I asked her not to do that. The next week, she triumphantly brought in a completed square, demonstrating that she had mastered that task and was clearly more competent than I. That ended yet another effort on my part to find some common ground between us.

Over that summer, the Dobsons went on a two-week vacation to visit their relatives who lived in Georgia and Mississippi. The family reported that they had a great time. The girls were easy to get along with and did some interesting things with their cousins. But when they returned, Denise assumed the same negative stance with me. She dutifully answered my questions about her vacation in bored monosyllables and then settled down to sleep.

This time, I decided to get out the bag of miniature items that we had used in our earlier work to make up stories together. Naturally, Denise refused to play, so I began playing alone. I put my hand in the bag and drew out a small horse. I told a story about a cowboy who fell off his horse and refused to get back on. It had hurt his pride to fall off in front of his friends and have them tease him about it. The second time, I drew a kangaroo with a baby in her pocket, and said the baby is refusing to leave the mother's pocket because it is so nice and cozy in there and that way no one expects anything of the baby. Then I commented that Denise reminded me of this little kangaroo who had found a safe place and was unwilling to explore the world.

She denied this and said in an angry tone that I didn't know anything about the way she was feeling. To which I replied, "I've sure been trying hard but somehow I seem to keep missing the mark." Then Denise asked when she could stop coming. I answered when she got better, which she seemed to have stopped doing ever since school was out. I added that I thought she had been angry at me for some time but unable to talk about it. She adamantly denied being angry, saying how could I know she was angry because I didn't know anything about her anyway. After that comment, she returned to her sleeping position. This time, I said she might as well leave because I wouldn't put up with her sleeping in my office any longer. She looked startled, got up, and disappeared into the bathroom where she stayed for the last ten minutes of the hour. When her father came to pick her up, she opened the bathroom door and left with him without saying a word to me.

I expected to hear from her parents during the next week, but they did not call. At the usual time the following week, Denise turned up on time and seemed less angry. She sat up on the sofa and thumbed through a magazine while I talked about what had happened the previous week and my feeling of having been wiped out by her continuing to sleep. It was as if I didn't exist for her. She said she didn't know what she was supposed to do here. I said her business was to get some of her problems worked out. Then she claimed not to know what those problems were. I mentioned two—getting along with friends and coming out of the box she had been hiding in. Then I added, "You know I can't help if you keep closing me out." At that point, she got up and found a large piece of poster paper and started drawing, telling me I was not to come and look at it until she had finished. This was obviously a spontaneous gesture because she worked quickly and seemed to be pleased with what she was doing. Then she showed me a large grinning face with a big open mouth and wide eyes, and told me in a delighted tone that this was a "cookie monster."

That gesture was a turning point in our work. It seemed to me that Denise had found an authentic part of herself and what appeared for the first time as a lively sense of humor. These changes were a welcome relief for everyone, because she was much more easygoing and flexible to be around.

Interplay of Family and Child Work. The course of treatment for Denise and her family proved to be a juggling act because of the discrepancy between all the negativism Denise expressed in our individual meetings and how well things were actually progressing in the family sessions. Denise's negative transference toward me coincided with what she must have perceived as my turning against her in the family sessions in order to reinforce her parents' authority and her enthusiastic identification with the young African American guidance counselor at her middle school. This turned out to be an *in vivo* experience in splitting because when Denise found someone else to idealize, she began degrading me— that is, giving me the same passive-aggressive treatment she gave her parents. My job was to hold both sides of this split together until she could learn to tolerate some ambivalence (i.e., both loving and hating the same person). In addition, I needed to make sure that the confidential nature of our individual work was maintained or Denise would lose the importance of the trust we had built up before she allowed herself to express her rage at me.

In our private sessions, Denise kept telling me she no longer needed to be in therapy and she wanted to stop coming. My response was that I did not think she was ready to do that yet. When she was, she would have to bring it up with her parents, or at least discuss her feelings at a family meeting. So even though she threatened to leave, Denise never carried it out.

By the same token, I never mentioned the extent of Denise's negativism in our individual sessions. The family, however, seemed well aware of the tension between us because of Denise's defensiveness and argumentative behavior in family sessions. Mrs. D. noted, for instance, that Denise seemed to treat me in the same way she did her family; that is, by ignoring me, avoiding issues, and talking back. What I did was to attempt to role model alternative ways of responding to her mixture of passive-aggressive and provocative behavior by using a calm voice when I needed to reinforce parental requests and, whenever possible, using a light touch of humor.

Stage V: Termination

It was interesting to note that during the time that Denise was acting out in her individual work with me, her parents were reporting that she was easier and more cooperative to live with at home. Apparently, the two sisters were realizing that they would be separated in the fall when Dora attended college. In a way, the girls switched roles. Dora seemed to be the one quarreling with her mother at this point. Denise sometimes tried to mediate, but at other times she just managed to stay out of the way and let them settle their own arguments. In the family meetings, they were acknowledging the pain of separation and how hard it was to be leaving home. So the family meetings became a safe place to express their concerns and caring.

That year, Denise was to return to a school situation that was familiar and predictable. She was back in the special homeroom and talking with Cherise Jones fairly regularly. Gradually, Denise's relationship with me improved to the extent that we could talk over the events of the week by having a two-way conversation. While Denise always kept a private part of her self protected, she did learn to identify more with another person and discovered that it could actually be fun to keep up with what was going on around her. While Denise never revealed a great deal about her inner life, she seemed much more content and mentioned friends she contacted about homework assignments and activities for the band. However, she was content to spend considerable time alone and will probably always be more of an introvert. That tendency does not seem to keep her from getting along with others when she is with them. She has continued to enjoy a few activities away from home. She now takes pride in doing things for herself, whereas in the beginning of our work together, Denise spent a lot of time balking, acting helpless, and expecting others to do things for her. Occasionally, when she is overtired or worried about succeeding, she has a relapse. By and large, she has learned to accept responsibility for herself and is more able to tell others what is troubling her.

After Dora entered college, Denise enjoyed being the only child around most of the time—except when it came to chores. How the chores got divided up remained the favorite topic in the family sessions that now only included Denise and her parents. In general, Mr. and Mrs. D. and Denise seemed pleased that their daily life together was going rather smoothly. Denise was having fun in her art classes, which tended to draw her closer to her father. Her father was especially proud of her artistic and musical talents and how well she was doing in school. We stopped the individual sessions first. Then, over a several-months period, we gradually tapered down on the family sessions also with the understanding that they were welcome to call if something came up that they wanted to talk about.

Case Discussion and Conclusion

This case illustrates how parent guidance, play therapy, and family therapy can be used together so that the work can be viewed as a whole. The Dobsons were dealing with many difficult issues simultaneously. As a couple and as a family, they had many strengths. Yet, because of the severity and extent of the presenting problems and their stressful life circumstances, treatment extended over several years. Denise was at risk of becoming a psychiatric invalid. Her problem was a mixture of genetic predeterminants and early attachment problems requiring a special school placement and much family work.

At the time Denise was born, the family was in a beleagured state because of the death of Mrs. D.'s father and mother. Consequently, they were ill-prepared to handle a vulnerable, demanding infant. Mrs. D. had not yet worked through the shock and grief from losing her parents and was in no condition to care for a child who probably would have had a hard time relating to any but the most extraordinary mother. Because culturally the family was upwardly mobile, there was no realistic way that Mrs. D. could afford to give up her job and stay at home with her infant. That might not have helped anyway because of Mrs. D.'s underlying situational depression.

In the beginning, it was crucial that the family learn to trust me enough to let me get to know their child, which meant understanding what they had been through in their long search for explanations about what was wrong with Denise. Fortunately, the difference in our racial backgrounds did not create problems for the parents. Denise, on the other hand, started with an overly idealizing transference toward me. She changed abruptly when she realized that I was not 100 percent on her side of the family controversies and after she found a young African American counselor at school whom she could idealize. Actually, these events turned out to be fortuitous. When the family realized that Denise was treating me like she had been treating the rest of the family, they found some alternative ways to deal with her difficult and off-putting behavior. Denise needed to discover for herself that I could withstand her hatred and still not want to leave her. However, the turning point in our individual work came when I insisted that she recognize me as a person with human feelings. Before Denise turned against me, we had shared a history together in which I had mirrored her emotional needs and helped her find words to describe something about what she was experiencing and feeling. In the beginning of treatment, Denise presented the side of herself to me that was a *Goody-Two-Shoes*, obsessively compliant and ingratiating. We began to make some progress when Denise felt safe enough to act out her anger, competitiveness, and stubbornness. Being able to work through that difficult period allowed her to get in touch with a more genuine, authentic part of herself and learn to live with her ambivalent feelings.

In a different way, her parents learned to understand themselves better and accept their own strengths and limitations. In the beginning, they needed a time to be seen by themselves to express and sort out their frustrations and disappointments. When they had regained confidence in themselves, they profited from what they learned from the family sessions. It was helpful to include Denise's sister in the family meetings because Dora was a good observer and sure enough of herself to speak her mind and come up with practical solutions to some of the family dilemmas. In the end, Dora profited from having a place to talk about her concerns about going away to college and to understand that she was going through a fairly normal transitional crisis. As different as the sisters were temperamentally, they managed to form an alliance. It was useful for Denise to learn to take Dora's side from time to time and not feel that the whole family was ganging up on her.

After my work with the Dobsons was completed, I continued to hear from them occasionally at Christmas or when Mrs. D. just felt like sharing family news. For example, they were pleased when Denise made the honor roll in high school and thrilled when she was salutatorian of her graduating class.

PART TWO

Assessment and Planning

6 Parent Interviews in Biopsychosocial Assessment of Children

As both science and art, the biopsychosocial assessment process involves collecting and analyzing information in a way that sheds light on the various developmental forces, social situations, and mental health problems that have played a part in creating the children's difficulties. The science of assessment is based in the substantive knowledge base of the clinical social worker; the art, in the ability to create a therapeutic alliance within which to elicit information not only about the developmental, familial, and situational facts, but also the feelings, relationships, and psychosocial climate in which the facts are embedded.

The substantive dimensions of assessment integrate knowledge about the developmental lines and possible developmental disturbances documented by child development theory, ecological theory, and research; multidisciplinary health and mental health knowledge; and the written and oral knowledge traditions of social work. Together, these substantive dimensions inform data collection in light of the presenting problem(s) and symptom array, and provide the conceptual outline structure along which information is organized, recorded, analyzed, and interpreted. Data interpretation, or biopsychosocial assessment and diagnostic formulation, in turn facilitates treatment planning and enables the clinical social worker to make sense of the unfolding therapeutic narrative in developmental play therapy and concurrent parent work.

Neither the art nor the science of biopsychosocial assessment of children is complete without the other. Nor is data collection complete without interviewing both parents and child. Therefore, this chapter focuses on the art and science of parent interviews in biopsychosocial assessment, followed by child assessment interviews in the next chapter. The parent interview material is applied in the case of Zack Amanto. A parent assessment interview checklist concludes the chapter.

The Art of Assessment

Ordinarily, children are referred to the clinical social worker by an adult. Generally, it is the parents, the real experts on their children, who see a problem and seek help. Sometimes, however, persons in authority outside the immediate family (e.g., teachers, clergy, judges, police, or relatives) identify a problem and make the referral when parents fail to do so. Whoever the referral source, parents are the primary historians and informants. Sometimes their memories are complete and fairly accurate; other times, incomplete and based on distorted perceptions.

Whatever the case, the art of assessment is rooted in the ability of the clinical social worker to respond to the normal anxiety of parents with sensitivity and empathy. This initial attuned response sets the tone for parents' comfort in revealing critical information and preparing their child to be seen. Because this introductory contact is usually by telephone, a reassuring and understanding telephone style is essential, as is the message that the clinician is a helper in dealing with children. While the parent is developing a mental image of the practitioner, so too the practitioner is collecting preliminary data through the small details of the call: Who called? How long did it take to return a call? What was the length of the call? The content? The conversational style? Did the parent cross-examine you? Did they view you as helpful, intrusive, or threatening? Were the responses due to anxiety or style and cultural norms? These and similar thoughts are merely noted in the practitioner's mind in preparation for the initial interview with the parents.

The dual purpose of the first interview is to create a working alliance with the parents and gather information about the child's presenting symptoms, as well as their developmental and familial history. In this interview, the clinician elicits their concerns, observations, understanding, and feelings and gives them credence. In responding to parents as the central persons in their child's life, the clinical social worker is initiating a beginning therapeutic alliance with them. As the clinician strives to provide a holding environment for the parents, she begins to engage them in better understanding and helping their child. This message is conveyed through a nonjudgmental stance that gives credence to the parents' concerns, feelings, and observations, and avoids blaming them for their child's difficulties. This latter stance is sometimes harder than it sounds because parents frequently want to know the cause of their child's problems—fearing, of course, that they are responsible. Because one parent will sometimes blame the other (explicitly or implicitly), it is important to strengthen their common bond as parents from the beginning. It is helpful for them to know that all children are complex and that there are multiple reasons and causative factors for their difficulties, possibly including genetic, neurological, developmental, temperamental, psychosocial, and cultural ones.

Establishing a therapeutic alliance with adolescent mothers or psychotic parents can present an especially formidable challenge. One clinician, for example, walked into a hospital room to assess a toddler for a possible feeding disorder. He lay crying in the crib while his fifteen-year-old mother sat in a chair across the room sucking on her baby's pacifier. In this case, observation was more meaningful than words could ever have been. A developmental play assessment was then conducted with the mother/child dyad and the developmental history of both mother and toddler was obtained from other sources. From the observation, the clinician immediately wondered why this mother did not hear her baby cry. Fraiberg, Adelson, and Shapiro (1975) wrote that such parents are repeating with their child what was done to them. That is, the "ghosts in the nursery" take over.

Thus, one answer could be that no one had heard her cries. In another case, the clinical social worker was talking with an adult schizophrenic mother who was terrified that she would harm her baby. This mother was immediately soothed when she understood that there is a difference between thinking and doing.

Another overwhelming task involves child-custody disputes in which parents "prep" the child to say libelous, often untrue, things about the other parent. The clinicians are well advised to know the boundaries of their own countertransference issues before beginning to work with such parents. Unfortunately, the clinician, like the child, may feel caught in the middle and rue the day she agreed to evaluate this child. Such a case brings up the necessity of knowing one's own limitations, as well as the limitations of the employing agency or institution. For example, some clinicians realize that they become overly anxious about abusing parents or suicidal children. In these instances, they need to work closely with their supervisors or refer the cases elsewhere. Some cases clearly need to be referred to another mental health professional, even on the first telephone call. For example, "I do not have expertise in doing child-custody evaluations, so please let me give you the name of three colleagues who do."

As art, the assessment can be likened to a road map with many different highways and byways to arrive at a destination. If one road is blocked, the driver detours to another route. In driving along the countryside, she may stop to explore unfamiliar terrain. Sometimes, she may prefer to take a more circuitous route and more time. Eventually, she arrives at her destination, a new city she anticipates knowing. So it is with alternative ways of conducting an assessment. Some clinical social workers prefer to take the psychosocial case history from the primary caregiver, others prefer to have both parents present. In an ideal world, the preference is usually one interview with the couple and then separate interviews with each parent.

Mindful of time constraints, many clinicians will ask parents to list and bring the significant developmental milestones and life events, as well as the baby book or photos of the early years. However the clinician proceeds, the developmental history usually takes about ninety minutes to complete. This said, however, the clinician takes particular caution in allowing parents to proceed at their own pace and ordering of the information. While the following outline of needed information is presented in question format to jog the clinician's thinking and organize the data collected, it is important not to bombard parents with questions. Instead, the style is one of a more leisurely, careful exploration of familiar and unfamiliar ground. For the most part, the narrative follows parents' lines of thinking and reasoning, which may or may not be congruent with the outline.

Data Collection

Identifying Data

Conducting a biopsychosocial assessment and writing one are two very different actions. The written form usually begins with identifying data, including household composition, and the name and nickname of the child with the identified problem. Sometimes it is in table format, sometimes in sentences. In the latter case, one sentence is usually used to present the child's name, age, birthdate, gender, race, religion, sibling order, school, and grade. A similar approach emphasizing the crisp, concise facts of demographic information is used for the parents, siblings, and others in the home.

Presenting Problem and History of Presenting Problem

During the first interview with parents, most clinicians prefer to begin with the presenting problem and the history of the problem. Thus, the study embarks with "where the child is" and "where the parents are" in relation to their child. It represents a beginning at developing a working alliance with the parents and answering the child's call for help.

What are the parents' current concerns? When did the problem start? Was there a specific event (or events) that triggered the problem? Why are they seeking help now? What happened that led them to the agency? What changes have been noticed in the child or family since the problem first began? What changes would they like to see? With these questions, the clinical social worker is seeking to understand the relationship between the current symptoms and biological disorders, adaptive or maladaptive responses to key life events, and the child's customary coping mechanisms. Does the child seem comfortable or uncomfortable with the presenting symptoms; that is, are the symptoms ego syntonic or dystonic for this particular child? Are the symptoms culturally congruent?

The answers to these questions provide an anchor for the assessment and a springboard to further thought about the presenting problem. By this point, the clinical social worker usually has a beginning hypothesis (or hypotheses) for further inquiry. Of course, a lot of the hypothesis testing depends on the relationship between the problem and the child's age and the developmental expectations for that age. For example, if the child was referred by the daycare center before the child's second birthday, the clinician first considers temperament and attachment problems. Or, if the child is slightly older and beginning the first weeks of preschool or kindergarten, the clinician thinks about separation anxiety. In this instance, the clinician also explores earlier attachment issues and responses to earlier transitions. If school avoidance surfaces in the later elementary school years, the clinician explores the possibility of depression along with separation anxiety. The first-grader who is acting out in school and referred by the teacher is certainly assessed for attention problems, whereas the third-grader referred for school failure is evaluated for learning disabilities. While exploring the initial hypothesis, the clinician does not rule out alternative rival hypotheses. She also keeps the possibility of co-occurring conditions in mind.

Early in the interview is usually an appropriate time to ask about other professionals and agencies that are involved with this child and family. How have others explained the problem? Do the parents agree? This also may be the time to ask about obtaining collateral information and seeking written permission to obtain it. Outside sources of information are important supplements for obtaining missing information, clarifying accuracy, and providing a basis for exploring discrepancies. With parental consent, existing information such as medical, educational, or legal records and new information may be obtained. New information usually consists of conferring with the referral source, meeting with teachers, and observing children in their classroom and on the playground. When possible and feasible, a visit to the family at home provides an even more complete picture of the child's world. The goal of all of this data collection is to gain a valid and reliable understanding of the child's cognitive, physical, psychosocial, and cultural world.

Parents have ideas about what they would like to see changed in relation to their child and school. The clinician needs to sort out whether these ideas are reasonable and feasible. Is it grades or behavior? Is it something about the child or the school? Are the parents concerned that a teacher's attitude is part of the problem? Or, has the school system let them down in preparing their child's Individualized Educational Plan (IEP) for specialized or supplemental services? In this way, the clinician gets a sense of the parents' expectations of the school, as well as the way in which they are managing the problem and information about it. Do the parents view the problem the same way? What have they tried at home? What works? What does not? Do both school and parents see the problem the same way? Does the child think there is a problem? What is the child's view of it?

What services are the parents requesting of the agency and the clinical social worker? It is important that both parents and clinician have a clear understanding of the social work tasks and the tasks of other professionals in relation to the current problem situation, the services requested, and the outcomes expected.

Developmental History

As the clinical social worker continues the interview, she directs the parents' attention to the developmental history. Although it is presented here in chronological fashion, in reality it rarely follows such a predetermined course. In mapping out the history, there are both direct and alternate routes. The most important thing is to obtain information about significant developmental issues, especially as they shed light on the child's problems and parent/child interactions. The clinician is trying to enlist the parents' aid in determining the child's position along the range of motor, language, and cognitive development, as well as the ability to relate to others, regulate affect, and adapt to new situations. In this way, the clinician identifies the presence of any developmental disturbances or onset of any mental illnesses.

Pregnancy, Delivery, and the Neonatal Period. In assessing early development, the clinician usually begins with the pregnancy, delivery, and neonatal period. Was this pregnancy planned and welcomed by both parents? Was there a reason for the particular timing of the conception? One mother responded that the stars were in a certain constellation that predicted harmony for the child.

How did they decide on the child's name? When asked the meaning of a certain name, a parent responded, "Warrior, and that is why he is so oppositional." Another responded, "Queen of the Nile and she certainly has begun to act like one." A third replied that the child was named for her uncle and he seemed more and more like him, to which the clinician replied, "Tell me more." What were the parents' hopes and dreams for their child? Their fears? Was there a preference for a given gender? Did they know the gender prior to birth? One father was gravely disappointed when told that this child would be his fourth daughter and not the longed-for son; hence, the name Josephine and some of the father's expectations about her abilities.

Were there marital difficulties during this period? Any family changes or stresses? What was the mother's health during pregnancy? Any complications that could have threatened the pregnancy, such as bleeding, hypertension, or gestational diabetes? Any use of medications, alcohol, tobacco? What was the course of labor and delivery? Did anything seem unusual to the parents? Was the baby premature, in intensive care, on oxygen? Other? What were the APGAR scores identifying alertness and well-being? Were any congenital anomalies or illnesses noted at birth? What were the parents' fantasies and fears about the infant at birth?

Temperamental Characteristics of Early Infancy.   Infants are often remembered for certain temperamental characteristics that parents consider to be constant throughout childhood. For example, the parents of an overly active six-year-old may recall the newborn period as a time when their infant was hypervigilant, difficult to soothe, or seemed to be swimming in his sleep. Clinicians usually find it useful to explore information about selected temperament attributes along the lines of Thomas and Chess's (1977, 1986) classification:

Activity Level	Is your child constantly on the move or does he or she prefer quiet activities?
Rhythmicity	Does your child eat, sleep, have bowel movements according to a relatively predictable schedule?
Approach/Withdrawal	Does your child approach new people, food, or situations willingly or with reticence?
Adaptability	How does your child tolerate change and respond to new suggestions, change, and discipline?
Intensity of Reaction	How does your child react to setbacks or delight? Are the reactions muted or euphoric?
Quality of Mood	Is your child mostly cheerful, negative, or down?
Persistence/Attention Span	How long does your child spend engrossed in one activity? If he is challenged, does he give up easily or persist? Is he easily diverted?

Distractibility Are you able to distract your child when he is upset? Can he easily turn his attention to another activity? Is it easy to calm him or does he continue to whine no matter what you do?

Threshold Level How does your child respond to external stimuli, such as noise, light, touch, or texture of clothing?

For example, one family who brought their six-year-old daughter Josselyn for assessment described temperamental characteristics beginning in infancy. They described her as "the most perceptive baby in the nursery," a precursor they felt to her wonderful creativity that found its expression in her marching to the tune of her own drummer. Josselyn was an active infant, awakening at least five times a night, screaming and crying. She was inconsolable even after her mother gave her a bottle. Nevertheless, her mother described her daughter as happy in every way, a jolly baby who was very friendly. Josselyn was so friendly and fearless that by age two she frequently wandered off from her parents, often disappearing in the grocery store. As young as eighteen months, Josselyn would play her own games, her own way, by her own rules. She was unable to adapt to any situation that required her to adjust or acquiesce to rules or norms. Josselyn was referred to the clinical social worker at age six when she wandered off the playground at school after the teacher asked her to wait to take her turn in the game "Four Square."

Other important issues concern the emotional presence of her mother and the way in which she encountered this time in her child's life. The clinician may ask about how her mother experienced the mutual, visual gazing or smiling between mother and infant. Attentiveness is in order as such memories do not always trigger immediate pleasurable emotions. Allowing parents to take their time in describing and processing their affective experience helps them empathize with their child and their child's current problem.

Attachment in the First Year of Life. While the first year of life is heralded by major developmental milestones often recalled by the parents, the clinical social worker also wants to determine the nature of the attachment with the primary caregiver. Were the infant's proximity-seeking behaviors of clinging or crying met with reciprocal maternal responses, such as holding, rocking, and soothing? Were there frequent changes in caregivers at home and in daycare centers? Because young children are so susceptible to separations and loss, it is important to note the dates of such events and the child's responses to the changes. How did the child react to even minor separations from mother?

Information about the baby's feeding schedule, likes, and dislikes is also important. Was he breast- or bottle-fed? Was he fed on demand? Was food used to quiet the child? When was he weaned? Were new foods tolerated or met with refusal? How about sleep patterns? How did the parents respond to any difficulties in falling or staying asleep? How long was it before he established a fairly predictable routine?

In one instance, the clinical social worker wondered about attachment problems when she first met with the mother of a four-year-old. Mrs. Olivera appeared distressed and tired as she slumped in the chair and talked nonstop about all of her problems. Finally, after repeated prompting, she explained how her daughter acts like a monkey, marks on walls, and used to bite her doll's fingers until mother bit Eliana's fingers. Now Eliana bites her own fingers. She also plays with matches in the closet. Mrs. Olivera, who is currently taking "pills for being way up and way down," reported that she disciplined Eliana whenever she cried for food during her first two years of life by scratching and beating her and holding her upside down to shake the devil out. Because the mother/child interaction was unpredictable, threatening, and abusive, Eliana's development was disrupted and her attachment would be classified as disorganized.

As the inquiry moves into toddlerhood, clinicians ask about motor milestones such as sitting, crawling, and walking. Clinician and parent also explore visual, fine-motor skill, and gross motor/muscular development.

Socialization in Toddlerhood.   As the infant turns into an upright child, he is able to explore and manipulate the world in new ways, so the clinician wants to know about his reactions to things and people. Was he timid, fearful, or exuberant as he tackled new challenges? How and when was he toilet-trained? To find out if there is any history of encopresis or enuresis, the clinician asks about any problems with soiling his underpants or having accidents. Did he take to the demands of toilet-training easily or not? How did the parents handle the experience?

U.S. society stipulates that children be clean. However, because the child is not yet civilized, he may react with horror at the thought of a bathtub, fearing that he too will disappear with water down the drain (Fraiberg, 1959). How did the child adapt to bathing? Did the bathtub become a playground or battleground? Did you bathe your child alone, or with siblings, or with you?

Because sleep patterns may change at this age, the clinician explores how the child separates at bedtime. Is there a transitional object? How does the child respond to the demands of parents? Was there a power struggle? Was he oppositional? How do the parents remember the terrible twos?

Clinicians next ask about language development, specifically when the child said the first words and began to speak in sentences. Along with locomotion, language promotes separation and individuation as the child encounters the self in social interaction, including the capacity for symbolization and play. The child's response to peek-a-boo games and capacity for pretend are examples of his or her symbolization ability.

Discovery of Self in the Preschool Years.   During the preschool years, the child displays considerable curiosity about his body and mind. With singular interest, he inspects his own genitals and wonders about sexual differences. What are his ideas about conception and childbirth? What have his sexual experiences been? How do his parents and caretakers respond when he plays with his genitals?

What about playing doctor with other youngsters? Children wrestle with these issues through play and imagination. Their rich fantasy life may usher in sleep problems such as dreams, fears, nightmares, or sleepwalking. Does he sleep in the parental bed or his own? Do the parents worry about any of his behaviors?

By the age of three, youngsters realize that desires and wishes are involved in emotions like joy and contentment, and that others have their own beliefs and subjective experiences. By age four, they consider the opinions of others as they grow to understand their own mental processes and those of others in relation to behavior. Given these developments, the clinician inquires how the child makes sense of the circumstances of his life.

Many children head off to daycare or preschool about this time, so the clinician explores how they handled the separation experience. What was the teacher's view of his interaction with peers? How did he handle transitions within the classroom? Was he invited for playdates? What was the quality of his play? Between ages three and five, many children experience the profound insult of having to share their parents with a newborn or newly adopted sibling. How did he react to this "intruder"? Did he have imaginary friends?

The School Years.   The educational history not only includes the child's academic strengths and weaknesses, but also his ability to relate to teachers and peers. Although the parents' perspective is invited and respected, the most objective informant frequently is the teacher. The educational history includes the types of schools attended and the dates of attendance. Have there been frequent moves or changes in schools? If so, why? What is his attendance record? Is education valued in the home or is the child left on his own with schoolwork? Is he motivated, attentive, or distractible? Is he slow to develop in one subject area? Does he excel in others? What is his learning style? What is his favorite activity or subject? How does he spend leisure time? What are his hobbies? Has he received any supplementary or special educational services?

What is the quality of his play both on and off the playground? Does he prefer to play with boys, girls, or both? Is he a welcome playmate or is he considered to be either a bully or class clown by his peers? Do other children make fun of him? Does he follow the behavior of others or is he a leader? Does he do well in a group situation, or does he prefer to be with just one peer? Does he have a best friend? Is he invited to birthday parties?

What is his relationship with the teacher? Is he respectful or disruptive? Does he respect rules, regulations, and property? Is he an active participant in classroom discussions or more withdrawn? Does he understand directions, or do they need to be broken down for him?

If school problems are identified, the clinician then explores the level of current functioning in comparison with past performance; specifically, his ability to concentrate and attend to academic endeavors, motivation to perform, and degree to which potential is reflected in actual achievement. Learning disabilities present in different ways. They tend to be most apparent when there is a manifestation of educationally significant discrepancies between estimated educational potential and actual achievement. Some school systems require a child's achievement to be two years below grade level before educational assessment and services can begin. Fortunately, clinical social workers are in a position to identify such discrepancies before a child falls so short of academic expectations. For example, indicators of learning disabilities may include some or all of the following:

- hyperactivity
- short attention span
- visual perceptual disorders that may present with reversal of letters or numbers, inadequate reproduction of geometric designs, or poor handwriting
- auditory perceptual disorders that may show up as poor discrimination between gross sounds or speech sounds, centering on target sounds in a noisy background
- motor problems, as evidenced by low muscle tone, clumsiness, or poor motor coordination
- memory problems, as indicated by an inability to acquire and retain information, difficulty remembering sequential information, an inability to repeat words or numbers in sequence, an inability to repeat sentences
- language disorders may present subtly as when the teacher explains to parents that the child may have a hearing impairment or attention problem; in other instances, there may be an inability to internalize and organize experiences to provide a basis for later spoken or written language, expressive language difficulties (oral or written), receptive oral or written language problems, auditory closure problems, or coding irregularities
- difficulties relating to teachers or peers
- disruptive classroom conduct
- participation as either instigator or victim in school incidents
- absences associated with truancy, school avoidance, or diagnosed physical illness

By the end of this section, the clinician should have a fairly good idea about how the youngster relates and responds to others, his capacity for impulse control, and his cognitive strengths and weaknesses.

Medical History

The medical history begins with a general description of the child's physical progress and current health. The clinician makes sure that the child has had a recent physical exam. After obtaining written parental permission, consultation with the child's pediatrician is often a good idea. Are the child's height and weight within genetic, age, and gender expectations? The clinician also asks about physical disabilities, chronic illnesses, or other differences that may challenge the child. The types of illness and age of onset are noted, along with the types of medical interventions or accommodations required. What was the child's reaction to being sick? Are there any reports of high fevers, seizures, accidents, hospitalizations, or surgeries? Current or past medications are noted, along with type, purpose, dosage, and any reported side effects. Is there a history of asthma, allergies, or other problems that may interfere with the child's activity and exercise patterns? Are there concerns about substance abuse?

Legal History

Have there been any custody issues? Has the child ever been in trouble with the law? Why? Note the approximate dates and court dispositions. Is the child currently on probation? Is any legal action pending? If indicated, the clinician obtains collateral information after obtaining written permission.

Cultural and Socioeconomic History

Cultural norms and values have significant impact on the child and family in the context of extended family, school, neighborhood, and community, as well as in the interaction with the clinical social worker and agency. What is the cultural background, educational status, religion, and racial/ethnic identity of each parent? Of their extended families? Of this family unit? What is the child's social identification? How does he feel about his race or ethnicity and that of others? Have there been moves, relocations, or immigration? If so, what was the nature and response of the child and family to these experiences? What are the family cultural patterns, traditions, and myths? What is the fit with their local community?

What is the family's economic status? Do both parents work outside the home? Is there a family business in the home? Have there been any recent problems related to employment? Is a parent in school or a vocational training program?

Family History

In taking the psychosocial history of each parent, the clinical social worker notes significant developmental problems and whether they are similar to the child's. The clinician is particularly interested in listening to the process of the narrative and understanding how the parents make sense of their past and current lives. Observation of their interactions during the family history speaks volumes, so detailed questioning about family interaction characteristics may not be necessary. These and other points in relation to the family history are meant more as guidelines to stimulate the clinician's thinking. For example, the clinician usually includes questions about the composition of the parents' families, the relationships of each to their parents and siblings, and whether family members are living or deceased. A major concern is the developmental history of each parent when they were the child's current age. What was going on with them and in their lives at this age? Is there a history of physical or mental illness for the parents or their extended families? Who in the family does their child seem most like? What are the characteristics of this person? The clinician also obtains information concerning relevant family members' educational, legal, and employment histories.

Courtship and Marriage.   What was the nature of the parents' courtship and marital relationship? What were the complementary needs of the parents prior to and following the birth of their children? Have they experienced sexual-adjustment problems? What are the significant issues in the parental role system, including dominance/submission, competition/sharing, and carryover patterns from their families of origin? The clinical social worker also notes the current quality and satisfaction of their marriage and/or relationship with the other birthparent. If the child was adopted, do they have access to the birthparents? What do they know about the birthparents' histories?

Appearance and Behavior.   The clinical social worker gives her impression of the physical appearance of the parents and their manner and attitude toward their child and the clinician. She notes the interaction patterns and styles, including verbal and nonverbal communication within the family household, and with extended family, neighbors, and social institutions (i.e., school, court, social agency, hospital, employing agency). She looks for predominant interaction patterns in relation to dependency/autonomy, dominance/submission, rebellion/conformity, mutuality/competition, giving/withholding, and participation/withdrawal.

Problem-solving Skills.   How are decisions made and conflicts resolved? For example, how does the parents' course of action about their child's presenting problem impact on their motivation for treatment? Are their attempts at conflict resolution based on either conscious or unconscious collusion or projective identification? Does the family identify any other problems? What were their attempts to solve them? Were they successful? Is there clarity and adequacy of communication in both crisis and routine situations? As the family deals with the social system, are there areas of conflict that result in stress? Do they call on other supportive networks (e.g., other family members, friends) to assist them?

Role Performance.   Significant issues in the family system include role relationships, particularly dyads, alliances, splits, reversals, and isolations. Role performance is assessed according to the multiple roles of each family member, family role integration, and role perception. The clinician explores the continuity and hierarchy of roles within the family unit, the extended family, and the community network, as well as role complementarity and attendant need-satisfaction patterns. Does each parent feel that his or her needs are being met? What is each family member's perception of their own and others' roles? Is there clarity? Who fills roles such as scapegoat, helper, disciplinarian, feeder, and revealer or suppressor of secrets?

Family as Social Environment

Because the care and socialization of children is a primary responsibility of parents, the clinical social worker pays special attention to both. For example, how does a family handle feeding, cleaning, and clothing their child? Are basic subsistence needs being met? What are parental expectations and training methods? How do they show approval or disapproval? Is there consistency of care for each child? What is the nature of social teaching and learning in the home? What is the family climate in which children are reared, including characteristics such as relaxation/ tension, satisfaction/dissatisfaction, trust/mistrust, intimacy/detachment, empathy/lack of understanding, love/hostility, overt/covert agendas, and differentiated/undifferentiated family mass or triangles? Is there adequacy of parental nurture, protection, guidance, and controls?

Household Procedures.   It is worthwhile to assess the adequacy of the physical facilities in the home and neighborhood. If there are problems in this area, what is the potential for change? What are the daily living routines, such as meals, bedtime, chores, and general household management? Do the children have their own beds or bedrooms? Do they have access to a study area apart from others? Is there adequate lighting?

Educational Supports.   How are the intellectual learning needs of the family members being met? Are children overindulged with television programs or computer games? Is there access to the value of reading, intellectual discussion, or the educational worth of computers? How does the family support intellectual curiosity and creativity?

Family Activity Patterns.   The clinical social worker considers the time the family spends both together and apart and notes the content of activities. Are they involved in either formal or informal associations? Are they flexible and spontaneous, or rigid or impulsive in planning activities? Is there room for compromise? For example, how do they arrive at decisions regarding finances, major household purchases, household duties, sex, leisure time, or family projects?

Family Values.   A family's values are reflected in the specific content and direction of their behavior, attitudes, interests, aspirations, goals, and fears. In addition to understanding these values, the clinician notes the consistencies and discrepancies among their values, ambitions, and actions; their espoused values; and their values-in-action. What are their moral, religious, cultural, intellectual, economic, and social values as they relate to the family unit, role behaviors, and parenting practices? Is there cohesiveness within the family unit and a sharing of values, goals, and lifestyle with the extended family? Or is there pressure from the extended family toward conformity? What is the degree of individual difference tolerated within the family unit in relation to family values, interests, and ambitions?

Developmental Stage of Family.   As referred to in the psychosocial case history, the developmental stage of the family reflects more than the family composition and the number of years together, although that information is important. The clinician might ask whether the parents solidified as a couple and then opened up the family unit for children. Is this a multigeneration household? Is this a single-parent family? Is this a remarriage and a blended family? How does this composition impact family development?

The major roles and nurturing patterns of the parents are of primary concern. Sometimes, there is a role reversal in which one child assumes a caregiving role and becomes the parentified child. To assess family roles, alliances, patterns, and barriers to identification, both the major content and process of their communication are crucial. It is also important to understand the parameters of family functioning in relation to level of anxiety, capacity and motivation to change, and role as symptom carrier.

Family Support System.   In exploring identifying information about extended family members outside the household, the clinician's interest is knowing who supports and who stresses the household. What has been the impact on the family support system of major family changes, such as losses, deaths, illnesses, moves, and changes in household composition? These events and their dates are best depicted as a time line of family life in relation to the identified child client. Significant also is who was living in the home at various points along the time line. What are the physical, psychological, social, and cultural factors affecting present family behavior and feelings?

Community Supports and Resources

Clinical social workers also inquire about the availability and involvement of neighbors, friends, members of the faith community, doctors, club members, or employers who understand and support the family's needs. Is the family involved in a social network or isolated? Are there one or two community supports or is there a large support system?

Data Consolidation

After all of this information has been obtained and summarized, the clinician has certain impressions and tentative hypotheses about the child and the environmental context of this family. These invaluable data help the clinical social worker prepare to interview the child.

The following case material demonstrates data collection from parents, community, and child. It illustrates the integration of data from these multiple sources into a biopsychosocial assessment of Zack in the context of his family and school and their expectations and pressures.

Biopsychosocial Assessment: Zack Amanto
by Elizabeth M. Timberlake, D.S.W., LCSW-C

Identifying Information

Name: Zachariah (Zack) Amanto   Sex: Male   Race: African American
DOB: 11/13/87   Age: 10.9 years
School: St. Catherine of Siena (auspice–Roman Catholic)   Grade: 5
Religion: Roman Catholic
Parents: Lila and John Amanto
Address: 300 Edisto Lane   Columbia, SC 20814   Tel: (999) 888-9999
Employment: Mr. A.: bakery manager $41,000
　　　　　　　 Mrs. A.: elementary school teacher $41,000
Household Membership: 2 parents, 1 child
Telephone Intake: Mrs. A. 6/15/98:   Referred for psychological and neuro-
　　　　　　　　　　　　　　　　　logical consultations prior to psycho-
　　　　　　　　　　　　　　　　　social evaluation
　　　　　　　　　Mrs. A. 9/1/98: Called to request appointment
Dates of Evaluation: Parents: Mr. and Mrs. A. 9/3/98,
　　　　　　　　　　　　　　　　　Mrs. A. 9/16/98, Mr. A. 9/17/98
　　　　　　　　　Child: Zack 9/18/98, 9/25/98
　　　　　　　　　Principal and Teacher: 9/8/98

Presenting Problem and History

Reason for Referral.   Zack, a 10.9-year-old African American male in the fifth grade at St. Catherine of Siena, was referred to the Child Service Clinic by his fourth-grade teacher on June 15, 1998, for failing written work, disorganization, and inability to complete assignments in his first year at this school. In view of his history of learning problems in public school and *petit mal* epilepsy, the clinical social worker referred the family for psychological and neurological consultations prior to psychosocial evaluation at the Child Service Clinic. After these consults, Mr. and Mrs. Amanto requested agency evaluation and treatment on September 1, 1998, as they remained concerned about his school performance "even though he was promoted to fifth grade."

Both parents agree that Zack has learning problems in school and that this needs to be addressed. Both project blame for many of the earlier learning and behavior problems onto the public school. When confronted, they respond that Zack does have learning problems. They perceive the earlier problems of fighting as public-school-specific. They view the problems as much less severe than school personnel view them.

Summary of Consultation Reports.

Principal and Fourth-grade Teacher: Sr. Joan Flaherty, Mrs. Mary Sheely
Zack was given a social promotion to fifth grade but principal and teacher were concerned that their school was unable to provide the educational supplements he needed to learn and perform up to his capability. He was failing written work, disorganized, and unable to complete in-class assignments. He completed homework with his parents' help. He was not a behavior problem. Sometimes he had trouble concentrating in class. He had no physical problems as far as they knew. Mr. and Mrs. A. were adamant that they wanted Catholic education for Zack, could not afford private tutoring, and refused to seek public-education supplements. The parish priest was supportive of Zack remaining in the parish school.

Neurologist: Dr. A. Johnson, child neurologist
Diagnosis: Petit Mal Epilepsy. Appointments every three months for medical management since age five. Medications for past three months: a.m.: 30 mgs. phenobarbitol and 100 mgs. dilantin with higher doses p.m. (50 phenobarbitol and 120 dilantin). Recent EEG and CAT scan have revealed abnormal brain patterns associated with epilepsy. Mild degree of disability. Physiologically based learning problems not surprising. Some specialized but mainstream educational approaches indicated if possible, but parents resist and little available.

Catholic School Psychologist: Dr. Judah, educational psychologist, 7/98
Problems learning and adjusting to new environment. Full scale (98), verbal (105), and performance (90) scores on the Wechsler Intelligence Scale for Children-Revised (WISC-III-R) within average range of intellectual development. The scatter suggests organically-based learning disabilities. Some spatial perceptual weakness with low tolerance for paper-and-pencil tasks. Adequate remote memory. High levels of distractibility for abstract concepts. Weakness in conceptualization. Weak in visual motor coordination and new learning ability. Bender–Gestalt score of 9 years 3 months (1.5 years below chronological age of 10.8). Weakness in spatial perceptual tasks may be organic in nature. Figures suggest depression and tendency to withdraw. Appears defensive and overly suspicious. Peabody Individual Achievement Test Scores: math 3.9, reading recognition 4.3, reading comprehension 4.5, spelling 4.3.

Public School Psychologist: Dr. Jackson, educational psychologist, 4/95
Problems in learning generally, math specifically, at the Learning Center. Partially mainstreamed. Age seven years five months. Intellectual testing showed Zack to be functioning at the average range in verbal and low average range in nonverbal performance, with a 14-point spread. Average ability in visual organization, interpretation of social situations, visual/motor coordination, and verbal-concept formation. Below-average ability in numerical accuracy in mental arithmetic, long-term memory, and ability to reproduce abstract designs. Zack's reproductions of Bender–Gestalt designs were deficient and marked by rotational integration and

angulation. Second-grade WRAT scores: reading 2.1, spelling 1.7, arithmetic 1.7. Fine motor control, particularly handwriting, was a serious problem. Lacked self-esteem and self-confidence. Probable depression. Diagnosis: Learning Disability NOS with Attention Deficit Hyperactivity Disorder.

Current Family Situation

Zack, an only child, lives with both parents in their own home in a middle-class neighborhood. Mr. Amanto returned home to live in May 1998 after living with his brother for nine months (September 1997 through May 1998). During that period, he came to the house from work, ate meals, saw Zack, did things around the house, and went to his brother's to sleep. Both he and Mrs. A. denied involvement with anyone else during this period. No family members or friends were told of this "sort of separation." At present, any marital problems are minimized.

Mrs. A. teaches second grade in a public elementary school. Mr. A. manages the bakery department at a large grocery store. Zack is in group family daycare after school (within walking distance of school).

Developmental History of Child

Health History. Zack began having *petit mal* seizures about age five. The seizures last anywhere from a split second to ten seconds. Although he loses his motor skills, he is often aware of his surroundings and of persons talking. He cannot speak and often loses his balance if standing or moving around. Seizures tend to occur when he is running on the playground or at times of high stress. On the playground, Zack either falls or runs into something or someone. He has a set routine for taking his medications and is good about following it. His parents believe that his seizures are well controlled. Neither parents nor Zack seem able to estimate how frequently he has seizures. According to both parents, they and Zack are open about Zack's epilepsy and "discuss it freely." (His Catholic school principal and fourth-grade teacher, however, did not know of the epilepsy until the end of fourth grade, when they asked about Zack's general health.)

Mr. A. witnessed the first seizure that they know of. They were playing and Zack could not move for a few seconds. Mr. A. knew what it was because he also has *petit mal* epilepsy, which is medically controlled; Mr. A.'s brother has similar epilepsy. Etiology is unknown for the three. There are no other family members with identified epilepsy. Mr. A. tends to see Zack and Zack's epilepsy as "just like me."

Zack has had no serious childhood illnesses or accidents. He has never run high fevers or been hospitalized.

Developmental History. Mr. and Mrs. A. wanted only one child so that they could afford to give this child the advantages of a good life (i.e., college, toys, vacations, house, clothes). They were pleased when she became pregnant. She was on no medication during pregnancy. After thirteen hours of labor, Zack was born by Caesarean section as "his head was turned wrong." She "lost 29 pounds of water when he was born." He weighed 7 pounds, 4 ounces, and was 19 inches long. According to the Amantos, the "doctors said Zack had very alert APGAR scores." They did not remember the numbers.

Zack was a good baby—an enjoyable, pleasant child with no feeding or sleeping problems. He did things early—laughing, holding up his head at three weeks, walking at nine months. Neither remembered when he began to talk, but were sure that it was "early."

He has always been a physically active child with good coordination except during seizures. Mr. A. thinks his timing may be a bit off in playing various ball games but associates this with needing to practice. Zack is good with his fingers in making models. He is left-handed and right-footed. His eyesight is good. When his eyes were checked, the doctor did not mention eye dominance; the Amantos have not noticed either eye being dominant. His hearing is good.

At times, Zack has been afraid of the dark, but has no big fears. He sleeps in his own bedroom but keeps the door cracked. He sleeps pretty well and does not have nightmares. He has always been a good eater. He was bottle-fed so that Mrs. A. could return to work.

Zack's maternal grandparents were his babysitters from birth until he entered school. He was not a clingy child. Zack and his maternal grandfather were awfully close; often shopping, playing, and gardening. When Zack was in first grade, his grandfather was diagnosed with cancer and died after two or three months (December 1993). Zack did not react overtly to his death, but fell apart—sobbing and carrying on—two days after the funeral when the eighteen-year-old family dog died.

Zack has never been an aggressive child and has never demanded a lot of attention. He has no friends in the neighborhood and has never seemed to have many good friends at school.

School History.   Last year at St. Catherine, Zack realized for the first time that they were serious about work in this school, so he began to try harder. According to his parents, he knows what is expected now and can do the work.

Zack has always been an immature child with a lot of play in him when it comes to schoolwork. His parents attributed his poor first-grade work to everybody's upset over the illness and death of Mrs. A.'s father. Mr. and Mrs. A. thought Zack did adequately in second grade and were surprised that he was referred for testing. The parents report that Zack was referred for educational evaluation because he was "experiencing difficulty meeting success academically." In Fall 1995, he entered a learning center for children with perceptual learning disabilities and attention deficits at the same school. He repeated second-grade material, although his parents reported that he was identified as being in third grade. His parents reported that he did well that year and blame the school for curriculum mix-up as he should have had third-grade work. The following year, he returned to the regular school program for third-grade. That was a "bad year" for Zack. The substitute teacher was poor in handling both academics and discipline. Zack fought and got beat up a lot at recess. Zack never started the fights. He was promoted to the fourth grade and transferred to St. Catherine at the beginning of the next school year. Mr. and Mrs. A. have given up on public school for their child. At St. Catherine, Zack tries to overachieve and do things perfectly. He never fights. His parents approve of these changes.

Mr. and Mrs. A. clearly value education and are concerned that Zack is not performing at grade level. They pressure him to improve.

Developmental History of Family

History Mrs. Amanto. Thirty-nine years old, African American, Roman Catholic.

Mrs. A. was born with rickets. She had rheumatic fever as a child and continues to have problems. During her first year teaching, she had a recurrence of rheumatic fever. During this time (age approximately twenty-three or twenty-four), she was living at home with her parents and taking twenty-five aspirin a day for pain and fever. While growing up, her parents and doctors had put a lot of restrictions on her when she was sick. But that last time, they were all so worried that she never got out of the house that her mother recruited Mr. A. as a boyfriend. Her mother met him in the grocery store. Doctors have mentioned the possibility of heart surgery within the coming year because her heart valve has stretched. She does not plan to have surgery even though the doctor told her she would die without it. She fears what shape surgery may leave her in. She has low blood pressure and no energy, but otherwise feels okay. Mrs. A. refuses to allow her husband or the clinician to talk with her doctor.

Mrs. A. describes her learning pattern as like Zack's, in that it seems as if she is not assimilating something when she really is. That is, she stores it and recalls it later. Given this pattern, it is hard to measure what she knows or what Zack knows. She always liked school and did well in subjects she liked. Mrs. A. attended Catholic elementary school and public high school. She prefers Catholic school for learning as "it gives one steadiness." Mrs. A. received her degree from State Teachers College.

Mrs. A. volunteered no information about her brother, either as they were growing up or currently. When asked, she shifted subjects. She spoke warmly of her father who provided well for his family. Her mother was strict, very religious, and fussed at her a lot.

Mrs. A. has taught lower grades at the same public elementary school for eighteen years.

History Mr. Amanto. Thirty-six years old, African American, converted to Roman Catholicism to marry.

Mr. A. grew up in Indiana with one brother two years older and one sister two years younger. His father died a few months ago. His parents had been divorced for twenty-five years and he had not seen his father for a long time before his death. He was about twelve at the time of the divorce. His mother was strict but fair with her children. His father was not around much.

Mr. A. failed second grade. He always did well in classes he liked. He attended State University for 2.5 years as an advertising/design major. In college, he was uptight and controlled, just like Zack. The finer the detail in school assignments, the better he liked it. Mr. A. would throw himself into any schoolwork, proceed along, but then stop before the end. He would not finish the last 1 percent because he feared that it was not perfect and he would fail. If he did not finish the work, he did not have to take time to worry about whether it was perfect. "It's scary to see Zack so like me. The difference is that Zack is slow and methodical in doing things throughout the process." Mr. A. talked at length about their perfectionism. He stated that if he is intensively involved and concentrating for a long time, he will have a seizure. Therefore, he has learned to pace himself and take breaks.

Mr. A. describes his epilepsy as like his brother's and son's. Onset occurred at age four; etiology is unknown. Seizures are mostly *petit mal* and controlled through daily medication at a minimum dosage level. Fooling with a lot of figures will set Mr. A. off. He did not know about his seizures until age fifteen, when he had the flu and a high fever that triggered a *grand mal* seizure and landed him in the hospital. His doctor told him that he had had seizures since age four. His mother refused to talk about either of her sons' epilepsy. She fell apart whenever his brother had a *grand mal* seizure, so Mr. A. handled it. Mr. A. did not respond when asked who helped him when he needed someone.

Mr. A. described his brother as a renegade in high school and always under pressure to get in line. He and his brother are opposites. His brother is argumentative in style, has been married and divorced twice, and is about to marry again.

Mr. A. describes himself as a person who sits back and observes life. He cares about people and real values. He does not like to see people torn down. He likes to help others (poor, elderly) and to rescue people. Mr. A. described his family as very light complected and the dominant family value as "if you can pass, do." He believes his family emphasis on and valuing of status has hurt people. Mr. A. would not elaborate on this.

Mr. A. has worked at the same grocery store for sixteen years and has been managing the bakery department for five years.

Marital History.   Mr. and Mrs. A. courted three months and have been married fifteen years. Their first marriage was a secret civil ceremony with both her parents present. For three months after that, he kept his apartment. She stayed some with him and some with her parents. They described this as a "let's pretend" marital state, with the real marriage occurring at the religious ceremony in November 1985. Prior to the religious ceremony, there were major arguments with the parish priest about his conversion process and premarital counseling. He put up with it for her sake, but felt like the priest and Mrs. A.'s mother were always after him.

During their courtship and early marriage, they were really close and have become so again. After the September 1997–May 1998 separation, they are back together in a "more mature" relationship. As Catholics, both believe in working out problems and have. Both state that the real problem all along has been her mother. Even though her mother chose Mr. A. as a boyfriend, she actually had not wanted her daughter to marry and "certainly not an epileptic." She does not understand and cannot accept epilepsy. Her mother saw a boy die during a seizure when she was a child. To their knowledge, her mother has not seen Mr. A. or Zack have a seizure. Mr. A. told Mrs. A. about his epilepsy before the marriage. According to both, his epilepsy has not been a problem for her.

During the recent separation, neither her family nor their friends knew about the separation because he was at the house on days off and evenings. He only went to his brother's house to sleep. Both thought that their difficulties were their business and no one else's. She kept her feelings to herself and little things got on her nerves and built up. Her mother was constantly at her that her husband no longer cared for her. Mr. A.'s style, by contrast, was to get angry, get a cup of coffee, and let the anger just boil out from inside him. He did not talk about it, but just let the anger peak and fade. This way, it did not disturb anyone else. He is a night person, she is a day person. He needs space and she is able to give him that now. He is better able to handle distractions now. She used to bring a lot of work frustrations home with her, would be full of anger, then just explode; he did the same. Each describes self as feeling better about work now and bringing home problems less often. Both still feel that a lot of the problems were not theirs but were associated with pressures exerted from outside. Although encouraged to give specifics, core problems were not explicitly identified as such—other than the difficulty communicating and different personal styles. They denied that their problems had any impact on Zack.

For the first year and a half of marriage, they lived mostly with her parents. Then they bought a house in the neighborhood. While living with her parents, she got anonymous phone calls that he was running around. These calls tapped into her low self-esteem, fears of losing him, and worries about being able to hold him. Mr. and Mrs. A. argued a lot then but not about the real issue—the telephone calls. She felt alone and that she had to carry this burden by herself. Mr. A. denied that he has ever stepped out on her. Although she is more open and direct today, she still needs time to work up to talking.

Family History Time Line.

1985	June, married in secret civil ceremony with her parents present
	November, married in church after disagreement with priest, mother
	Mr. A. 23, Mrs. A. 26
	Lived with her parents for 1.5 years
1987	Spring, bought house in her parents' neighborhood

Zack

1987	11/13	Zack born by C-section
1988	3 months	Mrs. A. back to work, her parents babysat until Zack entered school
1993	5 years	Winter, Zack's *petit mal* epilepsy diagnosed, began medications
	5.9	Fall, Zack entered first grade in public school
		December, maternal grandfather died, family dog died
1994	6.9	Second grade, failed
1995	7.9	Repeated second-grade content in special-education third grade
1996	8.9	Third grade, fighting, poor academic performance, substitute teacher
1997	9.9	Fourth grade, St. Catherine of Siena
		Parental separation; Mr. A. began sleeping over at his brother's
1998	10.2	February, Zack referred for psychological testing
	10.4	Spring, Mr. A.'s father died
	10.6	May, Mr. and Mrs. A. reunited and Mr. A. back at home
	10.7	June, referral to clinic, clinic referred for neurological, psychological workups
	10.9	Fall, Zack entered fifth grade St. Catherine
		Family seen at Clinic

Summary of Child Assessment Interviews

Zack is a tall, slender, 10.9-year-old African American male with a medium brown complexion like his parents. His breathing pattern is slow and heavy. His gums protrude and are swollen over his teeth (a symptom associated with his medication). He tends to present himself as younger than his age. His speech pattern is soft, slow, clear, and correct "formal, school-style" English. His movements in drawing are slow, methodical, and detailed. He waits for someone else to initiate activity and appears afraid of "not doing it right." On the school playground, by contrast, he seems enthusiastically alive as he plays ball and engages with peers. His movements seem somewhat awkward and not particularly coordinated.

Zack explored the knapsack of toys in a cautious, slow manner and seemed fearful of risking. His fantasy material included:

Favorite and best age to be: Teenager as can do a lot, go places with friends, see movies (affect lights up)

Three wishes: Have a spaceship to go away in; a new house with a swimming pool, game arcade, museum (perseverated a few minutes about what he'd fill house with); and having money because he'd buy a Ferrari and everything else

Saddest time: I don't know; when Grandpa (mother's father) died

Happiest time: I don't know, last birthday, more grownup

In response to the Despert (1948) fables used to elicit his projective thinking, Zack replied:

Baby bird fell out of nest, what will he do?: He'll stay there because he can't fly

Wedding anniversary party, why did child go off alone?: The boy doesn't like their getting married (became anxious and picked up war toys)

New baby lamb gets the milk, what will the older lamb do?: He'll go eat grass, feels jealous

Funeral, who is dead?: Can't answer that one; it might be grandfather

Anxiety, what is he afraid of?: Might be mean ghosts

Elephant with long trunk has changed, how has he changed?: Changed into an angel because he was magic

Child creation, will he give mother his clay tower?: He'd keep the tower

Walk, boy and mother go walking, why does dad look different?: A different man

News, what news will child tell?: Exciting, they're going to move

Bad dream, what did child dream?: Can't figure it out, he got lost

Zack's spontaneous play themes included playing war games and killing off bad guys; drawing spaceships and killing off spaceships; and building towers with blocks. When anxious, Zack picked up and held one or two toy soldiers and became verbally quiet while wiggling more in his chair.

His relationship style with adults is that of pleaser. His movements appear slow and deliberate. He begins an answer and perseverates until stopped. He seems afraid to end an answer for fear that it is inadequate. When he comprehends something, his whole being lights up.

Psychosocial Formulation

Zack

Zack, a 10.9-year-old African American male in the fifth grade at St. Catherine of Siena, was referred to the Child Service Clinic by his school for continuing educational problems: failing written work, lack of informational content in scattered areas, inability to complete work in school, and disorganization. The long-standing duration of the academic difficulty is evidenced by his having difficulty in first grade and repeating second grade. A history of *petit mal* epilepsy (identified at age five), high distractibility, spatial perceptual weakness, and mixed dominance, coupled with history of poor academic performance, point to organically based learning deficits. Psychological and neurological workups support this conclusion. The psychological testing also identified Zack's basic intellectual ability as average with identified visual perceptual and attentional deficits.

Diagnosis of epilepsy just prior to entering school not only impacted on Zack's own perception of his body image as different and defective, but also reflected a loss in his relationship with his maternal grandmother in that she was not able to accept either Zack's or his father's epilepsy and tends to deny its existence. With his parents, by contrast, identification of a physical defect in their child seemed to increase their identification with him on the one hand. On the other hand, it also increased their denial that Zack has organically-based learning deficits.

Zack's maternal grandfather was a major source of nurture and caring. His illness as Zack entered first grade and subsequent death in the middle of that school year provided additional stress for Zack's already overtaxed ability to learn in a mainstream classroom setting. This loss was further increased by his grandmother's inability to continue caring for him during this period and his placement in daycare. It seems likely that his mother's grief and probable withdrawal further compounded the nature of Zack's losses.

Zack experienced additional losses at age nine. During that academic year, he left public school and entered St. Catherine. His parents separated from September to May of that school year but kept it a guarded secret, shared only with Zack and Mr. A.'s brother.

The Amantos perceive and present themselves as a solidly middle-class African American family—that is, as homeowners, college background, white-collar employees, expectation of school success by only child, and active members of church and parish. Both parents exert pressure on Zack to perform in school and have created a psychosocial developmental environment within which he has internalized this expectation of accomplishment. The lack of congruence between his and his family's expectations about his performance level and the actuality of his academic performance have led to further reduction in his already poor self-esteem. This downward spiral is further exacerbated by Zack's obsessive defenses through which he strives for control and perfection by slow methodical work and excessive attention to detail. The result has been a behavioral pattern of not completing work; a pattern that his father perceives as reflecting a pattern of generation repetition of Mr. A.'s perfectionism and fear of failure.

Zack's primary psychosocial diagnosis is one of lowered self-concept that exacerbates classroom learning difficulties often associated with organically-based learning disability with visual and attentional deficits. Comorbid diagnosis is dysthymia and obsessive traits. It is clear that he had major depressive episodes associated with losses. There is clear identification with maternal depression. Zack's psychosocial dysfunction is further complicated by parental psychodynamics and marital discord.

Mr. Amanto

Mr. A. (age thirty-six) is a slender, medium-complected African American who presents himself as a white-collar manager, while at the same time denying that he has a drive to achieve and move up in the world. His employment pattern is stable and he has been promoted over the years. As he presents, his peer relationships appear good; authority relationships, to be tolerated. He frequently portrays himself as a compassionate, people-oriented person in terms of helping poor or elderly customers and rescuing them. This portrait contrasts markedly with his other description of self as one who sits back and observes rather than becomes involved.

He presents himself as having grown away from his family's values: money, achievement, social standing, and passing. Yet, as he talks, these continue to be conflicted areas.

With minimal support and encouragement, Mr. A. is able to share facts and feelings, think about issues during sessions, grapple with concerns, and bring ideas back to the evaluation. Affect is appropriate, although at times somewhat constricted. He seems to have a good understanding of his epilepsy and copes well with his minor limitations. It is likely that his rescue complex serves to boost his self-esteem.

The primary area of dysfunction in his relationship with Zack would seem to be his active projective identification on a verbalized conscious level, along with little real recognition of the strength of the projection. The content here includes the epilepsy *per se*, the obsessive-compulsive coping style, learning issues, some confusion of self-concept in relation to both the physical challenge and family of origin value system, and mild depression. Although some of the depression is clearly his own internalized difficulty, some appears to be in response to his wife's depression.

Mrs. Amanto

Mrs. A. (thirty-nine) is an average size, medium-brown–complected African American who presents herself as exhausted, physically ill, angry, depressed, and overwhelmed by life circumstances. The real state of her physical health in relation to her history of rheumatic fever/enlarged heart valve, pending surgery, current medication/exhaustion/depression, and future prognosis is difficult to gauge given her martyr style. She refuses to give Mr. A. or the clinical social worker permission to contact her doctor.

Her employment pattern is stable in that she has spent eighteen years in one elementary school. She currently appears to be receiving little satisfaction from her work and resents the demands made on teachers from all fronts. She adopts a mother-hen style when she thinks her second-graders are being short-changed, and sees herself as fighting for them and staying in an apparently rough school because the children "need a teacher of her calibre." She seems to be isolated from the rest of the teaching staff and to have few satisfying peer relationships.

Mrs. A. appears to be engaged primarily in hostile dependent relationships: with mother, husband, principal, clinical social worker, and Zack's school personnel. She often withholds information and presents this behavior pattern as supportive of a great secretive thing she will accomplish, as something belonging solely to her, and sometimes with a shade of "you already know what it is" (i.e., appearance of symbiotic merger with clinician, which seems to be the object-relations pattern with her mother). Her affect is consistently angry and depressed. She seems to have difficulty mobilizing herself to attend to details and small tasks asked of her, as well as to more major productions expected of her at school and home in the way of routine performance. Her self-esteem fluctuates wildly from minimal to grandiose.

The primary areas of dysfunction in her relationship with Zack include (1) active projective identification on an occasionally conscious but primarily pre- or unconscious level, no recognition of the projection related to health issues, poor self-concept, keeping feelings to self, and sensitivity to slights by others; (2) pattern of generation repetition of her own symbiotic relationship with and hostile-dependent tie to her mother; (3) style of keeping her feelings to herself; and (4) shifting the burden of her own chronic depression onto Zack.

Her primary psychosocial diagnosis would include dysthymia, physical health as a stress factor, and obsessive-compulsive personality traits. There is some fusion of self-concept with Zack through projective identification. Her psychosocial dysfunction in everyday life ranges from moderate to severe. She uses her Catholic background and religious beliefs to present herself as a martyr, whose life task on earth is to shoulder her burdens. If indeed her doctor has given her twelve months (eight have passed) to live without surgery, she appears to be actively suicidal on a preconscious level because she does not plan to have surgery. It is difficult to obtain facts from her about her health. Mr. A. does not have these facts and does not pursue them. The other possibility is that she has used the health issue to manipulate Mr. A. into returning home and also to reestablish the martyr/rescuer marital equilibrium.

Marital Pattern

Within the marital relationship, Mr. A. assumed the rescuer and Mrs. A. the helpless martyr roles from the beginning. Moving in with her family initially appeared to be associated with her inability to break the symbiotic hostile-dependent tie with her own mother, as well as her poor concept of self as a woman/wife/adult. Although issues of secrecy/privacy/wishful thinking would probably have become major marital themes regardless, they were heightened by living in Mrs. A.'s childhood home. Neither Mr. nor Mrs. A. tolerate open conflict well. He goes off and angrily stews alone; she withdraws into herself. Both describe their personal styles as opposites (night/day, active/quiet, just so this way/just so that) and have begun to work toward calibrating a joint couple style. Roles appear to be diffused and leadership patterns in various areas of family functioning are unclear. In many ways, this trio seems reflective of an undifferentiated family ego mass. Communication patterns are not clear, informative, affective, consistent, or mutually constructive/satisfying.

The timing of their separation repeats the pattern in Mr. A.'s family (he was also nine when his parents separated). Both continue to be quite angry about the separation, but have difficulty expressing their anger and addressing the separation issues. They convey their basic belief that trouble not acknowledged does not exist—which was the pretense maintained for outsiders during the period of actual separation. It is my impression that their reuniting is associated with their own hostile-dependent relationship, their projective identification with their son, their middle-class and Catholic value system of family / no divorce, and a mutually satisfying rescuer / martyr bond that the separation and her recent health problems rekindled. Both deny the existence of sexual problems (past and present) and their affect during this discussion conveyed mutual satisfaction on some level.

Ongoing Diagnostic Tasks

The major diagnostic task continues to be the monitoring of Mrs. A.'s depression. It seems probable that (1) as the couple are back together longer, her anger at Mr. A. will surface and may possibly be directed destructively toward herself in order to pay him back and make him feel guilty; (2) insertion of the clinical social worker as a buffer between Zack and Mrs. A.'s depression and resettling the depression back on Mrs. A.'s shoulders is likely to increase her depression; (3) Zack's approaching birthday may symbolically represent his growing up and needing her less, thus reflecting a loss for her with subsequent grief possibilities; (4) with the approach of the "year-to-live" deadline (whether real, medical guesstimate / threat, or fiction / fantasy), there is likely to be a sensation of anticipated loss (of self, wish, or fantasy); and (5) with the advent of the New Year, she may see it as a time for action of some sort.

The second diagnostic task is further clarification of the marital relationship and its impact on Zack's ability to learn and function in school. The third task is clarification and isolation of the nature of the depression for each family member so that it may be treated. The fourth task is further clarification of Zack's ability to function and learn in a mainstream classroom setting, and determination of the educational resources necessary for optimal learning on his part.

Diagnostic Formulation Identified Client: Zack

Axis I	315.9	Learning Disorder NOS
	314.9	Attention Deficit Hyperactivity Disorder (predominantly inattentive)
	300.4	Dysthymic Disorder
Axis II		None
Axis III		*Petit Mal* Epilepsy
Axis IV		Psychosocial stressors of marital discord, maternal depression, and death of maternal grandfather
Axis V		Current GAF 65

Treatment Plan
Zack

Weekly individual developmental play therapy appointments will be sched-uled to achieve the following goals:

1. Clarify learning needs and educational support services
2. Clarify self-concept confusion
3. Increase self-worth
4. Express feelings and fears
5. Alleviate depression re: parents' separation and history of losses
6. Buffer and begin to split the symbiotic fusion with
   a. Mother re: learning pattern and depressive-affect coping style
   b. Father re: coping with epilepsy and learning style of not completing work
7. Facilitate understanding and coping with parents' patterns of marital com-munication

Mr. and Mrs. A.

Weekly concurrent parent sessions with the couple will be used to achieve the following goals:

1. Improve the parent-child relationship by focusing on objectives of
   a. Buffering and splitting the symbiotic fusion with Zack
   b. Enabling them to communicate with Zack about their differences within their marriage, and that it is not his responsibility to hold the family together
   c. Setting age-appropriate autonomy objectives for Zack
   d. Handling health issues appropriately as adults, with age-appropriate sharing with Zack
   e. Helping them to increase Zack's self-esteem
   f. Facilitating their acceptance of Zack's problems as his; epilepsy as his health problem, his learning problems, his need for educational supple-ments
2. Improve the marital relationship as the context for childrearing by focusing on objectives of
   a. Increasing their communication of feelings, fears, and facts
   b. Increasing their ability to handle anger constructively
   c. Facilitating creation and provision of personal space for each partner within the marriage
   d. Facilitating their finding sources for self-fulfillment and emotional feeding
   e. Increasing their sense of self-worth as individuals
   f. Alleviating the sense of family depression
   g. Clarifying and facilitating coping with health issues and fears

  h. Clarifying and working through marital conflicts associated with prior separation
  i. Enabling them to communicate and open up family secrets and myths
3. Improve individual adult functioning by
  a. Centering the family depression back on Mrs. A. as the primary carrier and enabling her to acknowledge her need for individual therapy as a client in her own right
  b. Clarifying issues of individual identity within the marital relationship
  c. Clarifying health reality and dealing with issues of self-concept confusion and projective identification

Collaterals

Professional contact with key collaterals (principal, teacher, pediatrician, neurologist) already involved with Zack, with the parents' written permission and Zack's knowledge, to:

1. Facilitate their understanding of the reasons for Zack's learning difficulties and depression
2. Support educators' handling of a child who needs a great deal of individual work while he is mainstreamed and parents who resist educational supplements
3. Learn about Zack's epilepsy, neurological impairment, and medication regimen, and share information about his problems in day-to-day functioning
4. Request re-evaluation of medication in light of epilepsy, ADHD, and dysthymia.

Conclusion

The developmental perspective lays the foundation for the assessment and treatment of the biological, psychological, cultural, and social dimensions of children in their interactions with their family, school, and community environments. All of the data are gathered, organized according to the checklist in Table 6.1, and analyzed to come up with a case formulation of the child's problem, current family functioning, and parenting issues. The initial family assessment, however, is tentative and subject to change as more data are collected from the parents, child, and collaterals. While the parent and child assessment interviews are presented separately, materials collected are integrated to form a whole biopsychosocial assessment of child-in-family-and-school. The therapeutic change process both confirms (or changes) the original assessment and formulation and generates a need for updates.

TABLE 6.1   Parent Assessment Interview Checklist*

I. Identifying Family Data
  A. Family household composition
  B. Description of family members
II. Presenting Problem and Referral Source
III. Developmental History of Child
  A. Pregnancy, delivery, neonatal period
  B. Temperamental characteristics of early infancy
  C. Attachment in the first year of life
  D. Socialization in toddlerhood
  E. Discovery of self in the pre-school years
  F. The school years
  G. Medical history
  H. Legal history
  I. Cultural and socioeconomic history
IV. Developmental History, Structure, Functioning of Family
  A. Social history of each parent
  B. Courtship and marital relationships
  C. Appearance and behavior of family members
  D. Family problem solving, decision-making, and conflict-resolution patterns
  E. Role performance
V. Family as Social Environment
  A. Household practices and procedures
  B. Educational supports
  C. Family activity patterns
  D. Family values
VI. Community Supports and Resources
VII. Psychosocial Formulation: Parents
  A. Assessment of appearance and behavior
  B. Interpretation of current problem and symptoms as affecting each parent
  C. Assessment of social role functioning
  D. Assessment of parental maturational level, strengths, weaknesses
  E. Assessment of socio-environmental stresses
  F. Assessment of parent-child interactions and parenting practices

*Combine with Table 7.1 Child Assessment Interview Checklist (see Chapter 7)

7 Child Interviews in Biopsychosocial Assessment and Planning

In the art and science of biopsychosocial assessment of children, multiple variables from five developmental areas comprise the multidimensional data system that leads to a dynamic case formulation and treatment recommendations. Using data from both parent (see Chapter Six) and child interviews, a child's maturation is assessed along the developmental lines of object relations (Mahler, Pine, and Bergman, 1975), cognition (Piaget, 1952), the psychosocial life cycle (Erikson, 1959), intrapsychic development (A. Freud, 1965), and biological development. In the process, developmental disruptions and distortions are noted. Intervention using the developmental play therapy model conceptualizes progression in treatment as the unfolding maturation of each developmental line and their convergence into an interlocking whole.

A metaphorical world map provides a visual aid in depicting the cognitive, emotional, biological, social, and environmental realms of child development as the five continents of the child's world. The alternating periods of smooth seas and the tidal waves of disruption, turmoil, and conflict within a child's life are represented by the oceans, which also form distinct areas, yet an interlocking whole. In sum, this metaphorical map provides a notion of the ever-changing dynamism of a child's world and clues for understanding how to purposively correct imbalances in it.

This chapter focuses on the art and science of data collection in biopsychosocial assessment through child interviews. Attention is directed to the five developmental realms; assessment techniques with children; the mental status exam; and case formulation, diagnosis, and planning. This material is applied in the case of Molly Jones. A child assessment interview checklist concludes the chapter.

Developmental Realms: Concepts and Application

The Biological Realm

The biological realm centers on the child's maturing brain function, biochemistry, physical health, temperament, and genetic endowment. Information about these innate attributes that impact on the child's potential is obtained through a thorough developmental history provided by parents (see Chapter Six). An in-depth, three-generation family history of current or past mental disorders is also part of the parent interviews. Pediatric consultation is essential in determining the child's current and past physical health. In addition to this information, the clinical social worker also evaluates the biological realm directly for information about the child's physical health and well-being, observed physical challenges (i.e., a limp, a missing finger, overweight, or eyeglasses), less visible physical challenges (e.g., hard of hearing, difficulty breathing, difficulty with fine motor-muscular coordination), and physical attribute differences from the rest of the family (e.g., features, skin tone, hair color and texture, height, weight, size). Appropriate treatment recommendations may include medical, physical therapy, and educational referrals and play therapy to address issues of understanding biological issues, coping, and adaptation.

The Cognitive Realm

The developmental dimension across the cognitive domain measures the way in which the child applies language, memory, thought, and imagination in problem solving. The clinical social worker needs to have a thorough understanding of how such mental processes work for the child. If any of the processes are inhibited, delayed, or disrupted, they need to be restored so conflict or defense interpretation becomes more meaningful.

The clinician evaluates the child's cognition to determine the presence of representational thought. Is symbolic knowledge available or is the thinking prerepresentational and concrete? Even though prerepresentational play precludes the ability to link and elaborate ideas, wishes, and fantasies, is the child like the two-year-old who is able to recall memories and use imagination in play? Or is the child more like three- or four-year-olds who demonstrate the capacity to express and reflect on thoughts and feelings in themselves and others? When three- or four-year-old cognitive capability is reached, children are able to make something present that is not present through the use of internal symbols, as evidenced in their fantasy, play, and the shared communication of language. Such children are said to be capable of symbol formation and representational play. Their mental processes are intact and available for symbolic play. If there is a lag in memory, imagination, or representational thought, the developmental formulation in the biopsychosocial assessment will reflect the delay. Developmental play therapy is recommended for cognitive and behavioral change and dynamic developmental work.

The Social Realm

The stage of a child's play crosses the cognitive and social spheres through four levels: solitary, parallel, imaginative, and competitive/collaborative play. The level of the play is readily observable during the evaluation. If the play is solitary (such as that often seen in children with disrupted mental processes), the clinician notices self-stimulating play that usually demands immediate gratification. This sensorimotor play level is often centered around bodily concerns. The interpersonal encounters reflect a paucity in the linkage of beliefs, desires, and wishes to action. At this level, the child appears to be self-absorbed.

Play becomes more active with the onset of parallel play in the context of the dyad. As children play side-by-side with the clinical social worker, they are available and responsive and understand that their mind guides voluntary actions and behavior. They grasp the concept of pretend play. Imaginative play portends well for developmental play therapy because it connotes triadic and interactive connection. Creativity and innovation flourish. These children tell their story through talk and play. They are able to link ideas and fantasies to action. Their representational mind thrives.

The next level of competitive and collaborative play represents the capacity for meaningful interaction with the peer group. At this developmental level, the child (usually latency-age) may turn to board and card games in the playroom.

The child's social realm is apparent during the initial interview. Later, during treatment, the social world of the child is understood through the transference. In the beginning, the clinician notes how the child uses the self in the interpersonal encounter. Are the social behaviors age-appropriate? Is there a sense of mutuality? It is important to assess the potential for social relatedness in terms of the type and evolution of the therapeutic alliance. Specifically, is the child able to use the clinician for play and understanding? The youngster with really poor social relations is unable to do this and usually withdraws or becomes defensively overactive during the interview. The clinician feels how fragmented such children seem as they struggle awkwardly to organize their environment and display enormous difficulty in controlling their affect.

The Emotional Realm

The observation of play permits us to get an idea of the child's inner world and conflicts. Children recreate their life experience through symbolic forms, as seen in the displacement in fantasy and play. It is important to discern the full spectrum of affective reactions as seen in the child's play, words, and manner of relating. Emotional responses are conspicuous through motoric action, facial expression, verbal expressions, and quality of play. In the younger child, energetic activity is typical and not necessarily indicative of hyperactivity. Does the child's laughter indicate anxiety or joy? The clinician searches for the affect behind the child's actions, words, and mood.

The affective experience of the preschooler is more accessible than that of the school-age child. Normally, latency-age children will present us with their defenses rather than a discussion of their feelings or affect. The anxious child defends against something terrible happening in the future, while the depressed child thinks something awful has already happened and experiences guilt as a symptom. In both cases, the result may well be intrapsychic conflict. Because the defense is motivated by the need to minimize the anxious or depressed feeling, the clinical social worker explores the nature and purpose of the defense in coming to know the child. For example, a common defense seen in phobic children is avoidance of a stressful situation. Are children with school phobia avoiding school because they hate it or are they displacing anxiety from another source?

During the biopsychosocial assessment, the children's defensive structure is evaluated for its usefulness in protecting them from anxiety. The clinician analyzes the nature of the defense, whether it is primitive or more mature and whether it is ego syntonic or dystonic. In school-age children, the clinician expects an obsessional defense organization, while preschoolers present with more phobic composition. The more primitive defenses often used by youngsters include projection, incorporation, and projective identification.

Anna Freud's (1965) developmental lines were conceptualized to assess how the child matures in relation to expectable outcomes in order to understand the source of intrapsychic conflict interfering with that maturation. In brief, these developmental lines include the following:

1. *From dependency to adult relationships.* Here, an expectable biological harmony with mother gives way to separation/individuation and object constancy by age three, followed by oedipal concerns that are, in turn, relinquished so that six-year-olds may turn their attention and energy to school.

2. *From suckling to rational eating.* This line begins with the breast and moves on to self-feeding. There are a host of affective reactions concerning the symbolic meaning of food (see Chapter Three).

3. *From wetting and soiling to bladder and bowel control.* This line traces mother's efforts to instill control and the child's emotional reactions to this demanding task.

4. *From irresponsibility in body management to responsibility in body management.* This line addresses children's growing ability to care for their own bodies and health.

5. *From egocentricity to companionship.* In this line, the child's narcissism is relinquished in favor of gratification and satisfaction in relationships with other children. Empathic ability develops as narcissism is tamed.

6. *From body to toy and from play to work.* This developmental line tracks the sensorimotor play first associated with the body, followed by the attachment to a transitional object, and then to toys that represent various feelings and fantasies. Eventually, the child chooses certain toys for displacement of oedipal feelings. Finally, the child takes pleasure in play and satisfaction in a job well done.

These developmental lines help the clinician to understand the spectrum of developmental play and assess where the child needs the most help. Affective reactions that are seen in a child's fantasy and play are understood in the context of the overall emotional realm. Through following these developmental lines, the clinical social worker comes to understand how children have used their environment, especially their parents, to facilitate their maturation along each line.

The Environmental Realm

Environment concerns the child's external world in the family, neighborhood, and school. There are a host of environmental factors that children use to mature in their other realms or that negatively impact their biopsychosocial functioning. For example, the foster child who has had multiple placements has experienced trauma associated with loss, separation, and abandonment. Poverty impacts on child well-being directly and through parents' stress as their struggle to provide food, clothing, and shelter leaves little energy for nurturing and caregiving. The realistic concerns caused by crime and violence may find expression through phobias, anxiety, or acting out. Marital discord taxes a young child's ability to cope. The substance-abusing parent engenders fear in the child. Inadequate schools where a child's unique needs are not addressed bring about despair and often a sense of failure. Thus, sometimes the environmental realm provides a good-enough supportive holding environment for developmental maturation and sometimes it does not. In addition, some children are resilient in the face of adversity, while others are vulnerable to situational conditions beyond their control.

Child Assessment Techniques

Observation

The child interview normally begins in the waiting room as the clinical social worker walks out to greet the child. On the way, the clinician observes the interaction between mother and child, level of activity, eye contact, motor capabilities, and physical appearance. Is the child disruptive, clinging, or quietly engaged in play? Hopefully, the parents have followed the clinician's recommendations for preparing their child for the interview by saying something like, "Mommy and I met with Ms. Smith to talk to her about your nightmares. We arranged for you to meet her too so she can help you with your worries. You and she will talk and play together in her office while Mommy waits for you in the waiting room." Once in the waiting room, the clinical social worker introduces herself to the child, calling him by name, "Hello, Joe. I am Ms. Smith. Let's go into the office while your mother waits for you right here." At this point, the observation continues to note the appropriateness of the child's separation from mother. Does he jump into mother's lap or separate with ease? Does mother remain silent, encourage him, or look longingly after him? One child left mother readily as he ran to kiss the clinical social worker's leg. Such behaviors in separating speak volumes. The child's physical appearance can be just as notable. The clinician simply makes a mental note of these and proceeds with further observation of the child in the office or playroom.

Engagement

Once inside the office, it is usual to inquire about children's names by asking if that is what they like to be called or do they have a preferred nickname? One five-year-old boy proudly stated his first, middle, and last name followed by, "And I'm a big, tough man!" His proclamation certainly broke the ice and opened the way for an easygoing interview. At this point, the clinician clarifies what she or he does to help children with their worries or problems and adds that they will talk and play with the toys. Depending on the chief complaint, many clinicians make clear that the child can do or say just about anything, so long as he or she does not break the toys or hurt anyone. It is also helpful to let the child know that whatever is discussed will stay between the clinical social worker and the child. Of course, the caveat about danger to self and others is worked into this discussion as appropriate.

The clinician assesses the quality of the child's object relations and the capacity for engagement from the very beginning. It is useful to grasp children's understanding of their problem early on, as well as their understanding of what the clinician will do. After some difficulty separating from his mother, an eight-year-old boy said, "I'm here because when my father was a young child he didn't have anyone to talk to about his worries, so my parents want me to have someone to talk to." Not only was he well prepared, he readily acknowledged having worries. Other children are not so easily engaged and may respond with a shrug of the shoulder, "I don't know," or hiding under the desk. The psychotic child may be responding to internal thoughts or processes as he smiles mysteriously. In such instances, it is usually helpful to say something like, "Your mother and father brought you here because you keep getting into trouble at school" (or a similar paraphrase of the child's problem, as reported by the parents). Such comments clarify the reason the child was brought for an evaluation without asking the child directly why he is here.

At about this time, the clinician shows the child the play materials letting him know that he can choose whatever he wishes. The anxious child looks for direction. The hyperactive child pulls many objects off the shelf. The depressed child may wander aimlessly or just sit there. If children experience any difficulty at this point, they will be relieved by a simple suggestion to draw a picture or play with the clay. If the suggestion is an open, "You might like to play with one of the toys here," the choice of toy has diagnostic value. The clinician notes how the child uses and associates to specific kinds of play materials, whether a doll family, puppets, soldiers, drawings, or other toys (see Chapter Three). Through the child's creative expression, the clinician notes the child's clinical themes and patterns of aggression, separation/individuation, trust, and so forth. This introductory, unstructured phase of the assessment sets forth the ongoing observation of attention, motor tone, activity level, cognition, affect, curiosity, and imagination. The clinician notes the rate, rhythm, and amount of the child's speech and proficiency in receptive and expressive language, as well as any oddities of speech (e.g., perseveration or echolalia).

Play gratifies and engages the youngster in the language and work of childhood. It is for this reason that clinical social workers prefer to have several sessions to evaluate the depth, intensity, and recurrent nature of the narrative themes in the play drama. Through this displaced format, one gets a sense of the child's mental processes, interests, fantasies, and conflicts. One nine-year-old girl, who was referred by her recently separated parents for temper tantrums and low self-esteem, told the clinician how she was unable to talk to any friends or adults about her parents' pending divorce. She blamed her mother for the separation. As she played with the social worker's cat family, the child disclosed how she confides in her cats at home who exhibit human-like qualities. She said, "When I am sad or angry, my cats speak back and tell me not to worry—that things will get better." In the play scenario, she (as the baby cat) went outside to lie in the grass and cry. The sibling cats came to her and comforted her. Meanwhile, a toy car careened into mother cat, smashing her against the dollhouse and killing her instantly. Baby cat blamed herself for mother's demise. This narrative continued through three sessions via cat play, drawings, and dream exploration. Because time was devoted to getting to know the child in some depth, the clinical social worker's initial hypotheses were confirmed by the child. Her mental processes were assessed as being fully developed, her fantasies explored, her interests illustrated, and her conflicts expressed. At this point, the diagnostic question posed is whether the conflict is primarily conscious and brought on by a clash in her environment or whether it is intrapsychic and stems from earlier maladaptations. The answer determines how developmental play therapy will be used to resolve the conflict.

Exploration

As clinicians appraise children's engagement and expression in play, they move forward with more structure and direction in order to understand the child's sense of self at home, in school, and in the community. This appraisal is accomplished by taking a sincere interest in the child's world and saying something like, "You mentioned your baby sister earlier, I wonder what you think about her?" After the child talks about her, the clinician might ask, "And then what did your Mom do?" as an entry into family interactions and discipline. Alternatively, the comment might be, "Oh, I see. What about other people living with you at home?" This avenue of exploration helps to make known the child's view of self within the composition of the household. It may well open the door to describe a family member or loved babysitter outside of the home (e.g., an estranged father, loved grandparent, or departed caregiver). The use of open-ended comments and questions helps the child elaborate. For example, one young boy volunteered, "Well, I'm not supposed to tell you this, but my father's in jail." In commenting, the clinician is listening for the fantasy and reality elements that lie behind this statement. Before moving on to the child's school life, the clinician will want to know who the child gets along with best and least at home.

The clinical social worker wonders about the child's transition from home to school. "Tell me what it's like for you leaving home in the morning." A phobic seven-year-old girl commented, "That's when my tummy starts hurting." The clinician explores this symptom further before moving forth to discern the child's least and most favorite teachers, class subjects, and friends. The clinician gets an idea about sports, use of leisure time, and hobbies by saying, "What do you like to do?" The clinician appreciates any child's peer interactions and so might remark, "I'm wondering about what games you like to play on the playground." A nine-year-old bully exaggerated with intricate detail about the secret gang he started, the kids he hated, and how he wanted to tie them to a tree. Needless to say, this narrative led quite naturally to additional study of his attitudes toward aggression, the reasons for them, and his defensive structure through both his verbalizations and soldier play.

The clinical social worker turns attention to the exploration of fantasy material as a way to understand the nature of children's defenses and the symptoms that brought them for evaluation. This exploration continues through both free play and controlled situations. After considerable aggressive play with the toy soldiers, a seven-year-old boy explained, "They fight with guns, but I fight with words. I feel silly and content when I'm annoying. It's my nature. I'd like to change into normal, but I like my annoying skills. It's my self-defense." This youngster was using his fine intellect and well-honed verbal skills to rationalize his denial of the presence of annoying acting-out behaviors, which included pushing and shoving the more dominant boys in school and beating up his four-year-old sister at home. The clinician suggested he draw a picture of anything he liked. He drew a picture of the biting-shark family, in which mother and baby shark were devouring the water snake placed in between them. There he was sinking to the bottom of the ocean as he watched the two girl sharks above. Mother shark actually killed the water snake because she was afraid and wanted to feed him to the baby shark. As usual, daddy shark was away at the Biting Shark Convention Center. This artistic production reproduced the reality of his traveling father, preoccupied mother, and attention-seeking sister. It also represented his fears that mother would not be available for him and symbolized his inadequate masculine yearnings. His fantasy was that they would all forget about him . . . thus, better to be annoying. In the next session, he drew "the story of the boy who wants to be noticed."

Structured psychometric tests that involve drawing and can be formally scored include the Harris-Goodenough Draw-A-Person, House-Tree-Person, or Family. More often, the clinical social worker uses these tests as less-formalized clues to a child's projective expressions. For example, the child is given a piece of paper and a pencil and asked to draw a person. The clinician notes the figure's gender and the presence, absence, or exaggeration of detail. These projective expressions are added into the growing body of the evidence of the developmental level reached by the child in the multiple realms of maturation. Once the child has completed the picture, it is helpful to elicit a story about the figure. "What is going on now? What happens next? How do you think she feels?" Previously undisclosed gender issues arose when one six-year-old boy drew a bizarre picture of himself, saying it was a girl. The clinician also notes any fine motor or visual perceptual problems the youngster displays in drawing. The Draw-A-Family picture is useful in ascertaining some of the family dynamics through the inclusion/exclusion, placement, and size of various family members.

Dreams and daydreams open doors into the child's inner world. The clinician says, "All kids have dreams . . . good and bad. Can you tell me about one you have had?" One six-year-old girl who was referred for separation anxiety said, "Daddy was invisible in the bedroom. Then he changed into a big scary thing that was painted red. He took Mommy to the dungeon and she couldn't get out. Then, I found the key and took Mommy right home to take care of her. I couldn't go to school the next day." Sure enough, this child had extreme problems separating from her depressed mother, feeling she had to protect her, even from Daddy. In another situation, a six-year-old boy who had been physically abused by his mother reported dreams in which monsters were after him. He explained, "Mom and the kid were swimming and Mom drowned him . . . watched him drown."

The clinician asks children if they were granted any three wishes in the world, what would they be? Sometimes, children name materialistic objects for the first two wishes, but with a little prodding may disclose an inner thought that is troubling or a wish that cannot be granted as their third wish. For example, one boy wished that his dead mother would come back to life. Another wished he could be a girl because girls don't fight as much as boys. It is likewise helpful to ask what the child wishes to be when grown up. A six-year-old boy from a crime-ridden area announced he would be the President of the United States. At first, the clinician worried about his grandiosity, but then asked what he would do as President. He replied, "That way there will be no more crime. Did you know there is more crime in the United States than anywhere in the world? First comes Miami, then Washington, then New York, Detroit, and L.A." The clinician quickly realized this was more an expression of his realistic worries and fears than an aspiration.

Fantasy unfolds through the completion of fables. In the Baby Bird Fable and others adapted from the Despert Fables (Despert, 1948), the clinician begins the story and asks the child to end it. "Once upon a time, there was a bird family that lived in a nest high up in a tree. There was Daddy Bird, Mommy Bird, and Baby Bird. One day Mommy Bird left the nest to look for food for the baby. After a while, Daddy Bird was worried because she had been away for such a long time. So he flew away to look for her. There was Baby Bird all alone. She (or he, depending on the child's gender) hadn't quite learned to fly yet, so she hopped to the top of the nest. She was hopping around and started falling and tumbling down. Now you finish. What do you suppose happened to Baby Bird?" The completion of this fable provides quite revealing projective material about children's fears in relation to trust, nurturing, abandonment, and autonomy issues, to name a few. For example, the eight-year-old daughter of a professional woman who worked fourteen-hour days elaborated, "Well, the baby fell down to the ground, but she realized she wasn't hurt. She walked down the path and bumped into a squirrel and said, 'Are you my mother?' . . . and on she went meeting all the animals on the forest floor. She never found her mother and was very sad. Instead, she was adopted by the Happy Mouse Family." While this baby bird did not master the task of flying the way some do, she did have an autonomous streak about her. The story is tinged with sadness, but a "good-enough" outcome in that she does, at long last, find a family that is happy. Both her wish for an available mother and fear of desertion are depicted. It is interesting to note that her father is not even mentioned.

The Anxiety Fable is used to explore anxiety and self-punishment. The clinical social worker says, "A child says softly to herself (or himself), 'Oh, I am so afraid!' What do you suppose she is afraid of?" One youngster in the midst of a bitter custody dispute announced, "Why, she's afraid she'll have to live with Daddy and he won't let her see Mommy." The News Fable surfaces wishes and fears. "A child comes back from school and his Mommy tells him, 'Don't do your homework right away. I have some news to tell you.' What do you suppose the Mommy is going to tell him?" These Despert Fables and other short vignettes have been found to be clinically useful over the years as projective techniques to stimulate thoughts, feelings, and fantasies. As projective clinical tools for individual children, they are esteemed, even though validity and reliability have not been established through rigorous empirical research.

The clinician also asks about children's favorite television shows or movies. Who is their favorite character and why? How about books and music? The young boy who wanted to be noticed reflected about his favorite song and looked longingly around the office for a CD player, which the clinician did not have. He replied that he would think about it. The next session, he brought his own boom box, inserted his favorite CD, started singing at the top of his lungs, and began dancing around the office. He certainly gained the clinician's notice—and probably that of the entire building.

Yet another projective technique is the deserted-island story in which children are asked to pretend that they are going to go far away to live on a deserted island. No one else lives there, but they can take one person with them. Who would they choose? The usual expectation for a preschooler would be mother; for a mid-latency child, a close friend. Sometimes children come up with other people, or even pets, from which the clinician draws inferences about attachments, dependency and autonomy, and interpersonal relationships. Again, it is the whole of the interview material and the summation of inferences that come together in the dynamic case formulation.

The Mental Status Exam

At about this time, the clinical social worker completes the psychological study, or Mental Status exam, an integral part of the child interview that is interwoven throughout the evaluation. The exam is presented here in full even though the information is rarely gathered as a distinct entity.

In interviewing children, clinicians become adept at systematically compiling the data gained through observation, projective work, and direct questioning, and then recording it in the standard hierarchical format used in the particular service setting. In the Mental Status exam, the hierarchical format proceeds from the basic mental functions attributed to the brain stem upward to the more elevated cortical functions (Lewis, 1991; Strub and Black, 1980). A general description of the child's physical and psychological characteristics is followed by nine categories, including level of consciousness, attention, behavior, speech, thought form and content, memory, orientation, cognitive processes, and judgment and insight. While the material is conceptually organized and reported in outline format, the mental status exam rarely proceeds in such a direct way.

General Description

The social worker first notices the child's age, sex, and race, followed by the physical observation of the clothing, hygiene, and grooming. Does the child's appearance correlate with age and gender? Does the child appear neat and tidy, careless or unkempt, healthy or sick? Are there any odd or unusual mannerisms, facial expressions, or unusual or identifying features?

Next, the clinician appraises the child's cooperation and attitude with the interviewer. What kinds of interactions occur? Is the child hesitant or forthcoming, hostile or engaging? The clinician begins to have subjective feelings about the child and their interaction, and describes the manner of relating both initially and over the course of the interview. The clinician also notes any correlation between their relationship and the child's interaction style with others.

Level of Consciousness

Level of consciousness is readily observable. Is the child alert, lethargic, stuporous, or in a coma? If the child is not alert, the clinician determines what is needed to arouse the child. For example, if the child is drowsy, is there a response to a subdued mention of his or her name, or is a light shake of the shoulder needed? A stuporous youngster is disoriented and will require vigorous talk or physical contact before responding in a remote and incoherent way. Children who are unconscious or comatose are, of course, in need of immediate medical attention because they cannot be awakened.

Attention

Attention is the ability to focus on a given stimulus without distraction. It may well be caused by anxiety, depression, or disorders of attention. Children with attention deficits experience distractability, inattention, and difficulty with concentration (see Chapter Ten). Such difficulties are measured by history, classroom observation, interview observation, and psychological testing. Some children are aware of their difficulties in paying attention in class, others are not.

Behavior

The clinician describes the child's level of activity, affective expression, and mood. Psychomotor activity is observable in gait, posturing, mannerisms, and unusual bodily movement. Is the child agitated, hyperactive (i.e., speeded up), or hypoactive (i.e., slowed down)? Are there either excessive or decreased motor movements? Is there pacing, handwringing, tics, or unusual mannerisms?

Affective expression is the immediately visible and expressed emotion associated with an experience. Some readily observable affects include joy, anger, sadness, or anxiety. The range or continuum of affect goes from broad to flat.

- Broad affect is characterized by a normal fluctuation in the expression of emotion through the tone of verbalizations, variability in facial expressions, and appropriate gestures.
- Restricted affect is observable through a marked decrease in the availability and intensity of affect.
- Blunting of affect (e.g., in the severely depressed) presents with an extremely limited range of affective responses.
- Flat affect is seen in clients (e.g., in schizophrenics) who have no real affective responses. For example, responses to questions may be through a nod of the head. Verbalizations are monotone and with an absence of gesturing.

Whether it be appropriate, labile, or inappropriate, the quality of the affect must be described. Labile affect is noted through sudden and inexplicable changes in emotional expression. Affect is inappropriate when it is obviously contrary to the content of the situation or interview, conflicting with the child's mood, or discordant with the child's culture.

While affect is immediate, mood is pervasive and sustained. It colors the child's view of the world. Predominant moods are generally described as dysphoric, elated, euphoric, normal, expansive, irritable, or anxious. The clinician can both observe and directly question the child about mood. What is the depth, intensity, fluctuation, and duration of mood throughout the interview?

Speech and Language

A child's spontaneous speech is measured by its flow and quality. Variations in the rate of speech (slow, normal, pressured, or rapid) may indicate developmental, attention-deficit, anxiety, or mood disorders. Are the rhythm and clearness of speech normal or is there presence of stammering, stuttering, or slurring? Vocabulary and the amount of speech is correlated with the child's age, culture, and language acquisition. Are certain classes of words omitted? Is there an overabundance of simple nouns and verbs? The clinician notes the quality of speech through the quality of articulation, spontaneity, pitch, and production.

Receptive language is gauged through a child's understanding of complex directions. The clinical social worker may ask a child to complete a task that involves three sequential steps. Sometimes a teacher or parent will wonder about hearing or attention deficits in a child who seems not to understand such complex directions. Expressive language is assessed through the spoken and written word. Some children will be able to communicate verbally with seeming fluency; yet, when special attention is paid to grammar, syntax, and style, the examiner may wonder about an expressive language disability. Further evidence may be found in a disorganized writing style. When speech and language issues are noted by the clinical social worker, further testing for language disorders is indicated.

Thought

Ordinarily, children's stream of thought is organized, logical, and goal-directed. Their thinking can be followed and understood. Children with disturbances in thought process, however, may show abnormal patterns through circumstantiality, tangentiality, perseveration, looseness of associations, flight of ideas, thought-blocking, or neologisms.

- Circumstantial thought: The child has a definite point to make but only after a wandering narrative and many digressions.
- Tangential thinking: Goal-oriented associations are not present; thinking is rambling; the child is unable to get from point A to point B.
- Perseveration: The child repeats the same word or phrase over and over again, no matter what the question.
- Looseness of associations: The rapidly shifting flow of thought is loose, disjointed, and disorganized. The child thinks the comments make sense.
- Flight of ideas: There is a continuous flow of thought with sudden changes in ideas. It seems as if the person is responding to internal stimuli.
- Thought-blocking: The child is expressing a thought and stops in mid-sentence.
- Neologisms: New words are produced by the child for emotional reasons.

The content of thoughts is evaluated by its appropriateness to the situation. Certain thought-content patterns in children include irrational fears and phobias, preoccupation with unwelcome obsessional thoughts, repetitive rituals, somatic concerns, and feelings of inadequacy or guilt. Some children present with suicidal ideation and need to be questioned specifically about the content of such thoughts, whether there is a plan, and whether there have been prior attempts. Their thinking about death also needs to be explored. Similarly, homicidal thoughts, ideas, and plans need to be thoroughly examined. Some children get so mad they want "to kill" someone. What keeps them from doing it? Are they clear about the difference between thinking, fantasizing, and doing?

Other examples of abnormal thought content that cause significant concern are delusions and hallucinations. A delusion is a false, fixed belief that is maintained rigidly by the child, even in the face of firm evidence to the contrary. The three major types of delusion are somatic, grandiose, and paranoid. If the child responds positively to questioning about delusions, it is necessary to assess the type.

Hallucinations are characterized by hearing, seeing, feeling, or smelling things that are not really there. Correspondingly, the four types include auditory, visual, tactile, and olfactory. The clinician might begin the exploration by saying something like, "Sometimes kids' eyes or ears play tricks on them. Do you ever see or hear something that isn't really there?" Some youngsters will respond positively as they recall a dream or imaginary friend. Thus, it is obviously important to explore the nature of these occurrences in depth before pronouncing a child psychotic. It is also important to discern whether such sensory perception is an illusion in which something may be perceived or misinterpreted, such as the mirage of wet pavement on a sunny day.

Memory

Memory complaints can indicate an acute or chronic neurological condition caused by infection or brain tumors. They also may be indicative of substance or alcohol abuse, learning disorders, anxiety, attention deficits, mood disorders, and psychotic processes. Clinical social workers test four different kinds of memory: immediate, recent, recent past, and remote. Immediate memory retention and recall can be tested by walking into a room and saying, "Hi, I'm Ms. Smith. I'm going to say four words and ask you to repeat them in a minute and then again later. The words are house, scarf, cat, table." Then, Ms. Smith asks, "Now, what is my name?" Within a minute, she asks the child to repeat the words. This simple test is repeated again after five and ten minutes to test for recent memory. Most school-age children will remember three words. Another common test is the digit span, which also helps evaluate the child's attention. When asked to repeat a sequence of numbers, most school-age children can remember four to seven digits forward and backward.

Recent memory refers to recollections of the past few days. What did the child have for breakfast, lunch, and dinner yesterday? What did the child do in school? Can the child repeat the four words again? Because recent-past memory measures the child's recall over the past few months, the clinician might ask about the activities of a certain holiday. Remote memory is determined by youngsters' ability to recall the names of teachers from years ago. Can children remember their birthdate?

If children are found to have memory impairments, it is important to find out how they compensate for the deficit. They may pretend through denial that nothing is wrong or they may act out to cover up their problems.

Orientation

Along with memory, assessment of orientation is conducted to rule out organic brain disorders. Orientation is often ascertained without asking any questions. The clinical social worker needs to know if the child is oriented to time, person, place, and situation. Time is measured by the children's correct understanding of their age and the date, including day, month, and year. Younger children may be asked the day of the week or the time of day. Orientation to time is the first to go in brain disorder; the last to go is orientation to person; that is, in knowing who they are—name, age. Orientation to place is evidenced through knowledge of where they are—place, city, state. Orientation to situation is determined by children's understanding of why they are here. Some clinicians eliminate this last type of orientation because children may legitimately wonder why they are here.

Cognition

For purposes of the mental status exam, cognition is usually measured by testing for similarities, mathematical calculations, and proverbs. For example, children may be asked how an apple and an orange are alike to see if they understand similarities. Or, perhaps they may be asked about a desk and a chair, a monkey and a tree. Calculations are determined by answers to simple addition and subtraction problems. Older children can be asked to subtract 7 from 100 and then 7 from each subsequent answer. Younger children are asked to subtract by 3's. Proverbs are a little trickier because they are biased by culture. The cognition part of the mental status exam focuses on the level of concrete or abstract thinking. The clinician may ask the child to comment on the saying, "You can't judge a book by its cover" or "What goes around, comes around" or anything else that is age and culture appropriate.

Judgment and Insight

One outcome of this final part of the mental status exam is to gain an idea of the child's social judgment. Often, the history will suggest a certain level of judgment. Nevertheless, the clinical social worker might ask, "If you found a wallet with $100, what would you do with it?" or "If you found a stamped, addressed, sealed envelope, what would you do?" The other outcome is to gain a sense of the child's capacity for insight by figuring out whether the child recognizes the nature and degree of his or her own difficulty. Thus, the clinician asks what the child thinks the problem is. Does the child have any ideas about what will make it better? How upset is the child about the problem?

Further Diagnostic Examinations

Additional diagnostic workups by specialists are needed to confirm a clinical impression of learning disorders, neurological problems, or physical conditions. Consultations with physical, speech, or occupational therapists add to the data and help with service planning for some conditions. Psychoeducational testing is necessary for appropriate educational planning for the child with special learning needs. Psychiatric evaluation may be indicated to help with assessment of some conditions, as well as to assess the necessity of medication trials when medication may be indicated.

Case Formulation, Diagnosis, and Treatment Planning

DSM IV Diagnosis

Diagnosis of a mental disorder is tied to the symptom-cluster taxonomy of psychiatric disorders found in the *Diagnostic and Statistical Manual, IV* (American Psychiatric Association, 1994). Using this classification system, diagnosis is based on the following multiaxial system:

- Axis I: all clinical disorders including learning disorders and V Codes for other conditions, such as a parent/child problem that may be of concern
- Axis II: all personality disorders and mental retardation
- Axis III: any general medical conditions
- Axis IV: psychosocial stressors and environmental problems
- Axis V: measures the global assessment of psychological and social functioning on a mental illness/health continuum; the Global Assessment of Functioning (GAF) scale ranges from 0, inadequate information, to 50, serious symptoms, to 100, superior functioning

All five axes should be recorded. The confirmation of the diagnosis, including any comorbid disorders, is based on the chief complaint or symptom cluster, the personal history, the family history, the mental status exam, and any laboratory findings or testing. The treatment plan should reflect a biopsychosocial orientation. For example, the biological element might include a referral for medication or assessment; the psychological might include individual, parental, or family therapy; and the social might include school planning, social, and recreational supports.

Developmental Case Formulation

The developmental case formulation summarizes the findings of the biopsychosocial assessment by placing the child's current difficulty squarely in the context of his or her life experiences. Specifically, the formulation includes an interpretation of the current problem in which the child's symptoms are explained. The state of the child's maturational development is presented from biological, social, environmental, emotional, and cognitive perspectives. A summary of the psychodynamic factors is presented to facilitate understanding of the child's defenses and personality organization. There is also a formulation of current anxieties, areas of conflict, and intrapsychic strengths and weaknesses.

Children's basic character structure is reflected through their cognitive abilities; that is, their basic intelligence, judgment, and presence of representational thought. There is an explanation of the affective reactions that reveal how the child manages anxiety. There is an explanation of the child's social world, as mirrored in play and interactions with the clinical social worker. A description of the impact of any environmental forces on the child's current functioning is likewise delineated.

Treatment Plan

After completing both child and parent interviews, the clinical social worker meets with the parents to discuss the child's strengths and weaknesses. Beginning with the good points is helpful in assuring the parents that the clinician sees the whole child. It is also helpful to be reassuring about the parents' positive efforts in helping their child. Then the clinician discusses the child's difficulties and condition, including the causes when known, and the prognosis. The parents are encouraged to ask questions. Treatment recommendations and options are explained. The parents are encouraged to take their time in thinking about this and to call as they think of additional questions.

Biopsychosocial Assessment: Molly Jones by Marika Moore Cutler, M.S.W., LCSW-C

Presenting Problem

Molly is a nine-year-old who was referred by her divorced father's psychologist after Molly pleaded that she wanted to see a therapist because she was tired, missing school, and fearful of everything. She was extremely isolated, had academic difficulties, and complained that she couldn't remember things. Her only friend was her academically gifted and beautiful eleven-year-old sister, whom she hated. Recently, Molly stopped speaking to her father and refused to stay at his house.

Mr. and Ms. Jones, who had divorced when Molly was six years old, both appeared depressed as they recounted Molly's history and current difficulties. Father spoke of the divorce with tears streaming down his face, while mother listened with a blank expression. She explained that she had fallen out of love and told Mr. Jones to move out. He felt the children blamed him for the divorce because he was the one who actually left home. They were poor family historians, but agreed that Molly's problems stemmed from the separation and divorce.

When asked about academic performance, Ms. Jones did report that Molly currently has difficulty with math and English. She tests below grade level and has difficulty completing her homework "neatly." Molly does enjoy reading. Mr. Jones thought that Molly has difficulty expressing herself, often not knowing what to say. Ms. Jones stated that Molly does not make friends, seems withdrawn, and prefers mother's company.

Developmental History

Ms. Jones described Molly's birth as easy, following a four-hour labor. There were no reported pregnancy or neonatal difficulties. She was the 6 pound, 14 ounce, product of a nine-month gestation. From the beginning, Molly was fussy and eating too much. She was breast-fed until she was weaned to the bottle at four months, when mother returned to work. Mother did not remember if there were sleep problems until father recollected sleep disturbances in the form of constant awakening beginning at this time. Mother resented having to remain with Molly until she finally fell asleep, only to be awakened two hours later. Mr. Jones volunteered that Ms. Jones had postpartum depression following the birth of both children, which might explain her trouble remembering the early days. Because of Ms. Jones' depression, Mr. Jones enlisted the help of maternal grandmother, who was Molly's primary caregiver until she died following a prolonged illness when Molly was two. Thereafter, Molly was in four different daycare homes until she went to elementary school. Huge separation problems in the form of temper tantrums and hysterical crying were noted at this time. Either Molly stayed home or mother stayed with her through morning kindergarten.

Mother reported all developmental milestones to be within normal limits. Molly toilet-trained herself, although mother did not remember when this occurred. Father pointed out that Molly's language seemed unclear and delayed to him. Neither remembered when she started talking, although mother stated she used some words by one year. The parents were uncertain about her past and present grades in school. They denied any past or current psychiatric, medical, or school problems. They were not concerned about Molly's lack of friends.

Teacher Interview

Molly's fourth-grade teacher described her as a lonely child who did not volunteer to speak in class. Her mind seemed to wander aimlessly as she peered out the window. Once in a while, the teacher noticed a "weird smile." She did not have any behavior problems, although she spent considerable time in the nurse's office. Her grades were average, even though she was characterized as a poor student with organizational problems. She did have a hard time with transitions during the day. Her fine-motor skills were mildly impaired. Molly had never been referred for resource help or psychoeducational testing.

Family History

Mr. and Ms. Jones share joint custody of Molly and her only sibling, Andrea. They spend four days a week with their thirty-three-year-old mother and the remaining three with their fifty-three-year-old father. Mr. Jones, who has retired from the military, is currently employed as a computer operator. Ms. Jones works as a nurse. They met at an Army base party and married within six months. Mr. Jones was eager to marry quickly because of his advancing age and recent divorce. That marriage had produced three sons. He seemed to wish to replace this first family with a new one because his wife had sole custody of the children, whom he missed.

Mr. Jones was born and raised on a farm in Kansas. He is the second child with one older and one younger brother. His parents have been married for sixty years. Ms. Jones was born and raised in Pennsylvania. She is an only child. She recalls that her parents had a happy marriage until she was twenty-two. At that time, her mother suddenly left the family to live with her boyfriend. Ms. Jones didn't see her for six months and didn't know where she had gone. Her mother later married the boyfriend and reconciled with her daughter. Her mother died when she was twenty-six (Molly was two).

There is a history of depression in the families of both parents: alcohol and substance abuse in maternal grandfather, paternal grandfather, and uncle; bipolar illness in maternal grandmother.

Child Interview

I was immediately struck by Molly's masculine appearance when I first saw her in the waiting room. She was overweight and wore black hightops, mismatched socks, baggy pants, a black basketball jacket, and baseball cap. She had short, cropped hair. There were none of the feminine accessories usually seen in a girl of this age.

Molly entered the office holding her mother's hand. Ms. Jones asked if she should remain, but Molly said she would be okay. After mother left, I asked if Molly needed to have her mother present. She quickly answered, "No." She walked slowly with a shuffling gait and slumped comfortably into a chair. Then Molly started moving around a lot in the chair, displaying signs of agitation such as facial grimaces and ear-pulling. She did not maintain eye contact and appeared extremely self-conscious.

I began the interview by explaining I had met with her parents, who told me she really wanted to have someone to speak with about her fears. In a halting manner, Molly said, "Yes." I waited to see if she would elaborate, but sensed a tentative and held-back quality in her manner of relating. So I asked if she might like to tell me about some of them. She replied, "I'm afraid of everything." I suggested she might want to give me an example. "I'm afraid to be alone. I'm afraid to be away from my parents." She also worried that something would happen to her mother; that she wouldn't come back . . . that she'd get lost and "I will end up in an orphanage." Molly did not offer spontaneous verbalizations, even with encouragement. I suggested that she might like to play and showed her the toys. She looked around with a blank expression and said, "No." At about this time, she started rocking herself in the chair, her way of showing me that she was feeling uncomfortable. In an effort not to overwhelm her, I decided to provide more structure by being direct and concrete.

I asked her to tell me about her day. She couldn't remember. Instead, Molly offered that she hated school, especially the work. She was afraid she'd be killed or shot. She just wanted to grow up so there'd be no more school. I asked if there was anything she liked to do. Molly liked to stay home and watch television, especially one show about a man who has magical powers to make things happen. She wished to be this man because he is a hero and a genius. I commented, "So you've thought a lot about being this man." Then, she explained how she dreams about him and wants to be a boy. "I feel like a boy, always have. I wish I could play with boys. They have more fun." I replied, "I wonder what it would be like for you to be a boy." She explained she would be taller, smarter, and stronger, "So tall I would reach the sky and talk to the birds. And if I were a grownup boy, I wouldn't have to get married. I would be smart." Sometimes, she pretends, even thinks, she is this television character and gets a funny feeling between her legs.

"So you're all set to be a man," I opined. She said, "Well, I'd like to be a baby boy. That way my mom would have to stay home all day and take care of me. I'd like that." She started rocking and holding herself again as she continued,

"Yeah, this time my parents wouldn't get divorced. I wouldn't have a sister and I would be a boy." She began flexing her muscles as she looked at me for the first time. "I'd be like you. You're a boy." I replied, "That way I would understand how you must feel." Molly answered, "Right. I'm clairvoyant too. You're like me. My mother and father can read my thoughts too . . . that way I don't have to tell them nothing . . . they know how I feel. Like you. . . you can read my thoughts."

At this point, I decided it would be wise to reestablish reality and decrease her anxiety. So I changed the focus by suggesting she draw a picture of anything she liked. I explained that I was really interested in her thoughts, her feelings, and her drawings too. She walked over to the desk and asked for many directions about what kind of picture. I said anything she wanted would be just great. After much deliberation and with great hesitation, she finally drew a bleak, primitive, and stark picture of a boy lying on a bed in the nurse's office at school. My major concern was not the content, which would lead to further exploration, but the significant visual-motor deficits. There was a clear, organic component to the drawing. Her next two drawings of a person and then a house were equally limited. One was a stick figure of a boy with limbs but no other details. The house was a box with a triangle on top. Her fine-motor skills were seriously impaired as well. Her printing style when she wrote her name on the bottom of the drawing was similarly awkward. She was clearly self-conscious and feeling rather defeated by her efforts. I found myself thinking how sad and shocking it was that the school system had never identified any learning disabilities. Her low self-esteem and insecurity were clearly reflected in these drawings.

Because she had drawn the boy in the nurse's office at school, I inquired about his health, attempting to keep this line of exploration in a displaced-metaphor format. Molly explained that he had stomachaches and headaches everyday at school. The boy was hoping he would be sent home to his mother, where he could watch television. I agreed he probably loved television, but what about other things? Did he have any favorite books? He loved the *Hardy Boys*, just like she does. His favorite thing to do was to do nothing . . . just be lazy. He didn't have any friends at all. He did like to play with his dog and cat.

Because we were clearly in the realm of reality, I decided to go ahead with further exploration of her fantasy world through various projective techniques. She wants to be a policeman when she grows up. If she could have any three wishes in the whole world, she wished for all the money in the world to spend on boys' clothes because she hates dresses, to have a dog, and to live in a nice and peaceful place. The baby bird fell down and couldn't fly. If she could take just one person to a deserted island, she would take her cat.

Mental Status Exam

Molly is a nine-year-old, Caucasian, fourth-grade girl who was dressed in masculine attire. Throughout most of the interview, she evidenced psychomotor agitation through rocking, facial-grimacing, and ear-pulling. Her manner of relating was hesitant but compliant. In the beginning, she would answer questions with a simple yes or no. She seemed vulnerable and overly self-conscious. As time went on, she became more engaged, especially as she spoke of her fantasy world.

Molly was alert and oriented to time, place, and person. Most of the time, she was attentive to the content of the interview. However, when she experienced anxiety, she seemed distractible and retreated to the self-soothing behaviors of rocking and holding herself. Anxiety was the most notable affect that was expressed through psychomotor activity. There was a definite sadness about her demeanor, with a blunting of affect that limited her affective responses. Her affect was inappropriate to the content of the interview, especially when she was overly optimistic in talking about her parents' divorce and when she spoke with resolute conviction of being a boy or clairvoyant. Molly described her mood as sad most of the time. Her depressed mood is pervasive and penetrating. There is an emptiness that is pronounced. Her mood remained constant throughout the session.

At times, Molly was verbally noncommunicative with definite weaknesses in organization and in processing information. There was a paucity of vocabulary and limited amount of speech. She was especially hard-pressed to formulate speech on demand or process language in a logical and flexible way, difficulties that probably interfere with social interactions and academic expectations. Her expressive language is constrained and lacks the degree of creativity normally seen in a child of her age. Her written language, which was informally assessed when she wrote a five-sentence story, is lacking in organization and detail.

Usually, Molly's thought processes appeared intact and organized. Occasionally, she evidenced some tangential thinking with rambling thoughts that were not purposeful. Other times, there seemed to be a flight of ideas as she would change direction suddenly, as if responding to some internal thoughts. Thought content was negative for obsessions, illusions, suicidal or homicidal ideations, and compulsions. She denied hallucinations and delusions, but there was a clear blurring of fantasy and reality. Molly's thought content was positive for many pronounced fears, somatic complaints that cause her to stay home from school, and feelings of worthlessness, especially regarding her gender identity and intelligence.

Despite Molly's complaints about memory, her immediate and recent memory were normal with a digit span of five digits forward and backward. She could recall three words at one and five minutes, and two words at twenty minutes. There were some impairments in recent past memory having to do more with her depression than an underlying neurological condition. Remote memory was normal.

Her cognition, as tested through similarities, calculations, and proverbs, was impaired. Serial 7's could not be done, so she was asked for serial 3's, which she was unable to do. She did complete serial 2's back to 90. There was limited understanding of similarities and impaired ability for proverbs. Her intelligence appeared to be in the low-average range, with the probability of a significant learning disability that is not caused by emotional factors.

Molly's judgment and insight also were impaired, especially concerning the nature of her difficulties. However, she did evidence good judgment in asking her parents to bring her to therapy. She readily acknowledged some of her fears, but was unable to voice her discomfort about other issues.

Further Diagnostic Studies

Psychological testing is recommended to determine the presence of perceptual-motor, particularly visual-motor, learning disabilities. Specific language subtests will be requested. Projective testing is necessary to rule out psychotic processes and to better understand her gender confusion.

A psychiatric consultation will be requested to see if a trial of medication is warranted to help treat her depression, especially given the depression patterns on both sides of her family and possible biological involvement.

DSM IV Diagnosis

Axis I: Dysthymia, 300.4, early onset, severe

Gender-identity disorder in children 302.6

Rule out specific learning disorders

Axis II: No diagnosis V 71.09

Axis III: None

Axis IV: Divorce of parents three years ago

Inadequate social supports

Academic difficulties

Axis V: GAF (current) 40

Developmental Case Formulation

Molly presents as a youngster who is compromised along several developmental lines, including gender identity formation, cognition, language, motor, and separation/individuation. Her long-standing depression is a reflection of both the biological and emotional factors that have impinged on her development. Her significant learning disabilities have not been addressed and have resulted in her social isolation, poor academic performance, and low self-esteem.

She does not have a clear sense of who she is or where she is going. The important people in her life, including her mother, father, teacher, and therapist, are experienced as symbiotic mothers who can read her thoughts and feelings. Molly does not evidence a joyful mirroring of relationships but rather the depressed constricted affect that was clearly present during the evaluation. Because of her mood, temperament, and maternal depression, Molly has not been able to elicit empathic responses from others. She has not acquired the capacity for self/other differentiation, nor is she able to firmly distinguish fantasy from reality. Her untapped potential for play leaves her on the solitary level of sensorimotor play as she self-soothes through rocking and self-holding. She is unable to represent her affective world through logic or play. Instead, she imagines herself to be fused with a caring adult through incorporation as she rekindles pregenital conflict. At the same time, she wants to know everything and nothing; yearns to be both autonomous and dependent; wants to be a baby and an adult; and ultimately, to be a girl and, then a boy.

The cognitive processes of language, memory, and thought are not appropriately available as Molly struggles to cope with her internal and external worlds. Her capacity for meaningful social interaction is seriously jeopardized as she retreats into magic, fantasy, and social isolation. She yearns for an empathic environment that will address her needs both at school and at home. It appears that mother was psychologically absent most of Molly's life. However, with the breakup of the marriage, Molly's father became more involved in her care. Molly experiences abandonment by her father. She defends against these troubling feelings by turning passive into active as she now attempts to reject father, while at the same time identifying with him as she desires to be a boy. There are significant biological concerns that present as low-average intelligence, learning disabilities, very concrete thinking, and no creativity. While her cognition seems to fall into the preoperational stage normally seen in two- to four-year-olds, there is limited capacity for symbolic activity and make-believe play. This deficit undermines her reality testing.

Her therapy will need to be geared to developing her mental processes to enhance skill maturation and cognitive growth. Therapy will be conducted in the context of a trusting relationship, where she can use fantasy and play as she learns to represent her life in symbolic ways.

Treatment Recommendations

When I met with Mr. and Ms. Jones to interpret the results of the evaluation, I began by addressing Molly's strengths. I noted how much I enjoyed getting to know Molly and that I found her to be a very pleasant child. She was gentle, cooperative, and kind-hearted. I was impressed with her request for help and with their efforts to secure it. I then agreed that she did, indeed, have multiple fears and that the divorce had been problematic for her. But I also had other concerns and questions that I wanted to discuss with them. I started with her low academic performance and noted her difficulties with fine-motor and perceptual tasks. She had spoken of her love of reading, but showed visible distress when asked to draw a picture. Perhaps this is why it takes her so long to complete her homework in an organized way. I thought it necessary to have further testing done because of the likelihood of learning disabilities that were interfering with her educational progress. I also thought they could be impacting on her ability to make friends because she had difficulty expressing herself and reading the social cues and nuances of her contemporaries. The parents were cooperative and agreed to pursue testing. We wondered together why the school had not addressed this issue earlier. They were relieved to know that appropriate help was available.

I attempted to elicit some empathy as we discussed Molly's depression and her need for psychotherapy in which she could establish a trusting relationship with an adult to discuss her worries and fears. I also noted my concern that Molly didn't seem to enjoy pretend play and noted that we would also work on that. The father seemed to identify strongly with Molly's inadequacies and readily agreed to twice-weekly therapy. Mother was less certain, but agreed to give it a try.

Because the parents did not voice any concerns about gender identity during their first interview, I asked how they saw Molly's view of herself as a girl. They readily acknowledged that since the age of two, she has talked about wanting to be a boy. Frequently, she would say, "I am a boy." I asked about nudity in the home and learned that father walked around naked and bathed the girls. I firmly suggested that he put a stop to both the nudity and bathing, which he agreed to do. I then asked about any games or toys she enjoyed playing. She would play Barbie dolls with her older sister. In this play, Molly often took the part of Ken. She also liked to play with transformers and G.I. Joe.

Before delineating the treatment options, I asked if they had any questions. Father asked whether he should force Molly to visit him when she was supposed to. I thought he might want to respect her opinion about this until we had a chance to get under way in therapy. A possible compromise could be that she wouldn't have to spend the night, but they could do something fun together during the day. We then talked about ways to help Molly develop age-appropriate interests, like soccer or Girl Scouts, outside the home. Mr. Jones then asked if I had any other suggestions, so I went over the following recommendations:

- Twice-weekly developmental play therapy
- Biweekly concurrent parent sessions
- Psychological testing to determine the nature of possible learning disabilities, including projective testing to better understand her internal world
- Referral to a child psychopharmacologist for a trial of antidepressant medication
- Consultation with school personnel to begin the process of educational evaluation for appropriate educational placement and programming
- Tutorial support
- Extracurricular activities to foster social-skills development and friendships

Before Mr. and Ms. Jones left the office, we scheduled twice-weekly appointments (that were to continue for four years).

Conclusion

The biopsychosocial assessment of the child focuses on the developmental progression of biological maturation, cognitive growth, social relatedness, emotional issues, and environmental factors. They are intertwined and represent the child's internal and external worlds. Developmental delays, disruptions, or distortions are measured through the mental status exam during the child's interview. Fantasy material is elicited through projective questions and the displaced format of play.

These variables, along with the developmental history given by the parents, school observation, teacher interview, and pediatric consultation, are then assessed according to expectable age, gender, and cultural norms. The developmental lines as outlined by A. Freud, Mahler, Piaget, and Erikson help determine whether stage-specific expectations are currently being met. All of the data are gathered, organized according to the checklist in Table 7.1, and analyzed to come up with a diagnosis, case formulation, and appropriate treatment plan for this child.

TABLE 7.1   Child Assessment Interview Checklist

    I. Initial Observation
        A. Level of activity, motor capabilities, and physical appearance
        B. Separation from mother
   II. Presenting Problem and Reason for Referral
  III. Choice of Play Materials
  IV. Child's Thinking and Feeling about Environment
    V. Exploration of Fantasy
        A. Controlled and free-play scenarios
        B. Dreams and daydreams
        C. Three wishes and who/what wish to be when grown
        D. Happiest and unhappiest times
        E. Earliest memory
        F. Fables, storytelling, writing, television, movies, music
        G. Drawings (free, self, house, family)
        H. Favorite age and why
  VI. Mental Status Exam
        A. General description
            1. Physical appearance (size, coloring, hair, distinguishing physical traits, clothing, grooming)
            2. Manner of relating
        B. Level of consciousness: alert, lethargic, stuporous, coma
        C. Attention: distractible, inattentive, or difficulty with concentration
        D. Behavior
            1. Psychomotor activity
                a. Hyperactive, hypoactive, agitated
                b. Gait, posture, mannerisms, unusual motor movements
            2. Affect
                a. Range of affect: broad, restricted, blunted, flat
                b. Quality of affect: appropriate, labile, inappropriate
            3. Mood
                a. Kind: dysphoric, elated, euphoric, normal, expansive, irritable, anxious
                b. Depth, intensity, fluctuation, duration
        E. Speech and Language
            1. Spontaneous speech through flow and quality
            2. Rate of speech: slow, normal, pressured, rapid

3. Rhythm and clarity
4. Receptive language
5. Expressive language
F. Thought
  1. Thought process: circumstantial, tangential, perseveration, looseness of associations, flight of ideas, thought-blocking, neologisms, other
  2. Thought content
    a. Obsessions, rituals, fears and phobias, somatic concerns, feelings of inadequacy, guilt
    b. Suicidal/homicidal ideation and/or plan
    c. Delusions, hallucinations
    d. Thought appropriate to situation
G. Memory: immediate, recent, recent past, remote
H. Orientation: time, place, person, situation
I. Cognition: similarities, calculations, proverbs
VII. Further Diagnostic Studies
VIII. DSM IV Diagnosis
IX. Developmental Formulation
X. Treatment Plan (and Parent Interpretation)

PART THREE

Alternative Model

8 Integrating Cognitive-Behavioral Theory with Play Therapy: An Alternative Model

BY BARBARA PEO EARLY, D.S.W., LCSW

Clinical social workers have an opportunity to create an alternative model of play therapy with children that reframes and blends the social work tradition of the person-in-environment paradigm with newly developing knowledge within the profession about the strengths perspective. In the person-in-environment paradigm, the fit of child clients with their social and physical environment is a central concern. In the strengths perspective paradigm (Saleebey, 1996, 1997; Weick and Saleebey, 1998), social workers seek and build on their child clients' existing capacities and both personal and social resources. For clinical social workers who wish to build a play therapy model that anchors child treatment in these two interlocking paradigms, a cognitive-behavioral conceptual framework is useful. Although weak in addressing children's psychosocial development, cognitive and behavioral theories provide the conceptual means to reframe and firmly establish social work's contribution of the person-in-environment and strengths perspectives to work with children.

This chapter first traces the roots of cognitive and behavioral theories and notes their current application with children. Then it integrates these theories into a strengths-oriented model of clinical social work with childhood problems. The model is illustrated through four case vignettes.

From the Roots of Cognitive and Behavioral Theories to Current Application to Children

Cognitive therapy with adults has gained favor among mental health practitioners over the past generation. The work of Beck (1979) in psychiatry and Ellis (Dryden and Ellis, 1988) in psychology has introduced cognitive theory to the practice of outpatient psychotherapy with adults who experience a variety of disorders, from depression to anxiety to substance abuse (Beck, 1979; Beck, Rush, Shaw, and Emory, 1979; Beck, Wright, Newman, and Leise, 1993). With children, social learning theory and behavioral analysis and therapy have dominated the fields of special education and residential treatment (Ayllon and Azin, 1968; Braukmann and Wolf, 1987; Phillips, 1968). While slower to embrace these conceptual frameworks than their colleagues in psychology and education, clinical social workers have begun to incorporate behavioral (Gambrill, 1995; Stuart, 1996; Thyer, 1989; Thyer and Wodarski, 1990) and cognitive theories (Granvold, 1996; Nurius and Berlin, 1994) into clinical work with adults and families.

Further, some specific cognitive techniques originally designed for adults, such as thought records, are also being used with children with internalizing disorders (Braswell and Kendall, 1988). Other cognitive methods, such as problem solving and self-instructional training (Meichenbaum, 1971), have been aimed at teaching children with externalizing disorders to develop cognitive mediating strategies where none existed before. Behavioral techniques, especially contingency management, modeling, and role playing, are used to encourage children to learn new adaptive behavioral patterns that compete with their less adaptive ones.

Although these and other tools from cognitive and behavioral therapies have been drawn into therapeutic child work, child therapists—with rare exceptions (Knell, 1996)—have failed to integrate this knowledge and technique into play therapy methods with preschool and school-age children. If play therapy is to better reflect social work's traditional person-in-environment and emerging strengths perspectives, then cognitive and behavioral theories should be integrated not just into adjunctive work with parents and consultative work with teachers or residential staff, but also into the direct therapeutic model itself. For example, behavioral techniques, especially those based on the reinforcement aspects of operant conditioning, are inherently interactive and designed to facilitate change, not just change in the office or playroom, but also change *in vivo*, in everyday life. Thus, parents or caregivers, other family members, and teachers who represent a child's natural environment are integral to the treatment. Similarly, any changes in thought or behavior may be enhanced by the therapeutic context of strength. The paradigm shift in the profession toward constructivism and the use of the narrative is particularly appropriate within the creative thinking and imaginative play of the child. Thus, cognitive and behavioral theories provide the conceptual framework for this traditional yet emerging platform and add a uniquely social work foundation to play therapy.

A Conceptual Context for Understanding Cognitive and Behavioral Theories: A Cyclical Model

Cognitive and behavioral theories and therapies have become lumped together as cognitive-behavioral. However, cognitive and behavioral theories reflect two very different philosophical origins and, therefore, two very different ways of understanding behavior and of viewing change. Because each informs clinical social work in general and play therapy with children in particular, it is important to understand their distinct conceptual foundations.

A common conceptual context for this understanding is characterized by a behavioral social worker, Richard Stuart (1996). He describes a cyclical model of human behavior in which (1) thoughts and feelings give rise to (2) behavior, which leads to (3) intended or unintended social experiences or consequences. These social experiences, in turn, trigger subsequent thoughts and feelings, and so on. While Stuart says that all social and psychological systems accept this explanation of human functioning, he notes that they differ in their emphasis and in where in the cycle of thoughts, feelings, behavior, and social consequences a helping person should enter to facilitate change.

One View of Change: Information Theories and Therapies

One broad category of theories, known as information theories, assumes that the most salient explanation of behavior is the thoughts and feelings that underlie it. As a result of social experiences earlier in life, a person responds with patterns of thoughts and feelings, often unavailable to consciousness, that influence behavior. It is the lack of awareness of the thoughts and feelings that inhibits change. Once persons understand their thoughts and feelings through the intervention of a helping person (whether a therapist or friend), they will experience a change of behavior and find their social environment responds differently. Thus, the information therapist intervenes in the cycle at the point of the thoughts and feelings and seeks the *why* of behavior. Change comes through information or insight. Insight into thoughts and feelings leads to change in maladaptive behaviors.

Certainly, the therapeutic models that derive from psychoanalytic theory are the most typical information therapies. However, because cognitive theory is also an information theory, its therapeutic models also fall within the information therapy tradition. The cognitive therapist is mainly concerned with the thoughts of the client and pays less attention to behavior, except as a measure of change in thoughts or cognitions. To facilitate change, cognitive therapists enter the cycle at the point of mediating thoughts. They help clients to examine and restructure their thoughts. Then the feelings and behavior change as a result.

Basic Concepts of Cognitive Theory.   In cognitive theory, "We are what we think. If we are to feel or do things differently, we must come to think differently." Thus, the most central concept of cognitive theory is the mediational model (Dobson and Block, 1988), which assumes that cognitive activity mediates between the events that occur in a person's environment and the emotional or behavioral responses that follow. Unlike with psychoanalytic theory, it is assumed that cognitive activity is available to the conscious mind and that this activity is amenable to change at the willing of the person. Therefore, changes in behavior or feelings may be effected by changing or reconstructing the mediating thoughts. The cognitive theorist believes that the ways that persons attend to, store, and interpret information become the filters or lenses that focus their understanding of the world. Therefore, observation is subjective; that is, subject to the biases of the observer. For example, a youngster who is ill and exposed to painful medical procedures comes to interpret such interventions as dangerous and begins to feel fear, an affective response that resulted from the cognitive mediation of the painful stimuli. In this situation, it is the thinking more than the procedures that triggers the fear response. For this child no longer to feel fear in the face of similar medical procedures, she must come to interpret the feared stimulus differently.

A second central concept in cognitive theory is the interfering presence of cognitive distortions. Beck (1979), for example, described depression as a thinking disorder. To him, depressive affect was the result of negative cognitions within the cognitive triad of a person's views of self, world, and future. Thus, from a cognitive intervention perspective, a therapist should seek a client's views of self, world, and future to help challenge and replace distorted views with more accurate ones. Ellis (Dryden and Ellis, 1988), too, says persons disturb themselves and identifies the major contributor to disturbed feelings as *musturbation* or a tendency to believe that things must or should be a certain way. He suggests that to feel better, a person must let go of the *shoulds* that dominate feelings. The philosophy of preference replaces the philosophy of desire. Cognitive restructuring, therefore, involves a conscious change in thinking, which results from either looking at the evidence for certain conclusions and considering alternative explanations, or accepting the conclusion but seeking the meaning behind it.

A Second View of Change: Action Theories

The other broad category of theories of human behavior is action theories (Stuart, 1996), which focus on the maintaining role of the social consequences that precede or follow behavior. The therapist intervenes directly at the point of behavior or by helping the client set up systems to manipulate the social experiences in order to encourage different action. Although the presence of thoughts and feelings is acknowledged by the action therapist, they are viewed as of little importance to the change process. Change comes through different action. From the action theory perspective, insight is not necessary.

Structural and strategic family therapies may be considered action therapies. For example, a family therapist may interpret the interactional patterns of behavior within a family in order to encourage new patterns to emerge, regardless of the *why* of the thinking and feeling behind them. The most obvious example of the action therapist, however, is the behavioral therapist. In behavioral therapy, it is assumed that some experiences trigger predictable behavior; that is, the stimulus-response paradigm of reflexive behavior. The other major paradigm of behavioral theory involves the notion that many voluntary or operant behaviors are maintained by the experiences or consequences that follow. Thus, the behavioral therapist intervenes at the point of the social experiences in the action cycle that either precede or follow a behavior in an attempt to stimulate or reinforce new behaviors. In action therapy, it is the change in action that ultimately can change thoughts and feelings.

Basic Concepts of Behavioral Theory.   Behavioral theory and its more contemporary sister, social learning theory (Bandura, 1977), explain human functioning in terms of observable behavior that is learned: "We are what we do. Thus, to change who we are, we must change what we do."

Applied behavioral analysis, behavior modification, or behavioral therapy presents approaches and techniques for practitioners to use to help clients unlearn maladaptive behaviors and to learn new positive behaviors or skills that are incompatible with the maladaptive ones. Thus, unlearning and learning are done through various forms of contingency management, in which the relationship between actions and the maintaining contingencies in the environment are rearranged (Gambrill, 1994).

Behaviors are learned through various means: respondent conditioning, operant conditioning, and modeling. Each of these three forms of learning reflects a separate historical, theoretical, and empirical root, and each has distinct methods of change associated with it.

Respondent Conditioning. Early in the twentieth century, Russian physiologist Pavlov (1927) described reflex or respondent behavior as involuntary responses driven by the central nervous system rather than the skeletal muscles. Respondent behaviors depend on the stimuli that precede them. A behavior is elicited by stimulus changes in the environment. Pavlov's dog salivated when presented with meat. This reflex behavior in itself was not learned; rather, it was an instinctive automatic reflex. However, animals and humans can learn to emit the same reflex behavior in response to a formerly neutral stimulus in the environment through pairing. Pavlov noted that a dog that involuntarily salivated on seeing food could learn or be conditioned to salivate when exposed to a formerly neutral stimulus, a bell tone, through the process of respondent conditioning (sometimes known as classical conditioning). Repeatedly pairing the sound of a bell with the presentation of meat to the dog would eventually come to elicit salivation when presented by itself without the meat. Thus, the dog has been taught to salivate. In this manner, respondent conditioning creates a conditioned or learned stimulus for the response. By pairing a neutral stimulus with a natural eliciting stimulus several times, the previously neutral stimulus will come to elicit the same response; therefore, it becomes a conditioned stimulus.

In more human terms, clinical social workers work with clients who are distressed about affects; for example, fear and anger. These affects also may be described as respondent behaviors. From a behavioral point of view, the young child who was hospitalized for pneumonia with painful medical treatments responded with fear. These painful medical treatments (natural stimuli for fear) were administered by white-coated medical professionals in a hospital with specific sounds and odors (neutral stimuli). Later and for many years, this child felt fear when she came into contact with people in white coats or smelled the smells associated with hospitals. She had become conditioned to fear white coats, hospital smells, and so on. Unlike the cognitive theorist who emphasized the role of thought, the behaviorist sees a reflexive response to pain paired with a neutral stimulus.

Several behavioral techniques developed to facilitate change have been based on the concept of respondent conditioning, or deconditioning. Systematic desensitization, in which a person is gradually exposed to the feared stimulus, or pairing the feared stimulus with a competing state of relaxation tend toward reducing the power of the conditioned stimulus to elicit the fear response (respondent extinction).

Operant Conditioning.   Operant behavior is voluntary behavior of the skeletal muscles with which persons choose to operate on their environment. The acquiring of operant behavior depends on the reinforcing consequences that follow it. Thorndike (1933) articulated the law of effect that an act may be altered in its strength by its consequence.

In operant conditioning, new operant behaviors can be taught or, more accurately, their probability may be increased by manipulating the reinforcing consequences that follow. Skinner (1953) demonstrated this principle with his Skinner Box, in which a white rat learns to press a lever because that behavior is followed by the release of a food pellet. Skinner observed that the rate of a behavior may be increased or decreased by altering the consequences of that behavior.

Various methods of reinforcement increase or decrease the probability of operant behaviors. Positive reinforcement increases behavior by applying a positive or pleasant consequence; negative reinforcement increases it by removing an aversive consequence. Behavior is decreased in probability through removal of reinforcing consequences (extinction), through removal of an object or privilege (response cost), or through punishment.

Modeling.   The third and last form of learning is observational learning or modeling. Bandura (1977) rounded out understanding of behavior and learning by adding what may seem obvious—that human beings and other higher animals also learn operant behavior through the process of imitation or modeling. This concept is important for social work because it further solidifies the importance of the social environment in understanding and helping people change. Social learning theory suggests that conditioning of operant behavior need not be directly reinforced but may take place vicariously. That is, a person may observe another being reinforced or punished and, therefore, change his or her behavior accordingly. Observation may be direct, as in witnessing the dire results of drinking and driving, or more abstract, such as through reading or watching a video. Modeling is the basis for change through mentoring, role modeling, and much teaching.

Integrating Cognitive and Behavioral Theories into Clinical Social Work with Childhood Problems

The Strengths Perspective

The strengths perspective deemphasizes attention to pathology and emphasizes a risk and resiliency paradigm. Cognitive-behavioral theory can further this value through its portrayal of human problems. Cognitive-behavioral treatment models avoid using terms such as *disorder* or describing difficulties as individual traits or characteristics; rather, the focus is problem behaviors. Behavior is viewed broadly as encompassing both overt easily observable behavior and covert behavior that includes thoughts, feelings, and physiological responses. Braswell and Kendall (1988) provide a useful typology of child problems by dividing them into:

- *internalizing behaviors:* mainly covert, including depression, guilt, somatizing, and anxiety
- *externalizing behaviors:* such as aggressive or violent actions, overactivity, and impulsive behaviors

The authors point out that internalizing problem behaviors result in part from distorted mediating thoughts. This explanatory concept is familiar in adult therapy. People who are depressed are seen to have deeply held negative beliefs within the cognitive triad or views of self, world, and future (Beck, 1979). On the other hand, externalizing problem behaviors result in part from a deficiency of verbal mediating thoughts. Rather than thinking negatively, children who act out fail to think. For these children, problematic action results from a lack of intervening thought.

Because internalizing behaviors are associated with cognitive distortion, it is appropriate to use techniques such as self-monitoring, cognitive restructuring, behavioral activation, and skill-building with the overall objective of disputing and restructuring distorted thinking. Externalizing behaviors that result from cognitive deficiency require cognitive coping skills and reinforcement strategies with two overall objectives. First, the therapist wishes to help the child slow down the process by introducing thinking where there is only impulse. Second, the therapist encourages the direct decrease of maladaptive behaviors and the strengthening of adaptive ones.

Person-in-Environment

A basic tenet of social work is the understanding of people as inextricably embedded in their social and natural environments. This tenet is especially true for young children who, despite their circumstances, live with some family structure, be it their biological or adoptive families or others who represent family to them. They live with parents, grandparents, foster parents, or the group parents of a group home, to name a few. Indeed, much of a child's life is shaped by teachers in schools, nurses, and therapists in hospital settings, or counselors in residential treatment centers.

Given children's embeddedness in their familial and educational environments, parent work and teacher consultation are viewed as integral aspects of the child work, in that all are part of the same client system. This contemporary view of child-in-environment is consistent with social work valuing of strengths and resiliency, keeps the child and family together within the client system, and expands the view of client to include the resources of the family and immediate environment.

Client Self-Determination

Perhaps the most fundamental value of the social work profession is the support of the self-determination of the client. Here, the constructivist paradigm—in which cognitive theory is based—becomes most useful. In this paradigm, the person constructs reality. Thus, there is no one, true, stable reality, but rather many realities reflecting the different views of various individuals—and it is the client's reality from which the social worker works.

Understanding the conceptual basis for this stance requires understanding the constructivist view of mind. Granvold (1996) characterizes constructivism as a motor theory of the mind, a theory in which the mind is an active, constructive system. Most theorists would agree that the mind produces output; however, in the motor theory of the mind, the mind produces input as well. That is, the interior structures, built from a person's earlier experience, filter and interpret information from the environment. Berlin (1996) further expands this view by describing human beings as essentially meaning-makers. Our cognitive structures produce cognitive products that reflect individual, family, cultural, and societal thinking patterns. Not surprisingly, two individuals such as therapist and client may see the world in very different ways by imposing entirely different meanings on the same event.

Thus, cognitive-behavioral theory provides a conceptual foundation for three social work principles: strengths, person-in-environment, and client self-determination. From these conceptual underpinnings, the clinical social worker expands the cognitive-behavioral model of child therapy by moving through the social work processes, from engagement through treatment and evaluation.

The Model

Engagement in the Therapeutic Relationship and Problem Identification

The initial stages of clinical social work involve engagement of the client in a therapeutic relationship and coming to a shared understanding of some problem. To build that relationship, a cognitive-behavioral social worker takes a collaborative role, in which she explains her method to the client. Social workers often find themselves working with mandated clients with whom they must first seek a shared reality in problem definition and perhaps broaden their view of the client system.

The cognitive-behavioral therapist begins work with a child client by supporting the child's self-determination and attempts to view the world through the child's eye by avoiding the role of adult expert. That is, the clinician avoids the role in which the therapist has knowledge that the child and parent do not have or of which they do not have conscious awareness. Instead, the cognitive-behaviorist takes on a collaborative role. Such a shift in thinking is difficult enough when the therapist and client are both adults. When the client is a child, however, and inherently less powerful than the adult therapist, the child's inevitable transference may place the therapist in the parent role. To counterbalance this difficulty, cognitive-behavioral therapists describe their view of the therapeutic relationship as an educative experience, thereby diminishing the importance of transference to primary relationships in their model of therapy. That is, the therapist would encourage the child to relate more as child to teacher than as child to parent. Thus, although the power relationship is still unequal, the familiar but more distant relationship expectations of the teacher role diminish the emotional nature of the relationship.

One way that the collaborative and educative role is developed in the engagement phase of cognitive-behavioral therapy with adults is in explaining the method. Therapists are careful to explain their understanding of what triggers and maintains problematic behavior. That is, they explain the environmental triggers and reinforcers of overt behavior or of internalized cognitive structure and patterns. They also explain what they intend to do to facilitate change and why these techniques should work. The objective of insisting on "no mystery to the method" is no different in the initial work with a youngster or an adult. The only change is to aim the explanation at a level of understanding appropriate to the age and developmental level of the child.

For the youngest clients of between three and six or seven, the explanation may be nothing more than saying, "Mommy is worried that you are sad" or "Your teacher tells me that you get pretty upset with your friends in school and she wants you to learn how to put on your brakes." Older children are fully capable of understanding that reinforcement provides "something in it for me" as they take on new behaviors, even when they have not progressed to age-appropriate levels of cognitive or moral development. Also, they can be taught by the therapist about the fascinating inner dialogue of thoughts that mediate between events in their world and the feelings and behaviors they display.

Further, a clinician's approach to any new client, young or old, depends on some level of shared understanding of the presenting problem and the motivation of the client to change it. While social workers have long worked with mandated clients, they sometimes fail to understand that, for the most part, all children are mandated clients. Braswell and Kendall (1988, p. 170) say, "adults tend to seek care for conditions that are causing pain to themselves . . . children are most likely to be brought into care when they display behaviors that are causing pain or irritation to the adults in their lives." If a clinical social worker has been open and honest about her understanding of the problem for which the concerned adult has brought the child for treatment and yet the child initially sees the situation differently, then it is imperative for the clinician to gain an understanding of the child client's cognitive schemata that comprise that child's world view. The child's view then can be compared to the views of others who have authority over him or her. Engagement with a reluctant child client may be illustrated with the case example of Miranda.

Engagement in Relationship and Problem Identification with a Child Client with Internalizing Problem Behaviors: Miranda.   Ten-year-old Miranda was referred to a clinical social worker at the community mental health center by the teacher in Miranda's Gifted and Talented class. She and the other teachers were concerned because Miranda was extraordinarily slow in her classroom work production and completed very little of her homework. This behavior was reflected in a flat grade trajectory that hovered close to but never quite at failure.

Miranda presented herself as sophisticated and detached from peers. She bristled at the teachers' offers of help, saying, "I know how to do that." Psychological testing at the age of seven revealed a child with superior intellectual ability overall and very superior verbal cognitive ability, but substantial weakness in nonverbal cognitive functioning. She was also found to be distractible and have low frustration tolerance. Thus, she had been receiving learning disabilities support for her visual-spatial skills. Over time, the intensity of her work with the learning-disabilities teacher had steadily decreased while her time in the Gifted and Talented Program had increased. In short, her learning-disabilities teacher surmised, "I don't know what Miranda's problem is at this point, but I do know it is not learning disabilities."

The assessment concluded that Miranda's problem behaviors were largely internalizing ones. She worried about not finishing school. Her adaptive behaviors were weak and infrequent. Because it is assumed that internalizing behaviors are associated with cognitive distortion and that these cognitive distortions are amenable to monitoring and restructuring, reaching the point of uncovering those thoughts depends on the building of a relationship and on the coming together of a common understanding of the problem.

Building a relationship with Miranda was a challenge. When first approached by the clinical social worker, Miranda answered questions in a cryptic monotone. She described herself as "an average student with an average amount of work completed in an average amount of time." While her parents were very concerned, Miranda was not.

Establishing an educative role with a child client is aided by the strong presence of teachers in children's lives. The therapist is often seen as another 'special' teacher who comes to take a student from class. Establishing a collaborative relationship, however, is often made more difficult due to the hierarchical nature of the school organization and the lack of choice children have about who their teachers are. Once the social worker explained clearly to Miranda that her only reason for interacting with her was to help her behave differently, it was important to determine a collaborative goal that would be accomplished by such a change in behavior—one that could be shared by Miranda and the parents, teachers, and clinical social worker. It seemed essential to explore the underlying cognitive schemata that comprised Miranda's world view so that it might be challenged.

Berlin (1996) describes human beings as essentially meaning-makers. Because of their internal patterns of thinking, individuals filter and interpret information from the environment in different ways. Miranda and the adults in her life interpreted the information about her behavior and her performance quite differently. Her mother saw Miranda as depressed and thus unable to do her work. Her teachers thought that she was afraid to fail. Miranda, however, thought differently. While often adult clients are simply asked for their interpretation of a situation like Miranda's, children tell their stories in less direct ways. Freedman and Combs describe the danger of interfering with a client story:

> When therapists listen to people's stories with an ear to "making an assessment" or "taking a history of illness" or "offering an interpretation," they are approaching people's stories from a modernist, "structuralist" world view. In terms of under-standing an individual person's specific plight or joining her in her world view, this approach risks missing the whole point. (1996, p. 31)

The initial stage of establishing the relationship and defining the problem—or the meaning of the problem—involved simply allowing Miranda to "story." Within a short time, Miranda revealed the following:

> Once on a time, there was a microwave oven. Microwave ovens are those things that can produce a lot of heat, but they always stay cool. The microwave worked very well until one day. Each time it was turned on, it turned off. The repairman was called to take a look at it. He checked the wires, but they were fine. He checked the switches and they weren't fine. The heat sensor was turning the oven off. It was supposed to turn off the oven if things begin to get too hot. If it didn't, the oven would break down or blow up.

While all three were interpretations of reality—depression, fear of failure, and damaged machinery, it was Miranda's interpretation that provided the clue for the thinking patterns that drove the angry feelings and avoidance behavior. With this understanding of Miranda's underlying self-view, distorted automatic thoughts, such as "Learning-disabled kids can't do that," became readily available for challenging and restructuring.

Assessment, Goal-Setting, and Intervention

Perhaps more essential than any other aspect of clinical social work treatment from a cognitive-behavioral view is the emphasis on clarity of assessment and defining of objectives in observable, measurable, and behavioral terms. Following this assessment and goal-setting process is an emphasis on monitoring and mea-suring progress. This empirical focus derives from the positivist paradigm and reflects the positivist foundation of behavioral but not cognitive theory. From the positivist perspective, reality constructs the person (Goldstein, 1990), as may be seen by the "bucket theory of mind" (Granvold, 1996). That is, information from one true external reality flows into the mind from the senses. There it is maintained as is, deposited in a bucket and unchanged by that bucket.

Behaviorists emphasize that current behavior, while it may have been learned in the past, is maintained in the present by environmental antecedents and consequences. From their perspective, human behavior is originally learned through conditioning interactions with antecedent and consequential events in the environment. These cues and reinforcers represent a stable, singular reality. Difference in human behavior and understanding is assumed to be due to each individual's being exposed to a different set of these maintaining conditions in the environment.

Assessment in cognitive-behavioral treatment involves addressing the following three questions:

1. What is the behavior?
2. What is getting in the way of the client solving it on his or her own? That is, what is maintaining the behavior?
3. How can the problem be operationalized so that it can be observed and measured at the point of initial assessment and in an ongoing way to monitor progress?

The process of monitoring provides the client with feedback. Feedback is effective in promoting change because it is a powerful reinforcer for strengthening the new behaviors that lead to the objectives.

Problem behaviors may be overt and easily observed by others or covert, including cognitions, feelings, or physiological responses (Persons, 1989). Typically, children's problematic overt behaviors include those that require a decrease in intensity or frequency, such as aggressive or overly active behaviors. For some children, problematic behaviors might be more subtle behaviors, such as avoidance behaviors, procrastination, or a deficit in skills. Especially with children, the presenting problem is seldom covert problem behaviors and troubling cognitions such as self-defeating self-talk, negative and damning automatic verbal thoughts, visual images, or dreams. However, covert behaviors may be the focus of attention if they are the mediating triggers for problem feelings or behaviors. More typically, problem covert behaviors include moods (e.g., depression, anger, guilt, or anxiety) or physiological responses (e.g., racing heart, sweaty palms, or even crying or tearfulness).

The first step in identifying the problem with child clients and their significant others is to generate a problem list with little censoring. Next, the clinician helps the client system to define these problems in behavioral terms. This defining means only that the problem may somehow be observed. Either the behavior may be observed directly or indirectly through standardized or idiographic instrumentation or by client self-recording and monitoring. From the list, the two or three most pressing target problem behaviors are selected and redefined as objectives in terms of increasing or decreasing their frequency, severity, or duration.

The second question to be addressed involves exploration of what is impeding clients from solving the problem on their own. Problems are considered to be normal occurrences that, for the most part, people solve on their own without outside help. Part of the behavioral analysis seeks a determination of the environmental or internal antecedent cues that trigger and thus maintain the regular and problematic display of the behavior. In addition, the analysis seeks the reinforcing contingencies that follow the exhibition of the behavior and strengthen its probability. While it is crucial to understand the problems and circumstances that surround them, it is also important to ask when the problem behaviors *do not* occur (DeJong and Berg, 1998). Reflecting the profession's growing interest in client strengths and solutions, the clinical social worker must also search for the exceptions to the behavior: "When does he not hit his sister?" "When does she go to school without tantrumming?" or "When do you feel less sad, or angry, or upset?" Here, the clinician needs to work with child, parent, and teacher in exploring the child's environment and observing the transactions between the child and all aspects of the social and physical environment for antecedents and consequences that reinforce those positive behaviors competing with the problem ones. In behavioral theory, it is assumed that two competing behaviors cannot exist at the same time.

Cognitive theory, as well as behavioral theory, inform assessment. One of the impediments to a child's solving a problem independently is the potential for distorted underlying cognitive patterns. Previously, in presenting a more radical behavioral view, antecedents and consequences were depicted as environmental only. More contemporary cognitive-behavioral thinking recognizes that among the powerful maintaining conditions for problem behavior are the internal cognitive structure and products that mediate between external event and behavior. The clinician's hypothesis about these underlying psychological mechanisms guides the intervention strategy in the same way as does recognition of the environmental antecedents and consequences of both the problem behavior and positive behavior.

The third and final step in assessment determines the means by which the child client and network of supportive adults may observe and measure the problem for the purpose of monitoring progress. Numerous instruments used with and for child clients include (1) behavior checklists, (2) self-recording and monitoring via charts, and (3) structured environmental observation in which a teacher or clinician records frequency of problem behaviors in the classroom at predetermined intervals.

The dimensions of the target behaviors should follow simple logic—either frequency, duration, or intensity. Tantrums, for example, might be tracked for frequency, duration, or intensity, while aggressive acts or words would more likely be measured by frequency. Finally, a reasonable frequency of measurement should be determined. At the least, behavioral objectives should be measured at the beginning and end of treatment. Ideally, however, if instrument reactivity does not affect validity, measurement should take place multiple times to provide data for an effective single-system research design, if desired.

Assessment, Goal-setting, and Intervention with Internalizing Problems: Brenda. Four-year-old Brenda was brought to treatment following a trauma.

Despite early development that proceeded without incident, Brenda's behavior changed from outgoing and happy to clingy and tearful after she experienced a frightening event. Late one evening, Brenda's mother was preoccupied with caring for the nine-month-old baby who had a severe ear infection. To relieve the burden on his wife, Brenda's father took her along when he drove to the pharmacy to pick up a prescription for the baby. As the car turned the corner, an inebriated homeless man stepped into the street and the father's car struck and killed him. The man was thrown facedown onto the windshield of the car, terrifying both Brenda and her father. Neither the girl nor her father were injured. In the ensuing chaos, a medivac helicopter, police cars, and ambulance arrived. Because the father had to stay and fill out a report, a policeman drove an exhausted and frightened Brenda home. It is not clear what Brenda understood about the incident in general or the man in particular. She had, however, not talked about it and her parents had not raised the issue.

Not surprisingly, Brenda's play at preschool soon involved crashing and breaking. She regressed to nighttime wetting and had a difficult time leaving her mother to go to school. Parents and teacher hoped that the anxiety would abate on its own, particularly because she was working through the trauma in her play. After six weeks, however, the mother brought Brenda to the clinical social worker for evaluation. In one remarkable play session at her home, Brenda repeatedly told her story to the clinician. With each retelling, the distorted thoughts (in the form of Brenda's visual images) underlying the anxiety changed such that their power to produce anxiety weakened.

After Brenda showed her room and toys to the clinical social worker, she settled down with toys provided by the clinician. These toys included cars, trucks, and an ambulance, as well as small dolls. At first, Brenda chose to race cars about and simply crash them into one another. She added nothing but car sounds. Later, she crashed two cars together and commented that she had a crash like that. When asked who was driving, she replied her Daddy was. No mention was made of the man who died. In subsequent crashes, Brenda found the ambulance and said an old man rode in the ambulance. When asked what happened to the old man, she said he broke his leg. She did not reply when asked if he was now okay.

As time and crashes went on, Brenda became more agitated. Reaching for the play doh, she asked the social worker to make a monster. When the monster was formed, Brenda pulled off his leg and then squashed him. She said that the monster was dead. This prompted the clinician to ask Brenda if she knew about death and its permanence. Not surprisingly, these were not concepts well understood by this four-year-old as she explored the usual experiences with dead bugs and dead guinea pigs at school. Soon, Brenda was saying that the monster was the old man and that he died. She did not understand, nor did it matter for a four-year-old, that the dead man would not return.

It did matter that she had confused the monster with her father. Clearly, her father had been upset at the time of the accident. Brenda was having difficulty differentiating between the father's upset and the sights and sounds of the dying man. The clinical social worker and child returned to playing out the scene more accurately with dolls representing father, Brenda, and the old man. While more work needed to be done with Brenda, she was able to play out much of her confusion during the initial session.

This process can be described via psychodynamic therapy as abreaction and the beginnings of working through. In cognitive-theory terminology, the confused and distorted images that Brenda had constructed were, perhaps, the beginnings of schematic products that could have colored her future affective reactions to angry or violent behavior, or even to male figures. Thus, the process in the play session could be looked at as surfacing, challenging, and reconstructing cognitions of a very young child.

Assessing, Goal-setting, and Intervention with Externalizing Problem Behaviors: Nathan. Nathan was an enigma. Having arrived after many years of a childless marriage and a difficult pregnancy, Nathan was the delight of his parents. He was clearly bright, engaging, and active. He also seldom slept, but this only gave his proud parents more time to enjoy him. Until he entered pre-school, he never gave his family a moment of concern. At age five, he was not the delight of his mature and experienced kindergarten teacher. By spring, on the advice of the teacher, mother had Nathan examined by the pediatrician for possible medication. Taking a conservative stance, the physician and parents decided not to introduce medication so late in the school year. They hoped that some maturity over the summer might help. Desperate, the teacher asked the parents to meet with the school social worker. They finally relented when Nathan began to report to his mother, "No one likes me."

The social worker arranged to assess Nathan within the context of his school environment. Beginning with the first step in cognitive-behavioral assessment, the clinician inquired of the parents, "What is the problem?" They were genuinely puzzled but, trying to be cooperative, said that the teacher thought Nathan was a behavior problem. The teacher answered the question with, "Nathan is wild." Neither of these answers addressed the problem in clear, observable, measurable, and behavioral terms, so the clinician worked toward narrowing the focus.

From two play interviews with Nathan, an observation in school, an interview with both parents, and consultation with the teacher, the clinical social worker facilitated agreement among the adults that Nathan poked, stepped on, or otherwise invaded the space of other children. He either ignored the directions of the teacher or responded with a silly remark while still not complying. When engaged in interaction with other children, he appeared to get so wound up that he would still be running when all the others had lined up to move on to the next activity.

These problems could be characterized as negative behaviors in need of decrease. Taking a more positive view, by contrast, would involve seeking competing behaviors in need of increase. In Nathan's world, all agreed on stating the three objectives as follows: (1) hands and feet to self, (2) follows directions without words, and (3) freezes. The last behavior was to be thought of as a game similar to "Statue" that would be taught to all the children. That is, whenever the teacher called "freeze," everyone was to stand still. At first, Nathan was slow to learn this game, but soon his peers helped teach him to play the game.

Looking at the second question, "What is getting in the way of Nathan's solving these problems on his own?," there were certainly many variables involved. Among them might be an underlying neurological condition contributing to the overactivity and perhaps warranting a diagnosis of Attention Deficit with Hyperactivity. Both these possible contributors might have included a lack of limits set at home. These contributors could be addressed with medication and parental counseling. What remained, however, was to explore the environmental antecedents and consequences of the problem behavior that existed in the school environment.

When assessing a child situation involving externalizing behaviors like Nathan's, it is assumed that these behaviors (unlike the internalizing ones displayed by Miranda) result from cognitive deficiency rather than cognitive distortion. That is, underlying thinking was lacking rather than distorted. Thus, the goal is to introduce thinking where there has been only impulsive behavior, in addition to decreasing maladaptive behaviors and increasing adaptive behaviors.

When asked the circumstances under which Nathan's problem behaviors occurred, the teacher predictably replied, "All the time." Focusing this frustrated response, the school social worker determined that the kindergarten day was divided into six periods and that the problems only occurred in three of them: when outside at free play, in circle time, and at snack time. She then began to engage Nathan in individual play therapy. As expected, the problem behaviors did not occur in that situation. However, the clinician was able to use dolls to set up school-like situations in which Nathan played out his classroom and playground behavior. This play provided the opportunity to establish a contract with Nathan. Consistent with the educational and collaborative relationship of cognitive-behavioral therapy, the clinician explained her role as helping Nathan learn how to help his friends like to play with him—his view of the problem.

The next steps involved developing an instrument with which Nathan could participate in monitoring his own progress. Together, they made a chart, cutting magazine pictures and pasting them in a vertical row on the left side of a paper. They found hands and feet to represent "hands and feet to self," an ear for "follows directions," and an icicle for "freeze." Across the top were pictures to represent the three difficult periods of time. He chose trees to represent "outside," drew a circle for circle time, and found a picture of a glass of milk for snack time. Photocopying of this chart provided multiple copies that could be dated. Nathan used stickers indicating smiley, neutral, and frowning faces and, with the teacher's help, evaluated his own behavior after each period of the day. The charts were returned home and the feedback loop was complete. It was initially intended that backup reinforcers be provided, but the feedback of this self-evaluation proved to be powerful enough to dramatically influence Nathan's school behavior in a positive direction.

Using Cognitive and Behavioral Theories to Focus on Strengths in Child Therapy

While cognitive and behavioral theories can provide a clinical social worker who works with children with a rich variety of interventive techniques, their basic assumptions flow from the traditional position of psychological theories, in which the focus is on deficit and dysfunction. The emerging perspectives of strengths (Saleebey, 1996, 1997) and of risk and resilience (Werner and Smith, 1982) offer a position in line with the core values of the social work profession. However, practice techniques, especially for work with children, are still being developed from these new conceptual foundations. Certainly, solution-focused brief therapy (DeJong and Berg, 1998) is beginning to operationalize the strengths perspective. This approach, however, still remains atheoretical in explaining the effectiveness of its techniques. In fact, the developers of this approach have stated that they do not know nor do they care why solution-focused questions work (DeJong and Berg, 1998). Cognitive and behavioral theories provide the conceptual foundation for strengths-based work.

The mediational model in cognitive theory posits that thinking structures filter and influence the information provided us by the environment, strongly influencing the resulting feelings and behaviors. Returning to the cyclical model of human behavior (Stuart, 1996), cognitive therapy as an information therapy seeks change in problem behavior through changing thinking. For the most part, traditional cognitive therapy focuses on negative and dysfunctional thoughts. However, social work scholars have demonstrated that clinicians can work with the often neglected positive schema resources (Nurius and Berlin, 1994) that also drive our thinking. This perspective helps explain the solution-focused emphasis on the positive exceptions to the problem behaviors. That is, positive thinking structures and core beliefs exist but may not be as available as negative ones, especially under difficult circumstances. The strengths-based cognitive clinician urges the client to call on existing positive cognitive patterns in the form of recollection of things done well in the past and positive images of the possibilities of the future, and not to dwell on or reconstruct negative thinking.

Behavioral therapy offers additional conceptual explanations for solution-focused and strengths-oriented work. For the behaviorist, change comes through action, not through changed thinking. Problem behaviors are maintained by current antecedents and consequences. Traditional behavior therapy asks a client to consider the times that problem behaviors are occurring and determine what environmental influences might stimulate and reinforce them. A solution-focused therapist makes the same assumption, but shifts the focus. What is happening before and after the times that the problem behavior is not occurring explains the maintenance of the exceptions. The clinician then calls on the client to "do more of it." A series of solution-focused questions contains two steps. The core question asks the client to envision something positive, a cognitive function. The follow-up, or satellite, questions ask the client to do something more—that is, behavioral activation.

Solution-focused questions may be divided into present exceptions, past coping, and future envisioning—all following the same pattern. A series of questions seeking present exceptions for a child client might be, "You are telling me about how angry you get at your teacher; tell me about the times when you are with her but are not so angry?," "What is happening during those times?," "What are you doing differently?," and "How could we work on you doing that more often?" A past coping series of questions for a parent might be, "I see that two years ago, you had your child returned to you from the foster home; what were you doing then that made that happen?," and "What can we do to make that happen again?" Future envisioning involves the "miracle" question (DeJong and Berg, 1998) or some variation of it. In it, the clinician asks, "If you went to sleep tonight and a miracle happened and all of your problems were solved, what do you suppose you will notice that is different in the morning?," "What would your mom see?," and "What would your brother be doing?"

Another useful solution-focused series includes scaling questions, "On a scale of 1 to 10, with 10 being as good as you can imagine and 1 meaning that the problem is just awful, where are you now?" This question involves quantifying the client's present perception—a cognitive process. Then the clinician asks, "When were you higher on the scale?," "What was different then?," and "What would you have to do to move up a couple of points?" These satellite questions seek previous or future action that will enhance functioning.

With each of these series, there is a positive cognitive envisioning and a request for positive behavioral activation. In essence, these techniques combine information techniques with action techniques to enter the cycle of change at two points, and combine the effectiveness of cognitive and behavioral intervention.

Using Cognitive and Behavioral Theories to Focus on Strengths in Child Therapy: Jerry.   At nine years of age, Jerry had already spent two years in a special-education class for seriously emotionally disturbed students. He had a persistent problem with responding to the slightest taunt or perceived slight with his fists. As an externalizer, Jerry did not stop to think between event and action. In his therapy, two techniques seemed to help. The first involved envisioning rather than engaging in retaliatory action against his tormentors.

Jerry was particularly upset with another boy in class named Sammy. Discussion in therapy revealed that Jerry wanted to levitate Sammy. That is, he would practice stopping any overt action when he felt the urge to hit Sammy and instead would imagine him floating up to the ceiling and banging his head. While this particular image might not appeal to another child, it did to Jerry. With practice during the therapy time, he came to be able to do this sometimes on the playground or in class when he found himself being taunted by Sammy.

The other effective technique involved work with exceptions. While initially listening and supporting Jerry in his frequent problem-talk, the clinical social worker consistently refocused him on talk about exceptions. She methodically helped Jerry to identify the environmental situations in which he was able to function well in class, as well as the types of behaviors he was engaging in that interfered with aggressive ones. This information was used with Jerry to help him "do more of it," as well as with his foster mother and teacher to manage the environment as much as possible to maximize the times when he did well. Both the cognitive envisioning and the behavioral activation were useful in helping Jerry put thinking in place where it was previously absent, and to self-cue behaviors that led to positive experiences.

Conclusion

Contemporary pressures render child therapy as practiced by clinical social workers more difficult and complex. Managed care demands that change be rapid but substantive and that change be capable of being observed, monitored, and measured. Home- and community-based services provide new situations in which clinicians may provide needed child treatment, but they must often do so within models that are decidedly short term, structured, and behavioral. Finally, the social work profession is reviving interest in some of its values from the past—particularly its interest in client self-determination, client strengths, and community resources. If structured change involves thoughts and feelings triggering behaviors that result in social consequences, cognitive and behavioral theory must come out of the shadows in the profession of social work and take their place in the mainstream of child work. Miranda, Brenda, Nathan, and Jerry are four children who changed—some more than others. Each, however, benefited from the contribution of cognitive and behavioral theory to move them toward the goals they shared in common.

PART FOUR

Clinical Application

9 Attachment Problems

Although the diagnostic nomenclature has changed over the years, social workers have always been concerned with the impact of family neglect and inadequate caregiving on children's development and psychosocial functioning. Today, clinicians are dealing with more and more children whose disrupted development, distorted relational patterns, and general psychosocial dysfunction arise within the disordered attachment matrix of severely neglectful family environments, are compounded by their subsequent experiences in foster care, and are so severe that remediation by adoption alone is not likely. Therefore, the focus of this chapter is severe problems with attachment, including reactive attachment disorders of childhood. It is important to note, however, that not all attachment problems are pathological in degree or indicative of clinical diagnoses, nor are all attachment problems associated with child neglect.

Problems with Attachment

Attachment Matrix

Attachment theory addresses the social, emotional, cognitive, and behavioral components of the parent/child relationship and takes into account its reciprocal affiliative nature (Bowlby, 1982, 1988). This relational bond serves as the attachment matrix within which caregivers convey availability and caring; responsively attune themselves to their children's affects and behaviors; and sensitively attend to their children's physical needs, emotional well-being, and sense of security (Lyons-Ruth, 1996). Within this matrix, children seek human contact and connectedness with their primary caregivers and develop a sense of their caregiver's helpfulness and accessibility. In the process, they learn how to modulate their affect, soothe themselves, and establish relationships with others.

The parental-attachment matrix also serves as the relational base from which young children explore their physical and social worlds, and form their own internal working models, or dynamic mental representations, of self and other in these worlds (Bowlby, 1982). Derived from the earliest real-life attachment experiences, these internal working models become the interpretive filters through which children come to understand themselves and their important social relationships. Because these representations and understandings are dynamic, they shift with changing caregiving experiences and corrective psychosocial relationships.

When young children have experienced their caregivers as available, responsive, and helpful, their attachment bonds are secure and their mental representations are adaptive. These children then go on to develop a sense of autonomy and achieve a balance between individual mastery and collaborative social relationships with peers and adults. In some instances, however, barriers inhibit caregiver availability to a particular child and, consequently, the child fails to develop a secure attachment bond. For example, parent-related barriers may include physical or mental illness, addiction, pain and anguish, immaturity, stress, and marital violence. Child-related barriers may include prematurity, developmental disability, physical illness, and hypersensitivity. Environmental barriers may include poverty, unemployment, inadequate housing, and community violence.

Research

Developmental attachment studies using Ainsworth's Strange Situation Procedure with paired infant/mother research populations have confirmed and added to her research classification of attachment strategies (Ainsworth, Blehar, Waters, and Wall, 1978; Biringen, 1994; Goldberg, 1993; Main and Solomon, 1990; Zeanah and Emde, 1994):

1. *Secure Strategies.* Infants balance exploration and proximity-seeking behavior, evidence appropriate distress during separation, and are easily soothed upon reunion.
2. *Avoidant Strategies.* Infants display relatively active exploration and independent behavior with attentive but not obvious monitoring of mother before separation, minimal distress and protest during separation, and avoidance upon reunion.
3. *Avoidant-Resistant Strategies.* Infants remain in close proximity to their mothers prior to separation, are quite distressed during separation, and combine tantrums with contact-seeking and avoidance behaviors upon reunion.
4. *Disorganized-Disoriented Strategies.* Infants lack a clearly organized attachment strategy in coping with the strange situation. Their fluctuations may include freezing upon reunion, staring dazedly, and intense proximity-seeking followed by intense avoidance behavior.

A recent meta-analysis of multiple research studies in Ainsworth's tradition yielded an infant distribution pattern of 55 percent secure, 23 percent avoidant, 15 percent disorganized, and 8 percent ambivalent attachment strategies (Van Ijzendoorn, 1995).

For clinicians, a note of caution about these studies and their protocols is in order. Protocols for identifying infant attachment strategies by means of the

Strange Situation Procedure were designed as observation and classification tools for developmental research studies and not as diagnostic tools for assessment of individual infants in clinical settings. The classifications, however, may be considered as possible indicators of risk for psychopathology (Zeanah and Emde, 1994). Of the identified attachment strategies, the disorganized-disoriented classification is found in greater proportions in high-risk samples and most closely approaches a designation of clinical psychopathology (Main and Solomon, 1990).

More recently, several researchers (Lieberman and Zeanah, 1995) have combined major findings from developmental research with clinical observations to create an alternative attachment classification:

1. *Disorders of Nonattachment.* Infant behaviors (up to twelve months of age) indicate no evidence of a preferred attachment to anyone. Subcategories of nonattachment include withdrawn and inhibited, as well as indiscriminately social, youngsters.

2. *Disordered Attachments.* Infant behaviors depict distortions in their use of caregivers as a secure attachment base from which to explore the world and return in times of danger. The symptomatic behaviors are relationship-specific, confined to disordered attachment relationships, and may include inhibition, self-endangerment, and role reversal, in which the child worries about the attachment figure.

3. *Disrupted Attachments.* Infants and young children (under three) react to the loss of a major attachment figure and convey their grief response through crying, refusal to be comforted, and withdrawal.

For the most part, developmental-attachment research has been grounded in a risk and protective factors approach. Taken together, this body of work has confirmed Bowlby's (1969, 1980) premise that insecure attachment in infancy is associated with psychosocial maladaptation in the early and middle childhood years (Cassidy, 1988; Lyons-Ruth, Repacholi, McLeod, and Silva, 1991; Troy and Sroufe, 1987). In an effort to increase the clinical usefulness of these research classifications, Zeanah, Mammen, and Lieberman (1993) proposed that attachment problems identified through these classifications would become psychiatric disorders when the emotional and social behaviors evidenced in attachment relationships become so disturbed that they substantially increase the risk of persistent distress or disability.

Problems of Neglect, Foster Care, and Loss

Neglect

Child neglect may be defined as a condition in which a caregiver responsible for the child either deliberately or by extraordinary inattentiveness permits the child to experience available present suffering and/or fails to provide one or more of the ingredients generally deemed essential for developing a person's physical, intellectual, and emotional capacities (Polansky, Hally, and Polansky, 1975, p. 5).

Neglectful families tend to be families only in the biological sense. The parents are centered on themselves and indifferent to their children's well-being and basic growth needs. The parent/child relationship is emotionally barren and contains scant acknowldgment that the children belong to and depend on their parents. Indeed, neglectful parents often leave their children and stay away with little or no provision for their children's food, safety, and shelter. Many seek to avoid reality and its associated problems through alcohol and drugs. Their indifference and neglect may be moderate to severe, and either consistent and chronic or episodic and stress-related in duration (Polansky, Chalmers, Buttenweiser, and Williams, 1981).

Within neglectful families, children's lives are chaotic and without order or structure. They eat as they can and horde food whenever an excess is available. When necessary, they steal food and rummage through garbage cans. They sleep whenever possible. They are dirty and unkempt. Family members seldom speak to them, set no limits on their behavior, and offer no rewards for being good. Neglected children tend to wander about alone and find themselves ignored by an indifferent world that offers them little warmth, caring, or hope of a better life.

As a result, neglected children tend to be underweight, constantly hungry, tire easily, be inappropriately dressed for the weather, and have untended medical problems. They display little curiosity, do not know how to play with toys, and often destroy any play materials provided (Young, 1981). They are frequently scapegoated, have no idea how to make friends, and rarely turn to their parents or other adults for comfort. They have little sense of self and rarely cry or laugh. Some appear apathetic, quiet, and withdrawn; others display uncontrolled and hyperactive behavior.

School-age neglected children usually come to the classroom tired and have difficulty concentrating. They seem to take one of the extremes of depressed and withdrawn or hyperactive and destructive behaviors. They may act impulsively, be defiant, lie, and steal. They lack comprehension of their impact on other persons and have little concept of the future consequences of their actions. They often fail in school and tend to believe that this failure is inevitable.

The National Research Council (1993) documented 55 percent of reported maltreatment cases as problems of neglect, and reports an incidence rate of 14.6 per one thousand children. In terms of age, more than half (51 percent) of the victims of neglect are seven years of age or younger.

Foster Placement and Loss

When severely neglected children are removed from their families and placed in foster care, there are both positive and negative aspects to be considered (Wasserman and Rosenfeld, 1986). The positive aspects include (1) ensuring the child's immediate safety, protection, and nurture; (2) providing a living situation in which the child is valued and wanted; (3) setting limits on destructive parental behavior;

and (4) providing parents with respite from childrearing responsibility, as well as an opportunity for change. The negative aspects include (1) separating children and parents whose attachment bond is probably not secure to start with; and (2) creating a sense of inadequacy and failure by parents and children alike.

For children, the move into foster care and each subsequent move disrupts their established life relationships, routines, and adaptations. The moves also necessitate coping with the sadness and anger associated with loss, learning new routines, building new relationships, and terminating with old ones. All too often when moving from home to home, however, little time is allowed for mourning and emotionally discharging their feelings of grief and rage. When the affective processes of these moves and losses is truncated, a defensive attachment is likely to develop, wherein children deactivate the distorted attachment matrix and fail to work through their need for the lost object, the reality of the loss, ambivalent feelings, and the yearning for reunion (Bowlby, 1973b, 1980).

For neglected children in foster care, the all too frequent pragmatic practice of terminating contact between the child and parent or foster parent without adequate resolution of the loss encourages the child to idealize these earlier caregivers and fantasize about reunion. The serial placements and repetitive losses often result in an accumulation of unprocessed experiences of separation and loss. Thus, the internal mental representation of the foster child's attachment bond eventually becomes made up of distorted, missing, and fragmented parts and cumulative feelings of grief and emptiness. Once established, the pattern of unresolved loss intensifies and creates a hypersensitivity to future losses. In time, these cumulative losses engender a sense of being unable to sustain caregivers, and lead to an unending search for ideal substitutes but with little hope for success. This search pattern interferes with secure attachment to any new caregivers who may appear on the scene (Eagle, 1994).

Pathology

In the absence of corrective mediating factors, disrupted caregiver relationships may lead to negative psychosocial and cognitive consequences for children's later development (Gonick and Gold, 1992; Hortacsu, Cesur, and Oral, 1993). For example, there is often pervasive failure in socialization and severe difficulty in trusting, making, and maintaining basic human connections. There is difficulty modulating affect and verbalizing feelings to relieve emotional pain and gain insight (Shapiro and Gisynski, 1989). There are likely to be cognitive, linguistic, and emotional developmental deficits that influence the capacity to process and come to terms with past and future separations (Eagle, 1994). Failure to negotiate critical developmental tasks, such as conscience development, is also common, as is difficulty delaying gratification and tolerating frustration.

On the feeling level, neglected children in foster care often feel responsible for their placement and loss experiences, and evidence strong feelings of shame, guilt, insecurity, and inadequacy. They convey a sense of knowing that they are bad and unworthy of love (Gonick and Gold, 1992; Samuels, 1995). In an effort to cope with these negative feelings, neglected children bring various defenses into play. They may, for example, turn passive into active in an attempt to regain a sense of being in charge of their young lives. To avoid becoming aware of painful aspects of their reality, they may shut off and deny strong emotions about their past. In so doing, they no longer have to deal with their feelings of anger, hopelessness, despair, and grief (Crittenden, 1992; Shapiro and Gisynski, 1989). In addition, they may project negative aspects of themselves onto others as a way of splitting off and disowning that particular unacceptable part of themselves. Not surprisingly, they also may displace their developmental conflicts onto foster parents, teachers, and peers, as well as new adoptive parents.

Reactive Attachment Disorders

To be diagnosed with Reactive Attachment Disorder of Infancy or Early Childhood, the symptomatic behaviors must be evidenced before age five and be apparent in the child's caregiver relationship, reflect disturbance in the child's ability to use the caregiver as a secure base for exploring the world, and be congruent with the *DSM IV*'s depiction of one of the interpersonal conditions in which attachment is the principle disturbance. It is important to note that, to date, there are no published studies about the validity of this disorder (Zeanah, 1996).

Clinical Syndrome

According to the *DSM IV*, children with reactive attachment disorders neither initiate nor respond to interactions with other persons in developmentally or socially appropriate ways. More specifically, they evidence one of two distorted relational patterns in most social contexts. In the inhibited-type relational pattern, the children are suspicious, watchful, and resist comfort. They evidence highly inhibited, excessively vigilant, and often very ambivalent or contradictory responses. In the disinhibited-type relational pattern, children are excessively familiar with strangers and indiscriminantly sociable with others. They also display a pattern of diffuse attachments with little selectivity among adult figures. By emphasizing that one of these two relational patterns is evidenced in most social contexts, the *DSM IV* deemphasizes the child's behavior with the primary attachment figure (Zeanah, 1996). Some clinicians suggest that attachment disorders represent pervasive and profound disturbances in children's feelings of security and safety. They propose that attachment disorders exist when the emotions and behaviors evidenced in caregiver relationships indicate persistent distress or disability in the young child (Zeanah, Mammen, and Lieberman, 1993). These researchers focus on the distorted feelings and behaviors within the child and consider persistent distress and disability to be core clinical features of the attachment disorder.

Prevalence

Neither community-based nor clinical epidemiological studies have been conducted to establish prevalence rates, comorbidity rates, or the course of reactive attachment disorders (APA, 1994; Zeanah and Emde, 1994). Comorbidity rates are odds ratios of the following:

# of times disorders occur in the presence of another disorder

---

# of times disorders occur without that other disorder

While it is thought that 40 to 50 percent of abused and neglected children display distorted attachment behaviors, researchers note that it is not clear how many are actually diagnosed as having reactive attachment disorders (Zeanah and Emde, 1994). For maltreated infants alone, some researchers have estimated that 82 percent demonstrate attachment disorders (Lyons-Ruth, Repacholi, McCleod, and Silva, 1991), but again, there is no established comorbidity rate.

Still other researchers have explored the association between maternal availability and attachment. Focusing on maternal depression, they found that children of depressed mothers were assessed with clinical attachment problems about 24 percent of the time in middle-income families (DeMulder and Radke-Yarrow, 1991) and 62 percent of the time in low-income families (Lyons-Ruth, Connell, Grunebaum, and Botein, 1990).

Clinical Etiology

Children with reactive attachment disorder may experience assorted problems with attachment and social relatedness throughout childhood. Much of the time, these problems are mild to moderate in intensity and are associated with their efforts to cope with caregiving patterns and family changes in the face of acute stressors (e.g., moves, illness, and death.) In other instances, however, the intensity and complexity of the feelings and tensions connected with attachment issues are associated with youngsters' efforts to cope with out-of-the-ordinary caregiving experiences, such as abuse, neglect, alcoholism, clinical depression, or the chronic stressors associated with extreme poverty. In any case, attachment issues become clinically significant only when the accompanying affect and behavior patterns become excessive in amount, intensity, and persistence.

Biopsychosocial Development of Attachment.   Ideally, the parent-infant attachment matrix enables children to feel safe and secure as they explore their various social environments. The development of secure internal attachment models with their primary caregiver enhances children's psychosocial development by facilitating their social exploration, first of others and then of self in relation to others. Good social exploration skills, in turn, lead to interactive peer play and the development of social competence. By contrast, children with insecure internal working models of attachment have experienced their early parental relationships as unresponsive and unsafe. In turn, they have learned to either retreat from or fight with their social environment (Bowlby, 1969, 1973a). They are unlikely to interact affectionately and cooperatively with their caregivers or others. Both retreating and fighting coping styles impede attachment, psychosocial development, peer play, and social competence.

Psychopathology.   Researchers have noted associations between attachment problems in infancy and subsequent behavior and impulse-control problems, parent-child conflict, peer-relationship problems, and lower self-esteem (Cassidy, 1988; Easterbrooks and Goldberg, 1990; Lyons-Ruth, 1996; Main and George, 1985; Troy and Sroufe, 1987). Comorbidity rates, however, have not been established for clinical or nonclinical populations.

Family Issues

Pathological caregiving is viewed as responsible for children's reactive attachment disorders. Such parenting is likely to be evidenced by ongoing neglect of basic physical needs, by disregard of emotional needs for affection, comfort, and stimulation, or by repeated changes in a child's primary caregiver that inhibit formation of stable attachments. By the *DSM IV* definition, parental maltreatment or the absence of stable caregiving is a prerequisite for a diagnosis of attachment disorder.

In view of their life experiences, some children with attachment disorders may be unwilling to seek help from adults and may avoid their caregivers when hurt or distressed. Others may depend excessively on their caregivers. Still others may evidence role reversal and excessive caring for others.

Support for Treatment Selection

Pharmacology

To date, there is no evidence that medications directly eliminate behavioral symptoms associated with attachment problems and reactive attachment disorders. However, if a comorbid condition of Attention Deficit Hyperactivity Disorder (ADHD) is diagnosed apart from the behavioral problems associated with attachment, a trial of stimulant medication seems indicated (Evans and Borenzweig, 1996).

Supportive and Rehabilitative Family Services

Supportive and rehabilitative family services for neglectful and abusive parents and their children take many forms—protective services, intensive home-based services, family preservation services, Early Head Start Services, therapeutic nurseries, and family respite services. Various studies have documented their usefulness in preventing the dissolution of families in acute distress and in rehabilitation efforts with moderately dysfunctional families (Barth, 1994; Kagan and Schlossberg, 1989; Peccora, Fraser, and Haapala, 1992; Tower, 1996; Zelman, 1996). In cases of chronic, severe maltreatment or drug abuse, however, there is little evidence that intensive wraparound services or child-development services alone produce long-term gains in family functioning and child well-being. In these extreme instances, removal from home and placement in foster care are frequently viewed as the preferred options for child protection, nurture, and development. Yet, these environmental changes by themselves are not always sufficient for overcoming early deficits in attachment and promoting further childhood growth and development.

Empirical Evidence

Limited data are available to support the usefulness of specific interventions with children evidencing attachment problems associated with neglect. The National Clinical Evaluation Study found that 70 percent of the neglected and abused children and youth served in nineteen research and demonstration projects showed gains in their overall progress, a decrease in clinical assessment of the likelihood of recurrence of abuse, and a decrease in the extent of reccurrence of abuse during treatment (Daro, 1988). Unfortunately, the reported data do not distinguish between abused and neglected children or children experiencing both abuse and neglect.

Psychotherapy

Whatever the family situation, children with developmental-attachment problems confuse the past with the present, in that they bring past neglectful and abusive experiences and their expectations about relationships with adults to the therapeutic tasks and the working alliance. That is, they perceive the words and actions of their clinical social worker to be rejecting, and seek through their responses and behavior to recreate old familiar interactional patterns. Thus, the initial task is to build a therapeutic alliance that can serve as a reparative attachment matrix with a secure relational base. Within this matrix, the clinician provides the corrective experiences necessary to accomplish three goals: (1) ameliorate the developmental disturbances associated with early bonding disruption and later relationship distortions; (2) decrease the severity of the presenting symptoms; and (3) enhance the child's ability to attach securely to a new primary caregiver.

Building a reparative attachment matrix and accomplishing these goals involves a twofold process: first, attachment substitution; then, parental attachment inducement (Lieberman and Pawl, 1990). The process of attachment substitution involves creation of a warm, consistent, nonpunitive holding environment within which the child and clinician can slowly build a sense of mutual recognition and trust, and start the process of attachment formation. Techniques may include the following:

1. Being with and responding to the child to convey that the therapist is present and attuned to the child's developmental needs.
2. Creating increased socioemotional interactions that serve to correct the child's expectations that earlier negative experiences will be repeated.
3. Responding to the child's agitation, anger, and distrust with verbal and nonverbal calm attentiveness, soothing, and creating a sense of safety and security.
4. Supporting therapist/child linkages verbally and behaviorally, *albeit* always being mindful of professional boundaries and ethics.
5. Actively gratifying the child's early unmet developmental needs through the symbolic metaphor of the good-enough holding environment (Winnicott, 1965a) for the expressed level of psychosocial development.
6. Responding (within appropriate professional limits) to the child's basic bio-psychosocial needs and modeling for the child that caregivers can provide physical and psychological nurture, protection, and stimulation.
7. Achieving object constancy with the transitional attachment substitute of the clinical social worker (Fraiberg, 1961; Lieberman and Pawl, 1990; Timberlake, 1979).

The process of parental-attachment inducement involves enabling the child to present self in a more favorable light, thereby eliciting attachment responses from a primary caregiver and significant others. Techniques may include the following:

1. Enabling the child to improve the presentation of self—personal hygiene, mannerisms.
2. Decreasing aggressive and increasing friendly verbal and nonverbal social behavior.
3. Transferring the object constancy achieved with the transitional attachment substitute (i.e., clinical social worker) to the parental attachment object, increasing the comfort level with the parent and decreasing the clinging behaviors.
4. Promoting attachment behaviors by the child and encouraging the child to induce attachment behaviors from others.

While attachment substitution processes occur in the early treatment stages of creating a therapeutic alliance and identifying narrative themes, they rarely become solidified before the later stage of developmental growth and change. Nor are they likely to be completely resolved before termination, because children with attachment problems rework old losses in new ways at this time. This last therapeutic stage also ideally engages the child in the final working through of the child's other developmental disruptions that were compounded by the attachment problems.

Course of Treatment: Ryan L.
by Karen Block, M.S.W., LCSW

Stage I: Biopsychosocial Assessment

Presenting Problem.   Ryan, a six-year-old male child, was referred to the community mental health center by his pediatrician to be evaluated for ADHD. According to his parents and teachers, Ryan was demonstrating hyperactivity, distractibility, low frustration tolerance, aggression toward peers, frequent nightmares, and irritable mood. When asked about his social relatedness, Ryan's adoptive mother described a pattern of excessive familiarity with strangers. She noted that Ryan moves away from her too easily and expressed fear that she could lose him in large public places. With grave concern, Mrs. L. stated, "Ryan thinks that every stranger is his friend; he will go anywhere with anyone."

History of Presenting Problem.   Ryan was adopted by Mr. and Mrs. L. at age five, one year before he entered treatment. After many years of infertility and after wading through the bureaucratic structures of a local adoption agency in a large Midwestern city, Mr. and Mrs. L. were thrilled to receive a child. They reported that the social worker at the adoption agency had told them Ryan would be a challenging child to raise due to his history of documented neglect, probable abuse, and behavioral difficulties. According to the Ls, agency psychological reports and interviews with his foster parents indicated that Ryan's difficulties with hyperactivity, distractibility, insecure social relatedness, poor impulse control, and low frustration tolerance preceded the adoption.

At the time of the referral to the community mental health center, Mr. and Mrs. L. described significant improvements since Ryan first entered their home. His hyperactivity had decreased and his aggression toward them when limits were set had ceased. Ryan no longer hoarded food under his bed. He had adjusted to the structure of their family life and was generally cooperative with age-appropriate chores and self-care tasks. Yet, despite these improvements, his adoptive parents were still concerned about his emotional well-being and his school performance. Mrs. L. stated that she rarely saw Ryan laugh. He constantly expressed fears that he would be taken away from them. His teachers and school administrators had pressured the Ls to seek professional help because Ryan's behaviors were becoming increasingly difficult to manage in his first-grade classroom.

Developmental History.   According to his documented psychosocial history, Ryan's biological parents were never married. Both mother and father had a long history of addiction to drugs. At age four, Ryan was removed from their care due to significant neglect involving lack of supervision. It was reported that Ryan was often locked out of his house and was left wandering the streets late at night. His meals were inconsistent and he was found looking for food in garbage cans.

Some evidence suggested that Ryan may also have been physically abused by his birthparents. No information was available about Ryan's early developmental milestones. After numerous placements and separations from foster parents in his year in foster care, Ryan was adopted by Mr. and Mrs. L.

In the initial interview, Mrs. L. demonstrated a loving, nurturing presence but appeared somewhat anxious. She was currently employed part-time in a daycare center while completing an advanced degree in early-childhood education. Mrs. L. described herself as growing up in a warm and loving family with supportive parents and siblings. She acknowledged that family members had a difficult time expressing feelings of anger or distress because her mother would become anxious or upset. Mrs. L. described the process of adopting Ryan as very difficult at times. She had to come to terms with her strong feelings of sadness and sense of loss about the couple's inability to conceive a child. She recalled meeting Ryan for the first time at his last foster home, feeling immediately attracted to his big smile and his cheerful disposition, and sensing that he was the child for them.

Although described by Mrs. L. as a firm disciplinarian, Mr. L. appeared to have a warm and soothing presence. Currently an employee of the federal government, Mr. L. described a traumatic personal history. At the age of eleven, both his parents were killed in an automobile accident. He and his younger brother were then separated and sent to live with relatives in different towns. Mr. L. became tearful as he recalled his own history in connection with Ryan's early experience of family loss.

Initial Child Interviews.   Ryan separated easily from his mother, readily joining me in the walk down the hall to my office. He was of average height and weight with dark brown hair, was casually dressed, and appeared to be his stated age of six. He had a high level of motor activity as he entered the office and quickly began to explore the toys. Immediately, Ryan invited me to play with him. Dumping a box of blocks on the floor, he asked, "Will you build a house with me?" As he started to build, Ryan directed me where to place each block. He was frequently dissatisfied and instructed me to "Put the block right there. No, not there." Ryan ordered. "Do it like this!" Then he took the block from me and placed it himself. Fantasies of omnipotence and a need to be in control were clear as he stated, "I'm the boss!" (*I was fascinated that his choice of play materials reflected my last name—Block.*)

Through displacement in this initial stage of therapy, Ryan revealed developmental themes, fears, and anxiety in the context of a stressful, unsafe make-believe play situation. For example, he noted, "Let's put the gorilla family into the house. This is the mother, this is the father, and this is the son. They are all locked in the house. Let's put people in the house too. The people are in with the gorillas!" I probed, "I wonder how the people feel in there with the gorillas?" "They are very scared," Ryan responded. "And there is no superhero to save them!" When asked about his mood and his worries, Ryan articulated, "Sometimes I feel sad. When I think about my old family, I feel sad." He expressed worries about school and added, "I hate school. Some days I don't get any stars because I am bad." Ryan's affect appeared to be full range and was appropriate to the interview content.

Aggressive themes emerged as the play continued the following week. "Let's build another house. And let's put the gorillas and the people inside." Ryan then added, "This time I am going to make the house fall down. Is that okay? I am going to knock it down." After checking with me to see if I could tolerate his scary, aggressive feelings, Ryan kicked the house over and it fell to the ground. "Will you help me build another house so I can knock it down?" Ryan and I worked together building house after house, all of which he kicked to the ground. At one point, Ryan stated, "If a kid kicked you like that, you'd be dead." I responded, "If a kid kicked me like that, I would think that the kid had angry feelings inside and that these feelings were very scary to him. I would also hope that the kid would use words to talk about these feelings." Feeling more safe for the moment, Ryan closed the session by sitting close to me on the floor and asking for my help in tying his shoes (*and coping with his rage*).

The following week, Ryan was eager to get into my office. He began the session with a thorough examination of the toys in the room and then decided to draw. In the process of drawing, Ryan expressed more of his emotional world. Holding up a crayon, he stated, "I know what your favorite color is. It's yellow, isn't it?" "How come you guessed yellow?" I inquired. "Because yellow is my favorite color. I know it's a girl's color, but I like it. I know you like it too." Acknowledging Ryan's fantasy of a common boundary between us (*characteristic of Mahler's normal symbiotic phase*), I commented, "It would be nice if we had the same favorite color." "Yes, it would," Ryan replied. Ryan reflected upon his drawing, "This is a picture of a yellow car. It is going to your house. Your father is driving the car." (*To myself, I noted Ryan's wish to be with me.*) It was difficult for him to clean up and leave the session that day.

Aggressive themes occurred in the next session as Ryan smashed toy cars into the wall and each other, crushed a toy play-doh figure that I had made, and killed families of toy people with falling houses and animal attacks. (*I thought that his lashing out was associated with his ambivalence about and fear of our developing working alliance.*) Within the metaphor of his play, I employed techniques of empathy, clarification, and reflective verbalization regarding his play content, process, and associated affect, thus providing a holding environment for Ryan.

Assessment and Diagnosis. Ryan was an intelligent child with the relational capacity to make connections with others and the ability to express his inner conflicts through the metaphor of play. Ryan enjoyed and invested in his initial sessions of therapy. He appeared capable of entering into a therapeutic alliance and, within the context of our working relationship, revealed developmental themes comprising his emotional world. Ryan's mental representations of his early attachment relationships were revealed in his interactions with me and symbolically in his play.

Upon evaluation, Ryan's basic ego apparatus appeared to be intact in the areas of memory, perception, speech and language, and appropriate control over bodily functions. While Ryan has the cognitive and linguistic abilities needed to perform at the expected developmental level at home and in school, deficits in his performance were apparent. Because his early childhood experience was characterized by grossly negligent care, unempathic mothering, and insecure attachments, psychosocial dysfunction was apparent in multiple developmental areas. Specifically, Ryan was unable to control his impulses, his frustration tolerance was low, and he was not able to sublimate aggressive impulses. In addition, he displayed defenses of acting out, displacement, regression, identification with the aggressor, and projection. Secure attachment and object constancy had never been achieved due to the documented early maternal neglect.

The developmental themes Ryan enacted in this initial stage of treatment most closely resembled those of Mahler's normal symbiotic phase (Mahler, Pine, and Bergman, 1975). The essential feature of this phase is the illusion of a common boundary between infant and mother, an omnipotent fusion of the self-representation with the internal representation of the mother. At this stage, the mother's holding behavior is the symbiotic organizer of the infant's inner experience, as that experience begins to be organized into categories of good and bad relative to the maintenance of homeostasis. In his play, Ryan enacted omnipotent control over me as he directed me where to put each block. He also expressed his dissatisfaction and frustration about my ability to meet his needs. Through metaphor, his play often reflected his fantasy of a nonindividuated relationship between us. Aggressive themes frequently accompanied this fantasy.

Ryan met the *DSM IV* criteria for Reactive Attachment Disorder of Early Childhood. He displayed lack of developmentally appropriate social responsiveness, specifically indiscriminate sociability, excessive familiarity with strangers, and highly ambivalent and contradictory responses to attachment figures. He had a history of grossly pathogenic parental care in the form of numerous lengthy deprivations and repeated changes in primary caregivers, as evidenced by numerous foster-care placements. Ryan also demonstrated additional features not identified in the current *DSM IV* criteria, yet shared by many children with attachment problems: poor attention and concentration, hyperactivity, attention-seeking behavior, impulsivity, and oppositionality. Conceptually, these impairments appeared to be associated with the inability of his parents to attune themselves to and meet Ryan's physical and emotional developmental needs as an infant, orient him in space and time, and provide him with a secure base from which to explore the world.

Treatment Plan.   I met with Ryan's parents to discuss his treatment plan of weekly developmental play therapy with a psychodynamic orientation, bimonthly parent guidance, and consultation with the staff psychiatrist to assess and monitor his medication needs. Within the therapeutic holding environment of developmental play therapy, short-term and overall goals were identified.

Reduction of disruptive behavior in school was identified as the primary short-term goal. With his parents' permission, I consulted with Ryan's classroom teacher to help her understand him developmentally and create a management/ teaching plan to address his most salient classroom behavioral issues.

Early in his treatment, a trial of stimulant medication was prescribed for Ryan by the staff psychiatrist to address a possible biological component to his hyperactivity symptoms. That there was no noticeable reduction in hyperactive behavior associated with the medication trial suggested that these behavioral symptoms were more likely associated with his attachment issues. The medication was discontinued after three months with no noticeable effect.

Ryan's overall treatment goals involved stimulating the process of psycho-social growth and change to return him to a normal developmental pathway. Consistent, safe objects in the therapeutic holding environment were expected to facilitate the development of frustration tolerance and accurate mental representations of self and other. This, in turn, was designed to promote movement toward reattachment and object constancy. Techniques of empathic support, acceptance, and reflective verbalizations within the context of the therapeutic alliance were planned to facilitate exploration of conflictual material and the associated affect.

Stage II: Creation of a Therapeutic Alliance

This second phase of treatment was characterized by Ryan's engagement in the therapeutic process and the creation of a working alliance with me. Separation/ individuation themes emerged throughout this period. For example, Ryan symbolically enacted the emotional refueling that characterizes Mahler's practicing subphase (Mahler, Pine, and Bergman, 1975). He built an extensive highway for a toy car, set up obstacles for the car to drive around, and opened several gas stations for refueling. He commented, "This car needs a lot of gas," as he filled up at one station, declared the station empty, and then proceeded to the next.

The following week, Ryan physically moved away from me as he walked into the bathroom in the office and closed the door, thus separating himself from me. Although the boundary line of the bathroom door had been tenuously established between us, it was clear that Ryan did not appreciate me as fully separate from him. He continued to experience himself as omnipotent, calling me to reenter his space and meet his emotional needs. He cried, "Will you come in here, please? I want to show you something. I have two teeth loose, one on top and one on the bottom." When I did not join him in the bathroom, but stated, "I am still here and I will be here when you are finished to look at your loose teeth," Ryan erupted with aggressive feelings in response to my separateness and his inability to control me. He banged on the garbage can in the bathroom and stated, "If a kid hit you with his hand like this, you would be dead." Finally, Ryan resolved his immediate struggle with our separateness by employing a transitional object, a frequent occurrence during the early practicing phase. He asked, "Will you bring me a block to play with in here—in the bathroom?" After I gave him the symbolic toy object, Ryan seemed comfortable with the door closed between us. When Ryan returned to his play in my office, I reflected, "I think you wanted to have me with you in the bathroom so that you would know that I am still here with you . . . that I haven't left." Ryan kicked a stack of blocks over and responded, "Now I can see that you are still here." Issues of power and control characteristic of both individuation and autonomy conflicts also were seen in this session, as were efforts toward mastery of these conflicts.

Ryan's mental representations of himself, me, and our relationship were revealed and explored in his play. He displayed a marked ambivalence toward me during this period, vacillating between proximity-seeking behaviors and resistance to contact, avoidance, hostility, sadness, and fear. Shortly after entering the office on one occasion, Ryan stated tearfully, "I want to leave now. Can I leave? I want to go to school. I didn't want to come here today. I am **not upset!!**" exclaimed Ryan. "I just want to leave." Ryan then walked toward me and sat on my lap. "Can I see your watch?" he asked quietly, taking my hand and peering into the watch. "I think I can see my face in your watch. Look."

The following session, Ryan took the glue out of the art box. "I am going to make something," he announced as he started sticking paper together, then sticking crayons together, and then gluing his hand to the table. I observed, "You really are sticking things together." "No kidding, stupid," Ryan retorted. Wondering about his hostility, I reflected, "Hmm. I wonder if you feel angry at me today because we did not see each other last week due to the snowstorm." Ryan responded, "I missed you" as he moved his chair closer to me. "Now I'm going to draw a picture of a cat. **Don't** look at me! And **don't** say anything!" he commanded. During this stage of treatment, Ryan often attempted to control me by offering to help and by symbolically taking care of me. Using play-doh, he cooked pancakes for me to eat. He was quickly at my side when it appeared that I needed help removing play-doh from the container or putting two lego pieces together.

Frequently, Ryan entered my office and immediately assessed this environment for any changes. "Do you have any new toys in here?" he would inquire on a weekly basis. "No," I would respond, "these are the same toys that are here every week." After surveying his surroundings, Ryan settled on the play-doh, building and pounding it into shape without interacting verbally with me. (*I had the feeling that Ryan was pushing me away.*) I observed, "Today I see that you are working by yourself. Sometimes you want to play or work with me, and sometimes you want to play or work by yourself." Ryan commented, "I **do too** want to play with you. Well, no. I don't know." I reflected further, "It reminds me of how you like to come here, but at the same time you don't like to come here. That can be confusing." "No, it's not confusing," Ryan corrected.

Ryan continued to work with the play-doh. He made an impression of his hand in it and said, "It's my handprint. I want to give it to you. And I want you to keep it and let the clay dry like this. Put it somewhere so that no one else will mess it up. Can I put it here in your desk drawer?" With permission, Ryan put his clay handprint in my desk drawer. "Don't let anyone go in here," he ordered. "Only I can go in here. If someone wants to go in this drawer, tell them '**no**' in a very loud voice." For the duration of his treatment with me, Ryan periodically checked on the handprint, which had hardened, to see if it was still intact. The clay handprint served as a symbol of Ryan himself, held and protected by me, as the transferred mother, in the symbolic form of my desk drawer.

Despite his ongoing ambivalence toward me, Ryan appeared to be feeling increasingly secure in the therapeutic alliance. The following week, he built a couch out of blocks, which we sat upon. He expressed pleasure that the couch was "strong enough to hold us up." He then asked me to help him build a "tall chair" out of blocks. When the chair was completed, Ryan climbed on top, then asked me to remove a block from beneath him. "Take out a block!" he exclaimed. I carefully removed a block and stated, "Okay. I'll make sure you don't fall." "I won't fall," Ryan responded, "take out another one." "Okay," I said, "does it feel shaky or secure?" "It feels secure," answered Ryan. "Take out another one." I removed another block. Ryan declared, "It still feels secure." (*I thought to myself that this play clearly symbolized Ryan's use of the block, as a metaphor for me, to depict how we were building a therapeutic alliance that would provide him with a secure attachment base for exploring his world.*) As this session concluded, Ryan asked, "Will you help me clean up?" Inviting me to help him was a significant shift from his earlier helpful/controlling interactions.

For several consecutive weeks, Ryan rearranged the furniture in my office, climbing under a table or behind a couch to make a house or fort for himself and me. After each house was constructed, Ryan filled it up with items designated as food. Then, he and I would crawl inside and Ryan would listen for sounds or signs of dangerous creatures outside. "I think I hear a T-Rex," he would whisper. Monsters, black-widow spiders, sharks, and dinosaurs with big teeth frequently challenged the safety of the play household.

Through the use of symbolic metaphor, Ryan tentatively began to explore issues surrounding his early childhood trauma. In one session, Ryan suggested, "Let's set up all the dominoes in a row, then let's put the big blocks next to the dominoes so that the little ones can knock over the big ones. No, I mean the big ones can knock over the little ones." After the blocks toppled over the dominoes, Ryan attempted to exert some control over the "big ones" hurting the "little ones" as he ordered me to set them up again.

The following week, we spent most of the session rolling play-doh into little balls and putting balls into a cup, which Ryan designated as "the pool." Ryan stated, "Now, I'm going to make a really big ball. This one is the biggest . . . he is the king!" I inquired, "Is the king the most important ball?" "No," replied Ryan, "this little one is the most important. You made this one. It is the baby." With a story narrative most likely symbolizing his own early experience, Ryan continued, "The baby will guard the others, so he has to sit outside the pool." Ryan proceeded to poke a small hole in the king and placed the baby inside the hole. "It looks like the king is holding the baby," I observed. "He is," Ryan agreed. Ryan's play with the play-doh babies continued as he put all of them into an empty cup. "What is this?" I asked, referring to the cup. "It's a crib," declared Ryan. Ryan then dumped the babies from one crib/cup into another and then repeated the process. From crib/cup to crib/cup, the babies flew, faster and faster. Suddenly, one baby fell to the floor. "Well, that one got away," noted Ryan. "What should we do?" I probed. "You can pick it up," replied Ryan, "and after you get it, say 'bad baby.'" "Does the baby feel like he is bad because he got away?" I inquired. "Yes, he does," Ryan said sadly.

Stage III: Premature Termination and Transfer

Reassessment and Termination Plan.   Ryan had worked with me for a total of fourteen sessions over five months. Controlling and aggressive behaviors continued to varying degrees throughout his treatment. Ryan's controlling behaviors represented his attempts to take charge of the therapeutic alliance (or transferred mother-child interaction) by either controlling me through confrontational punitive directness or attempting to take care of me by offering help or comfort. Interpersonally and in his play, Ryan also displayed highly ambivalent and contradictory responses toward me, including elements of proximity-seeking behaviors mixed with incidents of resistance to contact, hostility, avoidance, anger, sadness, or fear. These persistent attachment-relevant behaviors, characteristic of children with attachment problems, increased in their frequency and intensity as Ryan's treatment evolved.

At this point in his treatment, Ryan's adoptive mother reported that he had begun to ask her questions about his biological parents and to talk about his memories of his most recent foster parents. His nightmares occurred very infrequently now. Ongoing parent guidance during this stage focused on supporting Mr. and Mrs. L. as they dealt with Ryan's temper tantrums, which occurred sporadically when he did not get what he wanted. Mother and father were skilled at providing a safe holding environment for Ryan as he experienced intense feelings of frustration, sadness, anger, and disappointment. At school, Ryan's behavioral difficulties were becoming less disruptive to his class and more manageable to his teacher. Peer relationships were still somewhat unsatisfying for Ryan. At times, he verbalized feelings of sadness to his mother that he did not always get selected by his peers to play on a team or in a game.

At this time, my life situation changed and I prepared to move out of state. Termination plans with Ryan and his parents included transfer to another therapist. During this final portion of our work together, the plan was to address issues associated with premature termination and transfer.

Termination and Transfer Process.   As the therapeutic alliance evolved and narrative themes in treatment began to emerge, I shared with Ryan my plans to move away in two months. Immediately, Ryan verbalized his feelings of disappointment and loss. "How come you have to leave? You are my favorite friend to play with. I like playing with you more than anyone else," he stated sadly. I met with Ryan's parents to prepare them for the possibility that Ryan's initial symptoms might resurface in response to the impending loss and to deal with their feelings of loss as well. Mr. and Mrs. L. expressed interest in finding a new therapist for Ryan. I educated them about available therapists and recommended that Ryan continue in developmental play therapy with a psychodynamic orientation. We addressed their feelings of loss indirectly as we discussed the implications for Ryan. They were unable to deal directly with their own feelings.

After learning that our work would soon end, Ryan began the following session stating, "Let's build a fort today." As he moved chairs, toys, and blocks around the room, Ryan narrated, "I need to turn these chairs upside down so I can make a door for the fort." After carefully turning the chairs upside down, Ryan proceeded to a small table, then to a box of blocks, then to a carton of toys, thoughtfully turning each item upside down. He dumped out a box of crayons and removed cushions from the couch. When it was time to clean up, I reflected, "It looks like this office has been turned upside down." "Yes, it has," Ryan replied. (*To myself, I thought that the upside-down state of the office symbolized Ryan's feeling state about the end of our therapeutic work together and the state of his world.*) "Will you help me clean up?" Ryan inquired. Working together, we put the office back in order.

Within the metaphor of his play, Ryan expressed some of his feelings about the end of our work together. In one of his final sessions, Ryan retrieved the clay handprint made earlier in treatment from my desk drawer. He held it up over his head and announced, "I am going to drop this and it will smash on the floor. Is it okay if I break it? Do you like it?" "Yes, I do like it," I responded. Ryan continued, "But I really want to break it. Will you be mad if I break it?" "No," I answered, "I won't be mad." After thinking it over for a minute, Ryan dropped his clay handprint to the floor and it shattered. "Oh no!" he cried, "I broke it! Are you mad?" Ryan was visibly upset as he fell to the ground himself to collect the pieces. "Are you going to miss it?" he inquired further. Knowing that the clay handprint symbolized Ryan himself, I responded, "I am going to miss it but I am not mad." After again reassuring him that I was not mad but would miss the handprint, I added, "I have a picture of the handprint in my mind to carry with me so that I can remember it, just like I have a picture of you in my mind so that I can think of you when I don't see you any more."

Although I hoped my termination with Ryan would provide an opportunity for him to begin to work through our termination and rework some of his issues with object loss, Ryan attended therapy only sporadically in the last weeks of his treatment. (*To myself, I thought that these absences were connected with Mr. and Mrs. L's own avoidance strategies for coping with the painful feelings associated with object loss.*) Mr. and Mrs. L. called regularly to cancel appointments. During one such call, Mrs. L. told me that Ryan would like to speak with me. Ryan picked up the telephone and said, "You missed my birthday. And I lost another tooth yesterday." Thinking about our ending therapeutic alliance and his absent biological mother, I remarked, "You really are growing up. And, I'm missing it." "I know," replied Ryan. Mrs. L. described Ryan's mood during this period as somewhat more irritable, with a decline in frustration tolerance and an increase in the frequency of temper tantrums. Following our last appointment, Mr. and Mrs. L. selected a clinical social worker in their community to work with Ryan.

Case Discussion

The Case

Ryan was constantly in motion. His difficulties with self-regulation were apparent in impulsive, uncontrolled behavior at home and at school. He was unable to tolerate frustration, modulate his affect, or contain his aggressive impulses that frequently broke through and were discharged toward peers and attachment figures. Through uncontrolled motor activity, Ryan attempted to ward off feelings of rage, pain, anxiety, and vulnerability. He turned passive into active in an attempt to cope with feeling small and powerless and to achieve a sense of control and mastery over external stimuli. Ryan moved quickly from one activity to the next, making it difficult to maintain connections with others. His distorted mental representations of himself and attachment objects interfered with the development of safe, trusting, and meaningful relationships.

In the context of a secure relational bond, mother is expected to serve as auxiliary ego for her infant. In turn, the infant is dependent on mother to organize his internal experience, regulate intense emotions, permit gratification of some impulses, and restrict gratification of other impulses. Gradually, the young child is able to take on these functions. However, without sufficient gratification and symbiotic bonding with his biological mother, Ryan, was unable to develop this capacity for self-regulation. For him, this mental process was disrupted. Because of his unmet needs along this developmental line, Ryan frequently enacted his fantasy of this early symbiotic relationship in therapy.

Fantasies of omnipotence and a need to be in control were apparent as he stated, "I am the boss. Do what I say!" The therapeutic task was to gratify a level of unmet developmental needs and disrupted mental process appropriate to Ryan's expressed level of development. The depth of his needs, however, often left Ryan feeling frustrated and enraged by my inability to meet all of them and by his inability to control me. At home, his frustration and intense negative affect led to temper tantrums and outbursts of rage. Empathy, consistent and clear behavioral boundaries, and reflective verbalizations regarding his affect served as a container or therapeutic holding environment for him as he tried to cope with his intense reactions to frustrations and disappointments. Through the process of identification, Ryan began to internalize controls, label his feelings with words, and tolerate frustration.

Characteristic of neglected children and indicative of his insecure attachment strategy, Ryan displayed a keen awareness of my affective state and an extreme concern for my acceptance and approval. He often asked questions such as, "What are you looking at?" as he vigilantly monitored perceived changes in my facial expression, the direction of my gaze, and the tone of my voice. That Ryan examined my office and the selection of toys each time he entered and noted any perceptible changes further suggests an internal working model of the other person in attachment as inconsistently available and the social environment as unpredictable and unsafe.

A critical therapeutic task in the work with Ryan was to create a consistent, safe, nonpunitive holding environment within which we could begin the process of building a reparative attachment matrix. Ryan's markedly ambivalent and contradictory responses to me were met with a high level of empathic support and acceptance in order to challenge and change his mental representations of self in relation to an attachment figure.

Premature Termination

Although termination ideally occurs upon completion of treatment goals, Ryan's termination in this instance was for therapist-related reasons. That it was his clinician leaving, not Ryan, did not preclude the importance of the termination process and event for Ryan and his parents.

In general, premature termination of therapy is a separation that children have great difficulty understanding. If therapy has had significant meaning for the child, it is natural that he or she will experience feelings of hurt, anger, and anxiety when faced with losing such an important person in their lives. They feel rejected, abandoned, and sad over the real personal loss of their therapist, as well as over the interruption and loss experienced within the transference element of the therapeutic alliance. This transference loss reawakens earlier experiences with separation and loss, and triggers replay within the context of the threatened loss of a meaningful current relationship. Needless to say, how the therapeutic relationship ends will influence whether treatment gains are maintained and how well the transfer takes.

As in all separation and loss experiences, children first experience grief and the full range of the grieving process—including grief and withdrawal, emotional neutrality, negative and hostile feelings, and ambivalence toward the departing therapist (Fraiberg, 1962). Transfer adds two new phases: detachment and attachment. Yet, for these last two phases to occur, the actual events of termination and transfer must first occur. For until the child detaches from the departing therapist, an emotional connection with the new therapist is unlikely to develop.

As could be seen, Ryan's adoptive parents also experienced their own problems with the premature termination and transfer—to the point that they were unable to attend or bring Ryan in for the last few appointments. While such avoidant strategies in the face of loss are not unusual, they do remind the therapist to attend to the parents' issues with separation and loss, as well as the child's. It is also crucial to attend to the interactive effect as the loss experiences of each compound those of the other.

Another key person in handling the separation and loss experiences of premature termination is the therapist because this process is likely to trigger countertransference reactions. As the clinician's own narcissistic grandiosity comes into play, she may think, "No one can help this client like I can." Simultaneously, she is likely to feel both sad at leaving someone in whom she has invested a lot of emotional energy and hard work, and guilty about the interruption of the therapeutic growth process before the work is complete. In Ryan's case, she is also likely to worry whether the effects of the multiple separations from parents, foster parents, and now therapist will be more than Ryan can handle—whether he will risk reaching out to yet another person.

Conclusion

Ryan's insecure attachment to his early primary caregiver and his subsequent experiences of distorted attachments and losses in the foster-care system contributed significantly to his multiple psychosocial difficulties. Through the use of symbolic play, Ryan began to uncover and process issues surrounding his early-childhood trauma. The transference permitted work around his early-childhood experience of neglect—of unmet needs, object loss, and abandonment. The defensive processes of acting out, identification with the aggressor, and projection—which served to support and maintain his early, distorted mental representations of self and other—were gently challenged through dynamic play and verbal interactions in the therapy. In the long term, developmental play therapy was expected to facilitate his intrapersonal development, particularly in the areas of self-regulation and self/other relationships. Premature termination with one clinician and transfer to another, however, interrupted the therapeutic developmental progress that had begun and necessitated a second start, *albeit* at a different level, with his new therapist.

10 Learning Disabilities and Attention-Deficit Disorders

BY CHRISTINE ANLAUF SABATINO, D.S.W., LCSW-C

In early childhood, the preschooler learns through sights, sounds, smells, tastes, and touch. This learning takes place in considerable measure by learning about one's own body and the bodies of others. Ordinarily, family members serve as the foreground and background for this learning endeavor, and have no equal in their significance in the enterprise. Thus, physical proximity to the family as a primary learning environment is central for preschoolers.

Entry into school, however, brings many changes. While family members remain central figures in the child's life, the learning process itself is less tied to the family. The child enters the worlds of childhood and school where nonbodily learning comes to the fore and peers and teachers assume far greater importance. The world of childhood brings peers, games, and rules; the world of school brings reading, writing, and arithmetic (Pine, 1980).

In school, learning becomes a formal and extraordinarily complex process that enables children to develop and record knowledge, thoughts, and feelings in symbolic form and to communicate with others. For most children, developing the ability to read, write, spell, and do arithmetic presents some challenges. For others, however, mastering these learning skills is extraordinarily difficult (Maughan and Yule, 1994).

This chapter presents an overview of two of the most prevalent problems in children's learning process—specific learning disabilities and Attention Deficit Hyperactivity Disorder (ADHD). First, a taxonomy of learning as information-processing is presented with a brief description for each category to help clinical social workers recognize symptoms and understand behaviors observed in treatment. Next, issues in understanding ADHD are discussed with attention to its different categories, medical treatments, and impact on school performance. ADHD is further clarified by contrasting it with other major disorders such as Tourette's Syndrome, oppositional defiant disorder, anxiety, and depression. A case presentation is provided that illustrates the psychosocial, behavioral, educational, and medical interventions undertaken with Sam, a child diagnosed with comorbid disorders, and the concurrent work with his parents. Finally, multiple theoretical perspectives are applied to assessment and intervention based on parent, child, and teacher interviews to aid clinical social workers in developing their own practice model for treating dually diagnosed children and their parents.

Understanding Learning Disabilities

The cause of learning disabilities is unknown. Research, however, has focused on fetal brain development; brain structure; genetic factors; tobacco; alcohol, and other drug use; problems during pregnancy or childbirth; and environmental toxins. What is known is that nearly four million school-age children have learning disabilities (Neuwirth, 1993). Almost half of the students served in federally funded programs for children with disabilities are those with specific learning disabilities. Indeed, this category of disability has increased at a faster rate than the total public school enrollment (Digest of Educational Statistics, 1977).

A person with a learning disability can learn. However, this disorder challenges a person's ability to interpret what is seen or heard or to link information from different parts of the brain. These challenges happen during daily activities at home, with peers, and at school.

Attention, Memory, and Perception

To learn, a child must develop primary skills in attention, memory, and perception that serve as the foundation for secondary skills in thinking and oral language skills. Problems in any of these areas are sometimes referred to as processing problems. In school-aged children, learning disabilities are experienced as academic problems, including problems in reading, handwriting, written expression, and spelling.

According to Kirk and Chalfont (1984), *attention* is the ability to select appropriate or pertinent factors from among numerous competing stimuli that may be auditory, tactile, visual, or kinesthetic in nature. It is the process of selectively bringing relevant internal or external stimuli into focus. This processing problem will be greatly expanded upon in relation to ADHD.

Memory is the ability to recall what has been seen, heard, or experienced. To learn new facts, skills, and ideas, one must retain, recognize, and reproduce past experiences. There are several classifications of memory problems. Short-term memory allows one to remember what has been seen, heard, or experienced after a short interval of a few seconds, minutes, or hours. Long-term memory refers to the retrieval of information after a day. Meaningful memory is the process of relating information to what one already knows. Rote memory is not anchored to existing conceptual systems.

Auditory, visual, and motoric memory are required for all areas of academic performance. For example, in reading, a child with an auditory processing problem may fail to associate sounds of vowels and consonants with written symbols.

Visual memory is necessary for developing spelling and written language skills. Motor memory is the storage, retention, and reproduction of movement patterns, and makes it possible to organize the body to perform a series of acts such as dressing, undressing, tying shoes, dancing, writing, or throwing a ball.

Perception is the psychological operation of deriving meaning from sensation. Perception organizes, structures, and interprets stimuli. Common types of perceptual disabilities include (1) discrimination disabilities, (2) closure difficulties, (3) visual-motor disabilities, (4) perceptual speed problems, (5) sequencing disabilities, (6) difficulties with perceptual modality, and (7) perseveration.

Discrimination disabilities refer to the inability to discriminate similarities and differences among related stimuli in what one sees, hears, touches, and feels in movement, touch and movement combined, or figure-background. Children who have normal visual acuity may still not see the difference between visual stimuli such as *b* and *d*. Spatial positioning problems occur when the child sees the word *was* as *saw*. Depth-perception problems make it difficult to judge distances and result in children bumping into things and falling off chairs. Tracking problems occur when children lose their place when reading.

A child with normal hearing may be thrown into confusion by pitch, loudness, rhythm, melody, rate, or duration of sound and, therefore, be unable to discriminate phonemic structures used to learn reading or spelling. Tactile discrimination allows one to use the sense of touch to provide information about the environment. Examples of difficulty performing tasks that require sensitivity to touch include writing, using eating utensils, or handling small objects. This form of discrimination also is necessary in learning to avoid things such as fire and sharp items.

Movement provides information about the location of objects in the environment in relation to the body itself. A disorder in kinesthetic discrimination interferes with sensory feedback and prevents mastery of basic developmental skills, such as dressing, and complex skills, such as bicycle-riding, handwriting, and sports activities. These children are like the proverbial "bull in a china shop" and may become disoriented and off-balance in open spaces.

Touch and movement stimuli used simultaneously (known as *haptic discrimination*) provide more information than either alone. Finally, *figure-background* refers to the ability to focus on selected relevant visual, auditory, or haptic stimuli in the presence of other competing stimuli (background). In other words, children learn to pick out a specific visual cue from the background in which the figure is embedded. Or the child can focus on the teacher's verbal instructions in the presence of other noise in the classroom.

Closure refers to the ability to recognize when one or more parts of the whole are missing. Visual closure problems make it difficult for a child to identify an object if part of it is missing or a word if a letter is missing. Auditory closure problems make it difficult to recognize a word if only part is heard. A variant form of this problem is sound blending, which requires the synthesis of isolated sounds so that one is unable to decode *c-a-t* to recognize the word *cat*.

A visual-motor disability is the inability to position the eyes or hands in contacting or manipulating objects. This deficit brings about difficulties in directionality, where the child is unable to distinguish between left and right in relation to their own bodies or to stimuli in their environment. Problems in visual-motor coordination are seen in all areas of paper-pencil tasks, throwing, catching, cutting, manipulating tools, or learning new eye-hand activities.

Perceptual speed refers to the length of time required to process an auditory or visual stimuli. These children may require an inordinate time to respond to what they see or what they hear.

Sequencing is remembering the order of events and things that are heard, seen, or done. A common auditory example of sequencing difficulty is the child who cannot follow multiple-step directions: "Go upstairs, get in your pajamas, and brush your teeth."

Perceptual modality refers to the child's preferred learning style, which may be auditory, visual, kinesthetic (touch or movement), or a combination of these. Most children learn through all modalities. However, some children have a severe weakness in one area and great strengths in another. Perceptual-modality skills and preferences are important when it comes to classroom instruction methods.

Perseveration refers to a child continuing an activity after it is no longer necessary. This behavior is sometimes described as the child being in a rut and having difficulty in moving out of the learned mode of response.

Thinking

Kirk and Chalfant (1984) also posit that thinking is a basic psychological process that may further or hinder the learning process. Thinking involves various mental operations such as judgment, comparison, calculations, inquiry, reasoning, evaluation, critical thinking, problem solving, and decision-making. Thinking itself cannot be observed. However, behaviors are indicative of thought processes, and children can be taught effective thinking habits.

Two major areas of thinking related to learning disabilities are concept formation and problem solving. To give meaning and structure to the many stimuli encountered, children must develop some form of order or organization to apply to objects, events, ideas, or situations. In other words, they must learn to impose some system or approach to help them recognize relationships among experiences and to classify stimuli in terms of their attributes. This learning requires multiple steps: (1) attending to characteristics of things experienced; (2) recognizing similarities and differences; (3) identifying common factors; (4) determining the criteria or rules for inclusion or exclusion in the concept; (5) validating the conceptual criteria or rule, which leads one to; (6) retaining and integrating the concept or modifying the concept. Conceptual problems, or problems in abstraction, are seen when the child is unable to make inferences or interpretations from the literal concrete meaning of a stimuli to its general connotation.

Problem solving is the application of reasoning to overcoming obstacles, answering complex questions, and finding solutions to problems-in-living. It is a multistage process that includes (1) recognizing that a problem exists, (2) deciding whether to solve the problem, (3) analyzing the problem, (4) formulating alternative approaches, (5) testing alternative approaches, and (6) resolving the problem or continuing the problem-solving process.

Oral language is an arbitrary code whereby ideas are represented through words and sentences that are communicated from one person to another. It involves the response to sounds heard as well as the child's own vocalizations. To master oral language requires a child to understand and use phonemes, root words, syntax, and semantics, and to know their appropriate function and use. Language development also may be analyzed according to its content, form, or use. Disabilities in oral language are classified as receptive language problems, integrative or inner language problems, expressive oral language problems, or mixed-oral language problems.

Silver (1976) offers another paradigm for describing and understanding learning disabilities. He identifies four tasks that must function for successful learning: input, integration, memory, and output. *Input* refers to information recorded in the brain through all the senses, individually or in combinations. *Integration* requires the information entering the brain to be organized and correctly interpreted. *Memory* requires information to be stored and retrieved. *Output* is the expression or presentation of the material resulting from the three previous operations. Consistent with Kirk and Chalfant (1984), these processing problems may be related to visual, auditory, or kinesthetic stimuli, or a combination of them.

Types of Learning Disabilities

The functional manifestations of these processing problems in the school setting are academic learning disabilities. One or more processing weakness may be associated with a specific academic learning disability. These academic problems are categorized as learning disabilities in reading (Kirk and Kirk, 1971; Lyon, 1995), writing (Hooper, Montgomery, Swartz, Reed, Sandler, Levine, Watson, and Wasileski, 1994), spelling (Ehri, 1989), and arithmetic (Fleishner, 1994).

Dyslexia is a term often used to refer to a developmental reading disorder. Reading skills involve oral reading, word reading, word discrimination, and silent reading that incorporate vocabulary, listening, sequencing, and inference. Comprehension problems are one of the major components of a reading disability.

Written expression is the communication of ideas to others by means of graphic symbols. Children with a writing disability experience difficulty in having ideas to communicate, having language to express these ideas, and translating oral language into written expression so that others understand what is being expressed. Many skills serve as prerequisites for written expression; among them are receptive oral language, expressive oral language, reading, and spelling. Children who lack these prerequisites are poor readers, have limited vocabulary, use poor grammar and syntax, and have difficulty in properly formulating their thoughts for written expression.

Although reading and spelling are different mental processes, many children are disabled in both. Spelling disabilities refer to errors in writing the appropriate sequence of alphabet letters for a word. For many, spelling is a much more difficult task than reading. Besides omission of letters, difficulty may include substituting letters or phonetically misspelling, among other problems. Spelling is particularly difficult in English because approximately 50 percent of the words in the language do not follow regular phonetic rules (Smith, 1991).

Arithmetic disabilities include errors in basic skill such as addition, subtraction, multiplication, and division, as well as higher order computations related to fractions, decimals, word problems, algebra, geometry, or trigonometry. Like reading, writing, and spelling, mathematics also requires multiple information-processing skills.

Intervention

As one can see from this overview of information-processing and academic performance, learning disabilities are not a homogeneous disorder. Although the federal government has designated specific learning disabilities as a handicapping condition (Public Law 94-142, The Education for All Handicapped Children Act), it is characterized by specific areas of weakness in a particular domain, but average or above average performance in other areas of functioning. Further, the field of learning disabilities is replete with disagreement about the definition of the disorder, diagnostic criteria, assessment protocols, treatment procedures, and appropriate educational policies (Lyon, 1995).

In all cases, however, a learning disability is identified as a disorder in information-processing that manifests itself in a child's academic performance. In a learning disability, there is a discrepancy between a child's intellectual ability and actual achievement in one or more academic areas that can be tied to a processing problem. Academic remedial methods for learning disabilities require a multisensory approach using visual, auditory, kinesthetic, and tactile elements.

Children with learning disabilities do not outgrow this brain dysfunction. They often know they are different or believe they are slow. They respond to their frustrations in a variety of ways, from withdrawal to belligerence. Their self-esteem may be severely damaged and their behavior may be an emotional burden for the family.

However, many learning-disabled children learn to adapt and manage their disability. Parents play a critical role in this work by collaborating with school personnel to learn about their child's academic, social, and behavioral strengths, as well as the information-processing and academic-performance problems. Using this information, the parents can structure homework tasks and the home environment in ways that allow a child to succeed. The goal is to help the child feel competent and loved.

Counseling and support groups may be helpful in assisting family members to explore their feelings or obtain information, support, or reassurance, thereby making it easier for the child and family to cope day by day. The goal is for parents and siblings to learn how to tolerate and cope with the learning-disabled child's intense personal pain in the presence of extreme distress.

Understanding Attention-Deficit Hyperactivity Disorder

Problems in learning often co-occur with disorders in attention (Lyon, 1995). The cause of ADHD, formerly known as hyperkinesis or minimal brain dysfunction, is unknown. Commonly suspected causes of ADHD include fetal developmental impairments, neonatal injury, and genetic endowment.

Recent brain research has found the specific areas involved in ADHD. Results indicate that the frontal lobe and basal ganglia are reduced by about 10 percent in size and activity. Genetic research has focused on dopamine pathways, which are the primary neurotransmitters that link the frontal cortex and the basal ganglia.

Further, neuroimaging research has found that ADHD is in part a neuro-developmental lag that affects "the prefrontal cortex (the outer layer of gray matter covering the cerebral hemispheres), the basal ganglia (four collections of neurons located deep in the cerebral hemispheres), and the cerebellum (a portion of the brain involved in the control and coordination of skeletal muscles for voluntary movements . . ." (Castellanos, 1997a, pp. 30–31; 1997b). These brain circuits are "modulated by monoamine neurotransmitters, principally dopamine, which affects the 'signal-to-noise' ratio of neuronal communications (Castellanos, 1997c, p. 382).

These brain circuits serve the executive functions that are defined as control processes involving inhibition and delay in responding. These functions allow an individual to initiate, sustain, inhibit/stop, and shift thoughts and actions (Denckla, 1996). In association with executive functions are the abilities to prioritize, organize, and strategize. Executive dysfunctions are often found in (1) initiation, the ability to plan and organize; (2) sustaining, the ability to concentrate and be vigilant; (3) inhibition, the ability to engage in self-control and self-monitoring; and (4) shifting, the ability to maintain cognitive flexibility.

These executive dysfunctions interface with learning problems in acquiring and using skills in listening, speaking, reading, writing, reasoning, mathematics, and social skills. Denckla's research has led her to posit that ADHD is a major developmental problem "that affects academic achievement in childhood and has equally if not greater psychosocial implications, which is why it is a major child psychiatric diagnosis" (Denckla, 1989, p. 156).

Incidence and Comorbidity

The incidence of this disorder in the school-age population is 1 to 3 percent with the full syndrome, 5 to 10 percent with partial ADHD syndrome co-existing with other problems such as anxiety and depression, and another 15 to 20 percent showing transient, subclinical, or masquerading behaviors suggestive of ADHD (CHADD, 1999). This prevalence reflects the heterogeneity of the condition and methodological differences in assessment (Szatmari, 1992; Baumgaertel, Wolraich, and Dietrich, 1995). Two to three times more boys than girls are affected and, on average, there is at least one child in every classroom in the United States who needs help for this disorder (Neuwirth, 1994). This disorder tends to be chronic with significant symptomatology in evidence into adolescence and adulthood (Ervin, Bankert, and DuPaul, 1996).

A small proportion of children with ADHD have Tourette's Syndrome, which is characterized by tics and other movements like eye blinks or facial twitches that they cannot control. Some children with Tourette's may grimace, shrug, sniff, or bark out words. Another comorbid condition is oppositional defiant disorder. These children are extremely stubborn, have outbursts of temper, act belligerently, or are defiant. A third group of children experience comorbid conditions of internal mental disorders, such as anxiety and depression. The anxious child feels tremendous worry, tension, or uneasiness that affect the ability to think. The depressed child feels sad, overwhelmed, and not hopeful about the future. Although the percentage of children with co-existing disorders is small, children with ADHD should be screened for each of these co-existing disorders to rule in or rule out the need for complementary treatment plans (Neuwirth, 1994).

Types of ADHD

According to Children and Adults with Attention-Deficit/Hyperactivity Disorder (CHADD, 1999), there are four subtypes of ADHD: ADHD–inattentive type; ADHD–hyperactive/impulsive type; ADHD–combined type; and ADHD–not otherwise specified. The CHADD subtypes are defined as follows:

- ADHD–inattentive type is defined by an individual experiencing at least six of the following characteristics: (1) fails to give close attention to details or marked careless mistakes, (2) has difficulty sustaining attention, (3) does not appear to listen, (4) struggles to follow through on instructions, (5) has difficulty with organization, (6) avoids or dislikes requiring sustained mental effort, (7) often loses things necessary for tasks, (8) is easily distracted, and (9) is forgetful in daily activities.

- ADHD–hyperactive/impulsive type is defined by an individual experiencing at least six of the following characteristics: (1) fidgets with hands or feet or squirms in seat, (2) has difficulty remaining seated, (3) runs about or climbs excessively (in adults, may be limited to subjective feelings of restlessness), (4) experiences difficulty engaging in activities quietly, (5) acts as if driven by motor, (6) talks excessively, (7) blurts out answers before questions have been completed, (8) has difficulty waiting in turn-taking situation; and (9) interrupts or intrudes upon others.

- ADHD–combined type is defined by an individual meeting both sets of attention and hyperactive/impulsive criteria.

- ADHD–not otherwise specified is defined by an individual who demonstrates some characteristics, but an insufficient number of symptoms to reach a full diagnosis. The symptoms, however, are disruptive in everyday life.

The *DSM IV* (APA, 1994) has set forth the criteria for a diagnosis of ADHD. Symptoms in either inattention or hyperactivity/impulsivity must have persisted for at least six months to a degree that is maladaptive and inconsistent with developmental level; been present before age seven; been present in more than one setting, such as school or home; significantly impaired function in social, academic, or occupational functioning; and not occurred exclusively during the course of other specific disorders. If both inattention and hyperactivity/impulsivity criteria are met, the diagnosis is ADHD–combined type.

Common Behavioral Descriptors

As can be seen from these listings of types of ADHD, three common descriptors appear: children who generally are excessively active, children who are unable to sustain their attention, and children who are deficient in impulse control for their developmental level (Barkley, 1996). They are restless, inattentive, distractible, and disorganized.

Taylor (1994) defines *overactivity* as an excess of movement that exists even when the child is asleep. It is likened to a train engine that only has two speeds: full throttle and off. Overactivity may manifest itself as an increase in the tempo of normal activities, an increase in purposelessness, or body movements that are inappropriate for a situation.

Attention deficit refers to behaviors characterized by orienting oneself only briefly to a task, changing activities rapidly, focusing on irrelevant aspects of the environment, and playing for brief periods. Barkley describes children with *inattention* as those unable to

> sustain attention or respond to task or play activities as long as others of the same age and to follow through on rules and instructions as well as others. It is also seen in the child being more disorganized, distracted, and forgetful than others of the same age. . . . Parents and teachers frequently complain that these children do not seem to listen as well as they could for their age, cannot concentrate, are easily distracted, fail to finish assignments, daydream, and change activities more often than others. (1996, p. 67)

He goes on to describe problems in *disinhibition* or *impulsivity* as problems with

> fidgetiness, staying seated when required, moving about, running, climbing more than other children, playing noisily, talking excessively, interrupting others' activities, and being less able than others to wait in line or take turns in games. . . . Parents and teachers describe them as acting as if driven by a motor incessantly in motion, always on the go, and unable to wait for events to occur. (Barkley, 1996, p. 67)

In other words, these children are unable to regulate their activity level, sustain their attention, and control their impulses to act. Consequently, they are unable to produce work consistently. Situational and contextual factors such as time of day, fatigue, task complexity, or absence of adult supervision during a task may affect symptom severity.

For clinicians working with school personnel, the following checklists are offered as operational definitions meaningful to a classroom teacher (Association for Exceptionality and Learning Disorders, 1988). These lists may be useful in collecting information from both family and school during Stage I: Biopsychosocial Assessment, and in periodic reviews of a child's psychosocial functioning at school.

Hyperactivity may be operationally defined when a child

- climbs onto cabinets and furniture
- is always on the go and would rather run than walk
- fidgets or squirms
- does things in a loud and noisy way
- must always be doing something or having to fidget

Inattention may be operationally defined when a child

- needs a calm, quiet atmosphere in order to work or concentrate
- frequently asks to have things repeated
- is easily distracted, confuses details, and does not finish what is started
- hears but does not seem to listen
- has difficulty concentrating unless in a one-to-one structured situation

Impulsivity may be operationally defined when a child

- calls out or makes noises in class
- is extremely excitable
- has trouble waiting for a turn
- talks excessively
- disrupts other children

These and other checklists are useful in their very detail about the number of symptoms currently present. They also can be used to assess the degree of symptom severity, history of onset, and the symptom triggers.

Treatment of ADHD

Children do not outgrow ADHD; they do, however, learn to adapt and cope with the disorder. ADHD requires a multimodal treatment approach consisting of medical, educational, behavioral, and psychosocial interventions. This disorder requires a coordinated effort among all the involved professionals in conjunction with the parents.

Medication.   Psychostimulants are the most widely used medication for management of ADHD. These include Ritalin (methylphenidate), Dexidrine or Dextrostat (dextroamphetamine), and Cylert (pemoline). Whether to prescribe medication, as well as the specific type and dose of medication, must be individually determined for each child by a specialist in consultation with the parents. It is important to note that although 70 to 80 percent of children respond positively to medication, periodic trials of different medications and ongoing monitoring of medication is indicated (Neuwirth, 1994).

There is a debate among professionals and parents about the use of medication. The most common concern is side effects related to reduction in appetite and difficulty in sleeping. It is a myth that these drugs lead to drug addiction in later life. Rather, they help children focus and be more successful at school, home, and play. It is also a myth that they will make a child jittery or sedated. They do help children control their hyperactivity, inattention, and impulsivity.

Education.   Children suspected of having ADHD need an educational evaluation, which public schools are required to administer at their own expense. Under the Individuals with Disabilities Education Act (IDEA), a child who meets the criteria for ADHD may qualify for special-education classes under the category of "Other Health Impaired." Children who do not qualify under IDEA may still qualify for services under the National Rehabilitation Act, Section 504, which defines disabilities broadly.

Many children with ADHD can be taught in a regular educational setting with adjustments in the classroom environment. Researchers have found that the following characteristics promote success in the classroom: (1) predictability, (2) structure, (3) shorter work periods, (4) small teacher-to-pupil ratio, (5) more individualized instruction, (6) interesting curriculum, and (7) use of positive reinforcers. They also suggest a number of teacher characteristics that are helpful in teaching children with ADHD: (1) positive academic expectations; (2) frequent monitoring and checking of work; (3) clarity in giving directions; (4) warmth, patience, and humor; (6) consistency and firmness; (6) knowledge of different behavioral interventions; and (7) willingness to work with a special-education teacher (CHADD, 1999).

Other more severely affected children may need specialized classrooms, programs, or schools. In either case, however, children with ADHD are likely to evidence poor school performance unless they receive appropriate educational assessment and intervention services.

Behavior Management.   Behavior management techniques must be used in conjunction with other interventions. Clear and consistent expectations, directions, and limits are mandatory. A proactive discipline program is one that teaches and rewards appropriate behavior, while eliminating or reducing negative behavior through appropriate methods such as time out, natural consequences, and loss of privileges. Behavior-management techniques are likely to be helpful with these children at home, at school, and in recreational settings.

Psychotherapy and Concurrent Parent Work.   Life is very hard for the child with ADHD. These children may experience low self-esteem, frustration, hopelessness, and confusion about being different. Although they may have an average or a high IQ, they may perceive themselves as being dumb and not really comprehend the difference between intelligence level and ADHD symptoms. In addition, their peers may make fun of or ostracize them. Thus, developmental play therapy tailored to their preferred learning style may be used to help them deal with their confused perception of self and clarify misinformation.

It is also hard to parent a child with ADHD. Parents may feel overwhelmed, powerless, confused, in need of guidance, and in need of sorting out their feelings and fears about having a child who is different. Depending on their mix of issues, educational guidance, parent support and advocacy groups, concurrent parent work, or psychotherapy may be helpful.

The following course of treatment for Sam illustrates the difficulties faced by a child experiencing ADHD with Mixed Anxiety and Depressed Mood and information-processing problems. The case also illustrates the problems in parenting and the parenting issues addressed in concurrent parent work.

Course of Treatment: Sam
by Mary C. Owen, M.S.W., LCSW

Stage I: Biopsychosocial Assessment

Presenting Problem.   Sam is an eleven-year-old Caucasian boy in the fifth grade who presented for therapy with very advanced verbal skills. His parents brought him for therapy after a parent-teacher conference indicated behavioral and academic concerns that included high distractibility, restlessness, poor organization, and incomplete homework assignments. Because Sam had participated in the school's program for gifted and talented students and had always reported liking school, his parents were surprised by the teacher's report. When talking with Sam about the teacher's concerns, he readily agreed that completing schoolwork had become more difficult in fifth grade, but argued that the subject matter was easy to comprehend. He felt as if he understood things more easily than some of his peers.

Family History.   Sam is the only child of parents currently working in highly technical fields that had required high academic achievement. After trying to start a family for several years, Sam's parents had him later in their lives. Until Sam was nine years old, his mother was a full-time homemaker and his father worked long hours. When Sam entered fourth grade, his mother accepted a full-time teaching position in her technical field and his father achieved a managerial position that allowed him to be home most evenings. His parents reported that someone was always available to help Sam with homework or school-related projects, but he rarely asked for help. Until fifth grade, he maintained a high-grade point average. History indicated no childhood trauma.

Further history indicated that Sam's mother had been treated for major depression during adolescence. Her brother (Sam's maternal uncle) experienced severe school failure when young and was recently treated for anxiety as an adult. Sam's father reported no personal mental-health problems, but indicated that his mother (Sam's paternal grandmother) had been receiving treatment and medication for depression for years.

Child Assessment. Sam presented with a cheerful disposition and repeatedly demonstrated a great deal of knowledge on a variety of topics through his almost constant verbal chatter. Although he was quite able to relate concrete information and facts, Sam became silent and appeared somewhat confused whenever I approached the subject of his feelings. When I asked "How do you feel about school?" or "What feelings do you have when you're sitting at your desk noticing everyone else working on their assignments?," his response was often, "I don't know" or a shrug of the shoulders. I changed from a directive approach to a more nondirective one and reflected some observations of possible emotions for Sam by commenting, "You seem a little disappointed when you talk about the change in your grades" or "I wonder if you were feeling frustrated over what your Dad said to you about your grades." Again, Sam would not make direct commentary on his feelings and would continue with expressing random thoughts he was having or relating details about objects in the room that caught his attention. If allowed, Sam would choose to spend his whole therapy hour relating disparate pieces of information and knowledge, while wandering around the room touching various toys but not playing with any of them in a sustained way. Consequently, the therapy hour was structured by the therapist to include (1) some free talking time; (2) a therapist-introduced activity focused on feelings, school performance, and task completion; and (3) follow-up parental guidance.

From the information provided by the classroom teacher, his first interview, and the initial parent consultation, Sam was given a diagnosis of ADHD, with my acknowledgment that Sam also showed behavioral symptoms that were not completely explained by the diagnosis of ADHD.

Treatment Plan. After hearing the parents' concerns in an initial consultation, it was decided that I would see Sam in weekly individual semistructured therapy for a trial of twelve weeks. His parents would receive weekly parental guidance.

Permission to contact Sam's classroom teacher was obtained at the initial consultation. The importance of gathering initial classroom behavior information through a standardized behavioral checklist to assess the problem and measure treatment progress was explained to the parents; they readily agreed. It also was understood that the therapist and teacher would exchange general information about Sam in order to develop classroom strategies that might help him improve his classroom behavior and school performance.

Stage II: Creation of Therapeutic Alliance

Child Work.   Sam appeared to enjoy coming to sessions and his parents reported no problems with getting him to comply with attending. However, Sam worked hard to distract me from moving the sessions from free talk to a focused activity or topic. Understanding the high level of frustration Sam experiences whenever he is in a structured setting that demands sustained concentration and effort on his part, I contracted with him as to how much of the therapy time would be "free talking time" and how much of it would be "working time." By applying effort during the "working time," Sam was guaranteed "free talking time" the following session. This plan helped Sam remain cooperative with the structured activities even when they drew upon skills in which he was weak.

It became apparent that Sam needed help both in finding ways to improve his behavior in the classroom setting and in his thinking process. Often he would explain his poor school performance as a byproduct of the teacher's behavior (*"She gives such dumb assignments." "She lets the kids ask too many questions when it's so obvious.")* or a byproduct of his classmates' behavior (*"Everyone is always worrying about homework, whereas I make it easy on myself." "Some kids want the teacher to think they're good so they do more than they should.").*

I first established some guiding principles with Sam to help him get an accurate perception of himself and his situation in the classroom. Together, Sam and I generated three principles: (1) everyone learns in their own individual way; (2) everyone needs respect and understanding; and (3) performance is based on desire and effort. Sam wrote these principles down on a 3 x 5 card and taped them to the inside cover of his notebook for an easily accessible reminder. It was determined that whenever Sam found himself feeling frustrated with himself, his teacher, or his peers, he would open his notebook and read through the principles to help maintain a positive attitude in the classroom setting and motivate him to apply additional effort to the task at hand. Sam reported that the card helped him stay more focused. He also began using the card at home as a reminder while doing his homework. Whenever he felt extra restlessness or lacked motivation to complete his homework, he would read through the principles as a way to refocus his efforts.

I determined that it would be helpful to increase Sam's ability to utilize self-talk as a means for strengthening self-control and decreasing anxiety. Through the process of play and with a variety of play materials, Sam was repeatedly asked to develop self-talk for the characters in his play. I would ask, "Now what is it that this soldier is saying to himself about that bad alien guy?" or "What is Allie (alligator puppet) thinking that makes him think it's okay to interrupt his dad?" or "How does the car know it's time to crash into the train?" When Sam could not answer the self-talk questions directly, I would transition to a nondirective approach, where I would propose self-talk for the characters that would either be accepted or corrected by Sam. For example, when Sam had the rabbit puppet bite the fox puppet and then run and hide, I proposed, "I guess the rabbit is saying to himself that it's not safe for anyone to find out about the bad feelings he has inside." To which Sam responded, "Yeah, but the fox knows because the fox is stronger."

Much of the work in the first twelve sessions involved helping Sam talk about his feelings of frustration and self-doubt when presented with what he knew was a reasonable task, but which seemed too hard or tedious for him to do. Most of the structured part of the sessions were activities common to many therapeutic settings, with modifications when necessary to specifically address Sam's particular behavior problems, emotional tendencies, and social difficulties. Included in the activities were (1) constructing a classroom setting out of blocks and figures, and playing out common school problems; (2) making a mask that had "inside" and "outside" thoughts; (3) writing and illustrating a book on *Seven Ways to Cure Restlessness*; (4) reenacting a *Homework War* with soldiers and aliens; and (5) making a list of a hundred positive things about himself and/or his life.

Sam displayed a range of emotional responses to the challenge of the structured activities, including frustration, anger, withdrawal, fear, sadness, and shame. Each time, I reassured Sam that our work together was meant to give Sam ideas about how to be aware of his feelings and, at the same time, continue to move through a task successfully. Often, I would acknowledge Sam's feeling with an empathic statement such as, "It's maddening to have to work so hard at keeping your restlessness under control" or "Not being able to do something that is easy for a classmate to do makes you feel ashamed." I followed up such comments with encouragement for continuing to try. As feelings were discussed, I introduced a simple cognitive problem solving model that Sam began to use more consistently by the end of the twelve sessions. The model included Sam (1) identifying the steps necessary to complete a task; (2) identifying the steps with which he needed help and the steps he could complete independently; and (3) asking for help when needed.

In addition, I helped Sam identify his emotional response to the task being requested, and spent time helping him find ways to think about tasks without getting anxious or annoyed. Some of Sam's willingness to work on task completion was due to my helping him understand how to pace himself by being aware of his emotional tensions in the earlier stages of their development, rather than waiting for his frustrations to become strong and overwhelming. Whenever I would observe Sam beginning to have a negative emotional reaction to the activity, I would say, "What are you feeling right at this moment?" and "If you're not sure what the feeling is, can you find a place inside your body that feels a little tense or upset? What does that feel like?" Because of his attention problems, Sam had difficulty paying attention not only to external cues, but also internal cues. Sometimes I would say, "Sam, you're beginning to look frustrated. Are you noticing anything?"

It was very important for me to attend closely to Sam throughout the structured activity to identify the subtle signs of emotional reactivity, including (1) increased breathing rate; (2) flushing or draining of color in the face; (3) increased moisture in the eyes or tearfulness; (4) increased rocking, foot tapping, or extraneous body movement; (5) change in rate of speech; and (6) change in rate of doing the activity itself. By helping Sam notice the early signs of emotional reactivity, he was able to learn how to constructively manage his emotional responses in stressful situations. Sam found that he could better control his behaviors by using his 3 x 5 card reminder, problem solving model, and self-talk at the onset of an emotional response and pace himself with reasonable expectations. For example, Sam learned to say to himself, "I'm feeling a little tense. I need to take care of this NOW. I'll read my 3 x 5 card."

Shortly before the end of the contracted twelve sessions, Sam initiated asking, "Is there anything that can help my mind slow down to a normal speed?" When I pursued this request with him, I discovered that Sam had heard of a boy at school who was going to the nurse's office every day for a pill to "calm down." After discussing this request with his parents, I referred the family to a child psychiatrist for a medication evaluation. Subsequently, Sam was put on a trial of Ritalin and reported that he thought it helped keep his mind from racing ahead of his intended actions.

Parent Work.   During the first twelve sessions, concurrent parent work included helping the parents structure a behavior-modification program at home that would reward Sam for improving school performance as well as completing chores at home. His parents realized that, in the past, they had expected very little from him at home and had not been aware of how many deficits he had in organizing his time and materials, maintaining focus, and persisting through times of frustration. They began to see the disparity between his verbal intelligence and actual behavioral performance when they saw how frustrated Sam became when he could not "*talk* the kitchen counter into being clean or *think* his dirty socks off the floor." It was necessary to help Sam's parents understand that improved school performance had more to do with developing good study and work habits than making good grades. It was stressed that Sam's innate intelligence and verbal strengths had carried him successfully through the lower grades of elementary school, but that good work habits were going to be necessary for him to succeed in the more demanding grades of upper elementary school and beyond.

If Sam had not initiated the idea of medication, I would have discussed medication concerns with Sam and his parents during the twelve-week session. Too often after a diagnosis of ADHD has been made, medication is introduced as a cure or is perceived as one by either the child, parents, or teacher. When a request for medication is immediately acted upon, this misperception allows the child, parents, and sometimes the teacher to ignore their responsibilities for addressing the behaviors, thoughts, and feelings that need to be managed and will not be changed by the use of medication. Understanding that medication is an aid and not a cure is essential if the parents and child are to realize how much therapeutic work must be done for the child to function well.

Consequently, I wanted to ensure that Sam's parents fully understood how to utilize behavior-modification techniques at home. In addition, I wanted to impress upon the parents their role in and responsibility for managing a behavior-modification program for Sam and the need to make a long-range commitment to meeting Sam's behavior-modification needs. Part of the success of a behavior-modification program for a child with learning problems is the parents' willingness to accept the child as having special needs that might last throughout the developing years. I helped the parents to identify some of their own discouragement and frustration with Sam's disability. Through this process, the parents were able to make the necessary adjustments in their expectations of Sam to ensure a continued commitment to an effective behavior-modification program. Medication then became an additional aid to help Sam progress in his management of his disability and not a substitute for Sam's behavioral and emotional work in therapy.

Evaluation of Progress.   At the end of the twelve sessions, Sam, his parents, and his teacher all reported that Sam's school performance had improved. Results from the second behavior checklist completed by the teacher confirmed that Sam had improved in comparison to the first behavior checklist results gathered at the beginning of treatment. He appeared to be more motivated to complete tasks and had begun to use the problem solving model from therapy at school with both his teacher and his peers. He appeared more relaxed in therapy sessions and was able to carry on conversations in which he did not talk constantly.

Stage III: Identification of Narrative Themes

Child Work.   Although Sam had found some success in the classroom setting and at home, he was willing to contract for another twelve sessions. (His parents had earlier agreed to this after discussing his needs.) Sam continued to find it difficult to manage sustained peer relationships and reported that he was being ignored by peers or overtly rebuked by them, even though he was a friendly and cheerful person. Through therapist-structured play, Sam developed and performed a series of puppet shows that related the problematic peer situations that he repeatedly experienced in the school setting. Sam taped two puppet shows entitled *How to Make Friends* and *How to Keep Friends*. I guided Sam in examining how the different puppets thought and felt in each situation. He was encouraged to focus on the puppets having empathy for one another and being able to take another puppet's perspective. I would ask questions such as, "What does the rabbit need to say to the fox so the fox will know that the rabbit is sorry about biting him?" or "How does the alligator know he has hurt the bear's feelings?" Because it was difficult for Sam to attend to such intricate details about relationships and emotional expressions, he took the tapes home and watched and rewatched them several times. (His parents were encouraged to watch them with him and discuss them as well.) Each puppet show ended with Sam and I determining a lesson or overarching thought about peer relationships that he could practice while interacting with peers in the classroom setting (*e.g., "Give others their physical space." "Wait, watch, and listen." "Stay on the subject."*). In addition, I recommended to the classroom teacher and parents that these particular lessons be emphasized at school and at home when applicable to an educational or social situation.

Sam reported that he was able to use self-talk to remind him of the lessons while interacting with peers and that he was able to maintain more positive peer relationships. Several sessions were devoted to Sam examining magazine and family pictures, and analyzing the emotional expressions on the faces of people in the pictures. Repeatedly, I pointed out signs of emotion (e.g., "How is this frown line different from this smile?" "Can you see how his teeth are clenched?" "Look at how deep the lines are in her forehead.") to Sam and have him guess what those signs might be conveying. Sometimes I would have Sam mimic the pictures so that he could get a stronger impression of how people communicate their feelings. These sessions helped strengthen Sam's empathy and emotional awareness of others.

Parent Work.   During this time, the parent guidance sessions focused on maintaining a consistent behavior-modification program at home. Although this program had proven to be very helpful in the initial twelve weeks of therapy, Sam's parents struggled with the need to continue thinking in behavior-modification terms as a new way of life in their home. Because both had been high academic achievers and highly self-motivated students, they found it frustrating and discouraging to think that Sam might need a form of external reinforcement to maintain strong school performance. It also was difficult for them to realize that even with external reinforcement and structure, Sam still might not achieve as much academically as his high intelligence would suggest. Parental guidance included making written materials on ADHD children available to Sam's parents and increasing their knowledge about the disorder with which Sam was struggling. Discussing and universalizing about the strong emotional reactions and difficulties parents often have when a child has a disorder with long-lasting effects helped them feel less isolated and become more accepting of Sam and his need for ongoing support and structure from them. Even though this issue had been addressed in the initial twelve weeks of therapy, it was not surprising that it reemerged during the second twelve weeks. It is to be expected that parents periodically need to reexamine their feelings about their child's disability. This reworking can be especially true when the child moves to a new developmental stage that might trigger parents' awareness of new expectations that will not be met.

Evaluation of Progress.   At the end of the twenty-fourth session, Sam and his teacher reported that his peer relationships were slightly improved. He had begun to develop some confidence in how to approach peer interactions in a more positive way. His teacher verified his attempts. However, Sam and his teacher thought that he would need to have much more practice in relating to his peers differently before the peer relationships would change significantly enough to be considered rewarding for both Sam and his classmates.

Upon further exploration, Sam revealed that he sometimes experienced high levels of anxiety and self-doubt in the classroom setting. His parents reported him to be more irritable and moody lately. At my recommendation, Sam and his parents agreed to continue participation in therapy and contracted for another twenty-four sessions. At this time, reevaluation indicated that Sam was experiencing Adjustment Disorder with Mixed Anxiety and Depressed Mood. I recommended that Sam and his parents discuss this added dimension of anxious and depressed feelings and symptoms with his child psychiatrist to determine whether there was a need for a medication change. After evaluation, Sam's psychiatrist decided to maintain the medication without changes and encouraged Sam and his parents to work on the problems in therapy first.

Stage IV: Developmental Growth and Change

Child Work. Although Sam initially identified his problematic thoughts and feelings and had agreed to continued therapy, he became reticent and more restless in our sessions. I failed to engage Sam in a variety of structured activities. Conversations again often ended abruptly with Sam replying, "I don't know," or shrugging his shoulders. He spent his "free-talk time" questioning why he had to be in therapy and exclaiming how dumb everything and everyone seemed to be. Empathic listening and responding to Sam during this time did little to abate his resistance to working therapeutically with me.

I initiated a mutual storytelling technique in which we created stories together by each taking turns telling a sentence. In addition, I encouraged Sam to use the toys in the room to act out the story at the same time it was created. I then wrote the story down as we went along. I interested Sam in the mutual story-telling process by starting a story with, "Once upon a time, there was a boy who noticed that everyone in the world was dumb and that everything went wrong." Over several sessions, we created a story that revealed Sam's extreme fears of failure and his confusion due to his belief that he was so different from his father that he no longer felt he deserved his father's love. Because he was so different from his father, he also questioned whether his mother could love him. Sam linked these thoughts and feelings to the fact that he had ADHD and that it would cause him learning problems throughout his life.

A teacher consultation confirmed that Sam was using compensatory skills in the classroom and for homework assignments to achieve academic success. Sam seemed unable to explain why he got so anxious and depressed about his school performance when his teacher and his grades seemed to indicate improvement. He identified his process of internal dialogue with its persistent themes of "not being good enough," "the need to be perfect," and "the desire not to exist if imperfect." I questioned Sam about "not wanting to exist" and determined that he was not an active suicide risk at this time. However, I alerted his parents to the necessity of being sensitive to possible varying levels of self-despair. Through the mutual storytelling process, Sam and I developed several variations on the original story that, over time, came closer to an acceptance of his strengths and weaknesses and a tolerance for his imperfections.

In addition, Sam did a series of artwork that identified personal attributes similar to and different from his mother and a series of artwork that identified personal attributes similar to and different from his father. Whenever Sam would identify an attribute (e.g., good sense of humor, careless, smart, loses things), I would ask, "How is this similar to or different from your mother? Your father?" or "Is this something that is unique about you or your family?" As Sam developed a more complete picture of himself, he was able to separate out who he thought he was from who he thought he should be. In this way, he also gained an understanding of what his parents might value.

Again, Sam was able to generate more positive self-talk. We developed a new 3 x 5 card to add to his first card. This new card focused on three principles about self-esteem: (1) I can be liked for who I am; (2) I can have strengths and weaknesses and still be a good person; and (3) I can be different from my parents and still belong to the family. By focusing on these cognitive reframing principles, Sam was able to decrease his anxious and depressive approach in situations. He reported being able to listen to criticism with a more open mind, and could see his parents' frustration with him as growing out of their desire to help, not out of a desire to reject him.

Parent Work.   During this time, the concurrent parent sessions became much richer and more intense in the quality and range of emotions being felt and expressed by Sam's parents. His mother identified her extreme fears that Sam was "going to turn out like my brother and amount to nothing." His father agreed that he thought that "he didn't have much in common with Sam." His parents began to explore and understand how their strong emotional reactions to Sam's diagnosis of ADHD, the loss of their idealized perfect child, and their subsequent feelings about Sam as a person could be affecting Sam and his thoughts and feelings about himself. Further exploration revealed how Sam's parents had experienced disappointment and frustration with each other as parents who were attempting and failing to meet the challenges of parenting a special-needs child. His parents actively sought more constructive ways to think about Sam's needs and their feelings. They became less perfectionistic about their parenting and focused on how to maintain a positive attitude toward Sam. They worked on believing that his difficulties were not an indication of their personal failings. With this work, they came to a sense of resolution about Sam, his needs, and their ability to parent him.

Stage V: Termination

Progress Evaluation.   At the end of forty-eight sessions, Sam, his parents, and his teacher reported marked improvement in school performance, peer relationships, and home behaviors. In addition, Sam reported feeling better about himself, showed no symptoms of anxiety or depressed mood, and evidenced a return to his general cheerful disposition. His parents reported success at home with the behavior-management system that they had agreed to maintain, and an ability to appreciate and enjoy Sam as an individual who was both similar to and different from them.

Child Work. Termination was set shortly after the forty-eighth session. As Sam reviewed what he had learned in therapy and the different ways that he now felt, he reported feeling good about ending sessions because he thought he had a good plan and skills for responding to difficult situations. He identified his 3 x 5 cards that he would keep using and the lessons from his stories that would help him with useful self-talk. Although Sam agreed that things were much improved and that he felt he had an understanditng of how to work with his parents and teacher to maintain school success, he appeared somewhat ambivalent about ending the sessions. I explored his feelings about terminating by asking, "What is it you think you will miss most about not coming to therapy sessions?" Sam identified that he would miss most being creative, that so much of his life was structured and made demands on him. I empathized with Sam about the frustration of having a disorder where extra structure was a necessary part of daily living. I then asked Sam, "Is there anything you can think of to do right now that would assure you that sometimes you can be spontaneous and unstructured and that it will be okay?" Sam decided to draw a picture for me as a "good-bye" present. I expressed much appreciation and congratulated him for finding a positive way to use his creativity and express his feelings.

Case Discussion

Diagnostic Issues

Before attempting to understand Sam on a biopsychosocial level, it was important to establish that his poor school performance was not merely caused by boredom and low academic challenge. Because bright children often understand academic material easily, sometimes they fail to understand that other children might require more classroom instruction and why homework assignments repeating material already learned in class should require their time and attention. Conferring with the classroom teacher was essential in ruling out the possibility that Sam's behaviors were caused by boredom.

It also was important to confirm that the focus of the teacher's concerns that led to referral for treatment had been accurately related by the parents. Without directly talking with a classroom teacher, it is impossible for a therapist to fully understand if a child's behavior is distractibility, frustrated irritability and disorganization suggesting ADHD or purposeful disruption, angry threats, and passive-aggressive noncompliance suggesting Oppositional Defiant Disorder. It was established that Sam's pleasant disposition was consistent in the classroom setting and that the teacher did not experience difficult power struggles with him. This finding confirmed that Sam's behaviors were not a product of oppositionality.

The classroom teacher also can be a source of information about the overall cultural climate of the classroom/school. If there is a mixture of cultures or ethnicity among the students or between the teacher and students, certain customary behaviors of one culture or ethnic group might be viewed as problematic while behaviors of another group go unnoticed. If children perceive themselves to be unacceptable due to cultural or ethnic reasons, feelings of low self-esteem and anger at feeling rejected can lead to acting-out behaviors and poor school performance. Sam's school in an upwardly mobile, middle-class suburban neighborhood had a very homogeneous student population; there appeared to be no cultural/ethnic components to Sam's case.

By having contact with the teacher at the beginning of treatment, the clinical social worker can establish a baseline for the child's behaviors. This baseline makes it easy to track behavioral improvement and treatment success over time. Such systematic tracking is helpful because it is sometimes difficult for parents to discern change in view of the slow progress of therapy and the inevitable inconsistencies of behaviors that children periodically evidence during treatment. In addition, it provides valuable information if parents want to consider having their child on medication. Too often, trial medications are suggested and used without data that fully establish specific symptoms or severity of symptoms. Consequently, determining the effectiveness of treatment or medication is a more difficult task for the parents and doctor monitoring the medical aspects of a case.

Psychosocial Issues

Drawing from psychosocial developmental theory, Sam may be seen as displaying difficulty in successfully managing the psychosocial crisis of the childhood stage of industry versus inferiority (Erikson, 1950). This stage finds children focused on task ability and skill, as well as task completion to attain a feeling of competence. Competition, in the sense of being able to keep up with or do better than one's peers, is a central theme of this developmental period. Along with performing as well as one's peers, a central skill is the ability to negotiate the politics of the peer group and develop a feeling of belonging and getting along that is based on competency and performance. This competency is measured by activity or action. Although Sam could understand the academic material being presented, he was not able to follow through behaviorally with the expected tasks of the classroom setting. For him, the classroom was a consistent reminder of how difficult it was to organize his thoughts into action. He repeatedly failed at task completion. When Sam compared himself to his peers, he repeatedly experienced a sense of failure and inferiority. These experiences were frustrating for Sam because he knew that he was just as capable as his peers intellectually, even though he could not produce as effectively as they could. This sense of being different led to his not feeling part of the peer group and resisting attempts to perform that might make others aware of his deficiencies. Creating a problem solving model for Sam, which included appropriately asking for help from an adult or peer, helped him build positive peer relationships regarding his difficulty rather than avoiding required tasks.

Also involved in psychosocial development for children of this stage is the process of identification with the same-sex parent. Sam began to feel alienated from his father because he feared failing in his father's eyes. His dilemma was compounded because his father's job change had made him more available and, consequently, more aware of Sam's behaviors. Sam not only feared rejection from his father because he was not able to perform academically the way his father had, but also felt confused about what or whom he should be emulating if he could not be like his father. Thus, the unconscious desire to identify with the same-sex parent was causing Sam additional stress. Helping his parents be more understanding of his learning difficulty and work through their own fears about Sam's future as a successful student was important for Sam's identification struggle. As his father became more emotionally available to him, more empathic toward his problems, and able to spend more time with him in other ways, Sam was able to find aspects of his father with which to identify that were not oriented toward academic achievement.

Psychodynamic Issues

Drawing from psychodynamic theory, Sam attempted to protect his sense of self by using the defense mechanisms of rationalization, displacement, and projection. He initially had been protecting himself from feelings of shame by using rationalization. By separating out his intellectual capacity from his actual task performance, he could keep up a pretense of success and competence because he understood the material. After admitting to school-performance problems, he then blamed his teacher and fellow students for his distractability and incomplete schoolwork. He displaced his frustration with himself and his anger at his own inabilities onto the teacher, claiming that her assignments were "dumb" or a "waste of time." He projected his desire to be seen as good and his fears of being stupid or incapable onto his classmates. As his parents worked with structuring his homework time and motivating him at home, Sam learned to be more organized and focused. Through these efforts and with treatment focused on exploring and resolving the feelings experienced when perceiving himself a failure, Sam began to experience success in school performance. By developing some successful strategies of coping and adaptation, he stopped having to defend against feelings of inferiority, and took a more active role in finding ways to compensate for his difficulties and achieve in the classroom setting as well as at home.

Cognitive Issues

Drawing from cognitive theory, Sam amplified some of his emotional reactions to the classroom setting in terms of his concrete operational stage of cognitive development (Piaget, 1952). During this stage, children focus their thinking on things that are measurable. Their understanding of themselves, others, and situations is most often based on that which can be identified through a step-by-step description of events and quantifiable information. Sam was limited in his perception of his problems in the classroom setting because of his concrete thinking process. He experienced enormous amounts of frustration because he could understand the academic material more easily than some of his peers but received lower grades than others not as intellectually capable. Also, Sam perceived his behaviors as being outside of his control and not being intentional on his part. Often in treatment his major complaints would be, "I spend twice as much time doing homework as anyone else in my class but I get a lower grade. It's just not fair. I'm not goofing off. I'm not leaving things out on purpose. My brain just doesn't work like their brain does."

Cognitively, this situation defied his concrete sense of justice and fairness. Consequently, it seemed extremely unfair and unjust to him that he continually had school-performance difficulties when others did not. Because Sam could not be reasoned out of concrete thinking, treatment had to focus on ways that Sam could use this thinking style to gain a better sense of control over himself and his impulses. Learning ways to approach tasks on a step-by-step basis and having very concrete self-talk helped Sam gain a calmer state in performance/competency situations. Sam was encouraged to remind himself to do behaviors that helped (e.g., "Stop, watch, and listen." "Ask for help." "Recheck my work.").

Biological Issues

Because ADHD has been identified as a biological process with explicit and identifiable brain activity different from the brain activity of those who do not display symptoms of ADHD, one must draw from biological concepts to fully understand Sam's case. In the brain, the cingulate nucleus connects the neocortex to the limbic system. Its main function is to regulate attention and impulse control. In addition, when these functions are performed sufficiently, it appears that it creates a soothing effect on the limbic system and helps maintain more regulated emotions as well. Sam displayed the symptoms of restlessness, distractibility, irritability, and disorganization common to those with a brain dysfunction in the cingulate nucleus.

It is important to note that in children who have experienced a series of traumatic events or live in a trauma-inducing environment, brain chemistry can change and mimic ADHD symptoms. Levels of adrenaline and endomorphines can be out of balance with the child's present surroundings, causing behaviors of hypervigilance, startle response, and irritability that need specific treatment and medication different from the ADHD child. Taking a careful history in regard to trauma by abuse, neglect, or medical stress is necessary to distinguish the difference between ADHD and Post-traumatic Stress Disorder and disorders of attachment. In Sam's case, trauma-induced behaviors had been ruled out in the initial parent consultation. Throughout treatment, there were no indications to contradict the original assessment.

Given the biological component of ADHD, it was important that treatment include accurate baseline and ongoing measures of improvement and lack of improvement. When Sam experienced some behavioral and emotional improvement, it was easily confirmed by the ongoing tracking that had started at the beginning of treatment. When Sam reported no improvement in the feeling that his thinking was still out of control (i.e., "racing ahead of myself"), this statement was important information. The referral to a child psychiatrist, use of medication, and the subsequent improvement in specific areas helped assure the parents and Sam of the usefulness of medication.

Behavioral and emotional treatment done before medication helped emphasize to all the family members that medication alone cannot fully treat ADHD. Sam and his parents learned through the process of their own treatment that successful treatment of Sam's learning problem was a complex, multilayered process that required all family members to examine themselves and participate in the change process.

11 Anxiety Disorders

Anxiety has been variously defined as (1) a complex emotional and physiological response to anticipated or perceived danger that seems irrational and out of proportion (Bowlby, 1973b; Chessick, 1993); and (2) feelings of apprehension associated with a sense of danger from an unknown source (Allen, Leonard, and Swedo, 1995; Hales and Yudofsky, 1987; Livingston, 1991). As a signal to avoid danger, anxiety is adaptive in helping children modify their behavior. When its intensity and persistence create a sense of diffuse danger, anxiety may become overwhelming and impair development and biopsychosocial functioning. To be diagnosed with an anxiety disorder, the degree of impairment must be congruent with the *DSM IV*'s (APA, 1994) depiction of one of the conditions in which anxiety is the principal disturbance or is experienced in confronting a dreaded situation or object. The most prevalent anxiety conditions among children include generalized anxiety disorder; panic disorder; obsessive compulsive disorder; and simple, social, animal, or situational phobias (APA, 1994; Hibbs and Jensen, 1996). The focus of this chapter is generalized anxiety disorder. The case of Julie illustrates application of developmental play therapy to a representative clinical case with a primary diagnosis of Generalized Anxiety Disorder.

Clinical Syndrome

Children with anxiety disorders usually evidence symptoms from five symptom clusters.

Psychological symptoms may include feelings of fright, tension, apprehension, restlessness, and being stressed, as well as insomnia, nightmares, and scary daytime fantasies.

Physiological symptoms (Livingston, 1991) may be associated with four systems: *Respiratory*—shortness of breath, hyperventilation; *Dermatological*—skin rash, perspiration; *Gastrointestinal*—stomachaches, nausea, diarrhea, urinary frequency; and *Cardiovascular*—tachycardia, increased blood pressure, skin flushing or pallor, chest pain, fainting.

Social/interpersonal symptoms (Livingston, 1991) may include clinging behavior, need for reassurance, social uneasiness, and under- or over-reactions to personal situations.

Cognitive symptoms (Reinecke, Dattilio, and Freeman, 1996) may include (1) preoccupying worry or rumination about one or more situations, objects, or psychosocial competencies; (2) an expectation that something negative will occur; and (3) difficulty concentrating and completing tasks.

Behavioral symptoms may include avoidant behavior for activities of any possible danger or counterphobic excessive risk-taking behavior.

Prevalence

Epidemiological and comorbidity rates are informative but not necessarily exact because the research methodology of these studies lacks sufficient reliability and validity for estimating the extent to which identified differences are associated with real differences or are simply sampling and measurement artifacts. For example, the source of information may confound the data because anxiety symptoms are more consistently reported by children than by parents (Angold, 1994).

Epidemiology

A review of sixteen epidemiological studies from 1987 to 1993 yielded prevalence estimates for community samples that ranged from 5.7 to 17.7 percent for anxiety disorders, with half of these estimates above 10 percent (Costello and Angold, 1995). Although not varying by gender (Lewis, 1991), these estimates do increase slightly with age (Costello and Angold, 1995). Within this syndrome, the three most commonly diagnosed—generalized anxiety disorder, separation anxiety disorder, and simple phobia—occur in 5 percent of all children (Costello and Angold, 1995).

In clinical epidemiological studies, anxiety disorders are the most common mental-health disturbance (March, 1995) with the most prevalent—separation anxiety—occurring in 13 to 27 percent of the sample (Last, Perrin, and Hersen, 1992). The next—overanxious disorder (merged with generalized anxiety disorder in *DSM IV*)—occurred in 12 to 13 percent of two study samples (Kashani and Orvaschel, 1990; Last, Perrin, and Hersen, 1992).

Comorbidity

Community-based epidemiological studies have not clarified patterns within the anxiety disorder syndrome but have established comorbidity rates with other disorders. In four 1988–1995 studies (Costello and Angold, 1995), anxiety disorders were diagnosed:

- three to four times as often in children also diagnosed with depressive disorders
- two to three times as often in children also diagnosed with oppositional disorders

- three times as often in children also diagnosed with tic disorders and enuresis
- no more often in children also diagnosed with attention-deficit/hyperactive disorder

By contrast, clinical epidemiological studies have noted that half of the children diagnosed with separation anxiety disorder as the primary condition had co-occurring conditions of generalized anxiety disorder—33 percent (Curry and Murphy, 1995) and simple phobia—37 percent (Last, Perrin, and Hersen, 1992). Estimates of co-occurrence of anxiety and depressive disorders vary too widely to be useful. However, children diagnosed with multiple anxiety disorder conditions have been found more likely to be diagnosed with comorbid depression (Strauss, Lease, and Last, 1988). Comorbidity estimates with conduct or oppositional defiant disorders range from 20 to 40 percent (Curry and Murphy, 1995). From 17 to 22 percent of outpatient children diagnosed with an anxiety disorder also met the criteria for attention deficit-disorder (Curry and Murphy, 1995).

Clinical Etiology

Youngsters experience assorted fears and anxieties throughout childhood. Much of the time, their apprehension and tension are mild to moderate in intensity, and are associated with their neurobiological endowments and efforts to handle their biopsychosocial developmental tasks. At other times, the intensity and complexity of these anxious feelings and physiological tensions are associated with their efforts to cope with both ordinary and extraordinary life experiences. As youngsters' verbal ability, capacity for symbolic thought, and ability to differentiate affective states mature, they become increasingly able to distinguish among a variety of emotions, and are more likely to report subjective and objective anxiety symptoms. Anxiety becomes clinically significant only when excessive in amount and intensity (Marks, 1987).

Biopsychosocial Development of Anxiety

Young infants (newborn to six months) experience terror that they will not be cared for and react accordingly to the loss of support and feeding from familiar caregivers. Initially, their anxiety is expressed through hyperarousal, inconsolable crying, and frenzied physical movements; later, through more differentiated and qualitatively distinct crying and body language. Older infants (six to twelve months) actively struggle with developmental issues of trust and object permanency. They fear parental loss, cling, and may be apprehensive with strangers. When their parents depart, they convey their need for tangible comfort and transitional objects to soothe their separation anxiety. For infants and toddlers (thirteen to eighteen months), defensive-adaptive coping responses of avoidance, freezing, and fighting come into play in the face of danger and deprivation (Fraiberg, 1980).

Even with good caretaking, however, innate neurological defects may make it hard for some sensitive youngsters to cope with their anxiety (Fish, Marcus, and Hans, 1992).

In dealing with developmental issues of individuation and autonomy, toddlers worry that their behavior may lead to parental disapproval and withdrawal of love and care. Their minds are now capable of turning internal impulses that seem dangerous into external dangers (dark rooms, monsters) that seem very real. Due to their talent for magical thinking and unformed capacity for reality testing, toddlers are unable to distinguish between internal anxiety about perceived danger and external fear of real danger (Keith, 1995). They express anxieties and fears indirectly through motoric restlessness, tantrums, aggression, sleep disturbance, and somatic symptoms. Over time, they develop their own cognitive schemas about environmental dangers (Piaget, 1954), learn to cope with these dangers, and learn to handle the risks associated with change. They become able to identify signals of anxiety and respond before being overwhelmed. For some toddlers, however, the internal anxiety may become incapacitating. Such children evidence multiple symptoms of apprehension and fear, unsuccessful ritualistic coping efforts, and behavioral inhibitions. Their developmental progression is likely to be disrupted.

The developmental processes of three- to five-year olds refocus anxiety about external dangers and parental disapproval onto internal concerns about aggression. At this age, they worry about bodily harm and whether their own thoughts, actions, and achievements are good or bad. They may express anxiety as fears of body damage, specific objects, and selected behaviors, as well as general distress (Stallings and March, 1995). In mastering anxiety, preschoolers develop defensive-adaptive coping mechanisms, such as turning passive into active, and are able to channel anxiety about aggression into various play activities. At times, however, the protective defenses are unable to contain the anxiety, the play is interrupted, the child regresses and then recoups by strengthening the protective defenses, and the play resumes. In other instances, children may become overwhelmed and inhibited to the point of becoming affectively, cognitively, and socially paralyzed. When such disruption occurs, youngsters are likely to evidence emotional constriction, social inhibition, lowered self-concept, and underachievement in preschool and school (Keith, 1995).

Specific fears, too, change as children grow and develop. Five- and six-year olds are concerned about thunder and lightning, physical danger, staying alone, and death. By age nine, children realize that death is universal, irreversible, and a personal possibility (Anthony, 1975).

In the elementary school years, children are coping with developmental issues of competence and self-confidence in and out of school. They are self-conscious about their academic achievement, interpersonal skills, and extracurricular performance. They constantly compare themselves with peers as to appearance, talents, activities, and accomplishments. They are concerned about approval and disapproval by adults, peers, and especially their own internal self-regulatory systems. They worry about being ridiculed or embarrassed and not fitting in. They fear academic failure, poor performance, social incompetence, and social rejection. Any of these issues can be a source of transient anxiety or can escalate exponentially into a focus for severe, dysfunctional anxiety and lowered self-concept. During these years, anxiety has the capacity to mobilize an array of coping maneuvers, which resilient children use flexibly. By contrast, vulnerable children tend to employ fewer adaptive defense mechanisms and use them inflexibly.

Psychopathology

As children grow and develop, their fears and anxieties become internalized and are incorporated into their subjective life narratives. Their internal conflicts of the mind give rise to anxiety that produces a sense of *unpleasure*. Protective defenses are then mobilized to minimize the anxiety. When children's defensive-adaptive maneuvers are unsuccessful, symptoms (i.e., tantrums, whining, and headaches, to name a few) result. There are also losses of function and gratification. For resilient children, the forces of developmental change, parental caregiving and support, and their own inherent strengths in coping and adaptation may come into play and, once again, serve to minimize anxiety. Vulnerable children, however, may experience either transient or more marked developmental disruption that requires professional intervention to resolve. These internal experiences of anxiety grow increasingly complex throughout the life of a child, with the result that symptomatic expression in the external world is likely to evolve over time.

Family Issues

Innate neurological vulnerabilities or temperament may make it difficult for some youngsters to cope with the anxiety inherent in normal growth and development and for some parents to cope with their anxious children. Many mothers date an anxious temperament to the hospital nursery, where the infant was quick to startle and responsive to the slightest noise. They characterize the first year of life as demanding and report difficulties in soothing their hyperalert infants. Thus, the stage is set for parental anxiety about their child not being on a regular day/night cycle, frustration that they are unable to satiate their child, and exhaustion as they rock or walk the baby.

In an effort to calm their infant and promote well-being, parents may get so caught up in trying to relieve the child's anxiety that they unwittingly become intrusive and foster additional problems. It is important to note that both children and parents bring their own temperamental responses, vulnerabilities, strengths, and resiliencies to the parent/child interaction. Sometimes, these mesh well; sometimes, they mesh only with a lot of hard work; and sometimes, they clash.

In some instances, one or both parents may have an anxiety disorder, thus raising question about a possible genetic basis for their child's anxiety (Last, Hersen, Kazdin, Finkelstein, and Strauss, 1987). In other instances, different mental disorders also may be part of the clinical picture. While some parents may feel discouraged or helpless in the face of the insistent demands of an anxious infant, they report that an understanding of anxiety helps them cope better and weather the storm. For example, they learn techniques to calm and soothe their child, remain available to mirror affective states, empathize with distressing social interactions, and comprehend the need for sameness. They also learn that calm responses are more likely to quiet their child's fright after scary nightmares and daytime fears. They also recognize the child's need for anticipatory guidance and preparation prior to separations or new experiences. Because the demands of anxious children are great at any developmental stage, parents sometimes describe themselves as always on the hot seat. Parenting for them is perhaps best described as a balancing act that tries to relieve their children's anxiety while maintaining their own composure.

Empirical Support for Treatment Selection

Pharmacotherapy

Prescribing and monitoring psychotropic medications for children with anxiety disorders is the purview of Board-Certified child psychiatrist consultants who conduct medical diagnostic interviews; evaluate the scope, intensity, and impact of the symptoms on biopsychosocial functioning; make educated judgments about the indications and contraindications, as well as the risks and benefits of using any medication or particular medications; educate children and their parents about the disorder and use of medications; and consult with the clinical social worker about the case. Although medications do not directly eliminate the anxiety, they may increase the comfort level of some children. Such relief may free children's energy for therapeutic work toward re-engaging disrupted developmental processes, working through developmental conflicts, and confronting irrational belief and behavior systems. It is important to note, however, that not all anxious children need medication to invest in therapy.

Several studies suggest that medication, when combined with psychodynamic therapy (Klein and Last, 1989) or with behavior therapy (Rapoport, 1989), is effective in managing childhood anxiety disorders. Although there are few carefully controlled efficacy studies, some consensus about the differential use of psychotropic medications may be emerging (Kutcher, Reiter, and Gardner, 1995). Many therapists, however, point out that, at times, medications mask the anxiety symptoms and inhibit resolution of the developmental disturbances associated with anxiety disorders. Clearly, further clinical research is needed with children of all ages and from all cultural backgrounds to resolve this debate.

Tricyclic Antidepressants. Multiple studies suggest imipramine in treating complex school-refusal cases (Kutcher, Reiter, and Gardner, 1995) and clomipramine for serious obsessive compulsive disorders (March, Johnston, and Jefferson, 1990). For children with comorbid attentional and anxiety disorders, the symptoms of hyperactivity and attention span may respond to tricyclics (Kutcher, Reiter, and Gardner, 1995). However, caution is clearly indicated, in that serious cardiovascular side effects may occur and rapid withdrawal may lead to a variety of symptoms (Wilens, Biederman, and Baldessarini, 1992).

Benzodiazepines. Benzodiazepines show positive results in panic disorder and clinical utility in generalized anxiety disorder (Simeon, Ferguson, and Knott, 1992). Again, caution is indicated in view of the multiple dose-related side effects and the major withdrawal symptoms (Biederman, 1987).

Buspirone. Buspirone is similar to benzodiazepine and evidenced significant improvement and relatively benign side effects with a mixed group of anxiety disorders (Simeon, Ferguson, and Knott, 1992).

Selective Serotonin Reuptake Inhibitors (SSRI). Fluoxetine has been found useful with obsessive compulsive disorder and Tourette's Syndrome. Low amounts of these medications appear to be well tolerated and have minimal side effects (Kutcher, Reiter, and Gardner, 1995).

Psychotherapy

An early study (Milos and Reiss, 1982) found that play therapy effectively lowered separation anxiety by breaking down anxiety-provoking situations into manageable pieces, thereby facilitating mastery and autonomy. For rapid relief of anxiety symptoms of relatively short duration, cognitive-behavioral treatment is considered effective (Kendall and Chansky, 1991; Levin, Ashmore-Callahan, Kendall, and Ichii, 1996). For children with entrenched anxiety disorders, however, psychodynamically oriented psychotherapy is recommended (Target and Fonagy, 1994). In a recent review of treatment protocols, the American Academy of Child and Adolescent Psychiatry (1993) concluded that psychodynamically oriented treatment is probably more effective with childhood anxiety disorders and should remain the primary treatment modality. Falling within this latter interventive tradition, Julie's intensive course of treatment illustrates application of developmental play therapy to a representative composite case with a primary diagnosis of Generalized Anxiety Disorder. This case represents the usual way of therapy with its ups and downs following multiple traumas and changes in the child's life.

Course of Treatment: Julie
by Marika Moore Cutler, M.S.W., LCSW-C

Stage I: Biopsychosocial Assessment

Presenting Problem.   A demanding and needy child, seven-and-a-half-year old Julie was referred to the clinical social worker by a psychologist who had performed a battery of psychoeducational testing. According to both parents during the initial interview, Julie ruled the roost through outbursts of anger, low frustration tolerance, insistence on being with mother at all times, and academic demands associated with "perfectionism." When asked how Julie tolerated change, mother revealed a history of constipation with voluntary stool retention for up to ten days when Julie was anxious.

History of Presenting Problem.   The mother, as primary historian, reported a history of oppositional and stubborn behavior, including tantrums that began during the toddler years. Although they recognized no separation problems when Julie entered preschool at almost three, both parents described an unusual sensitivity to change when they moved to a new city about this same time. Her first encopretic episode followed a successful toilet training. Nightly sleepwalking began at four and lasted until about seven. During these episodes, Julie's eyes were open and she called for her parents with considerable agitation. Roused from sleep, the parents returned her to her own bed. Julie also developed a strong attachment to her mother and insisted that they remain together during every waking moment, including meals, bathing, and homework times. She had four separate bedtime rituals. First, she and her father played high school with her stuffed animals, with Julie as teacher and father as the animals' voice. Mother then took over for an additional thirty minutes of reading to her in the parental bed and helping to record the wheel speed of her pet hamsters. Finally, Julie would pour two glasses of water that her father would place on either side of her bed.

Developmental History.   After years of infertility, Mr. and Mrs. K. waited two years before the New York adoption agency called to announce five-month-old Julie's impending arrival from a South American orphanage. While initially thrilled, mother recalled Julie's first night as the "worst of my life." She remembered feeling overwhelmed and worried since she had heard that South American babies were fed on demand. She reported that carrying Julie was left to father as Julie was so heavy.

Julie became the center of her new parents' life. Father had a warm but passive nurturing presence. Mother appeared mildly depressed and anxious about Julie's performance. The sixty-year-old German nanny who worked for the family upon Julie's arrival stated that "Julie was in control from birth," and was the only historian who dated stool retention to infancy. Severe temper tantrums made limit setting in toddlerhood impossible. Julie's early babblings were described as beautiful with tones and rhythms like musical echoes. The three adults saw themselves as responsible for reading to her and teaching her arts and crafts. Board games were begun early. Julie did not seem to mind losing. All developmental milestones were met within normal limits.

Medical History.   Julie was reported to be healthy, except for occasional constipation. Prolonged stool retention was resolved by diet and enemas. Mother gave the enemas, which resulted in considerable rage and crying fits by Julie. Mother described the stools, when they did come, as "humongous," causing toilet backup and plumbing problems. There was much ado about bowel movements, with the most recent technique involving Julie sitting on the toilet after each meal.

Social History.   Julie was a self-isolating child who spent all her time with her mother, father, or nanny. Considerable attention was directed to Julie's school history and academic performance by her high-school-teacher parents. As early as kindergarten, mother reported that Julie was overly aware of how she compared to others. She struggled with her mother to complete her homework perfectly and was an excellent student through first grade. Intelligence testing found her to be cooperative, focused, motivated, and quick to say "I don't know" or "I can't." With encouragement, she was able to master tasks. The WISC-III R revealed superior intellectual ability on all scales.

The second-grade teacher reported to the clinician that Julie "lacked confidence, was very needy, had no boundaries, was out of her seat asking questions of the teacher, and was overly dependent. She had no friends and was excluded from peer-group play because she always took over and wanted to be boss. Occasionally, Julie would engage in parallel play with a boy she had known since preschool. She was very intelligent, artistic, and perfectionistic."

Child Interviews.   Julie separated somewhat hesitantly from her mother as she walked into my office. Appearing younger than her age, Julie was petite with short black hair and an encopretic odor. She was compliant, oriented, attentive, and responsive to questions. Her stated chief complaint was "I am here because I'm upset. I'm upset about being lonely." She discussed how she must have either Nanny or Mommy in the room at home and lamented not having close friends. It bothered her when the kids teased her about looking so different from her mother.

Julie described her mood as worried. Although the range of her affect was restricted, the quality was appropriate to the interview content. She appeared anxious, tentative, controlled, and guarded. Her stark, bleak drawings were laboriously completed and portrayed her family members as identical in every way except height. There was an absence of detail in drawings of herself, her family, and her home. When asked who she might take to a deserted island, Julie immediately said, "Not a kid. I don't know. Mom." If a fairy godmother could grant her any three wishes, she wished for "a wish every day, a big castle with servants to give me breakfast in bed and cook and do laundry, and no chores." With the Despert fable *Baby Bird Story,* she said, "Then baby bird flapped her wings and learned to fly. In fifteen minutes, she found her parents sitting on a hill together where they found food. Then the three flew back to the nest together."

Two days later, I was surprised when a cheerful and enthusiastic Julie bounced into my office. Henceforth, Julie controlled the emotional and substantive tone of treatment. She quickly incorporated me into her play by introducing me to eighteen creatures brought from home. The cat family protected Julie and her parents by day and night. The large rabbit family looked after one another and were quite competitive with the cat family. Flopsy Rabbit played a projective function for Julie's fears of not pleasing. "Flopsy is being tugged . . . pulled apart. She doesn't want to say anything to Baby Rabbit because she doesn't want to hurt anyone's feelings. See, Flopsy is caught in the middle." King Rabbit sits up all night and watches over Julie and her creatures. Then Julie talked about her blanket as being a boy named Baba that she takes everywhere. Baba sleeps with her as she sucks her thumb.

There were many races in the play. Julie and I played flying and horseback-riding games with the repetitive theme of crashing and rescuing. At one point, Flopsy said, "I flew on a plane to my parents." Mr. Brown Rabbit, a cousin who belonged to me, responded "Was Flopsy in Mom's tummy or out when she arrived?" Julie answered, "Out, but she wanted to be in." The play ended with a plane crash that conveyed a feeling of doom followed by a rescue. The races were so competitive that many of the creatures were jealous. Others felt they didn't belong.

The play continued the following week when Julie bounced into the office with two huge bags filled with creatures. "Here, let me introduce you to Giant Rabbit and Baba. I brought them and the same creatures because everybody told them what fun they had. They couldn't wait to come back!" "Well, nice to meet you Giant Rabbit," I said as I shook his hand. "And Baba, you sure look like a loved blanket to me." "I am. Every night I go to sleep with Julie." Julie added, "Yes, I hold on to Baba while I suck my thumb. I wanted them to meet Brown Rabbit. Remember, Brown Rabbit flew on the plane with me when I came to live with you . . . I mean, I mean my parents." Then as her anxiety increased, she shifted to playing school, a significant choice because only she and her father played school games. Julie dictated every rabbit's move in the jumping and climbing classes. She looked toward me and shouted, "Teacher, I'm afraid. I'm too little to jump. You may be stupid, but I know you'll show me the way. Come on . . . help." Julie closed the session by saying she didn't want to leave.

Assessment and Diagnosis.   Julie was an intelligent youngster with a rich fantasy life. Her expressed feelings of not belonging were associated with her displacement from another family and culture. Her omnipotent fantasies centered around her desire to be the power behind the parental throne. From her seat of power, Julie was demanding in her stipulations for immediate gratification. Tantrums succeeded in keeping her mother from her father, in that her parents divided their attention in order to pacify Julie. She enjoyed her initial sessions and seemed capable of developing a therapeutic alliance.

Julie's emotional world was compromised along several developmental lines: emotional self-reliance, bodily independence, companionship, and play. Unable to let her mother out of her sight, this youngster had not successfully negotiated the separation individuation process that permits three-year-olds to carry a mental representation of mother during her absence. Negative ambivalence ruled the day as Julie's demands for closeness and clinging were met with physical withholding and psychological control of her interpersonal world. Her voluntary stool retention became a battleground. Even when she had a bowel movement, she left it in the toilet and insisted that her mother flush the toilet. Julie took great delight when the toilet overflowed. The conflicts of her mind were portrayed in her ambivalence regarding issues of dependency, control, and autonomy. Her behavior was replete with temper tantrums characterized by screaming, crying, foot-stomping, and throwing things. Julie's engagement in parallel play, rather than the more age-appropriate cooperative and imaginative play, handicapped her peer relations to the point that they were basically nonexistent. Although well into her eighth year, Julie continued to depend on transitional objects to sooth her at home, at school, and in the diagnostic interviews.

At home, Julie was the center of an adult world. Her incredible insecurity was played out even in her bedtime rituals, when everything had to be "just so." In school, she was lonely, worried excessively about performance and competition, and felt she did not measure up to her teacher's and parents' expectations. She was unskilled in social nuances. Her reported perfectionism was actually a need for control because she felt uncontrollable. Julie wanted her world to be predictable because change was intolerable. Her efforts to rule the world resulted in bossiness and, therefore, an inability to make friends. Anxiety so permeated her life that she could not take pleasure in a task well done, whether it was evacuation into the toilet, play with peers, or achievement in school.

Julie met the *DSM-IV* criteria for generalized anxiety disorder because of unrelenting worries about school and social performance that she could not control, irritability, restlessness, and inability to concentrate. She also met the criteria for Encopresis with Constipation and Overflow Incontinence, symptoms that contributed to her sense of shame and social isolation.

Treatment Plan.   I met with Julie's parents to outline a comprehensive treatment plan that included twice-weekly play therapy and biweekly concurrent parent work. I explained how symbolic and imaginative play would promote Julie's emotional development, provide a safe context from which to establish a therapeutic alliance, and enable her to manage her anxiety. I also explained that changes at home and in therapy would be in small incremental steps. Reduction of symptoms and resumption of normal bowel control were identified as the primary short-term goals. I advised the parents to refrain from talking about Julie's bowel control and to discontinue putting her on the toilet after every meal.

Long-term plans focused on returning this child to a normal developmental pathway. It was anticipated that the treatment techniques would stimulate internalizing processes and facilitate development of frustration tolerance and accurate mental representations. These changes would, in turn, establish object constancy, thereby permitting comfortable separation and successful individuation. The vulnerability associated with Julie's early deprivation and cross-cultural adoption gave rise to primitive coping mechanisms, such as tantrums, whining, and stool retention. Under stress, Julie reverted to these mechanisms as a way to cope with her pervasive anxiety. Through clarification and interpretation of her conflicts and obsessional defenses, she would eventually gain insight and develop more adaptive coping mechanisms for managing her anxiety. Helping Julie understand her mental states and how they contributed to her behavior would enable her to control her impulses and begin to be responsible for her own behavior. With this approach, it was expected that her anxieties would become manageable and her encopresis would resolve.

Stage II: Creation of Therapeutic Alliance

This early phase of treatment was devoted to the play of making families with the creatures and trying to sort out where they belonged. No matter what the configuration, the baby rabbit and baby cat simply did not belong. Occasionally, Julie would verbalize some of her difficulties at home. One night mother was interrupted by a phone call during the bedtime rituals. To make matters even worse, mother then took a shower. Julie continued, "So I, so I screamed and cried to get her to come back, but she didn't." I responded, "You were mad at Mom." "No, not mad, angry. Mad is worse than angry," she retorted. The dialogue continued, "Okay, you were angry, that's why you had a temper tantrum, sort of the way Baby Rabbit does when he can't be with his Mom." Julie then engaged in a play scenario in which Baby Rabbit screamed at Mother Rabbit for talking to Father Rabbit.

On another occasion, Julie opined, "This is the goodnight story I'll tell my kids. Once upon a time, there was a beautiful Baba. When she went to her Grandmother's, she had Baba. When she ate, went to school, or went to bed, there was always Baba. Then one day she took Baba to bed to nap. When she woke up, there was no Baba and the little girl was very worried. She asked her mother where Baba was and mother said, 'Don't you remember? Before you went to take your nap, I told you that I would take Baba away to wash while you were sleeping.' And so Baba came back and the little girl was very happy. I don't know if this is a true story."

I commented, "As you were telling the story, I was thinking how sad and worried the little girl was and that even today she might worry when she tries to go to sleep." "Yes," she agreed, "that could be possible." I continued, "She might worry about something terrible happening to Baba or someone else she loved very much." Julie responded, "Well, I said I didn't know if it is true." I said, "Let's not worry too much about whether it's true. It could even be pretend. What matters is how the little girl felt." Julie realized it was the end of the hour, gathered her creatures, and marched out the door.

The creature family continued to grow with new additions to the extended family. School games in which Julie was teacher and I was assistant teacher were repeated compulsively. The teacher took on a dictatorial and boisterous stance. Within a few months time, Julie turned the office into a fort with a secret hiding place, me into the mother, and herself into the eldest daughter. She continued to bring the rabbits and throw them into my lap. Where she was once the older sister/mother to the rabbits, she was now the daughter with make-believe friends and family. She busied herself making the fort and introduced me to her imaginary sisters, Chloe and Nicole. She started walking and talking to her sisters, and then looked to me as mother/therapist and said, "I have to go to the bathroom. Mom, don't look. I'm going through the kitchen door." She pretended to squat on a toilet, ran back to the fort, peered over it, and said, "Mom, ask whether it was . . . (held up one finger, then two) . . . you know, ddd or ttt . . ." I replied, "You tell me." She held up two fingers.

"Mom, I'm going to the bathroom again." She squatted, "Plop, plop, plop." Then she ran back to the fort, talked to Chloe and Nicole, and yelled, "I have to go to the bathroom." She ran to the imaginary bathroom, squatted, and repeated, "Plop, plop, plop. Mom, come and look what I did. Wait! I'll run back to the fort and then you just kinda walk into the bathroom and say, 'Oh my! Julie did ddd.'" I followed Julie's commands and then returned to my chair. Within seconds, Julie announced, "I'm going to the bathroom again. I suppose Mom wants me to flush the toilet. Ha, ha, ha! Oh . . . I'm having a hard time flushing. It won't flush." Then she looked at me and said, "That happens a lot in our house. Guess why. Come on, guess. Ohhhh, I have to go to the bathroom again." She repeated the entire scenario three more times. Then she looked at me and said, "I have to go to the bathroom for real." Julie flew out the door, used the toilet in about fifteen seconds, flew back into the office, went back to the imaginary toilet, and invited me in to take a look. I looked into the pretend toilet and said in a positive and engaging way, "Look at what Julie has done!" "Yes, Mom, I bet you didn't think I could make such a big one. That's why the toilet won't flush. Ha, ha, ha. No matter what, it won't go down." I exclaimed, "Well, you've done such a wonderful thing that it may be difficult to say goodbye to it and have it swoosh down the toilet. This way, everybody gets to see it."

"Mom, I sure have to go to the bathroom a lot, don't I?" I answered, "You enjoy going to the bathroom." Julie continued, "Yeah, it even smells, you know, you know, you know, ha, ha, ha, . . . it smells like ddd." I wondered if Julie couldn't think of a word for ddd. There was more laughter and exclamations of, "No! No! Whoops, here I go again. I'm running to the bathroom. Plop, plop, plop. I'm flushing. It just won't go down. Mom, go look at it." I decided to remain in my chair and asked Julie to tell me about it instead. Frustrated, Julie rejoined Chloe and Nicole and ordered them to look at how big it was. "In fact, it's bigger than anyone else's in the whole house."

Stage III: Identification of Narrative Themes

In time, the family-creation games turned into anal games of secrecy. There was a grandiose quality to the bigness of it all, which was repeated just about verbatim over two months. Julie taught me the secret language that she spoke with her imaginary friends and in therapy. She would pretend to sleep walk into the bathroom while sucking her thumb. Much to the delight of her parents and pediatrician, her encopresis resolved. The parents couldn't believe how happy Julie had become. They told me that I was a magician. Their friends confirmed how relaxed Julie's demeanor had become. The rituals were loosening up. Julie even asked her parents if her biological mother was coming to get her. I prepared the parents for the likelihood of resistance developing. The imaginary creatures and friends were all part of the family romance where Julie would create and re-create families. There was an idealization of the biological family and devaluation of her current family. In therapy, Julie idealized the therapist's family as she tried to create a family romance with the therapist. In this play, Julie was juggling her three homes: biological, adoptive, and therapeutic.

The imaginary friends, secret language, creature games, and toilet rituals grew to include compulsive eating games and classroom scenarios where Julie was teacher and I was her assistant, bound to obey her every command. She became increasingly boisterous and intrusive, trying to sit in my lap and messing up my hair. Once when we were deciding what to do, I commented, "Well, we could talk." Julie replied, "No, that's private." Instead, she played hide-and-seek with her creatures. Over time, she created a private box with a secret code that the therapist/mother did not know. She would coax me into her fort to see the secret box, and then quickly order me out. Toward the end of the session, I pointed out that it was time to go home. Julie replied, "I am home. This is my home." I commented, "You want to stay." "No, I am home," Julie confirmed. I replied, "For real, it's time to go home." Julie destroyed the private box as an act of retaliation and left without saying goodbye.

During the summer months, many hours were devoted to card-playing, where Julie cheated unmercifully and constantly changed the rules. Issues of control over the toilet gave way to control over Crazy Eights, Gin, Spit, and War. Normally, this phase of therapy commenced with Julie arriving with a bag of three creatures that she would throw at me and a deck of cards. Once in a great while, she opened up and talked a little about her daily life.

Autumn brought a change in Julie's school. While Julie insisted that she didn't miss anything from the old school, she did not wish to play with anything associated with school. After her initial day, she said, "I know you want to ask me 'How was your first day at school?'" I said, "I bet several people have asked you that very question, especially your Mom and Dad." Julie agreed, "Yes, but I'm not going to talk about it." She then displaced this discussion onto Astro Rabbit by saying, "I took Astro Rabbit with me to school today." I asked, "What did Astro Rabbit think about his first day at school?" Julie replied, "Well, it was hard for him to see because he was in my backpack and that was on a hook. But every now and then, he looked over the edge. He saw lots of strange kids and a big classroom." I responded, "It sounds to me like he was a bit worried about what he would see at first and that is why it took him a while to look over the edge. Plus, when you think about it, there were so many new people and things to look at." Julie retreated back into the real by saying, "He was on the hook. He didn't really look over the edge." I said, "I understand. Still, it's helpful to bring a creature you love from home to a new school." *(Here, I was thinking of the creatures as transitional objects between home and therapy and home and school.)* Julie wondered, "I don't know if I'll bring him tomorrow." I replied, "You'll see how you feel in the morning. It's okay to take him again." Julie agreed. We continued playing cards. Then she said, "It's so nice to be here. I can breathe." *(She was feeling relieved.)* We were then able to discuss recent changes in her life.

One day Julie talked about the death of her favorite hamster, whom she missed. Her father had helped prepare a funeral with a casket, prayers, and finally interment. "We put her in a tiny box. My Dad and I wrote something about her on the computer and we reduced it so it would fit on the box and inside too. Then I gathered a lot of flowers and put them around her grave." I attempted to get to the feeling associated with this experience. The most Julie would say was, "I miss Fluffy. I came home from school, and there she was . . . all stiff." *(How tragically prophetic this death scene would soon become.)*

While Julie's tantrumming, whining, and encopresis had resolved, pronounced fears of separation and abandonment surfaced. Once, her mother left the office to go shopping. Julie was to leave the office and take the elevator to the lobby where her mother would meet her. Julie agreed, but I noticed her worry as she checked her watch every five minutes. She asked to be walked to the elevator and voiced concern about getting into it. I said, "Let's talk about the elevator." She said, "I'm afraid the door will close on me." I responded, "And you seem worried that you wouldn't know what to do." Julie replied, "I'd be crushed." She agreed that Mommy protects her from such scary things happening. This session ended with Julie pretending that I was her mother who walked her to the elevator.

Two days later, Julie waited for her father to come home. She was extremely worried about his delay. Distraught, Julie heard sirens in the near distance and ran to get Nanny. Later, a police officer arrived and told Julie and Nanny that her father had been killed in a car accident. Mother was at work, but rushed home to be with Julie. I met with Julie and her mother daily to go over every single step many times as they prepared for the wake and funeral. Julie remained stonefaced and silent on the sofa. Only occasionally did she shed a tear. Instead, she held it in as was her custom. This was her worst fear come true. The father who nurtured her, played creature games, taught her cards, read to her, and adored her was dead. Of course, there were enormous rageful repercussions in therapy that took the form of resistance and a negative transference.

Shortly thereafter, Julie and her mother would arrive late to therapy. I could hear Julie's screams in the hallway of the office building as she yelled, "No, no." Once inside the waiting room, she turned around in circles and hung her head, shouting, "No, no, I won't go in. I don't want to. Go away from me. No, no." Her mother tried coaxing her into the office. Julie sat on the waiting room-couch with her back turned and chanted a kind of mantra, "No, no, no." I said, "You don't want to be here, I know." She agreed, "Right! I never want to be here. I won't talk, so there!" Then mother said she wanted to talk for a few minutes. I agreed that today they could switch for a few minutes, although I left the office door open should Julie change her mind. Mother acknowledged that I had tried to prepare her for this, but it seemed to come out of the clear blue sky. I responded that it was provoked by father's sudden death and explained that the resistance meant that Julie and I were doing the work of developmental play therapy. Mother reported that Julie was once again withholding her stools for many days at a time and re-fusing to flush the toilet. Other symptoms included baby talk, sleep disturbance, separation anxiety, fear that either she or her mother would die, and temper tan-trums. Once again, she was her mother's shadow. Mother was annoyed and angered by the return of these symptoms, even though I explained that they would go away in time. We returned to the waiting room and I asked Julie if she would like to come in to play some games. "No!" she emphatically stated. I responded that she wanted to be with mom. Julie reiterated, "I want to be with Mom. If I'm with Mom, I'll talk." I thought it would be a good idea to have the threesome return to the office. Mother needed to see how the therapeutic mother would handle the situation. Julie's mother wondered whether she was a good mother. She had tried so hard, and now she was left alone to deal with Julie. She felt inadequate.

As soon as the door was closed, Julie declared, "I'm not going to talk. I don't like to talk." I replied, "I think you really don't want to be here, and it's okay to talk about that." Julie retorted, "You're right. I don't." The physical ex-pression of her affect was even more compelling as she frowned with downcast eyes glaring at the floor. She wiggled in her seat as she pushed her feet into the carpet. I agreed that she didn't want to be here. She added, "I hate coming here. I don't like you." I said, "That's okay too. You're able to talk about not liking me." Julie said, "Okay, then I don't!" Mother intervened by saying, "Julie, you used to love coming here." I attempted to address Julie's ambivalence by saying, "Sometimes you like coming here and sometimes you don't. Sometimes you like me and sometimes you don't." At this point, mother asked if it was okay for her to play with the dollhouse. Julie and I said yes, whereupon mother sat on the child chair next to the dollhouse, exclaimed how cute it was, and added that she had always wanted one. (*I marveled to myself about the role reversal of mother on the little chair and child on the couch.*) Julie negotiated, "I know. I'll come here one day a week." I responded, "That's something we can think about, but I think twice a week is better, especially now when you're missing Daddy so much." Julie then turned to mother to negotiate possible Christmas presents, including a dollhouse. (*Not only did Santa bring her a dollhouse, but also the exact duplicate of the dollhouse, furniture, and dolls in my office with mother doing the same thing as her therapist. Thus commenced a long period of parallel play between Julie and "mother's dollhouse" and Julie and my dollhouse. In the process, I gained a new appreciation for the mother's identification with the therapist, the therapeutic value of the dollhouse, and the importance of concurrent visits with mother.*)

Julie created a rather intriguing dollhouse scenario that began with the marriage of the captain of the toy fort and one of the women in the dollhouse. She chose two dolls because they "go together . . . see, they look alike. They both have blond hair." The couple quickly had two biological children with blond hair. Julie was quite insistent that they all have blond hair lest someone think they're adopted. In a few weeks time, the doll parents divorced. The children lived with their mother (home dollhouse) during the week and with the father (therapy dollhouse) on the weekends. I played the part of her father; her mother, the part of mother; and Julie, the devious children. Normally, Julie would command what

I should do and say. A typical session would begin with Julie greeting me by saying, "Shut up, stupid. Let's play in the dollhouse." Generally, the first twenty minutes of each session were spent rearranging the dollhouse so it was exactly the same as the session before. This meant dumping the contents onto the floor and starting over from scratch each time. She would purposefully throw some things on the floor and order me to pick them up. Sometimes I complied; other times, not. If I didn't, Julie would either hit or kick me. Sometimes Julie would be quite rough with the dollhouse and insist that I fix it. I understood and reflected the underlying anxious feelings, but set boundaries on this aggressive behavior.

One Friday evening in Julie's home, there were many preparations for the marriage of Mr. Right to mother doll. On Monday, she came into the office and said, "Mr. Right married my mother. He's much better than you (father doll who lives in my office). The brother and sister dolls, Jill and Johnny, were talking together, when Jill said, "Boy, do we hate coming here. Mom's new husband is so much more fun than Dad. Mr. Right takes us places and buys things." Together, they started ordering the servant dolls to fix food and give them money so they could go shopping. Jill confided to Johnny, "Boy, do I hate him." While they were walking around the neighborhood, Julie—through Jill—ordered the servants to search for them. When the servants found them, Jill knocked them down and yelled, "Die, you fools." She looked at me and said, "The adults are so stupid! You're the adults." At this point, she threw a karate chop that was a quick sudden jab to my left hip. I exclaimed, "Julie, you may not hurt me. Stop! You know what Julie? You really do have control over your actions and when you're angry with something I do or say, you can tell me about it." She stopped the physical assault and wanted to sit on my lap. When I declined the offer, she threw her body on mine. I again told her to stop and reminded her that we could talk. She returned to the play.

Jill and Johnny asked father doll if they could do gymnastics on the porch. Father thought this was a fine idea, but Jill said, "No. Say no." Father still thought it was okay until Jill shouted, "Okay, we'll hang off the rooftop." I responded, "So, when Jill and Johnny get out of control, they want help to stop—like saying no." Julie retorted, "Shut up, stupid." As the play continued, father doll decided to invite over a new neighbor and her three children. Jill yelled, "No, no. No other kids in this house, just us. Get out." Father doll said, "Let's sit down and talk this through." Jill knocked down father doll and ran up to the roof. Johnny and Jill whispered, "He's jealous of Mr. Right. He wants to get married just because Mom did. Jealous, huh!" Father doll said, "Yeah, sure, part jealous and part happy for Mom. I'm also sad our marriage didn't work." Jill replied, "Well, just because your marriage didn't work doesn't mean that you have to marry her (new neighbor)." In another session, father doll announced he had married someone else, whereupon Julie yelled at the top of her lungs, "NO, NO, NO." She then started hitting and kicking me. "Daddy can't leave me," she chanted over and over again as she displaced her anger onto me. As she calmed down, Julie explained that "only the mother and father at my house are married. Not here, not here." There was some confusion about whether Jill thought of Mr. Right as a father. Jill contemplated this idea and said, "I can have two dads." I said, "The dad you used to live with and the new one."

When father doll said something spontaneously without direction from Julie, she lost her impulse control. Within seconds, she snapped my bra. Each time I attempted to interrupt the impulse by saying, "No, you may not do that." After the bra episode, she jumped into my lap and said, "I want you to hold me." I responded by saying, "You want me to be close to you and other times you get mad if anything unexpected happens . . . like when even the father doll does something you weren't expecting." She retorted, "I didn't tell you to say that." I interpreted, "You also didn't tell me to do that. You were caught by surprise, and you don't like that because you have been deeply hurt by certain things." Julie confirmed, "Like my father dying." I reiterated, "Like your father dying; suddenly, unexpectedly." She returned to the exact same play scenario and said, "Now, you do what I say." When it was time to leave, she didn't want to go. "I want to stay here." The two homes seemed to represent Julie's two families, her biological and adoptive ones. They also symbolized her representations of the mother on whom she clung for life support and the father who abandoned her through death. These split representations characterized parallel play without collaboration with the therapist. She wanted me to be completely in her control. If it were left up to Julie, I would not say anything. The play evoked her fears that her mother would find yet another husband. Anything that altered the mother/child dyad was threatening to Julie, especially since she had been sent away from one mother on a plane, her adored hamster died, and her beloved father died. Julie enacted her overwhelmingly painful affects with the therapist by hurting her. She used play as an escape from her painful reality. She continued to struggle with how she fit into families in general and my life in particular. After vacations, Julie would insist upon knowing about my family and whether my children were adopted. *(I found myself thinking of how nicely Julie had moved along in therapy when she was zapped by her father's death. It seemed we were starting from square one.)*

Meanwhile, Julie's creatures had been tucked away in a box in her bedroom. I took this to symbolize her father's death. The play materials that both he and I had used did not return to my office for many months. When they did, it was in the form of cards. Julie created new rules within each game and used games in a control battle. At one point when particularly frustrated, she threw a deck of cards into my face. There was much repetitive card-playing that was reminiscent of a ritual. There was also a frenzied quality to her play with phrases such as, "hurry up, hurry up," rule-changing, and cheating. *(I remember feeling like a sphinx sitting there in my chair. As I pondered this, I realized that a sphinx is an imaginary creature that has a human head on the body of a lion and holds its victims captive. I then realized that Julie may well consider herself the victim in life, therapy, her family, and her school.)* Ritualistically, Julie would immediately cross the room, roll over the ottoman, pull up the child chair, and ask what game I wanted to play. I responded whatever she wished. Once I commented on her use of playing cards as a way to make the time go by quickly. She took this as criticism and became mute with downcast eyes, so I backed off. The theme of therapy was intense competition with winning at all cost and remaining in total control. *(I wondered a lot about this card-playing and the battle it represented for her. Of course, a battle symbolized conflict, but I came to realize that it was I who was conflicted about card-playing. The battle was truly a testing of wills. With this new insight, I decided to change technique.)*

The next session, Julie came in and said, "I still haven't taught you Egyptian War, but I'm not in the mood today. We could play gin *(which I had taught her)*. No, let's play spit." *(I was rather intrigued by the idea of "Egyptian" since I had recently been thinking of myself as an Egyptian sphinx.)* With rapid motion, Julie cut the cards into two piles and ordered me to count my cards. I did. Instead of playing with my usual rapidity, I slowed down. Julie commented on this change in technique by saying, "You are going too slowly . . . Speed up, speed up." *(The object of this game is to see who can be the first person without any cards, so that at a certain juncture one yells "Spit," puts one's hand on one of two piles, and takes that pile.)* For Julie, this was a time of intense cheating and rule-changing born out of frustration. It was so hard for her to tolerate frustration, delay, and not being in control. In the past, I had commented on the rule-changes, but this time decided not to. Rather, we exchanged glances instead of words. Julie looked at me with a quizzical look and became wide-eyed.

I said, "You can play just the way you want to play cards in here." Once in a while, I would slip and say something like, "Hey, that's not fair," but, for the most part, I did not comment on the cheating because Julie viewed such comments as being so critical. It was also my way of letting her know that it was okay to cheat in here and okay to speak in her secret language or play the sleepwalking or toilet games. She decided on gin and became an active teacher and learner by checking out card books from the library and bringing them into the office to go over the rules. Because gin is a slower-moving card game than spit, it permitted her to talk about other matters. She began to use the cards to show her magic tricks, and I responded to her deftness with due elation. Then, much to my surprise, Julie demonstrated exactly how she was able to accomplish the magic. *(To myself, I started wondering about magic and how it related to this child. Isn't magic a way to assure control? There is an irresistible charm and power to it. It is mysterious. These thoughts helped me make sense of Julie's therapy—the secret language, her imaginary sisters, the creatures, and the cheating. I felt that Julie was slowly sharing her inner, private world by revealing the secret of her magic.)*

Stage IV: Developmental Growth and Change

Slowly, a reciprocity of play interaction developed through the hours of repetition, verbal exchange, and closeness / distancing interactions. Although the resistance continued and the transference stormed, Julie's relationships outside of therapy improved. Sadly, many school children did not take to Julie because they did not wish to be controlled by her; nor was she adept at reading social cues or nuances. Nevertheless, she did develop a few neighborhood friendships. The encopresis periodically reemerged throughout the year following her father's death. The anniversary of his death was compounded by the sudden and unexpected death of her only grandparent (maternal). The crisis seemed to interfere with the therapeutic process. Once again, there was a regression both in and out of therapy, with a return to stool retention, baby talk, elevator phobia, anxiety, and depression. In therapy, Julie did everything in her power to be thrown out. She took great delight in torturing me through withholding her emotions and verbalizations, and enacting her rage in repetition of the play scenarios described previously.

Mornings were a particularly difficult time, with Julie refusing to eat or go to school. Her screams, shouts, and tantrums at times provoked her mother into hitting her. There were frantic calls from mother who was at her wit's end. After an especially trying day, mother telephoned me crying, "If I knew where her birth mother lived, I would give her back." This was said in front of Julie, who then dissolved into tears and retreated to her room. In therapy, she verbalized her fears that mother would stop loving her. She explained how neither she nor anyone else could understand her; something she found to be quite upsetting. This incident served as a catalyst for therapeutic change, as Julie came to realize that neither mother nor I would get rid of her. She began talking about events in her life. Her affect changed one day when she walked in with a smile on her face. "Well, I agree with you about one thing. I really do. Camp. Mom says you think I would have fun at a sleep-away camp. I'm a bit worried about being away from home. It's such a big responsibility. Could I do it?" Along with the verbal discussion, Julie and I played more cooperative board games in which the object was not solely winning, but also collaborating; there was less ordering me around.

After two years of treatment, this morose, withholding, and guarded child became more related and engaged. She seemed to take enjoyment in playing cards, saying, "This time, I really won't cheat!" After two missed appointments over a holiday weekend, Julie wanted to know all about my children, particularly their ages and whether they were adopted. I said, "You know, I was thinking that we didn't meet last week. Perhaps you were wondering what I was doing." She responded, "Mom was sick. She's always sick." I wondered, "So she wasn't able to have the holiday meal the way other mothers do." Julie agreed, "True, but she never does." I said, "Sounds like Mom is having a hard time." She replied, "Yeah."

Another time my therapeutic heart leaped for joy when Julie humorously announced that they had hooked up with the Internet and now her mother could E-mail me when she got mad. There was much laughter. Looking at her and responding to her mood, I exclaimed, "I'm thinking she won't be getting mad as much." One day, Julie walked in, found a book about Abnormal Behavior, and said, "That's me." She acknowledged that she felt stupid. Julie peppered her language with obscenities but worried that I would tell her mother. She asked to meet me at the toy store to buy games. We talked about this and how she desired toys that only she would play with—not my other clients. I thought I could get a puzzle for us to work on. Julie said, "Well, you won't get it." I reminded her that I had gotten some cards she wanted. She said, "But you got the dollhouse for the other kids." "Hmm, you're wondering what I do with other kids," I replied. Julie agreed, adding, "But now I have my own dollhouse." The session ended with my saying, "And your own time here without other kids and without my telling your Mom what you said."

As Julie gradually grew to understand her internal mental states, she was able to engage in new social interactions with her peers. She was less rigid in her academic work and began to delight in interactive classroom projects. For the first time, other youngsters selected Julie as they divided into teams on the playground. She weathered the second anniversary of her father's death by organizing a graveside memorial with family and friends who read poetry and recited his favorite psalms. At home, she respected mother's need for private time. She looked forward to camp and understood that such an experience could be met with the heretofore incompatible affects of apprehension, anticipation, and excitement. Her encopresis resolved. In therapy, she continued talking about her dreams, fears, and worries. The appearance of empathy was a welcome surprise as Julie arranged for me to win games. The cheating ceased. Games of pretend and make-believe evolved into imaginative building, drawing, and other creative endeavors. While we occasionally played side-by-side, it was more in the service of resourceful, symbolic, and innovative productions. The creativity was truly a developmental leap forward. Finally, she delighted in her accomplishments. Play therapy had succeeded in promoting Julie's mental development and the transference affirmed her self-confidence as she engaged in new social relationships without a paralyzing fear of rejection.

Stage V: Termination

In view of the consolidation of growth and change achieved during Stage IV, Julie, her mother, and I agreed that it was time to think about termination. In consideration of the severity of Julie's problems and the length and intensity of her therapy, the four-month termination period was carefully planned. Once in a while, Julie and I encountered resistance, but it was short-lived. In one session, she displayed the dangerous feeling of "opening up" her private world, followed in the next by "I'll let you in." She accepted the interpretation of wanting her own private world as a declaration of independence. The problem was that Julie was too young to be totally independent. She understood the difference between the wish and the reality. Julie and I worked through her feelings of loss of her country and family of origin, as well as the hurt feelings when peers teased her about looking so different from mother. The loss of father was profound, but she explained that now he was in heaven and only two years old. The upcoming loss of her therapist was diminished by her realization that she would carry what she had learned within her. In the last session, she unearthed her creatures from home. When the session ended, Julie and I exchanged a heartfelt "Goodbye."

Case Discussion

Julie could not connect feelings with actions. "I think, I don't feel" is how Julie explained it. She had a tough time understanding how her beliefs, desires, and intentions impacted on herself and her relationships with mother, friends, and therapist. She could not make sense of her actions. Julie's internal representation of herself as unworthy of help interfered with the affective aspects of mental representation of herself and others. Her problems with self-regulation were abundantly apparent in impulsive actions at home and in therapy. Her difficulties in self-reflection had to do mainly with affective experiences. She seemed to lack the capacity to understand her behavior and how others would respond. Instead, there were split representations between the all-good mother and the all-bad self; the good father and bad mother; the good mother and bad nanny; and the good mother and the bad therapist. Her ambivalence was played out in the dollhouses, at home, toward mother, and in therapy, as one moment she would hate and hit me and the next, love me and sit in my lap. She alternately withheld her stool and emotion only to follow up with an explosive evacuation of feces or affect.

Julie's distorted representation of her mother as rejecting was based on her understanding of her biological mother's abandonment and her adoptive mother's avoidance of her insistent demands. To avoid the pain of rejection, she sustained an idealized conscious representation of mother as loving and an unconscious one of mother as rejecting. The unconscious representation endured as an intractable representation of the tormenting affective experience. While the representation of mother changed over time, Julie was left with an idealized picture of father because his death precluded a developing representation. Her trauma was exacerbated and compounded by father's death and again by grandmother's death. Thus, the middle stage (Stage III) of treatment focused on adaptation to traumatic life events, as well as on the identification of conflictual themes in the therapeutic narrative.

Father had been the exception to the rule in that he had comforted her. Julie turned to him for positive affective mirroring, which he provided—only to be taken away. Julie was then left with the model of two sets of rejecting and abandoning parents. Consequently, her negative affects were split off from conscious recognition to the point that Julie defensively inhibited certain feelings in order not to see, know, or understand them. This mental split resulted in enormous problems with correctly perceiving and experiencing interpersonal relationships. There was a primitive turning of passive into active—of projection of internalized anger onto mother and therapist, with no understanding of her own responsibility in causing another's distress. The therapeutic task was to enable her to understand and manage incompatible experiences; to understand, for example, that "maybe mother was sick, sad, or having a hard time, not because of Julie but because of mother's own mental states."

Julie's secret and scary inner world had huge ramifications in her social world, where she was belligerent one moment and the next clinging, impulsive, surly, or anxious. She had few successful social interactions with peers. Her teachers and I agreed that she had inhibited or disrupted the mental processes of feeling, as exemplified by concrete thinking, little curiosity about the world, and a paucity of self-reflection. That Julie lacked an integrated representation of herself explained why many therapeutic interpretations of defenses or conflicts did not work. These premature interpretations were met with "Shut up, stupid." There-fore, the therapeutic work was shifted to restoration of the mental and conscious process of feeling. This shift was accomplished through the many manifestations of the therapeutic alliance and play therapy that resulted in normal growth.

Developmental play therapy was chosen to help Julie master her anxiety and, thereby, cope with her biological, mental, and social concerns that (1) she could have regular bowel movements and flush the toilet herself, (2) she did fit into her adoptive family, (3) her internal world was not dangerous, (4) there was safety in relationship, and (5) her behavior was meaningful. Through clarification of her beliefs and desires, Julie came to understand how they led to certain actions and emotional reactions. I did this by letting her know I could understand and respond to Julie's affective signals without rejecting her. Through reciprocation and repetition in play, Julie reconstructed an internal view more consistent with the realities of her external world. Together, she and I found that she could control her affects; that her inner world was not that dangerous and did not cause her father's death or her mother's depression.

In addition, the play therapy evolved along conceptual developmental lines from limited capacity for age-appropriate play into socially acceptable play. The parallel play of the creature, bathroom, and dollhouse dramas gave way to co-operative card games, imaginative building scenarios, and, finally, interactive play that enhanced verbalization of anxiety.

The transference permitted work in both present and past, continuities and discontinuities, similarities and differences. Julie transferred and worked through her past experience of being uprooted from another culture and adopted into this one. She had an intense feeling of not belonging, of not being deserving of help at home or in therapy. Throughout three years of treatment, I never commented on her encopretic odor, thus helping her to feel accepted. The reciprocity of play interaction and verbal exchange made possible an identification with me that facilitated an internalizing process. Julie came to understand, explain, and make sense of what happened to her.

Conclusion

Julie's anxiety manifested itself through the maladaptive strategies of unrelenting worries, compulsive rituals, a simple phobia, tantrums, and encopresis. In these ways, she was attempting to control her environment and make sense of the traumas she experienced. Her suffering was enormous, especially because it re-sulted in social isolation. The therapeutic task was clear from the beginning. Julie needed to understand her representational world and her anxieties. She would need to find more acceptable, comfortable, and appropriate ways of managing her anxiety. The play therapy was augmented by frequent parent sessions and regular contact with her school.

I determined that empathic mirroring was the developmentally appropriate way of meeting Julie in her at times solitary and at other times parallel levels of play. In this way, we met in the transitional space that occurs between the therapist and child client (Winnicott, 1965a). Together, we came to understand the meaning of Julie's play as I worked to advance the play to a more symbolic, cooperative, and imaginative level. We proceeded gradually, as is the case in all of childhood development. Initially, this was accomplished through my seeming to be in the child's control as she struggled to create families and control her bowels. Through the repetition and mastery of play, Julie was able to control her bowels until a traumatic life event caused her to regress.

Exploration of her inner world was used as a technique to better understand conflicts of her mind that were played out in family creation and secrecy games. Her wishes for a private world were respected throughout treatment. Through exploration, Julie and I worked through the feeling of being caught between two cultures, families, and parents: "She wanted to be in (birth Mommy's tummy) but was out (with adoptive Mommy)." The issues of winning, losing, and competing between creature, dollhouse, and real families were better understood through the use of clarification and interpretation. The multiple additions (adoptions) to the rabbit and cat families were captured as a way to figure out where Julie belonged. She was able to grasp interpretations in the displacement of play.

As a way of handling anxiety regarding loss, Julie needed to control the therapy sessions, which I permitted in the beginning. One moment she was the autonomous teacher or mother; the next, an infantile creature or daughter. After her father's death, confrontation about wanting to be close and other times physically assaultive was followed by the interpretation that Julie had been caught by surprise and deeply hurt by certain things. Julie confirmed a certain awareness by associating to the death of her father.

Restoration of the mental process of feeling was accomplished through clarification and reflection within the play scenario as I helped Julie identify which feelings led to what actions. For example, feelings of anger would result in a temper tantrum, worry led to thumb-sucking, and loss of control ended in hitting. Feeling states were connected with action; for example, "I hate my father for leaving me, so I'll hit you, and I'll be the one to make you leave." Such turning of passive into active was rationalized as a way to have me get rid of Julie. Instead, I tolerated her considerable rage and despair, and responded with empathy to this very anxious child. Through identification with me, Julie was able to internalize these processes as she returned to a normal developmental pathway.

12 Post-Traumatic Stress Disorders: Sexual Abuse and Community Violence

Although the idea that catastrophic events can lead to traumatic reactions by adults is not new, the predominant view up to the 1980s was that children were minimally affected by exposure to such events. Research during the last fifteen years, however, has supported the view of earlier developmental theorists (Erikson, A. Freud, Mahler) that the experience of major life-stress events creates a psychosocial crisis in the lives of children and their families, and can have serious emotional and developmental consequences for the children (Benedek, 1985; Burgess, Hartman, and McCormack, 1987; Fletcher, 1996; Gold, 1986; Green, 1985; Pynoos and Eth, 1985a, 1985b; Terr, 1985). Current theoretical and empirical understanding suggests that the psychological sequelae of children's reactions to traumatic events are contextually based and individually determined. That is, the sequelae for a particular child are influenced by the nature and meaning of the event, personal characteristics and developmental stage, vulnerability and resilience factors, and the familial and social environment. Thus, the diagnostic classification for some children exposed to catastrophic events is post-traumatic stress disorder (PTSD); for other children, however, the distress is less severe and the symptoms less pronounced. The case of Tina exemplifies the distress and psychosocial dysfunction following four episodes of sexual abuse by a neighbor. The case summary of Kanessa exemplifies full-blown PTSD after she witnessed the death of her mother and brother and was injured herself in an episode of community violence.

Context of Traumatic Events

Events and Meaning

Traumatic Events. Traumatic events have been defined as those that involve "actual or threatened death or serious injury or a threat to the physical integrity of self or others" (APA, 1994, p. 427). Events of this calibre may include, among others, the following:

- natural disasters of fires, floods, hurricanes, tornadoes, and earthquakes
- national disasters of war, terrorism, and refugee experiences
- community catastrophes of school shootings, gang violence, and accidents, such as plane crashes or industrial explosions involving death or injury
- personal calamities in social relationships that involve being physically or sexually abused, shot, kidnapped, or forced to witness violence against parents

These terrifying events and the associated circumstances trigger stress reactions, direct children's attention to the immediate catastrophic experience, and require extraordinary coping and adaptive efforts. Often, adaptation to such an experience and the accompanying changes means giving up old, successful means of coping and establishing new ones that provide some sense of control and mastery. While the new coping style may be helpful in dealing with the traumatic event, it may or may not be adaptive in everyday living.

Meaning. The emotional response to a catastrophic event is mediated by appraisal of its personal impact. This appraisal constitutes children's evaluation of the event's meaning and importance to their own personal health, safety, and view of the world (Lazarus and Folkman, 1984). Some catastrophic events have little impact on a child. Others negatively impact children's well-being by destroying part or all of their real world—including, for example, the survival elements of food, clothing, and shelter; the physical and psychosocial elements of home, neighborhood, and school; and the social and emotional elements of family, friends, and teachers.

All catastrophic events that touch a child shatter to some degree that child's symbolic mental representation of the world and basic beliefs about self in that world. This personal destruction is associated with the actual and symbolic losses of significant persons and relationships, possessions and familiar things, and aspects of the self (e.g., loss of physical integrity, sense of security, and self-image). Thus, grieving becomes a part of the child's emotional reaction, along with the initial numbing and subsequent fear, anger, and guilt. In an effort to make sense of all that has happened, children struggle to integrate this new experience and its personal impact into their beliefs about their real and representational worlds and their place within these worlds.

Coping with the Stress and Distress

To handle the stress and distress generated by extraordinary life events, children use assorted defensive-adaptive coping mechanisms. Some involve cognitive information-seeking strategies that focus on understanding their changed physical, social, and representational worlds. Some involve managing or defending against their emotional responses through self-soothing, self-distraction, and avoidance strategies. Others involve seeking social support from significant persons, problem solving and direct action, or actual and symbolic flight. Sometimes these coping mechanisms are adaptive and functional in avoiding thoughts about or gaining mastery over a catastrophic event, sometimes not.

Developmental Variance.   Children's defensive-adaptive coping responses are influenced, in part, by the strategies commonly available at their age and developmental stage. After traumatic incidents, young infants and toddlers, for example, are likely to have vague preverbal and preconceptual memories and a heightened sense of arousal to danger. In response, they may withdraw, cling to their caregiver, or be inconsolable.

Preschoolers, on the other hand, see and understand only surface appearances of events and deny the permanency of change. They view the world, life events, and themselves solely from their own egocentric perspective. They tend to think about life in terms of obedience and punishment for disobedience (Piaget, 1954). All too often, this point of view places them in the position of falsely assuming responsibility for both ordinary and extraordinary life events and blaming themselves when bad things happen. Event-induced anxiety complicates matters by distorting their perception of time during and in the aftermath of critical incidents. This compression and/or expansion of time sequence further confuses their life perspective and creates a sense of inadequacy (Herman, 1992). In an attempt to clear up the confusion and regain a sense of control and mastery, preschoolers are very likely to use varying combinations of denial, distancing, regression, and repetitive reenactment (Cicchetti, 1989; A. Freud, 1966; Johnson, 1989; Rossman, 1992; Terr, 1985, 1991a, 1991b):

■ *Denial:* They may ignore the existence of certain facts, conditions, people, and issues. At times, they may seem to have either no memories of actual trauma-related events or self-centered perceptions that are evidenced as distortions, embellishments, or gaps in their memories.

■ *Distancing:* They may seem detached, quiet, and suspicious as they move apart from others, seek personal safe space and time to grieve their losses, and make sense of what has happened to themselves and their worlds.

■ *Regression:* They may attempt to handle the current situation by returning to earlier developmental stages and behaviors that elicited caring and produced a sense of comfort and well-being. For example, they may cling anxiously to significant adults, curl up in bed, whine, have tantrums to get attention, have night terrors and sleep disturbances, or display specific fears of selected objects, persons, or situations.

■ *Repetitive reenactment:* Preschoolers may attempt to re-experience and rework stressful events and associated life changes through the symbolic metaphor of various play activities, either in order to undo what happened or to regain a sense of mastery and control over the event. They often convey a sense of being driven to replay these themes over and over.

School-age children, by contrast, have a somewhat more realistic view of the complexities and nuances of events in relation to their real and representational worlds and themselves in these worlds. Yet, they too may experience distorted perceptions of time because youngsters under twelve do not possess matured time operations (Piaget, 1954). On the one hand, they face constraints on their inner lives similar to those of younger children. On the other, they also face additional constraints on their physical and social activity with their peers at school and in the neighborhood. While they may continue to use the more primitive defensive-adaptive coping strategies of preschoolers, school-age children are more oriented toward developing an inner plan of action to change what happened. Their maturing cognitive and language skills provide them with additional tools for grappling with the personal impact of catastrophic events, attendant changes, and disturbing recollections. Thus, school-age children's additional strategies for coping with stress and affective distress reflect their maturing ways of being and behaving, and may include the following (A. Freud, 1966; Johnson, 1989; Rossman, 1992; Terr, 1985, 1991a, 1991b; Vaillant, 1992):

■ *Avoidance:* Initially, school-age children may try to avoid facing their feelings and the full reality of a catastrophic event by becoming preoccupied with the way things were before. This preoccupation may lead to loss of interest and poor performance in school, sports activities, artistic endeavors, and hobbies. Sometimes, the mental processes and contents connected with the traumatic event may become closed off and not integrated into conscious awareness, memory, or identity. When taken to the extreme, the disconnect and lack of integration may lead to dissociation (Lynn and Rhue, 1994).

■ *Acting out:* They may convey their inner distress behaviorally by getting into difficulty, seeking attention through risky or unusual actions, or regressing to earlier externalizing behavior, such as obstinacy, tantrums, and peer problems.

■ *Somatic complaints:* They may complain of stomachaches, feeling bad, and not being hungry or sleepy.

■ *Complex repetitive reenactment:* As they seek to undo or master the event, school-age children's repetitive re-experiencing and reworking incorporate complex scripted narratives focused on selected mental representations of the event, associated life changes, and personal impact. Their perception of their circumstances, choice of foci, narrative themes, and various modifications are influenced by their personal history and developmental issues. Depending on their style, they may seek reversal of the changes or retribution through fantasy. They also may attempt to compensate for what they did or did not do. Periodically, their reenactments shift back and forth from symbolic play enactment in the representational world to thematic expression in their social transactions in the real world.

■ *Rumination*: When school-age children do open up verbally about their experiences with a catastrophic event, detailed information pours forth about the facts, their reactions, and their interpretations. Initially, the rumination appears to be a verbal purging of their distress. When taken to the extreme over a period of time, the rumination may be experienced as obsessive outpourings that isolate affect and afford no relief.

While these and their other coping strategies reflect school-age children's developmental maturation, regression to earlier developmental stages is also fairly common in the face of overwhelming life stress.

In summary, traumatized children evidence psychic numbing, specific fears, and anxious attachment as they strive to assimilate the event and search for reassurance, safety, and caring. Their individual coping responses are influenced by all of the strategies commonly available to children of their age and developmental stage, as well as those uniquely available given the particular child's subjective interpretation of trauma, personal history, and unique preferences. Traumatized children do not necessarily use all of the defenses available to them.

Dysfunction.   When catastrophic events overwhelm a child's strengths and resiliency, defensive/adaptive coping strategies, and social supports, the events become a source of tormented memory and evoke a sense of helplessness, fear, and dread. They can disrupt developmental processes of the mind, distort mental representations of self and other in the world, interfere with resolution of current life issues in general as well as those associated with the event, and impede further growth and developmental differentiation. Indeed, Erikson (1959) notes that critical life events and trauma may trigger psychosocial crises and disrupt or distort the development of internal mental processes that comprise identity strengths for a particular period; that is, trust, autonomy, initiative, and industry, to name those strengths relevant to children. Extraordinary events also may exacerbate poorly developed personal strengths and underscore regressive identity attributes, such as a sense of mistrust, hopelessness, or helplessness; shame or doubt, reactive impulsivity, or overcontrol; guilt, futility, or loss of social roots; and inferiority, incompetence, or performance paralysis.

Post-Traumatic Stress Disorder

Clinical Syndrome

Catastrophic events that may precipitate PTSD involve actual or threatened death, injury, or loss of physical integrity for the child or others important to that child (American Psychiatric Association, 1994). While experiencing, witnessing, or learning about such events places children at risk for stress-related biopsychosocial problems, not all children develop PTSD. Sometimes the presence of supportive factors, such as parents and relatives, mediates the stress and decreases vulnerability. At other times, however, proximity to a high-intensity stressor increases a child's probability of developing PTSD despite available supports.

To be diagnosed with PTSD, a child's response to the event must involve intense feelings of horror, helplessness, and fear that may be expressed affectively; verbally; through agitated or disorganized behavior; or through nightmares with themes of monsters, disasters, threats, or rescue efforts. The inner life becomes tormented and constrained, outer activity becomes constricted and bounded by fear. Sometimes there are vivid terror dreams. Sometimes there are intrusive recollections or dissociative flashbacks in which the children lose contact with reality and re-experience the event. There is usually clinically significant distress and impairment in many areas of psychosocial functioning—intrapersonal, inter-personal, emotional, cognitive, and/or behavioral. Critical symptoms likely to develop include increased anxiety or general state of hypervigilance, re-experiencing the trauma event, and persistent avoidance of event-related thoughts and other reminders. These symptoms must be present for more than one month and may be diagnosed as acute (duration less than three months), chronic (duration more than three months), or delayed onset (six months after the event). The duration and intensity of the symptoms vary greatly, with complete recovery occurring anywhere from three months to more than twelve months (APA, 1994; Famularo, Kinscherff, and Fenton, 1990).

Prevalence

There are no community-based epidemiological studies that explore the incidence of PTSD in children. For at-risk individuals exposed to trauma, however, prevalence rates range from 3 to 58 percent (APA, 1994). A meta-analysis based on 2,697 children from thirty-four samples places the average prevalence rate at 36 percent of exposed children (Fletcher, 1996).

Estimates of the number of children exposed to different traumatic events vary widely. Sometimes there are estimates of the rate of PTSD associated with particular events; more often, there are not.

Clinical Etiology

Initially, traumatic life experiences are likely to evoke psychic numbing; then intense affective reactions involving fear and anger. Caution is in order, however, in that children, at first glance, may appear to be all right and may not express their feelings directly. While it is clear that stress and anxiety are inherent in each traumatic life event, the degree of stress experienced by a particular child varies. The intensity of the experience tends to be associated with how overwhelmed their ordinary family lifelines, social support systems, and personal resiliency become. Stress and anxiety levels are also likely to be increased when the event is perceived as life-threatening, unexpected, not a sole episode, beyond their control, and either personal in nature or in the child's immediate proximity (Fletcher, 1996). Traumatic reactions and development of PTSD symptoms are especially likely to occur when no corrective action—such as fight or flight—appears possible. Over time, these traumatic symptoms may become disconnected from the source event and take on a life of their own (Herman, 1992).

Family Issues

Families provide children with a sense of safety and personal identity in connectedness with others and with certain beliefs and expectations about self and the world. One such expectation is that the family will be able to protect its children and shield them from harm. Traumatic events, by their very nature, breach this assumptive world view that families can provide safety for their members and an average expectable environment (Hartmann, 1939) for their children. Thus, the trauma and its associated consequences, by their very nature, impact on the child's course of development (Khan, 1963) and become the organizers by which children and their families view their lives and their worlds. Some families are able to provide social and psychological support that enables their children to (1) mobilize their strengths and resilience, (2) assimilate the traumatic experience, and (3) adaptively change their beliefs about self-in-the-world. When families are decimated by an event or cannot mobilize their strengths, and when children are especially vulnerable, PTSD is the likely result.

Empirical Support for Treatment Selection

Apart from case reports and clinical experience, there is little evidence to support treatment choice for children with PTSD. Naturalistic and quasi-experimental studies on the efficacy of treatments yield mixed and largely nonsignificant outcomes (Weisz, Weiss, and Donenberg, 1992; Salladin and Timberlake, 1995).

For national and community disasters such as school shootings or earthquakes, many professionals use preventive crisis-intervention models that triage acutely exposed children. These models seek to support and strengthen coping skills for dealing with the psychic numbing and anticipated grief/trauma responses, rapidly identify and treat mental disorders exacerbated in the context of severe stress, and provide brief focused treatment for children evidencing chronic PTSD symptoms. Case reports—but little empirical evidence of the outcomes of these interventions—abound in the literature.

Psychotherapy

With traumatized children in developmental play therapy, there are usually four major treatment goals: (1) processing the emotional, cognitive, and physical aspects of the catastrophic event(s) and the developmental ramifications; (2) addressing dysfunctional patterns of coping and adaptation; (3) restoring the sense of connection with others; and (4) repairing the self-concept (Herman, 1992; Salladin and Timberlake, 1995; Timberlake, 1978b, 1979, 1981). Work on these goals usually proceeds in tandem. The therapeutic process is likely to vary depending

on the type of stressor, the surrounding circumstances, the strength and entrench-
ment of the PTSD symptom array, and the time lapse between the event and
intervention.

Sexual Abuse

Prevalence

There were 3,126,000 reports of child maltreatment in 1996, a figure that represents
forty-seven reported incidents per one thousand children, and is double the 1983
rate (Wang and Daro, 1997). Of these figures, 60 percent represent familial abuse
(Tower, 1999). It is estimated that 14 to 15 percent of maltreated children have
been sexually abused; that is, approximately 468,900 children in 1996 (National
Center on Child Abuse Prevention, 1998). This figure represents a 300 percent
increase from the incidence rates during 1980–1988 (National Center on Child
Abuse and Neglect, 1988; Wang and Daro, 1997). While no distinct incidence rates
for sexually abused children diagnosed with PTSD were located, the clinical
literature clearly supports the existence of this mental disorder among sexually
abused children (Briere, 1992; Famularo, Kinscherff, and Fenton, 1990; Herman,
1992; Kendall-Tackett, Meyer-Williams, and Finkelhor, 1993).

Clinical Sequelae

Disasters and catastrophes are public events with the facts generally broadcast
repeatedly by the media. Sexual abuse, by contrast, is private, personal, and likely
to happen again. As defined by public law (Child Abuse Prevention and Treatment
Act, 1984), *legal sexual abuse* refers to an adult's (or a person five years older than
the child) use of a child for sexual gratification and includes the following:

> (i) the employment, use, persuasion, inducement, enticement, or coercion of any
> child to engage in any sexually explicit conduct (or any simulation of such conduct)
> for the purpose of producing any visual depiction of such conduct, or (ii) the rape,
> molestation, prostitution, or other form of sexual exploitation of children, or incest
> with children, under circumstances which indicate the child's health or welfare is
> harmed or threatened thereby. (Section 42)

The catastrophic impact of sexual abuse results from the abuse *per se* and
multiple other factors. It is heightened when it involves young children, frequent
episodes stretched over a period of time, penetration, bizarre factors, and either
multiple perpetrators or a significantly older perpetrator. The impact is further
increased when the child feels personal responsibility for the sexual abuse, powerless, betrayed, and stigmatized. That is, the child's emotional responses to the
abuse, together with parents' responses following disclosure and the child's prior
biopsychosocial adjustment, mediate how the event and associated processes tend

to alter or distort children's cognitive and affective representations of their world and themselves in it (Briere, 1992; Morrissette, 1999; Tharinger, 1990; Trickett and Putnam, 1993).

While sexual abuse of children has multiple clinical sequelae, it is sometimes difficult to separate out the effects of sexual abuse *per se* from other forms of abuse, the consequences of disclosure, or the assessment processes and legal proceedings. Although the intensity of the symptoms varies from child to child, sexually abused children are likely to evidence an array of the following:

- heightened sexual activities that include hypersexual and sexually provocative behavior associated with being eroticized by the abuse
- sense of powerlessness, guilt, and responsibility for not stopping the invasion of their body by the perpetrator
- fear of being identified as a victim and a sense of isolation from peers, siblings, and other family members (especially in incest cases)
- difficulty trusting
- depression often coexisting with pervasive anger, sense of helplessness and hopelessness
- somatic symptoms including difficulty sleeping, poor appetite, fatigue, and general malaise
- anxiety and fearfulness, hypervigilance, flashbacks and intrusive thoughts about the abuse, reenactment episodes, withdrawal from contexts where the abuse occurred
- outwardly directed aggressive behavior, antisocial acts, and chronic disobedience through which boys strive to reestablish their masculinity, but inwardly directed aggressive acts of suicide attempts and self-mutilation (e.g., burns, cutting, anorexia) through which girls seek to make themselves less attractive

Sometimes the child's clinical symptom cluster meets the *DSM IV* criteria for PTSD, sometimes it does not. States vary in reporting requirements.

Developmental Dysfunction

Abused children develop a mental representation of their social environment as unpredictable and threatening. This view of their external world complicates the usual developmental tasks of childhood by adding the element of self-preservation in the face of danger. More specifically, their tasks become the establishment of trust and safety in a dangerous environment; the capacity to soothe and regulate self in a harsh environment; an autonomous self in relation to abusive or helpless others; and initiative and industry in an environment demanding conformity to the will of the omnipotent abuser (Erikson, 1950; Herman, 1992; Salladin and Timberlake, 1995).

In seeking to preserve their self-concept, abused children develop adaptive patterns of avoiding danger, dealing with parental anger, and guarding against memories of abuse. They may avoid attention by running away or freezing in place. They may associate feelings of safety with hiding places, not people. They may escape by altering their mental representations of reality or by dissociating themselves from reality (James, 1989; Kluft, 1985; Salladin and Timberlake, 1995). These defenses allow abused children to block out and deny the reality of the abuse trauma, separate their feelings from their thoughts, and maintain the wish of parental adequacy. Dissociation adds the benefit of containing the abusive experience, acting as an analgesic for the pain, and allowing the child to retreat into make-believe and fantasy (Donovan and McIntyre, 1990; Kluft, 1985; Salladin and Timberlake, 1995; Timberlake, 1981). In time, these defenses solidify, expand into an internal system of rules that distorts cognitive thought and dynamic mental representations of self in the world, and become associated with increasing psychosocial dysfunction within and outside of the family unit.

Although abused children often identify with the omnipotent abuser and strive to comply with the rules and demands for secrecy, they are likely to become increasingly uncomfortable and self-conscious and eventually disclose what has happened or—in many cases—is still happening. They feel a sense of shame at failing to comply with the abuser's demands and a sense of blame and guilt at allowing the abuse in the first place. They feel betrayed by the nonabusive parent, or both parents in the case of nonfamilial abuse, who failed to protect and care for them and are likely to fluctuate between either loving or hating them.

The mixed feelings generated by abusive experiences distort children's sense of connection with significant caregivers and can be overwhelming. This, in turn, results in regression to the earlier developmental periods, in which self and object representations were distinctly separated into all good or all bad. By polarizing positive and negative images, the primitive defense of splitting keeps ideal objects apart from negative ones. By not allowing for ambiguity of affect and self/object representations, splitting prevents the integration of bad/good objects and the ensuing unbearable anxiety and guilt in relation to their parents (Chethik, 1989; Mishne, 1983). Finding fault with themselves rather than with their parents enables them to preserve their idealized parental image, their parental attachment, and the hope of eventually earning parental care and protection. Thus, the splitting defense mediates the child's internal conflict between the need for a nurturing and protective family environment and the painful rejection of self experienced in the abusive episodes (Salladin and Timberlake, 1995).

Through these situationally adaptive coping efforts, abused children are attempting to screen out or change what they bring into their internal mental worlds from their real environmental worlds. Thus, initially, these two defenses may serve children well in modifying their mental representations of their real experiences. Over time, however, abused children find it necessary to expend increasing amounts of psychic energy to guard against dissociation of self from reality and to maintain the split representations.

Family Issues

Some traumatic events, such as child sexual abuse, go beyond simply breaching the assumption that the family is able to provide a protective shield for its children. Especially when the perpetrator is a family member, sexual abuse violates not only the child, but also the integrity of the family unit. Thus, in a sense, both child and family may be seen as victims, *albeit* for different reasons. The abuse shatters the sense of connection and attachment among family members. It also undermines each family member's sense of self that was formed and is sustained in relation to other family members—who at best have failed to protect and at worst have violated their child. Sexual abuse especially emphasizes failure in the mother's role of ensuring child safety and protection. In this way, sexual abuse undermines family belief systems that offer connectedness and meaning to the human experience. In addition, the sexually abused child experiences disruption and distortion of progressive emotional development. In some instances, more than one child in a family is sexually abused. While all forms of maltreatment of children occur in all socioeconomic strata, maltreatment is found four times more frequently in poor families (Finkelhor, 1984). This finding is not surprising because abusiveness is almost always an act of parenting failure through acts of omission or commission, and the poor have fewer parenting supports and resources. Often the families of these children are socially isolated and the children themselves are frequently left alone while their parents work or are simply out (Finkelhor, 1984). In addition, half of maltreating families evidence substance abuse and many evidence marital problems (Trickett and Putnam, 1993).

In terms of sexual abuse, most victims are female, with the majority being ages eleven to fourteen and also being oldest daughters (de Young, 1982; National Center on Child Abuse and Neglect, 1995). Sexually abused males are most often four to six years old (National Center on Child Abuse and Neglect, 1995).

Perpetrators, whether family members or not, tend to have experienced deprivation and chaotic, dysfunctional families in childhood. Many were sexually abused. Many became independent at an early age (Faller, 1988). When the father or father surrogate is the perpetrator, he tends to view his daughter as his possession and submission as her duty. In some instances, the mother knows about the father's abuse, but tends to look the other way and rationalize about what is happening (Trickett and Putnam, 1993). Usually a perpetrator known to the child and family uses his or her power to dominate and threaten the child, thereby maintaining secrecy. The secrecy ensures that the sexual abuse can continue. Sometimes when the child discloses abuse by a family member or very close friend, other family members compel the child to recant. Their reasons usually involve fear of the perpetrator and dissolution of the family unit, rather than concern about what is happening to the sexually abused child.

Treatment

Supportive and Rehabilitative Family Services. When the child discloses physical or sexual abuse, the immediate priority is ensuring health and safety. In some instances, it is possible to modify the family environment and mobilize the support resources necessary for child protection and well-being. In other instances, when protection from abuse is not possible within the home, child protective services removes the child, places him or her in foster care, and develops an individualized service plan that includes permanency planning, psychotherapy for the child, and case management and restorative services for the family. Engaging the family with an abusive member, however, can be difficult because these families tend to maintain secrecy and distrust outsiders, especially service providers. In part, they resist exposure to treatment because treatment means the possibility of changing their dysfunctional family patterns.

When the sexual abuse is perpetrated by an outsider, some families react with anger and confrontation, some with denial, and some with a sense of futility that whatever will happen will happen. Often, it is difficult to engage these families in treatment—even crisis intervention. Some families, however, are more willing to expose their child to treatment if they perceive a problem in their child's coping with the traumatic event. In this case, it is often helpful to maintain supportive telephone contact with the parents or five- to ten-minute interviews around the child's appointment. The focus in these contacts is the child's coping and adaptation at home, at school, and in the neighborhood, and clarifying the meaning of the child's behavioral and affective expressions. The goal is to increase parental understanding of and empathy for their child, thereby strengthening their own ability to nurture and protect.

Psychotherapy. With sexually abused children in developmental play therapy, there are usually the same four major treatment goals noted for traumatized children generally: (1) processing the emotional, cognitive, and physical aspects of the abuse event(s) and the developmental ramifications; (2) addressing dysfunctional patterns of coping and adaptation; (3) restoring the sense of connection with others; and (4) repairing the self-concept (Herman, 1992; Salladin and Timberlake, 1995; Timberlake, 1978b, 1979, 1981; Tower, 1999). Work on these goals usually proceeds in tandem. As narrative treatment themes, they do not necessarily appear in the same order for every child; nor is one theme likely to be resolved completely before others appear.

Because they are accustomed to gaining adults' approval, children are likely to view the sexual abuse as punishment, even though they are often not sure why, how, or if they have been disobedient. When the sexual abuse is a relatively recent occurrence, elementary-school-age children evidence symptoms, but rarely major psychosocial dysfunction, maladaptation, and guilt unless other problems were already present. They may, however, reveal magical thinking, self-blame, anger, and a sense of feeling different. When time has lapsed and the symptom array has become more entrenched, children often begin to feel that they are different, somehow damaged, and no longer socially acceptable. The full array of PTSD symptomatic behavior then may begin to be evidenced.

Early on in treatment, the clinician elicits information about the sexual abuse and events that co-occur in time, because children may attribute cause and effect to events that happen in proximity. Children sometimes feel that adults are omnipotent and all-knowing and, therefore, know how they feel. Therefore, they may sense disapproval if the clinician does not talk about the abuse. They may need to reveal graphic details to reassure themselves and others that they are truly okay. As children talk about and replay the event, they become increasingly able to externalize the cause as apart from and having nothing to do with them. The danger, however, is that a child may pretend to understand what happened, thereby, encouraging their parents and other adults to close the abuse issue before it is resolved. Therefore, the clinician needs to attend to the possibility of premature closure in exploring and clarifying the sexual abuse. This needs to be done in simple sound-bite language that is developmentally age-appropriate; that is, in small dosage ideas and words that children can understand, digest, and keep in mind as a mantra. For example, repetitive aggression and pain issues in play and talk could be partially reframed to "sometimes good people do bad things to good children." Adult behavior also can be framed in terms of broken rules, punishment, and teaching adults to behave appropriately with children. When these and other ideas are in the clinician's mind, such statements are easily and appropriately worked into the play context. In time, it is often useful to co-create pictures, stories, and play that enable sexually abused children to move beyond split images of good/bad and achieve a resolution that incorporates nuance and achieves the notion of duality and integration of image, affect, and behavior.

Another important theme in the therapeutic talk and play narrative is that the child bears no shame because she or he has done nothing wrong. This theme is usually handled by metaphor until it is clear that a child really understands how the perception of sexual abuse, damaged goods, and stigma can influence concept of self, feelings, and behavior. Various play scenarios initiated by the child and elaborated in the therapy can be helpful in inculcating the concept of innocence. It is, however, important to note that children tend to absorb their parent(s), unresolved issues about the abuse and that parents also may need help in working through shame and guilt.

Often, sexually abused children are overwhelmed by their rage and become fearful when they vent their anger through aggressive play. They fear that this expression will have magical and destructive consequences. Thus, they need a safe holding environment to express aggression and act out even symbolically. As they work through their anger and cease provocative behavior, abused children begin to face the reality that what masqueraded as love and attention was really pain and abuse.

On a dynamic developmental level, the clinical social worker is rebuilding the child's perception of self so the child will be able to redefine abusive relationships for what they are and will be able to see themselves as lovable. Eventually, as therapy progresses, the play narrative is likely to incorporate stories, drawings, and games in which heroes and heroines vanquish evil monsters and fantasy figures. As children play out dangerous scenarios, the focus shifts from rescuing injured persons to preventing traumatic events and hurt. The clinician interprets these mastery themes in a way that enables children to relegate their feelings about the sexual abuse to the past, offers reassurance that their sense of completion is appropriate, and helps them move forward into the future. Through such mastery play, school-age children begin the process of closure and resolution.

Course of Treatment: Tina, a Case of Sexual Abuse by Jennifer Weaver, M.S.W., LCSW

Stage I: Transfer and Reassessment

Presenting Problem. Tina, an attractive, dark-complected, ten-year-old African American girl living in a very poor area of a large metropolitan city, was referred to our outpatient clinic because of sexually provocative behavior, frequent school absences due to illness, and aggressive and oppositional behavior patterns in her fifth-grade classroom.

Initially, she was seen in individual therapy for about three months. During that period, she played out themes associated with sexual abuse and need for a safe retreat. This work ended prematurely due to her mother's dissatisfaction with the therapist. She then was placed in a weekly psychodynamic group for school-age children with diverse histories and problem behaviors. Chart notes indicate that Tina was frequently verbally aggressive toward other children in the group, had great difficulty with impulse control, and was sexually provocative. She was asked to leave the group early a number of times and had to be physically restrained twice during angry outbursts. Further, the mother reported to the group leaders that Tina had been suspended from school twice in the past three months and her behavior continued to be a serious problem. After approximately six months in the group, Tina's mother and her group therapists determined that Tina's symptoms had not improved in any significant way, and agreed that Tina might benefit more from individual play therapy.

Although Tina's mother declined to meet me at the time of the transition due to her work schedule and the very real threat of being laid off in the office downsizing, we were able to talk by phone about some of her concerns for her daughter. She described Tina as controlling, manipulative, and angry. She stated that Tina had been fighting and verbally abusive with her siblings. Most importantly to Tina's mother, she was sullen and uncooperative in school, with occasional verbal outbursts that sometimes resulted in school suspensions.

History of Problem. According to her mother, Tina's behavioral problems at home and school—while always present to some degree—did not become a major issue until it was discovered that Tina had been molested by a neighborhood boy three or four times within a four-week period. She was eight years old at the time, the boy was thirteen. Her mother had responded to the discovery by taking her to a local hospital, where she was examined and released. The examination revealed penetration had occurred. Charges were filed but the boy was not prosecuted for a number of reasons, including Tina's mother's concern that Tina would have to testify in court. She thought it would be better if Tina just forgot the whole thing.

In the first few months after the incidents, Tina was clingy, fearful of leaving home, and cried frequently. She seemed depressed, did not eat or sleep well, and was sick a lot. Within six months, Tina's behavior shifted and she became oppositional, seductive, angry, and verbally abusive to her siblings and peers. At a teacher's recommendation, Tina's mother sought counseling for her. After three months of individual therapy and six months of group, her mother reported that she had seen no improvement in her behavior either at home or in school.

Developmental History.   Tina was the youngest of four children. Her seventeen-year-old sister was five months pregnant at the time of our first interview. Her fourteen-year-old sister and twelve-year-old brother were doing well in school. A psychosocial history, taken during her initial treatment phase at the agency and confirmed by phone interviews with her mother, indicated that her parents had marital problems during her mother's pregnancy with her. Her father left home permanently before she was eight months old and has had no contact with Tina or other family members. No prenatal problems were reported. Tina was described as willful and sickly from birth. She was unable to keep food down and was hospitalized during her first three weeks for failure to thrive. Tina was monitored closely for her first six months and was eventually diagnosed with a gastrointestinal-reflux problem. Her mother reported that Tina had medical problems until she was about three years old, but that her first years of developmental milestones, such as walking and talking, occurred either slightly early or about average for her age.

Tina has been attending the same school since kindergarten. Her mother described frequent complaints of illnesses and a poor attendance record throughout her school history. Educational achievement was described as a high priority within the family. Tina had been successful with As and Bs until this year when her grades dropped to Cs and Ds.

Initial Assessment.   The assessment and group intervention plan developed after Tina's first three sessions at the clinic had been updated quarterly by her group leaders. Tina was initially diagnosed as suffering from Post-traumatic Stress Disorder, chronic, as a result of sexual abuse by her neighbor a year ago. Following a current diagnostic workup, however, the mental health team noted that although Tina displayed some common PTSD symptoms, her symptom array did not fully meet the clinical criteria for the disorder. Thus, her revised biopsychosocial diagnosis was stress reaction of childhood induced by sexual abuse. Her initial anxiety and depression, and later sexually provocative, oppositional, and acting out behaviors, clearly reflected this symptom cluster. In one sense, these behaviors could be seen as adaptive in keeping others, including possible sexual perpetrators, at arm's length. Increasingly, however, her behaviors were becoming more maladaptive, causing poor peer and family relationships and difficulty at school. Her anger was increasingly getting her in trouble. She presented to others as sullen and unhappy.

Stage II: Transfer and Creation of Therapeutic Alliance

Within the first three sessions, Tina clearly established that she was hurting inside from the past assaults to the self. In addition to the oppositional and acting-out behaviors, she exhibited symptoms of repetition compulsion, hypervigilance, fear, and a strong desire for control, thus safety. Tina quickly established basic patterns of how she would be using her therapy time. She brought a snack, which she used for soothing when her emotions ran too high or she felt out of control. From the very first session, she used art frequently to express her feelings and fears, and to gain some sense of mastery over her trauma. Tina also used dramatic stories, metaphors, and dreams as vehicles for expression. All play sessions took place in my office; materials at her disposal included art supplies and toys meant to encourage projective expression of feelings, such as puppets, dolls, soldiers, dollhouse, blocks, and clay.

Tina's use of the available chairs was of particular note. She made it a practice to use one chair, near the door, at the beginning of each session. At that time, she most often talked about real material from her everyday life. As she moved into feelings and fantasy, Tina would often stand up (sometimes to give a dramatic presentation of a story) and sit down in a swivel chair in the middle of the room. It was in this chair that she related her fantasy life, metaphors, deeper fears, wishes, and dreams. Sometimes, she would then move to my desk chair and draw out fantasy material. At the end of the session, Tina would usually spend the last few minutes back in the chair near the door. She used this chair as a transition back to the real world before she left the office. Thus, in each chair, Tina allowed varying levels of anxiety and degrees of directness in revealing traumatic material.

In the first session, Tina moved quickly into the therapeutic narrative, telling me metaphorically how she was feeling, as well as what she hoped and expected from me. She started to talk about volcanoes, which she had recently been studying in class. She then decided to draw one for me. Tina was quiet during much of this session, letting her drawings speak for her. She started, unusually enough, with the lava pouring down from nothing; she then proceeded to draw the mountain from which it came. I reflected what I saw, and Tina expanded on her theme, telling me a number of times that the lava was very hot. She said, "It's spewing out here, you can't get too close, it could burn you." She showed how the lava pieces could land on people even if they were far away. As part of her educating me, Tina explained that if I were walking by this mountain, I would not even

FIGURE 12.1   Erupting Volcano

know that the lava was inside until it began to spray out "hot stuff" and hurt me. (*Along with this probable metaphor for male sexual functioning and her experiences with the perpetrator, I thought that Tina was, as importantly, telling me about all of the hot, angry, hurt feelings she carried inside that could not be seen from the outside until or unless she exploded into aggression. She also was warning me, letting me know that she felt dangerous, and suggesting that I might not want to get too close to her. Conversely, she was also conveying her mistrust and ambivalence about getting close to yet another therapist.*) When she finished, Tina offered me the picture to keep and "hang on the wall right here, over your chair where you can see it all the time. It would look good there." (*This offering reflected her wish for help and was a beginning in building our therapeutic working alliance.*)

Tina then proceeded to draw another picture. She instructed me about how one can draw a whole picture starting with only a couple of straight lines. While she filled the lines in, I was to guess what she was drawing. In this way, Tina structured and maintained control over our interaction. Her lines became a picture of a broken down car. She took great pains to show where one wheel was missing and where the windows were cracked. *(This picture showed me another side of how Tina felt about herself; not only full of anger and aggression, but also broken and cracked and with parts of her former pre-trauma self missing.)* When she finished this picture, I stated that it looked like that car could use a good mechanic so that it might feel better. Tina graphically replied, "The car might be able to be fixed up, but then again, it might have to go to a junkyard. I don't know for sure."

During the second session, Tina did not draw, but rather explored the toys and played with the babydolls and the blocks in a very flat but socially appropriate manner. *(It is likely that she felt very exposed after her first visit and needed to be more certain of me, her surroundings, and her ability to control what and how much she might choose to explore about her painful inner life.)*

In the third session, Tina began to play in a similar way, but became more focused once she picked up some of the toy soldiers. She then spent the rest of the session using the soldiers as a vehicle of expression. She first arranged the soldiers so that they were "prepared for war." This preparation involved having them face me. Tina told me, "The enemy could be anywhere—they have to be ready—they could be around any corner." *(Clearly, she worried about my status. Would I help or hurt her? Was I a possible enemy, another danger to be dealt with in her tense, bottled-up world? This narrative theme also was a clear depiction of her constant state of awareness of danger and her hypervigilant stance.)* Tina then had the good green soldiers shoot the enemy tan soldiers, collected the tan soldiers into the middle of a circle, and surrounded them with green ones. Next, she had the green soldiers discuss the situation. Tina had the one in charge announce to the others, "Good work men! Now let's begin the execution." The others asked him, "When do we shoot them?" He replied, "Soon, soon. . . . It's time! No wait, there has to be a trial. They know the crimes."*(I thought to myself how much this play reenactment paralleled her experience with being sexually abused. I wondered if it might reflect her own confusion about simultaneously being hurt and sexually stimulated. Perhaps it also reflected some sense of self-blame.)*

Tina then brought out a dollhouse figure of a grandmother and spoke in a very different voice, authoritative yet feminine. "The soldiers must die. I saw what they did to our children." This older female was protective of and sympathetic to children who might have been hurt. She most likely symbolized a magical caregiver who might be able to protect children from molesters (such as the boy who assaulted Tina), but could at least make sure the bad guys are punished. *(Perhaps this was Tina's wish about my role? Or for her mother's role? Deeper down, it is also possible that grandmother doll was a repository for Tina's own less acceptable angry feelings about the perpetrator's actions, her worry that she was responsible in some way, and her need for controls.)*

Tina waited in silence, appearing to hesitate to kill the soldiers despite the grandmother's orders. She put the grandmother figure back and inspected one of the green soldiers more closely, taking him out of the circle. She said, "This one has a hole in his back. See it?" The soldier did have an actual hole. I replied, "Yes, I do. A hole right there," and I touched the hole she had showed me. She said, "One of his friends might have shot him. This is something we have to check." *(Repetitive reenactment of the assault and investigation.)* Then she swept away the execution circle and brought out a couple of the other green soldiers. *(While her avoidance of the expected execution and subsequent change of the charges and crimes mirrored her real-world experience, it appeared to be more a form of repression or denial in her internal representational world. That she seemed unwilling or unable to play out the entire scene with a violent end also raised the possibility that the bad soldier represented a piece of herself, the part that had caused the perpetrator to sexually abuse her.)*

I reflected back to Tina, "He might have been shot by one of his friends?" She answered, "I think that is exactly what happened. We have to have a trial to see which one did it. We can tell by checking." She then had a conversation between two soldiers, with the one in charge asking, "Soldier, was it a friend or enemy that shot you there?"

"It was a friend."

"Which one was it?"

"I don't know . . . I don't know."

"Was it your best friend?"

"Maybe . . . it was a bullet from behind me."

"We will have to check."

She then put the point end of the gun of one soldier into the hole of the shot soldier. "No, this one doesn't fit." She proceeded to try to match up the size of the hole with the gun-barrel sizes of about six other soldiers. "This one is close. It could be him," and she set him aside. "Or this one. It could be either. How will we be able to tell which one did it?" I reflected, "They have the same size gun. It will be hard for you to tell who hurt him so bad." Tina (as herself) then questioned the first soldier directly, "Did you do it?" He answered, "No way. I like him. I wouldn't shoot nobody." She questioned the other soldier who was chosen from the circle, "Then, did you do it?" This one answered, "Yeah, he gets on my nerves." *(This play showed another part of Tina's world view based on her past trauma; namely, some people hurt others for no good reason, perhaps because they just feel like it. Thus, the world is truly unsafe. On another level, Tina may again have been expressing a desire to kill off a piece of herself that she, or others, finds unacceptable. On yet another level, perhaps the play symbolized the sexual abuse with the hole representing her vagina and the gun barrel, the perpetrator's penis.)*

Tina responded to the soldier who confessed, "Then you will have to be executed," and she began to arrange another circle of soldiers and placed the confessor in the center. I asked for clarification, and we discussed the situation she had created in her play.

"So he shot his friend?" (JW)

"Yep." (T)

"Because he got on his nerves?"(JW)

"It happens all the time. Except, sometimes it's suicide."(T)

"Suicide?"(JW)

"He could have done it himself, and his friend's just lying."(T)

"Oh, the friend could be lying?"(JW)

Tina directly questioned the soldier with a hole in his back, "Did you shoot yourself?" She had him answer her, "No, sir!" Tina herself asked him again, "Are you lying to me?" Again, he answered, "No!" She said to him, "Well, I think you are. You shot yourself. You will have to be punished." *(Her worry that she too had caused her own victimization.)* She put the soldier with the hole in the center of the execution circle, replacing the soldier who lied about shooting his friend. I asked Tina, "What will happen now?" She replied, "That's it for him. He's dead meat." I reflected, "He'll have to be punished for his crime." She told me, "They're gonna shoot him dead. Then it's over." Tina then had each soldier in the circle slowly, in turn, shoot the soldier with the hole in him. When they finished, she paused for a moment, then quickly swept up all the soldiers and put them back in their box. She next opened a bag of potato chips and, as she stuffed them in her mouth, asked, "You want some?" *(This abrupt shift to food and feeding signalled her need to self-soothe and get her overwhelming anxiety back in check.)*

In her first three sessions, Tina had played out a significant collection of feelings and fears. She showed me again some of the ways in which she felt damaged. Perhaps, like the soldier, she also felt different from others; that someone put a hole in her or that someone penetrated her. She brought to the play ideas of friends hurting friends, friends who lie, and people who even hurt themselves. She talked about danger and arranged for punishment of those who committed crimes. Tina briefly expressed her sense that I could also be an enemy to her and showed she would remain on her guard. Most importantly, Tina showed me that she was going to be able to express herself and her feelings clearly through developmental play therapy. To help her work through some of her post-traumatic stress, my main tasks were simply to create a good-enough holding environment; be present, hear, and accept the pain in her life; follow her lead in working through the traumatic events; and enable her to regain a sense of mastery and control of herself and her life.

Stage III: Identification of Narrative Themes

As we moved into the third working stage of treatment, Tina exhibited some of the same issues and narrative themes that she brought to the beginning sessions but in more depth. She developed scenarios in which she repeated over and over her sense of danger and fear, as well as her desire for safety. To stay safe, she continued to exhibit hypervigilant symptoms.

She also brought more of her deeper concerns about herself, not just about feeling broken, but also about feeling somehow bad, dirty, evil, and destructive. For instance, Tina clearly assumed she was somehow bad and deserved the trauma she experienced—a partially adaptive coping mechanism for trying to understand why the sexual abuse happened (and perhaps for even hoping that as long as she was good, she could have control over her life and prevent bad things happening to her again). These concerns about herself corresponded with her strict delineation of people and situations into either "all good" or "all bad"; that is, use of the defense mechanism of splitting. Underneath all of these powerful conflicted feelings was Tina's pervasive sense of shame.

As the working alliance strengthened, Tina began to trust and share more of her deeper concerns. My goals while she worked through her trauma included accepting every part of Tina, including those parts that felt aggressive, broken, or dirty; challenging some of her magical thinking that she was somehow bad or caused the assault to happen; supporting her coping mechanisms that allowed her to make some sense of the attacks or to feel safe from future abuse; allowing her to rework the trauma as many times as she needed in order to gain a sense of control and mastery over what happened to her; and helping her to connect some of her present feelings and behaviors with her past traumatic experience.

In one session, Tina spent much of the time drawing "her man" for me. This drawing was clearly representative of both the way she wished and feared to be seen by others. The drawing was also a visual representation of her use of splitting to cope with the aftermath of her trauma. In the drawing, a strong muscular man with tattoos, a gun, jewelry, and boots stood in the center of the page. Tina described for me what she was drawing and also talked some about the inner life of her man Tyrone. Her voice became rough and she used some street slang while she drew. Tina pointed to his necklace with the peace sign hanging from it and told me, "This necklace says 'Stay Away!' When people see him coming, they back off." She also informed me, "He could beat you up just by lookin' at you." *(This to remind me of the danger I was in by being near her scary feelings.)* She added boots to the drawing that were his "kicking boots," brand-name boots similar to the style she wore every day. Tyrone was a character who could keep people from hurting him just by the way he looked and by what he wore. He was strong and safe and able to protect himself with ease.

Tina told me in a tough voice, "This guy looks like he couldn't have no girlfriend; like nobody'd be a girlfriend to him. But he does. This is for his girlfriend." She drew a heart on one arm with the name "Tina" under it. "And this is for his best friend Mike." She drew a black gun with the word "Mike" on the opposite arm. "Now, I'm gonna give him his nine-millimeter." She drew the butt of another black gun sticking out of his shorts. I reflected back in a mirroring tough voice, "So, that's his gun, huh?" She replied, "Now the people know there's no messing with him." I again reflected, "The gun really lets them know to stay away," which she accepted without comment. She drew in more details and then worked hard to color him in. She wrote "TYRONE" in bold letters across the top of the page. Then I made a summary comment and asked some questions about what she had created. "So, let me see. The necklace and the gun and the boots and all the other stuff really let people know that they should stay away from this guy. This stuff keeps him safe. And, the tattoos are for his girlfriend and his best friend. I see a heart and a gun tattoo. He has friends even though people might not think he does. What do the people think when they see him walk down the street?" She answered, "They think, 'I'd better run or I'm gonna get kicked in the head.'" I replied, "Wow, they sound scared. And what does Tyrone think when he sees them?" She answered, "He thinks 'Why doesn't anybody like me?'"

"Sounds like he feels worried."(JW)

"Nah. He'll just keep on down the street."(T)

FIGURE 12.2   Tough Tyrone

"He stays safe but he doesn't like it that everyone is so scared of him. It would be better if just the bad guys were scared."(JW)

"Yup."(T)

Thus, Tina was able to again express some of her fears about the world and her desire to feel tough and angry so that no one would see her as a victim again. Yet, she clearly felt lonely and misunderstood inside when people took her protective facade to be true. Also, the splitting into "all good" and "all bad" was illustrated graphically through his gun tattoo on one side and his heart tattoo on the other. There could be no safety in any middle ground or compromises for Tyrone, and none for Tina right now as well.

In later sessions, Tina created a number of stories with themes of revenge and ultimately death, particularly death of a mother figure. She may have been expressing some of her anger toward her mother or anyone who was unable or unwilling to protect her from the abuse. She had a number of sessions where she drew her teacher's or her mother's funeral. In those scenarios, children who often attended the proceedings were secretly happy about their mother's demise (though this feeling was always projected onto a child other than herself). These stories brought out her fear of her own destructive anger and worry that her feelings were so powerful that they might actually come true. (*I wondered if she was also worrying about having gotten rid of two therapists and now was worrying about losing me.*) When these fears would sometimes begin to overwhelm her, Tina would try to soothe herself with food or "clean up" her feelings in some way, such as straightening up toys or picking up play materials.

In almost every one of the first twelve sessions, Tina brought some kind of snack she had saved from her lunch or bought at the small neighborhood market next door. She used this food, as in her soldier play, whenever she needed to nurture herself after a particularly difficult expression of feelings. Some of my magic markers were the kind that smelled like different fruits; she also used the smell of these markers in ways to soothe or nurture herself, satisfying her more oral needs. For example, she once described her anger at her teacher in detail and also how she planned to poison her in revenge for what she did. She then drew the gravesite, complete with coffin and tombstone. She added a little girl, "Mrs. Jones' own little daughter," who stood by the gravesite crying. Tina drew tears running down the child's face and made little "boo-hoo" noises as she drew. The crying was obviously fake, either mocking the child's grief at losing her mother or perhaps showing that the child herself was not actually sad that her mother had died. I noted in a more straightforward tone, without Tina's sarcasm, "She's crying and crying. The tears are pouring down." Tina replied ominously, "She'll never see her mother again." I reflected the child's (Tina's) wish and fear by saying, "My mother is dead." Tina was expressing anger at her mother that session using the metaphor of her teacher. Most likely, the anger stemmed from the fact that her mother did not protect her from the neighbor. Because this wish for revenge was too scary to stay with, Tina then made some serious efforts to change the angry revengeful tone. She held the picture up as if to get a better look at the whole composition, then added a sun in the corner and noted that it "was a sunny day." The cheerful sun was not soothing enough, however, and did not change the drama.

Tina looked around the room and spotted the fruit markers. She found the yellow lemon-scented marker and visibly cheered. "Mmmmmmm! Cleeeean!!!!" she said as she smelled it. I noted how good it smelled to her and how it felt good to smell something so clean after drawing such a sad picture. She pulled out another piece of paper and wrote in huge print with the lemon marker, "I AM A NICE GIRL AT ALL TIMES!!!" She smelled the paper with the scent on it. Then she rubbed the paper onto the drawing with the gravesite on it. She smelled the grave picture. I noted, "You hope your picture smells good now, too." She looked at me dejectedly and replied, "It doesn't work. The smell won't come off." I reflected, "You just can't make the gravesite smell clean and good, even though you really want it to." It was clear that she was trying to transfer the good feelings from her positive wish and self-statement, written in clean lemon scent, to the picture of her anger and desire for revenge. Tina continued to feel dirty from her trauma and the subsequent wishes and fears that it brought to her preconscious. Even a marker that smelled like cleaning solution could not make her feel less dirty and destructive that day. She was able to explore the feelings, however, and look at them without feeling judged in therapy.

Tina looked at the picture a minute more, then hunted for crumbs in her empty potato-chip bag. She put her coat on, signalling her need to have the session over for the day despite the fact that we had a few more minutes of time. In later sessions, we continued to explore her anger with her mother. In response to this theme, I looked for opportunities to convey to Tina that it was all right to be mad at your mother sometimes; that even bad feelings, worries, or dreams couldn't actually cause bad things to happen to her; and that lots of times people felt two ways at the same time—mad and glad, sad and happy, love and hate. "Maybe she sometimes felt both ways too." Tina was silent for a bit and then moved on with her play.

Tina also told stories and dreams about being threatened, chased, or followed. These fantasies directly showed the hypervigilant stance she took during much of her daily life, always needing to stay on her guard so that she might stay safe from further abuse. Some of these dreams seemed to be symbolic repetitions of her abuse that she needed to play again and again in her head in order to gain some control over them. For instance, in one session, she moved to the swivel chair *(where she most often presented more metaphorical material)* and asked, "You want to hear a dream I had last night?" I answered, "Sure." She began, "It was aaaawful!! This big hairy demon came in and tried to sweep up all my things. Then it took out the hospital blood and opened the bags of blood. They went everywhere, all over me and my clothes. But, I called to 'Jesus, Sweet Jesus' and the Holy Spirit to banish it. And then, they was speaking in tongues? Do you know about speaking in tongues? Ever heard it?" I responded, "No, I've never heard someone speaking in tongues. What's it like?" Tina started to sway in her seat. She answered, "Well, it's not a pretty sound. You'd get real scared if you heard it for yourself."

"It sure felt scary to you when you heard it."(JW)

"You bet it did. So it worked. The demon went away, thanks to our Savior."(T)

"Jesus came along and protected you from the awful demon."(JW)

"He did, all right!"(T)

"And then, how did you feel?"(JW)

"Well, I was still shaking, but I felt better."(T)

"It feels good to be protected."(JW)

"It sure does."(T)

(It seemed to me that Tina possibly used this dream as an analogy for her memory of her abuse with the "big hairy demon" representing her abuser and the "blood" representing "both her own physical hurt and anger." At this point in her therapy, she was able to speak only in metaphor of her past experiences, fear, and current need to feel protected.)

In another session, Tina described some fears she had while going to school. She told the story in the chair she normally reserved for dreams and fantasies, although she told it as though it was at least partly based on a real fear she had experienced that day. More importantly, she was using the story as a symbolic representation of her hypervigilance. She began with a general description of "Sometimes I feel something bad is going to happen. I can just feel it." When I asked her more about this, she explained, "Like something bad is going to happen. I feel it in my body. Want me to give you an example? Today, my Mom took the bus, so I walked to school. And I look back, and a car is following me. I can feel people looking at me. This old man, he'd been watching me for a long time. I noticed on the bus. It happens that he's been following me. He looked out his window. He walks out when I pass by. Then, he was on the bus. He knows my times. Then, in the car. He was with his friend. Then, the car stops just ahead on the corner of my street and Winslow. You know? There's nobody around, and the man, he jumps out. I'm just walking along, but I know he's out. He says my name, 'Tina!' He's got a map, like he needs to know where to go, but I know the truth." She leaned forward and whispered softly and ominously, "He's gonna try and snatch me up." She moved back to her regular voice, "So, I don't answer, and I just keep walking. So he yells, and I look and run to my friend Sharice's house 'cause she lives just around the corner with her mother. I know his license number, though, so he won't be after me anytime soon. It was 23 . . . let me see, it was 23 HOL, no, wait, it was 23 MHOL. That's it." I noted her feeling but focused on the coping mechanisms she used. "Wow. It was scary but you got his license number, and you ran to a friend's house where her mom could keep you safe." She replied, "Sharice's mother has hot chocolate." Again I noted her feelings by reflecting, "Hot chocolate could maybe make you feel safe too." She agreed, "It sure does."

This narrative represented a recurrent theme of shame, leading to a fear for her safety. She expressed foreboding feelings, danger, and a desire for protection from a mother figure. She also included the worry that others could be watching her. This shows not only her hypervigilance, but also her fear that other people can see her dirty, angry, bad feelings of which she is so ashamed. It was interesting to note that even in her dreams and fantasies, Tina used food to help soothe herself. My main therapeutic goal relating to her repetition of her trauma and her hypervigilance was simply providing a safe place in which to express, discharge, and work (and rework and rework) some of the dangers she felt. I also supported successful coping strategies and maintained a nonjudgmental stance in the face of her trauma. This stance gave her another, less shameful picture of herself as she worked through her fears and attempted to integrate her good and bad selves.

Stage IV: Developmental Growth and Change

Eventually Tina directly addressed her abuse with me. This verbal discussion seemed to conclude identification of the narrative theme stage of the therapy for her. She had just described, and drawn, a particularly violent fantasy (that she presented as real) of attacking a schoolmate. She had moved back to what I considered to be her "beginning and ending" chair and was putting on her coat. There were about four minutes left in the session. She then asked, "Do you know why I'm here?" I replied, "Hmmm. Why you come to see me? Why do you think you come to see me?"

"I don't know. Because of something that happened to me?"(T)

"Something that happened to you?"(JW)

"Yeah. Do you know?"(T)

"Is it something bad that happened to you?"(JW)

"REAL bad. REAL REAL bad."(T)

"Something that happened when you were eight?"(JW)

Tina looked up and smiled, appearing relieved. "Yup."

"Do you come to see me because you were molested when you were eight?"(JW)

(*My anxiety clearly got in the way. I should have waited for her to tell me. I guess I was trying too hard to make her comfortable because of my own discomfort. Why couldn't I have simply said, "Maybe you'd like to tell me about what happened"?)*

"Yes."(T)

"Is it okay that I know about that?"(JW)

"Oh, yes."(T)

We sat in silence for a while.

"Maybe you'd like to tell me about what happened when you got hurt."(JW)

"There was this boy. He lived down the street at my old house. He took me to these bushes, and then once to his room. His room in his house. I could take you there. I could show you all the places where it happened?"(T)

"You remember all the places where you were molested? It would be okay for me to see where?"(JW)

(*Tina clearly wanted me to believe her. I wish I'd stayed with her and invited her to tell me about the sexual abuse, that I'd like to hear from her, that I had conveyed my concern for her. I guess I worried about being too intrusive, worried that she might feel I was grilling her. I was trying to protect her from her own life experiences and feelings. I was also anxious and having a hard time hearing from a young girl that she had been raped. It was more comfortable for me to use the fancy word molested than to let her tell me about the experience in her words.)*

"My mother is really mad about those boys."(T)

"Some kids feel really mad too, when they have been molested."(JW)

"My mother says we can't do nothing."(T)

"What do you wish could happen about getting molested?"(JW)

"He should be in BIG trouble. He ought to get expelled."(T)

"He should really get punished for what he did?"(JW)

"Yep."(T)

Again, we sat silent for a while.

"Maybe there are other reasons why you might come to see me?"(JW)

(Now why did I change the topic? I could have stayed with being glad that we had talked a little about the molestation, that she could talk more about this with me whenever she wanted. Maybe I felt we had both had enough—or that I had?)

"Well, that's the big one."(T)

The tenor and themes of her therapy changed significantly after this session. *(I do not believe, however, that discussion with me of her abuse was the one and only breakthrough; that all that came before was simply a warmup for the main event. Many traumatized children never directly address what happened to them in any detail and yet still benefit dramatically from developmental play therapy. Tina did not share many details about the abuse with me. My own responses to her were quite clumsy at times. In fact, if I had the moment to do over again, I would not have asked so many questions. Instead, I would have responded that I knew some things but that I'd like to hear it from her. I also would have stayed with the moment more and been less quick to fill the silences [which felt a little like mourning]. Looking back, I realize that I was unprepared for her switch, after so many sessions, from fantasy expression to direct confrontation with the reality of what happened to her. However, I believe our "good-enough" relationship carried us through my not-so-good technique in handling direct expression of the traumatic experience. I believe that my nonjudgmental acceptance of the powerful "hot stuff" she shared with me in our earlier sessions led to her desire, even need, to feel unburdened of her particular shame about the assaults.)*

Tina's play began to change slowly after the session discussed previously. She did not move as much from seat to seat, but began to spend the time in only one or two chairs. She avoided the swivel chair (fantasy and metaphor chair) all together. Further, the stories and material she brought to the sessions began to change in quality from violent, fantastical dreams and fantasies to more reality-based material. For instance, in session twelve, Tina spent most of the time describing her frustrations with her brother and two sisters. She was clearly angry and hurt by some of their behavior, particularly when she felt they had left her out. However, she did not move into any violent fantasies toward them, other than saying she wished they would all move away. This was a drastic change from earlier sessions in which she might have launched into a revenge scenario complete with poison, gravestones, or blood, which could then be drawn out and discharged in picture form. It was a change in a larger sense as well—from overwhelming suspicion, anger, and fear to more age-appropriate frustrations, such as sibling rivalry and older/younger-sibling-role issues.

Tina continued to draw in the sessions, but the themes changed from fantasy material to more practiced pictures that she could have been drawing at school or with classmates. *(The drawings conveyed a sense that she was regaining her own equilibrium.)* Some of the drawings were also examples of the strong alliance and identification she felt with me by this point in the therapy. For example, she drew a bouquet of flowers, shoes and dresses, and her apartment with her friend's cat sitting in a nearby tree. She spent a full session drawing the layout of the apartment where she lived, showing me the rooms and objects in them that were especially important to her. *(Her play showed change, both by the material she did not bring to the sessions as well as by the new material she did bring. In terms of narrative process,*

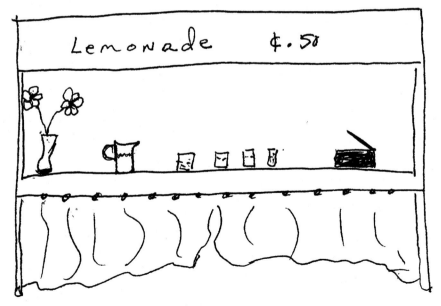

FIGURE 12.3   Lemonade Stand

I guess I was the watchful cat helping her to explore her apartment self, the whole and the parts, and helping her answer the question,"Am I okay?")

Stage V: Termination

In our last three sessions, Tina spent most of the time focused on the same project, a lemonade stand. *(For her, the lemonade seemed to represent the process of integrating sweet and sour, good and bad, thereby reflecting a decrease in her propensity to use the defense of splitting.)* Tina and a next-door neighbor had begun plans to make money over the summer. She described and drew her friend for me. This friend in and of herself was a wonderful change for Tina. Her mother had proudly told me just the week before that Tina and the other girl were spending many after-school hours together "without any fighting." Tina also carefully drew what the lemonade stand would look like and how it was to be built. One week, she even drew for me an example of the sign that might hang over the table to attract customers. *(The sign brought home to me another change; namely, that Tina, as the well-put-together lemonade stand, seemed interested and comfortable with the idea of risking interactions with customers who could possibly be strangers to her.)*

Through telephone calls, it was established that both Tina's mother and teacher were witnessing similar positive changes at home and at school, and that Tina's oppositional, seductive, and angry behavior had decreased significantly. Tina and I terminated our therapy three weeks before the end of her fifth-grade year.

Case Discussion: Tina

Tina brought some strong, frightening material to our sessions. While some of it was real and some fantasy, all of it was based on her fear, anger, and anxiety born from the trauma of sexual abuse. I accepted all of the information and surrounding feelings without judgment. I believe that most of her healing came from being able to expose all of her "hot stuff" within the therapeutic alliance. She found out that it did not hurt me and that, once out, it did not hurt her as much. Further, I continually took the supportive yet clarifying stance that I did not expect her to feel ashamed and did not believe she deserved punishment, either for what happened to her or from any of her subsequent wishes or fears.

In the end, Tina was able to discharge some of her powerful internal life and experience acceptance by me. By gentle questioning, I was able to help her explore some of her all-or-nothing thinking about herself and her significant others. Her hypervigilance and sexually provocative behavior decreased while her positive interactions with her peers and siblings increased. Her oppositional stance to life softened once she felt it was safe to sometimes let her guard down. Tina also learned that even her scariest wishes and feelings could be looked at without causing them to come true. Eventually, she was able to put the good and bad parts of herself back together and even begin to accept herself.

Community Violence

Prevalence

Although crime rates have been falling for the last six years (*The Economist,* 1998), school violence appears to have escalated or, at least, be more widely heralded by the media. Today, children continue to be involved as victims and eyewitnesses to interpersonal violence and aggression in their schools and neighborhood communities (Anderson, 1997; Burman and Allen-Meares, 1994; Richters, 1993), and to marital violence (Cummings and Davies, 1994) or parent/acquaintance violence in their own homes. Some families have even described themselves as living in battle zones (Dubrow and Garbarino, 1989; Lorion and Saltzman, 1993).

Two Chicago studies (Bell and Jenkins, 1993; Shakoor and Chalmers, 1991) reveal that 26 percent of 536 African American elementary-school children had witnessed life-threatening violence, with one fourth of this group having witnessed a shooting and one third, a stabbing. A Washington, DC, study of six- to ten-year-olds (Richters and Martinez, 1993) indicated that 165 children in a low-income, moderately violent neighborhood were between two and four times more likely than the national average to witness violence to others and be in violence-related situations involving others. These children tended to report higher levels of violence exposure than did their parents. Two additional studies of sixth-, eighth-, and tenth-graders in the northeastern United States found that 40 to 41 percent had witnessed at least one violent crime in the past year, with exposure being greater for African American and Latino/a students than for European American students and for students of low socioeconomic status (Schwab-Stone, Ayers, Kasprow, Voyce, Barone, Shriver, and Weissberg, 1995). Although parent(s) acknowledge the dangers their children face, they often feel powerless to do anything about community violence (Dubrow and Garbarino, 1989).

Death

Comprehension. Taken to the extreme, life-threatening violence results in death, an event that may or may not be fully understood. Not surprisingly, children's ability to comprehend death is mediated by their developmental stage and family belief systems. A review of multiple research studies suggests that children under five have little cognitive understanding of death, but that five- to seven-year-olds generally understand that death is final and universal (Speece and Brent, 1984). Their concrete thinking style and the strong emotions associated with death, however, often result in confusion by this age group about the deceased person, the irreversible nature of death, and the customs and rituals associated with death. By age ten, children usually comprehend the full meaning of mortality (Lewis, Lewis, and Schonfeld, 1996), but may have difficulty coming to terms with its irreversible nature.

Their coping with death is further influenced by their family's beliefs about and ritual practices for dealing with death, burial, and bereavement. Usually based in cultural and/or religious traditions, these customs and practices are intended to assist mourners by mediating specific aspects of death, providing psychosocial support, and facilitating the grief process. Often, caretaking adults try to protect children from experiencing the full impact of loss and bereavement by not explaining what has happened and not allowing their participation in funeral rites. In reality, however, such protection creates an emotional blockage between caretaker and child that inhibits the mourning process (Furman, 1996). Often, the caretaking adults are so caught up in their own sense of loss that they are unable to be emotionally available to a child. Without information and understanding of death in general and this specific death in particular, a child cannot mourn and then move on with living.

Death of a Parent.   For children of any age, the death of a parent is a tragedy and mourning is a painful task that is difficult to complete fully. However, not all parental deaths are traumatic in the sense of creating stress reactions that overwhelm the physical and psychological integrity of the child and trigger PTSD. Yet, when a parent's death is violent and unanticipated—especially when a child witnesses such an event—the resulting shock and stress usually do overwhelm and paralyze a child. In these circumstances, efforts to deal with the violent death and the initial emotional reactions (i.e., numbed feeling, depersonalization, and apathy) may paralyze coping and adaptive efforts and lead to full-blown post-traumatic states (Furman, 1986).

Malmquist (1986) interviewed sixteen children who had witnessed the murder of a parent and were diagnosed with PTSD. All reported intrusive, distressing recollections of the event and most reported nightmares. Among the group, there was also an increased number of arousal responses, including anxiety, restlessness, hypervigilance, and difficulty concentrating; school performance also had declined.

Clinical Sequelae

Violence.   The NIMH Community Violence Project (Martinez and Richters, 1993) found that exposure to violence was associated with symptoms of distress in both older and younger children. The symptoms in first- and second-grade children included depression, anxiety, intrusive thoughts, and sleep problems; those for children in fifth and sixth grade included depression and anxiety. Reports from the older children indicated that the majority of the violent incidents involved known persons (i.e., family members, friends, or acquaintances). In instances involving familiar persons, clinical distress was higher. However, parents in this study tended to underestimate their children's symptoms of distress. In a separate study, Bell and Jenkins (1993) found that family victimization was as strongly correlated with psychological distress as personal victimization.

In a study of elementary-school violence, Pynoos, Frederick, Nader, Arroyo, Steinberg, Eth, Nunez, and Fairbanks (1987) found that 77 percent of the children on the playground at the time of a sniper shooting reported moderate to severe

PTSD symptomatology with re-experiencing and numbing, post-event fear and anxiety, concentration difficulties, and sleep disturbance accounting for half of the variance among the children's responses. Others have documented acute responses to violent events and PTSD in multiple studies of children (Pynoos and Eth, 1985a; Terr, 1991b, 1991c).

Incomplete Mourning and Dysfunction. Failure to complete the mourning process fully tends to truncate the developmental process and may appear as a variety of symptoms. Initially, these symptoms may be masked and only become apparent in the next developmental stage, when it becomes clear that the child's energy is still tied up in mourning the loss and is not available for the new tasks and conflicts inherent in growth and developmental progression. Whenever symptoms do manifest, they indicate psychic struggle with the loss and represent a cry for help in coping and completing mourning.

Community and Family Issues

Community Structure. Family childrearing and management practices become intermixed with community practices in the social environment in which they live. Therefore, no exploration of children's exposure to and coping with violence is complete without a look at the organizational structure and values of their communities. In this vein, several research studies (Elliott, Wilson, Huizinga, Sampson, Elliott, and Rankin, 1996; Sampson and Groves, 1989; Simcha-Fagan and Schwartz, 1986; Taylor, Gottfredson, and Brower, 1984) support the view that three social characteristics of communities are associated with an increased risk of crime and violence:

> (a) anonymity and sparse acquaintanceship networks among residents, (b) unsupervised teenage peer groups and attenuated control of public space, and (c) a weak organizational base and low participation in local activities. (Sampson, 1997, p. 38)

Under these circumstances, the community structure is socially disorganized and unable to maintain an effective state of civility and social control.

Code of the Streets. In the inner city, groups of street-minded youth often dominate the public spaces. Although families may oppose the values of the street code with its prescribed way of responding aggressively and violently when challenged, they may encourage their children's learning the code as a defensive maneuver for taking care of themselves and negotiating an inner-city school and neighborhood. The issue of respect, deference, or being treated right is at the center of the street code. However, what a person deserves in the way of respect often requires intense negotiation and careful maintenance. If a person is insensitive to the code or slights another, they may inadvertently "disrespect" or "diss" someone, placing themselves and family members in real physical danger (Anderson, 1997).

Treatment

Supportive Intervention for Parent/Caregiver.   When their children are exposed to community violence that leads to someone's death, parents or caregivers often experience shock, grief, and anger. They also fear that another episode of school or neighborhood violence might lead to their own child's death. In addition, parents' own feelings of vulnerability and memories of prior violent events may lead to denial and avoidance of community intervention efforts and therapy for themselves and their children. Sometimes parental desires to protect children from pain may create initial resistance to therapy. If parents can be helped to explore the meaning that the violence holds for them, they may experience some emotional relief and accept the usefulness of intervention for their child. Parents often respond to crisis work that addresses their own reactions and frees up their emotional energy for supporting their child. Concurrent psychoeducational intervention enables them to understand and cope with their child's shock, grief, and mourning.

Parents and caregivers especially need help understanding youngsters' needs and age-related efforts to bind and master the violent event, associated stimuli, and overwhelming emotions through repetitive play, fantasy, storytelling, and dreams. In this way, children repeat the violence theme with variations that turn passive experiencing into active mastery and facilitate assimilation. Sometimes parents are concerned about what they perceive as their children's distortion of the actual violent episode and need to understand that faithful reproduction of the event is not the issue; rather, replication of the violence as the child perceived the event and his or her place in relation to it is the important factor. Parents also need to understand that, for a while at least, their child is likely to be highly sensitized to all around them, react strongly to changes in their lives, and insist on sameness. The goal in this work is to enable the parents to support—not truncate—their child's healing process.

Child Treatment.   In treating children diagnosed with PTSD following extreme violence and death of a significant person such as a parent, sibling, or close friend, multiple narrative treatment themes are likely to come into play as the clinical social worker and child address the treatment goals of (1) mourning; (2) processing the emotional, cognitive, and physical aspects of the violence and the developmental and familial ramifications; (3) addressing dysfunctional patterns of coping and adaptation; (4) restoring the sense of connection with others; and (5) repairing the self-concept. These narrative treatment themes do not necessarily appear in the same order for every child; nor is one theme likely to be resolved completely before others appear. Generally, it is important to address the trauma-related work themes initially as distinct from the grief-related work themes in order to decrease the likelihood that the violent images will interfere with and truncate the grief and mourning.

Trauma-Related Work Themes.   At times, children may play out or talk about certain parts of the violent event, but avoid others for fear of being blamed or becoming overwhelmed by painful feelings. When avoidance is apparent, techniques of modulated pacing and universalization of feelings may help upsetting material emerge more easily in the therapeutic narrative. By commenting on the child's reluctance to discuss certain memories, the clinician takes note of what is happening, but maintains the child's sense of being in control. It also may be helpful to clarify the nature of therapy—specifically, that the clinician can be helpful with difficult things and feelings. Over the course of treatment, the child needs to face the truth of what has happened, but there is no rush about this confrontation.

Through play reenactments, children release suppressed emotions and begin to modify the overwhelming nature of the violence. As children repetitively play out the violent event and re-experience both event and affect, they may allow themselves to experience the trauma more. Sometimes as this theme gains ascendancy, symptoms become exacerbated. In the long run, however, repetition in play therapy enables children to regulate their confrontation with the multidimensional aspects of the traumatic experience, modulate the dosage, and gain a sense of mastery so that they can come to terms with the experience and integrate it into their lives. Play therapy can help reduce their anxiety and make it possible to make conscious the connections between the play and the event. When the timing is right, interpretation of this connection and the event-associated affects permits greater exploration of emerging feelings and a greater measure of internal control as child and therapist more fully understand the event, actions, and feelings. When the intensity is too great to manage, it is helpful to supportively comment that such reactions are usual, and decrease the intensity of the play. It is often helpful to alert children to those aspects of their physical and social environment that intrude and remind them of the violence. Helping children anticipate their potential reactions allows them to establish a greater feeling of internal control over their lives and the violent event.

Especially with violence, revenge themes are a prevalent part of fantasy and play. These themes provide catharsis through safe expression of aggression within the therapeutic alliance. Initially, fears of safety may increase. In violent situations, children have become aware that adults are not able to protect them. Thus, their ability to identify with protective adults as a way of maintaining their own inner security is damaged. To help them regain a sense of safety and security in their inner and external worlds, the therapist helps them symbolically represent the experience through play and verbalization. Together, they explore the fear and anxiety in detail, the panic when they are left, the fear of further loss, and the anger about the deceased person's unavailability. The clinician symbolically introduces themes of protection and safety and helps the child develop alternative resolutions to the violent event. Introducing helping elements and teaching the child what to do in violent situations paves the way for the child to establish his or her own safety-enhancing identifications and coping mechanisms. The child thereby gains coping skills, an enhanced sense of self-efficacy, relief from self-blame, a greater sense of psychological distance from the event, and a greater sense of internal control. It is important to note, however, that this approach is helpful only if it is realistic, given the child's particular violent situation. Safety and trust themes are explored and accepted; preoccupation with them diminishes.

Often, children think that they should have done something to prevent the violence and rescue the deceased. They may compensate for feeling helpless as they did during the violent episode by imagining that they have a grandiose power. Such self-blame and guilt have protective functions and are often found in the earlier stages of treatment. It is important to elicit details of the context of the violence in which these feelings originated and to remind them of how small and frightened they must have felt. It is helpful to note that they used good judgment by not attacking the perpetrator because they then would have endangered themselves. Sometimes, sensitive explanation of reality may be helpful even though the child appears unresponsive at the time the explanation is given. Other times, their sense of power and responsibility can be cognitively reframed into a wish to be brave, accept responsibility, and take care of others. It is important not to use either of these techniques prematurely, however, as children also may develop internal cognitive action plans that involve unrealistic ideas about their thoughts and actions during this and future violent events.

Mourning-Related Work Themes. Coming to terms with loss of a loved one through death ties up a child's psychic energy in a three-fold psychic task (Furman, 1996) that includes the following:

1. *Understanding and coming to terms with this particular death:* This process involves knowing and accepting the facts and circumstances of the death and the disposition of the loved one's body. By incorporating pictures of the deceased into the work, the clinician can include nontrauma memories; restore a more intact image than that associated with the violence; and repair the child's narcissistic wounds through play, reminiscence, and role-play. To complete this process, children are dependent on adult caretakers' explanations, truthfulness, and reassurance that life will go on.

2. *Working through the detachment and identification aspects of mourning:* The process of detachment involves loosening the emotional attachments to the deceased by working through strong emotional reactions of pain and sadness, guilt and anger. It is important to deal with the anger in the context of loving feelings and ambivalence. This work also involves coping with the intense longing for the deceased and the frequent unexpected confrontations with his or her absence from the external physical world. Sometimes children take out their anger at being abandoned on the remaining parent or another adult caregiver. Other times, children withdraw and blame themselves for their parent's death because they have been bad or perhaps wished their parent dead at some point. To cope with their intense feelings, children need emotional support, caring, and acceptance of their feelings in their day-to-day lives. Working through the identification process involves the child's incorporating particular meaningful aspects of the deceased that soothe the distress of the loss and adaptively enrich the child's life. Children often need help in taking on aspects, characteristics, or belongings that will facilitate their coping with the loss and be adaptive for them.

3. *Picking up and going on with life:* This process begins when working through the trauma and mourning has freed up enough energy for the child to contrast the current feeling of isolation with the earlier feelings of connectedness and begin to reinvest in other persons and activities. As development proceeds, the child is likely to continue to work on mourning by expressing feelings, dealing with anniversary reactions, and working through loss and identity issues in subsequent developmental stages. The adults remaining in the child's life need to be available as supporters and facilitators in this process.

Case Summary: Kanessa, a Case of Community Violence by Marika Moore Cutler, M.S.W., LCSW-C

Problem

Kanessa is an eight-year-old African American female who was referred for treatment following the brutal murders of her mother and older brother, murders that she witnessed. They were horribly mutilated two months before her referral. Kanessa, too, was savagely attacked and left for dead by the drug gang that forever changed her life. Apparently, her brother had been a member of this gang and the murders were in retaliation for his alleged betrayal of this gang to the police. Her own wounds left her with a weakened right leg and a large scar on her forehead. Following discharge from the intensive care unit (ICU) of a West Coast hospital, Kanessa was sent across country to live with her sixty-year-old maternal great-grandmother, Mrs. Thomas. While in the hospital, there had been an outpouring of support from the staff, police officers, and members of the church where Kanessa had been a choir member and active participant in their after-school girls club. The church minister and his wife continued to be in touch with Kanessa after she moved.

Collateral Information at Referral

A *guardian ad litem* was appointed to recommend appropriate placement because there were no known relatives out west. The judge agreed she should be in the care of Mrs. Thomas because both Kanessa's mother and grandmother were deceased. The father was unknown to the family. The judge also thought Kanessa could have a fresh start in another city far removed from the crime scene and the murderers who had not been apprehended. Before meeting with Mrs. Thomas and Kanessa, I obtained collateral information from the police regarding the details of the homicides and attack on Kanessa, the hospital psychiatrist who had evaluated her in the Intensive Care Unit (ICU), and the *guardian ad litem*. The psychiatrist reported psychic numbing about the actual trauma, sleep awakened by nightmares, and a diminished interest in school or social activities. Kanessa was hypervigilant, especially when there were unexpected sounds in the ICU. She also had an exaggerated startle response when any intrusive medical procedures were conducted. Kanessa met the criteria for PTSD, Acute.

Treatment Summary

I became aware of my own anxiety regarding the enormity of the trauma this youngster had experienced. The magnitude of her loss was compounded by her own injuries and removal from the only community she had known. I imagined Kanessa's fear of the murderers being out looking for her, the only eyewitness. Of course, she hadn't attended the funerals because of her hospitalization. Now, in addition, she had to cope with a new family and school.

When I met with Mrs. Thomas, who was employed as a librarian, I was impressed with her gentle demeanor. She seemed a little shell-shocked to have a young child again, especially under these circumstances. Nonetheless, she wanted to do what was best for Kanessa. Unfortunately, she could not provide a developmental history because her own daughter had been estranged from Mrs. Thomas. Kanessa had been living with Mrs. Thomas for about one month and seemed agitated and depressed. Kanessa complained of nightmares and stomachaches. She did not speak of the horror she had witnessed. Otherwise, she seemed to be a regular kid, except she limped and was self-conscious about her scar.

Kanessa entered my office with an endearing smile and shook my hand. She was a very pretty girl dressed immaculately in a sweater and skirt with bright red ribbons in her hair. She immediately went to the small chair and desk and looked longingly toward me. I imagined she had spoken to many adults since the trauma, so decided not to ask her any questions. Instead, we looked around at some toys and she decided to make something out of clay. There would be many clay productions. This one became a rectangular box with a lid on it. (*I was thinking to myself this must represent a coffin, but then realized that she hadn't seen the coffins. On the other hand, this was an empty box; a wish fulfillment, I wondered?*) Kanessa asked me to guess what it was and when I failed, she said, "Why, it's a suitcase!" I exclaimed, "Of course, wonder where it's going?" She said, "It's already been . . . came on a long trip on an airplane." The drama that unfolded was that the suitcase, which was beautifully decorated with bright red play doh, had gotten lost on the plane. It really didn't know where it was going. It had been bumped and beaten up on the plane. Then some nice old lady took it to the lost and found. Nobody wanted it so the nice old lady took it home. I said, "Gee . . . what do you think was in it?" She said sadly, "Nothing." So it turned out to be a lonely and empty suitcase. I thought it probably was very lonely, but together we could fill it up. (And that's exactly what we did over a period of many months. First, we filled it with sad memories and, later, with happy ones.)

From the beginning, I was impressed by Kanessa's resilience, ability to relate, and capacity for creativity and imagination. The murderers had not taken that from her. As Kanessa came to trust me, she confided that her mother and brother had died. Actually, she explained, that is why she limps. She pretended to be dead while those men were in her house. "See this scar . . . it's from that." Over time, she decided to grow bangs to camouflage the external scar on her forehead. The internal one was not so easily covered up, although she tried mightily to put on a happy face.

The inner scar expressed itself through violent dreams that awoke her nightly, leaving her terrified. The nights were the worst because she felt all alone. One recurring nightmare was of a black monster with horns who chased her around the bedroom. She would hide under the bed, but he would find her. Then she would wake up. As she drew the dream in a picture, we decided to give this monster a name. She named him Mr. Hornhead and gradually started to laugh at both his name and his silly appearance in the pictures. Bit by bit, he removed himself from her dreams. One day, she marched in and announced, "Mr. Hornhead is gone. I should have named him Mr. Pain-in-the-Neck since that's what he was . . . a pain in my neck, no . . . maybe he was a pain in my head." *(I was wondering about the pain still left in her heart.)*

Shortly thereafter, Kanessa told me she had seen her mother last night. She talked to her saying, "I love you." I responded how much she must miss her. "Oh, yes," she replied. "It was really awful . . . you know . . . that night. But last night she was okay." We talked about how she could remember her mother this way . . . peaceful and loving. Kanessa liked that idea even though her life had been filled with chaos. Then she drew a picture of her mother as an angel flying to heaven. Another series of pictures depicted the devil and reminded me of Mr. Hornhead. At first glance, I thought the devil represented the murderer, but came to understand him as symbolic of her brother, who neither rescued her nor prevented the savage attack. Later, I came to realize that the devil was a condensation of all the evil in her life. The therapeutic goal was to heal the split between a loving but idealized mother/angel and the hateful, bloodthirsty brother/murderer, a daunting task.

An external event that triggered continuous reenactment of the homicides was the arrest and indictment of a murder suspect. Kanessa had touched on her anxiety about such an occurrence earlier in the therapy. Her terror of being found by the murderers was replaced by the fear of testifying in court, a realistic possibility. Unbeknownst to Kanessa, the prosecutors wanted to subpoena me to disclose the contents of her therapy. Fortunately, a psychologically minded judge was persuaded otherwise by my attorney.

Clay and drawings dominated the play with two different scenarios. The clay figures created were of her mother, brother, two murderers, and Kanessa. She pointed out that only one of the guys had been arrested. Where was the other one? He would find her. Fortunately, the second suspect was apprehended a couple of weeks later. The drawings were of a court scene with judge, suspects, attorneys, Kanessa, and me. Would I be there to protect her? The same clay dolls were used in the dollhouse to portray the actual crime scene. The terror of what happened was repeatedly depicted in great detail and verbatim over twenty sessions. As she worked through her feelings of dread, revulsion, and guilt about what actually happened, Kanessa began to take some satisfaction in preparing herself for any courtroom testimony through drawing. This time she felt like she had some control, or at least she wouldn't be caught off guard.

Meanwhile, Kanessa had difficulty fitting into her new school. Sometimes the kids would make fun of her limp. Neither they nor the teachers knew the reason for it. To me, Kanessa also seemed lonely. While Mrs. Thomas made every effort to provide a nurturing home, it was just the two of them "rattling around in that big apartment."

Kanessa was now able to talk about how much she missed her old school friends and her minister and his wife. Maybe she could go back, she told me. We started talking about happier times. Kanessa had been an A student and loved the choir.

With all the discussion about the impending trial, we made plans for where she would stay. The church minister, who had four children, opened his home to Kanessa and Mrs. Thomas. Kanessa's testimony was videotaped in the judge's chambers. She experienced a sense of mastery and vindication when the guilty verdict was announced. After the trial, Kanessa decided to stay with the minister and his family and was eventually adopted by them. When I last spoke with Mrs. Thomas, Kanessa had returned to her old school where she was once again an A student. She also had many friends and was quite active in many extracurricular activities.

PART FIVE

Practice Accountability

13 Evaluating Therapeutic Change

BY MICHAELA Z. FARBER, D.S.W., LCSW-C

The twenty-first century mandate for professional accountability in clinical social work practice calls for case-by-case evaluation of intervention effectiveness. In developmental play therapy and concurrent parent work, practitioners routinely examine and record their assessment of whether treatment goals for children and their parents have been met prior to the final treatment stage of termination. Usually, however, this preliminary outcome assessment is couched as anecdotal narrative and theoretical reflection. Only rarely have clinicians integrated outcome assessment as a formalized systematic evaluation of case outcome.

In part, the reasons reflect philosophical concerns about research intrusiveness into the therapeutic process and a concern about quantifying the complex process of human change. In part, the reasons are pragmatic because "how to do it" in a clinically meaningful way remains something of a mystery. Can human feelings, actions, and relationships be reduced to a few desired outcome variables that really capture the depth and nuance of human experience? How can the clinician attend to evaluating practice when the sessions need to focus on client issues, therapeutic alliance, and treatment process?

Yet without systematic practice evaluation, it is difficult to assess what works for whom under what circumstances, thereby subsequently improving practice. In addressing this dilemma, this chapter presents general issues and principles in practice evaluation, and concludes with an illustrative evaluation of Jack's developmental play therapy. After exploring meaning and measurement, the chapter explores issues in creating practice outcome questions, conducting systematic measurement, analyzing data, and drawing conclusions.

Incorporating Meaning into Measurement

Practice evaluation through measurement of the treatment outcomes of one client in multiple environments first involves translating treatment goals to outcome objectives, and then specifying systematic measurement procedures for gathering information that operationalizes these outcome objectives in ways that are measurable or observable and both valid and reliable. To be useful to a clinician concerned about a particular case, the informational data need to be organized or classified in a manner congruent with the explanatory and change theories being applied to the problems, issues, and desired outcomes of this particular client-in-situation. Once the conceptual and operational classification systems have been developed, the measurement and observational protocols may be qualitative, quantitative, or some combination of the two. Various forms of narrative and statistical analysis organize and summarize the data into themes and patterns from which to make inferences back to the child and family. Quantification of client objectives and statistical analyses facilitate systematic tracking of client changes over time. Qualitative narrative analyses provide rich clinical descriptors of the treatment process themes and clinical benchmarks that denote change. Thus, together they provide more systematic detail about what has or has not been happening, both in treatment and outside of treatment. In a nutshell, incorporating clinical meaning into outcome measurement is the aim of single-subject research methodology.

Systematic observation and measurement of clinical process and outcome also offer a way to compare observed practice with prescribed standards of practice. Quantification of outcome objectives reveals the direction of the desired changes. Qualitative information supplies the material for reflecting on what is facilitating and impeding clinical progress and achievement of best-practice standards (Tripodi, 1995).

Actually incorporating measurement into clinical social work practice with children and their parents requires that the practitioner become:

1. precise in helping the child and parents clarify the problems and desired goals
2. nonjudgmental in helping them determine treatment outcome objectives that reveal progress, or the lack thereof, against some acknowledged benchmark
3. skilled in recordkeeping and ways of documenting change through tools that provide information about client progress at the different stages of intervention—tools such as clinical notes, process recordings, video or audio tapes, graphic recordings, and measurement scales
4. competent in clear and comprehensible communication with children and their parents, and able to translate this competency into a common frame of reference for translating the treatment goals into observable and measurable outcome objectives

The meaningfulness of the translation of client outcome objectives to both client and clinician relates to their congruence with the therapeutic changes desired and possible.

Creating Practice Outcome Questions

Through the rich symbolism of play in therapy, children reveal their experiences, problems, developmental levels, strengths, and therapeutic needs. When this symbolic and verbal communication is juxtaposed against the material gathered from parents, teachers, and multiple other sources, information is revealed about every developmental line and every environmental domain of the child. This clinical material is analyzed and consolidated into a dynamic case formulation, diagnosis, and treatment recommendations. After completing Stage I: Biopsychosocial Assessment, the child enters Stage II: Creation of a Therapeutic Alliance, and progresses through this and subsequent ones—Stage III: Identification of Narrative Themes, Stage IV: Developmental Growth and Change, and Stage V: Termination. Yet, to answer the question of what a particular child and parent actually take away from developmental play therapy and concurrent parent work involves going beyond the clinical formulation to develop focused practice outcome questions and intervention hypotheses specifying the area, degree, and type of change anticipated. In general, these outcome questions specify the particular problems, symptoms, and developmental issues targeted for change, the degree and the direction of the change expected, and the impact on children's strengths and resiliencies.

- Will developmental play therapy impact on the child's problems, symptoms, developmental issues, and strengths? In what ways? To what degree?
- Will concurrent parent work impact on parenting this child? In what ways? To what degree?

As operational definitions of treatment goals and recommendations, these anticipated or hypothesized clinical changes must somehow be meaningful and discernible to both the practitioner and the client. They also must be analyzed clinically and statistically in relation to the level of change desired, and provide specific information about what has gone well and not so well.

Children express their problems in a variety of ways. Thus, clinical manifestations of change may include shifts in behavior, affect or mood, action, thought, and expressed feeling as related to problems, symptoms, developmental levels, and strengths. These changes may be apparent in their play themes, at school, with peers, and at home. To decide which clinical manifestations of the difficulties should be tackled, when, and to what degree, the practitioner prioritizes the treatment goals by selecting those that:

1. are of most concern to the child and parents
2. have the greatest likelihood of being resolved within a reasonable time frame
3. can be addressed through the practitioner's repertoire of knowledge and skills
4. need to be resolved before other client goals can be met

5. are likely to produce the most negative consequences if not attended to in the immediate future;
6. can be identified through specific observable behaviors, including mood, action, and communication of feelings
7. are likely to yield the expected change

Developing Client Objectives from Treatment Goals

To select the client problems and treatment goals that will guide the development of treatment outcomes necessitates clear, concise operational definitions of the difficulties and desired outcomes. For example, a general problem statement that was presented as "C.J. is having lots of trouble at school" or "C.J. is always upset about something" may turn out to be that C.J. cannot read the expected third-grade material, has difficulty recognizing letters and their related sounds, has recently begun hitting classmates, and has been unable to sit still. Thus, during biopsychosocial assessment, the clinical social worker finds out specific details of how the problem is defined, by whom, and in what situational circumstances. For example, assessment questions (about which behaviors, what mood, what actions, what feelings, and what thoughts are communicated by C.J. in what situations) clarify the when, where, toward whom, and to what extent a particular problem or concern exists. To determine the scope, duration, and intensity of the clinical difficulties, both qualitative and quantitative measurement is needed.

When the actual details of the child's difficulties have been identified, the next task involves connecting the clinical concerns with the treatment goals and expected outcomes through carefully specified outcome objectives. For example, although the goals of enabling C.J. to read grade-level material and behave appropriately in school may seem obvious, the treatment goals remain abstract. That is, these goals must become more precise and stipulate what is to be achieved, under what conditions, to what extent, by what method, and by whom, as well as how and by whom any changes will be tracked and documented. In developmental play therapy and concurrent parent work, clinical social workers are accustomed to tracking treatment changes in their heads and reporting outcome in hindsight narrative form. While accustomed to spelling out treatment goals, clinicians are not used to identifying specific outcome objectives in the early sessions. Nor are they accustomed to formally identifying the current state of particular outcome objectives during the course of treatment.

What Is to Be Achieved?

The outcome objectives that fully or partially operationalize a particular treatment goal should be achievable. For example, perhaps one of C.J.'s outcome objectives is that he be able to express his wants and needs appropriately. To achieve this still quite complex outcome objective, further partialization into smaller steps is essential. For example, C.J. may have to learn appropriate skills to express his desires, gauge his mood, and control his anger. Similarly, his parents may have to learn a consistent way of responding to his requests. Each of these smaller steps may have a further set of specific activities that are aimed at achieving one or several small objectives. For example, to improve C.J.'s communication, C.J. may be involved in several activities. He may become involved in storytelling in which he is asked to describe a make-believe character's feelings or draw pictures illustrating his or others' feelings. He may become involved in creating a story that has a conflict requiring him to process different solutions. Each of these activities, thus, is in the service of achieving a specific objective, and the degree of accomplishment of the activity provides a gauge of the degree of success in completing the activity. For example, C.J. might be expected to be able to describe his own feelings as well as those of others, comprehend and communicate feelings in various situations, and use appropriate words to label feelings and behaviors. Although the direction of client change can be implicit, the account of "what is to be achieved" in the client's objectives need to be made specific. It is important for the clinician in developmental play therapy to understand that these small steps represent a clinical research way of thinking that parallels, complements, and supplements clinical practice thinking.

Under What Conditions Is It to Be Achieved?

Considering the conditions under which an outcome is to be achieved also involves the details of where, when, how often, how long, and with whom. For example, where will C.J. practice his storytelling? Will this activity take place—during play therapy, at home, at the sitter's, or at school? How often will it occur—only once, or on a specific day during the week? How long will this activity be practiced— once, several times, or for the next three months? Who will be present at this activity—only the therapist, parent(s), or others? Itemization of conditions usually helps to reveal the client's environmental domain which influences and is influenced by the practice objectives.

To What Extent Is It to Be Achieved?

How much improvement is needed before the child is considered "better" or what behavior would suggest that the child is getting "worse"? For example, how well does C.J. need to be able to express or describe his feelings or the feelings of others in order to be assessed as improved? The first issue is the degree to which the problem occurs before intervention is attempted. What is C.J. like before treatment? What benchmark will be used to determine that C.J. is making desired progress? Is it possible to obtain a baseline of C.J.'s problems and/or strengths prior to treatment? If not, how else could changes in his progress be monitored? Should C.J. be able to correctly identify and expressively label all feelings or just some? Which feelings? Should it happen occasionally or always? Under what conditions? How will this information be collected, recorded? By whom?

The second issue is the desired level of outcome to be achieved. Does C.J. need to be able to correctly label nuances of expressive feelings or just be able to tell when someone is upset with him? What repertoire of skills and communicative expressions does he need to be able to demonstrate that he has achieved an acceptable level of expected outcome?

What or who will decide the desired level of outcome? Will C.J. score in a certain range on a test that measures his ability to identify and label feelings correctly? Will his teacher report satisfaction with his behavior in the classroom? Will his parents report that he is more cooperative? Will the therapist, in some way, observe and quantify the differences in levels of possible outcomes?

Although the desired level of performance need not necessarily be spelled out by the end of the formal period of biopsychosocial assessment, it does need to be outlined at the point that the parents and child accept the treatment recommendations and explicitly enter into the therapeutic alliance toward some purposive end.

Creating Measurable Client Objectives

The conceptual definition of expected client outcome objectives describes clinical problems and issues in the theoretical and clinically meaningful terms that are part of the practitioner's repertoire. The operational definition simply restates the outcome objective in terms of what can be observed and measured; that is, as proxy indicators of change taking place in a child's abstract theoretical condition and clinically descriptive behaviors. Such proxies, from which direct or indirect inferences are made, may include subjective conditions, observed behaviors or activities, verbal statements, observed process themes in the therapeutic narrative, and scale scores on paper-and-pencil instruments. Thus, it is important that the concepts be operationalized in such a way that the referents accurately represent the clinical issue of concern, become clearly observable to all parties, and—in some way—also be countable, whether in actual number frequencies or a rank ordering of more/less, higher/lower. Multiple sources of information about an outcome objective (from child, parent, teacher, therapist) provide a more rounded picture about what is happening or not happening, and verify the accuracy and reliability of data about therapeutic change.

A client outcome objective is not useful unless it is specific in defining clearly what is supposed to happen before the treatment goal can be achieved. For example, suppose that the goal for C.J. is reducing his aggressiveness to his sister and other children. While the clinical issues and dynamics may differ in these aggressive patterns, reasonable objectives may be no hitting, less frequent purposive destruction of their toys and school materials, and some play in which he does not create a conflict.

Whatever outcome objectives are chosen, their meaning must be agreed to by all involved. Hitting, for example, may be described along the range from tapping a shoulder to pounding with a hand. Specificity facilitates tracking and measuring. Along these lines, Gabor and Grinnel (1994) offer several useful criteria for planning outcome objectives for children and their parents:

- The change that is to be achieved should be one that the client is capable of achieving.
- The change should be viewed positively by the client.
- The therapist needs to anticipate potential unintended consequences that may result in the achievement of the client objectives.
- Whenever possible, the outcome objective should describe what the client will do rather than what the client should not do.
- The outcome objective should describe what change is to occur, to what extent, and under what conditions.
- It should be clear to all involved who is going to do what.
- Some means of measuring change should be established that clearly indicates when the outcome objective has been reached and to what extent.

Selecting Systematic Measurement Designs

Although some clinical social workers argue that measurement tends to oversimplify a client's problems, distorting their true meaning and robbing them of the rich clinical context in which a client's life takes place, seasoned therapists view measurement—when properly done—as a complement to their clinical skills and as adding precision, objectivity, and an organizational system for documenting a client's needs and goals.

There are various means and tools through which to track clinical change. That is, there are different research designs that each provide a particular set of plans for making systematic observations and collecting information about the change or lack thereof. There are also different instruments for making client observations and collecting information about outcome objectives.

Selecting Designs

In selecting designs or ways to conduct systematic client observations, the clinician typically asks three related questions:

- What type of design would best fit the developmental play therapy model, client goals and circumstances, and repeated collection of information over time?
- How will the information be measured?
- From whom will the information be collected?

Needless to say, this same set of questions is asked in relation to concurrent parent work.

In clinical practice, single-subject designs are deemed useful in that they provide the opportunity for a systematic look at the treatment process with repeated data collection over time, as well as a look at the extent of the client outcome. While the data-analysis approach focuses on a single unit —the client—

the focus can be expanded to the single case unit of parent and child. That is, it is possible to apply separate single-subject designs to a child in developmental play therapy and to a parent in concurrent parent work, and understand how each has changed. Then, the two recorded graphic depictions of parent and child patterns are juxtaposed in order to explore treatment outcome parallels or dysfunctions in the parent/child system.

Qualitative Single-Subject Designs

The qualitative data approach to tracking change is part of a long-standing tradition in clinical social work. This approach uses theoretical concepts and clinical descriptions from the biopsychosocial assessment that the clinical social worker views as relevant to change. From the natural experience of the person-in-situation, the therapist keeps track of subjective themes, categories, classifications, and topologies that denote a client's understanding (Laird, 1994). Because social facts are embedded in social action just as social meaning is constituted by what a client does in everyday life, clients' meanings are most often discovered by being with, watching, and asking clients why they do what they do. In other words, children's actions are viewed as inseparable from the meaning of their social contexts (Miles and Huberman, 1994).

Case Study.   Case studies involve gathering large amounts of qualitative information about the client's problems as related to their life before, during, and toward the end of treatment, and describing their change in as much detail as possible. Case studies may use client observation of their behavior, mood, and actions, as well as reconstruct information from interviews and existing case notes. The clinician evaluates the collected information in view of the observed client relationships, communications, actions, or mood, and then constructs ideas and hypotheses about the pathways of change that are occurring. The narrative description of the intervention is deemed especially useful when there is little prior information, paucity of research, and minimal theory available. The outcome objective in a case study represents a tentative working hypothesis about a client's management of the day-to-day life situation.

In developmental play therapy and concurrent parent work, case-study information is usually collected through multiple sources, an established practice that provides for triangulation of perspectives about the change that may or may not be occurring. Case-data analysis is accomplished through pattern-matching to assess the degree of fit between a template of what is actually happening and the theoretical template depicting the pathways to change (Yin, 1993). The advantage of this approach is the rich context that is used to describe the process of client intervention and change. Case-study analysis is strengthened through linking the client's problems to grounded explanatory and change theories, while simultaneously using select quantitative measures to lend further support to the qualitative theoretical hypotheses about the client's situation. The main objection is the natural bias of the therapist as the narrator who subjectively elucidates the trials and tribulations of the purposive therapeutic process of facilitating change.

Target-Problem Scaling.   This qualitative design (with some quantitative elements) involves assessment of the degree to which the child's present problems are reduced or eliminated. The child, parent, and clinician have clearly identified the problem through their own assigned meaning. Problem severity and frequency are repeatedly rated and tracked over a period of time. The scaling is often a five-point scale (ranging from no problem to very severe problem) based on the client's and therapist's perceptions. Improvement in the client's problems is tracked in a similar way (ranging from being worse to greatly improved). The advantage of this approach is that it can be very quickly instituted across therapeutic sessions. However, it can easily fail if the problem's meanings are not clearly defined or if there is a marked difference between the client's and therapist's definitions of the problem. Its main drawback is that it focuses mainly on problems and not on desired outcomes (Alter and Evens, 1990).

Goal-Attainment Scaling.   Goal-attainment scaling is a widely used method for specifying and tracking client outcome objectives (Kiresuk, Smith, and Cardillo, 1993). It is considered a flexible design, which incorporates qualitative goal statements along the continuum of a quantitative scale. Specifically, the procedure requires that a client's problems and treatment goals be identified and outcome objectives be developed for each treatment goal. Each outcome objective is assigned a weight on a scale, from most unfavorable outcome thought likely to expected level of success to most favorable outcome likely. The procedure is then scored by developing a composite score based on the assigned weight of the importance that a particular objective be met and how successful the client is at reaching it at any given point in time.

For example, Sarah is a four-year-old child who was traumatized by the murder of her older brother on the front stoop of their row home, where she was playing at the time. Biopsychosocial assessment revealed that until the incident, she was a typical kindergartener who enjoyed playing with dolls as much as climbing on the playground and listening to stories. She did not have specific health problems nor were there any concerns about her developmental progress. Following the parents' report of Sarah's persistent nightmares, avoidance of playing outside voluntarily, some regression in toilet training, and overall fearfulness, the diagnostic assessment focused on the trauma and Sarah's problems in coping with the murder and expressing her grief appropriately. The parents needed help in coping with their grief while attending to Sarah's needs. The parents and Sarah accepted the treatment recommendations for developmental play therapy and concurrent parent work. The therapist developed three outcome objectives to be used in goal-attainment scaling for Stage II: Creation of Therapeutic Alliance—reducing Sarah's symptoms of suffering, creating a reality-oriented working alliance with Sarah, and increasing the parents' understanding of Sarah's needs as a four-year-old trying to cope with this trauma.

Each outcome objective for goal-attainment scaling was assigned a weight and then scaled on a continuum of expected outcomes, as shown in Table 13.1. As these goals were achieved during the subsequent treatment, they were modified or renegotiated to reach Sarah's overall treatment goal of being able to master her shock and grief so that it would not impede her further growth and development.

In the beginning of the intervention, the therapist calculated a beginning goal-attainment-scale score as a composite of all three weighted outcomes. That is, in the first few sessions, Sarah actually began showing signs of further withdrawal (-2×10), she showed no eye contact or interest in the therapist, and she did not respond to any available toys (-2×5). Although her parents were able to discuss her developmental needs, they were overwhelmed by their grief and had difficulty focusing on Sarah (-1×7). The beginning composite score was a total of $(-20) + (-10) + (-7) = (-37)$. This score was placed against a possible range of the composite score of the worst outcome (-44), somewhat worse outcome (-22), expected outcome (0), somewhat better outcome (22), and best outcome (44). As the therapy continued, the clinician scored each session to keep track of the progress.

The most difficult aspect of setting up the goal-attainment-scaling design is operationalizing problems and goals into realistic outcome objectives. The advantage is its flexibility, individualized nature, and usefulness in measuring process and change occurring during the course of treatment, as well as at outcome. Although the goal-attainment outcomes are anchored quantitatively, they are described qualitatively and, therefore, may incorporate clusters of symptoms and behaviors to be monitored, not just single behaviors. In goal-attainment scaling, the symptoms and behaviors also can be described by using quantitative (standardized) measures and a given range of expected scores for each scaled outcome (Bloom, Fischer, and Orme, 1999).

Quantitative Single-Subject Designs

Moving from a qualitative to a quantitative approach to tracking change involves a different way of operationally defining client behaviors, feelings, and actions. Numerical indicators of client functioning are used as observable referents of behavior. For example, client characteristics may be assessed based on a developmental and behavioral profile, repeatedly measuring problem behavior and symptom level from the beginning baseline period to the end of the intervention (and perhaps later follow-up), recording, and displaying the changes in client functioning. The items selected for tracking are monitored across stages of treatment, as well as across social situations within and outside of the treatment sessions. The information is then graphically recorded in a way that usually displays the outcome objectives along the ordinate (vertical) line, while time (interviews or treatment stages) is plotted on the horizontal line. It is customary shorthand to use the alphabet to designate different treatment periods (A = baseline or period before intervention; B, C, and D = phases of different interventions; B_1 and B_2 = the same intervention but with varying intensity).

TABLE 13.1 Goal-Attainment Scale for Sarah

Levels of Predicted Attainment	Scale #1 To Reduce Sarah's Distress	Scale #2 To Develop Rapport	Scale #3 Parents Display Understanding of Sarah's Developmental Needs	Percent of Anticipated Progress
WEIGHT	WT. 10	WT. 5	WT. 7	%
Much Less Than Expected Level of Outcome (2)	Sarah shows more signs of withdrawal	Sarah shows no eye contact or interest in the therapist	Parents ignore and neglect Sarah's needs as well as their own	0% Change Client is worse off
Somewhat Less Than Expected Level of Outcome (-1)	Sarah continues to have nightmares, but is generally cooperative	Sarah shows occasional eye contact and interest in the therapist	Parents are able to intellectually recognize Sarah's developmental needs, but have some difficulty in attending to her basic needs; they are unsuccessfully coping with their own grief	25% Change Client is slightly better off
Expected Level of Outcome (0)	Sarah is able to begin expressing her feelings without being overwhelmed by distress	Sarah becomes engaged in a cooperative activity with the therapist	Parents are able to appropriately parent Sarah's needs, as well as attend to their own needs	50% Change Client is about halfway through the ultimate goal
Somewhat More Than Expected Level of Outcome (+1)	Sarah is able to express her feelings appropriately	Sarah asks questions or verbally responds to questions	Parents resolve their acute grief and start anticipating Sarah's needs	75% Change Client is close to reaching her goal
Much More Than Expected Level of Outcome (+2)	Sarah has regained her confidence and has stopped being fearful	Sarah responds appropriately to therapist's requests	Parents are able to cope with their grief and anticipate Sarah's new developmental needs	100% Change Client is ready to terminate treatment

339

Outcome measures selected for single-subject designs need to be reliable, be consistent, be easy to gather, and have good inter-rater reliability. Preferably, they should be brief and standardized and have satisfactory validity. Equally important, they should be sensitive to change. Because the clinician has little control over extraneous factors in children's lives that impinge on treatment outcome, single-subject designs in the real world of practice are exploratory and the findings are always interpreted with caution (Tripodi, 1995).

Exploratory Designs.   The main purpose of exploratory designs is to monitor client's changes over time during the course of treatment without attempting to prove a causal link between outcomes and process activities believed to have engendered them. They address the question: "Is change occurring?" This design is easy to set up because it does not track descriptors of clients prior to entering treatment nor does it establish baseline behavior. Rather, it uses a client's subjective self-report or records from other professionals (e.g., teachers) to establish a description of the client's problems prior to seeking help. This design then operationally tracks the accomplishment of outcome objectives throughout treatment. The focus is monitoring whether the client's objective is changing in the desired direction. While this design is quick, is simple to implement, and systematically monitors change, no conclusions can be drawn. The findings serve as one piece of evidence that change is occurring. They are reported as supporting the clinical evidence of change, or not, as the case may be.

Quasi-Experimental Designs.   These designs are set up in such a way that tracking allows for collecting baseline information prior to implementing treatment. To show that it was the intervention that was responsible for the client change, information is collected about what the client's difficulties and strengths were like before the intervention began, during treatment, and after the intervention ceases. Needless to say, the before and after treatment data-collection requirement poses special problems for the clinician.

The most common quasi-experimental design is the descriptive AB design, in which baseline information (A) is followed by intervention (B). It is expected that the clinician will be able to collect baseline information about the client's outcome objectives at three different points in time before initiating intervention (Alter and Evens, 1990). Obviously, this design is not appropriate for clients in crisis or great distress. This design considers the developmental play therapy model to be a whole treatment package individualized to meet the needs of a particular child. The design's main advantage lies in the ability to draw some inference about client change based on comparison of the outcome objective from baseline to the end of treatment. Many variations on this and other single-subject designs exist for use in special circumstances, in which treatment begins before a baseline is established, in which multiple problems are targeted, or in which multiple interventions are used.

Overall, the choice for using qualitative and quantitative measures of client outcomes is guided by adherence to standards of practice in providing quality therapeutic services to children and their families. The rigorousness of designs is underpinned by the client's need for responsible feedback in treatment, as well as by the therapist's need to be able to identify, select, and augment treatment to match the client's needs. Most therapists know and use nonempirical methods for evaluating change, and many are becoming skilled at employing variations on exploratory single-subject designs to monitor change. In child treatment, it has long been the expected standard of practice that data will be gathered from multiple sources; qualitatively described over the course of treatment; and interpreted to children and their parents at assessment, during treatment, and at the end.

Measuring Outcomes

The operational definition of the outcomes desired restates the outcome objective in view of what can be measured, as indicators of change that represent the abstract theoretical condition. These proxies are collected by using tools or measuring instruments that record or capture the client's feelings, thoughts, perceptions, social relationships, and behaviors. Again, multiple sources, including several instruments or instruments plus observations, help safeguard the verity, consistency, and comprehensiveness of the information obtained.

Case Process Notes

The clinician's treatment notes provide a written record of therapy events, interactions, thoughts, and feelings from the clinician's point of view. Content-analyzing (or categorizing) this material provides a way of focusing and reducing a large amount of data. Obviously, the extent of thoroughness in recording the sessions has an impact on the quality of the information that may be obtained.

Direct Measures or Observation Protocols

Direct measures for evaluating client changes involve observations of clients in their natural environments. They also involve use of measures that represent clients' natural behaviors, such as analogue situations (role-playing) and self-reports.

Behavioral observations represent one of the most direct ways of measuring client behaviors during therapy sessions, as well as in real-world situations. Typically, the content and process of the behavior are observed as to frequency and duration or occurrence during some specified intervals. To assess frequency, the behavior has to be operationally defined, identified, and gauged for continuity. The clinician observer must be clear about what behavior to look for and how to recognize it when it occurs. Sometimes the participant observations are the usual ones of the clinician during an interview. Other times, videotapes are used to record treatment events. Frequently, a protocol or a written list of items may serve as a guide for observing, including a checklist of problems, developmental issues, symptoms of mood and affect, and specific behaviors, to name a few.

Although using one observer (i.e., the clinician) limits the scientific reliability of observations, it nevertheless remains an important measurement indicator in practice evaluations. Sometimes it is possible for teachers, parents, or other professionals to observe as well; more often it is not. It is not always necessary to record every occurrence of the identified behavior, nor must the observation be for long periods of time. To analyze recordings, intervals can easily be converted into percentages by dividing the number of intervals during which the behavior occurs by the total number of intervals observed and then multiplying by 100. Examples are shown in Tables 13.2 and 13.3.

Direct behavioral observations remain one of the most effective tools for measuring client behavior. When used with two or more observers (with interrater reliability of 0.80 or better), observations meet the claims of scientific rigor (Jordan and Franklin, 1995).

TABLE 13.2   Sarah's Style of Play Activity in Sessions by Ten-Minute Intervals*

Play Activity	1	2	3	4	5	6	7	8	9	10	11	12	13	14
None	4	4	2	2										
Solitary	1	1	2	2	2	5	2	1						
Parallel			1	1	2		3	4	3	2	1		1	
Cooperative					1				2	3	4	5	4	5

*Fifty minutes per session, or five ten-minute intervals

TABLE 13.3   Sarah's Amount of Eye Contact in Sessions*

Eye Contact	1	2	3	4	5	6	7	8	9	10	11	12	13	14
None	X	X				X								
A Little			X	X			X	X						
Some					X				X	X	X		X	
A Lot												X		X

*X = Eye contact present

Indirect Measures or Questionnaires and Scales

These measures are assumed to be signs or symbolic representations of the problems and behaviors targeted for change. Projective tests such as the Despert Fables, Draw-a-Figure, Three Wishes, and Story Completion Task are examples in the clinical repertoire of assessment tools with children. There are also many standardized indices and inventories for depression, anxiety, hyperactive behaviors, and oppositional behaviors, to name a few (Fischer and Corcoran, 1994). Because it may be difficult and expensive to set up direct observations, these proxy measures often serve as gauges of client change. It is preferable, of course, to use items that are scaled; have established age-related norms; measure several dimensions of the behavior in question; have established validity and reliability; are culturally sensitive; and have alternative forms available for parents, teachers, and children (Bloom, Fischer, and Orme, 1999).

When clinicians cannot use a standardized instrument, a self-anchored rating scale may be developed to evaluate the outcome objective under consideration. Such a scale represents a continuum, ranging from a very low point to a very high point on a given item. Typically, there are as few as three scaled points for an item and as many as one hundred scaled points for all items. Although a client may be asked about the presence or absence of the targeted behavior, mood, or something else, a question that has been scaled and anchored permits the clinician to detect subtleties in the client's response. For example, a preschool child is likely to be able to select a response from three items if they are made age-appropriate: "Tell me, were you upset not at all, upset just a little, or upset a lot?" Sometimes picture composites with varying facial expressions or picture sequences of events provide graphic illustrations from which children are able to identify the feeling relevant to the situation. Or children may be asked to draw how they felt, what they saw, what happened, and what they wish would happen in the future. Understanding the cultural background and developmental cognitive and emotional abilities of the child determines the accuracy with which a child will respond to scaled or anchored questions (Kirk, 1999). The advantage of anchored scales is that they can measure a range and intensity of feelings, attitudes, and thought patterns. The disadvantage is that they must be constructed to be meaningful to a particular child or parent, salient, developmentally appropriate, and minimize client reactivity. Asking unbiased, open-ended, or structured questions to elicit meaningful responses is an art, as well as a skill to be mastered by every social work clinician (Tripodi, 1995).

Analyzing Data

When deciding on which statistical procedures to use in evaluating the client's outcome objectives, the key questions for the clinician involve the following:

- Based on current standards of practice, which tools or instruments will be used?

- What designs will be applied?
- Which statistical findings will complement and substantiate clinical observation?
- How will this process hinder, support, or enhance the client's understanding of progress?

Choice of evaluative tools may guide the direction for linking clinical assessment to intervention, as well as for tracking treatment progress. At the most basic level lie the clinical interview notes or process recordings that underpin the clinical judgment offered the client as clinical feedback about how the contractual treatment goals are being met. This clinical judgment, grounded in theoretical understanding of the patterns of client behavior in relation to contractual goal achievement, may be complemented by symbolic graphic depiction and statistical analysis, and may enhance client feedback.

Graphic Analysis

Graphic analysis is usually used in single-subject designs with both qualitative and quantitative components. For example, the clinician may use content analysis to document the presence or absence and degree of observed targeted behaviors (seeking behavioral patterns through case notes and video recordings) and mathematical process (chi-square, two-standard deviation) to demonstrate progress. Graphic analysis typically requires quantifiable depiction of the outcome objectives along the ordinate and time referent (i.e., points of frequency during which the targets were collected: minutes, days, weeks, treatment stages, sessions) along the abscissa. The client's outcome objectives are symbolically recorded at each of the cross-reference points between the time referent and the amount of target behavior manifest. This recording creates a scatterplot picture with cross-referenced points of outcome behavior available for the following:

- inspection for visual patterns
- comparison along treatment stages by using percent change in the amount manifest
- comparison against statistical benchmarks that are either age-norm-related or denote statistical significance
- evaluation for the salient features that demonstrate or support the achievement of clinical and theoretical significance

Visual analysis requires that the scatterplot graph be examined for slope, drift, and variability. For example, eyeballing scatterplot points is usually informative as the clinician contemplates the effects of treatment. No change in the slope or level of the client's targets suggests that the intervention was not effective. Or it may be that the targets were not appropriately selected, not relevant to client goals, too difficult to record, or too infrequently recorded. As long as the graphed points representing the targeted behavior sufficiently approximate a line, then the level of change in the desired direction of effect, slope, drift, and variability of the points along the line may be visually inspected. Visual inspection can raise awareness of whether treatment is proceeding in the desired direction.

For example, Sarah (whose outcome objectives were discussed in relation to goal-attainment scaling) and whose eye contacts were recorded by the therapist in Table 13.4 affords the opportunity to see whether the treatment proceeded in the expected direction. The expected objective was to engage four-year-old Sarah in a trusting therapeutic alliance in order to help her deal with her feelings about the violent incident she had witnessed. This objective was supported theoretically, as well as by the developmental play therapy model, which posits that the therapeutic alliance is prerequisite to change. It also was supported by best-practice standards in work with children who have experienced trauma. As the symbolic proxy for trust and engagement with the clinician, Sarah's lack of eye contact was quite apparent, easily observable, and assessed as a developmentally inappropriate emotional response that allowed her to avoid visual input.

Sessions 1–5 represented the initial period of treatment; Sessions 6–10, the middle; and Sessions 11–14, the final period in facilitating Sarah's eye contact. Examining the scatter of the presence or absence of her eye contacts on the graph permitted easy demonstration that her eye contact—as symbolic of her engagement with the therapist—had proceeded in the desired direction. It also supported the therapist's hypothesis that developmental play therapy would initially increase her anxiety, but that the ongoing process would increase her level of comfort and engage her in a way that would allow further goals to be set. The simple visual inspection supported the therapist's hypothesis.

Percent Proportion

To further address relationship-building with Sarah, the therapist chose to examine and quantify the kind and degree of her style of play during the sessions. These data were depicted previously but are reproduced again in Table 13.5 for ease of reference. The therapist used a simple quantification or percent proportion to compare her engagement in a developmentally appropriate style of play (parallel, cooperative) with compromised play (none, solitary). Sarah engaged in

TABLE 13.4   (Repeated for Clarity) Sarah's Amount of Eye Contact in Sessions

Eye Contact		1	2	3	4	5	6	7	8	9	10	11	12	13	14
None	4	X	X				X								
A Little	3			X	X			X	X						
Some	2					X				X	X	X		X	
A Lot	1												X		X

TABLE 13.5   (Repeated for Clarity) Style of Sarah's Play Activity in Sessions by Ten-Minute Intervals

Play Activity	1	2	3	4	5	6	7	8	9	10	11	12	13	14
None	4	4	2	2										
Solitary	1	1	2	2	2	5	2	1						
Parallel			1	1	2		3	4	3	2	1		1	
Cooperative					1				2	3	4	5	4	5

predominantly age-inappropriate play in Sessions 1–5, in that twenty of twenty-five acts (60 percent) resembled those of a developmentally younger child. Her age-inappropriate play was reduced to half (56 percent) of her total recorded play acts. In the last phase of treatment, Sarah began engaging fully in age-appropriate play. The sessions indicated cessation of the developmentally younger play and an increase in her ability to engage in cooperative interactive play with the therapist. Clinically, the engagement objective was fulfilled because the change in Sarah's approach to play was deemed clinically and theoretically significant. This change was seen as necessary for pursuing further goals.

Proportion/Frequency Comparison

To assess statistical significance, the therapist also can use two approaches: (1) a proportion/frequency comparison of desired and undesired targets (acts) between the beginning and later phases of treatment; and (2) a mathematical procedure to calculate a chi-square statistic to address whether there might be a significant difference between the expected and observed frequencies in different phases of treatment or against an expected norm. Sarah's play acts in the early, middle, and later sessions may be compared. First, the therapist decides the direction of the desired change; in this case, the desired improvement (outcome objective) includes more play acts that represent a predominantly cooperative play rather than parallel play alone. The undesirable change would be in the direction of predominantly solitary acts of play or no play at all during the sessions. Second, the therapist counts the number of desired and undesired acts for the beginning and ending periods, and cross-tabulates these play acts into a 2-by-2 grid, as shown in Table 13.6.

Third, the therapist calculates the proportion of desired acts for the beginning period as $5/25 = 0.20$ and the total number of play acts (forty-five) for the ending period. Fourth, the therapist consults a table for "Cumulative Binomial Probability Distribution" (as seen, for example, in Rubin and Babbie, 1997). This table is organized to find the minimal number of desired intervention points (play acts) necessary based on the constraints of the proportion of desired points in the baseline or beginning period. For Sarah, the beginning period demonstrated a

TABLE 13.6 Cross-Tabulation of Sarah's Number of Play Acts by Phases of Treatment

Phases of Treatment	Undesired Play Acts (–)	Desired Play Acts (+)	Total Number of Playing Acts
Sessions 1–5	20	5	25
Sessions 6–14	8	37	45
Total Number of Playing Acts	28	42	70

proportion of 0.20 to be cross-referenced with the forty-five total acts of the ending period. Cross referencing identified fourteen to fifteen minimum acts needed to fall in the desired range of types (parallel, mutual); Sarah demonstrated thirty-seven desired play acts. This result suggests that there was a statistically significant increase in the proportion of her desired play acts from the beginning to the later intervention period, and that this result has about a 95 percent chance of being accurate.

Chi-square. To use the second mathematical approach of chi-square statistic in evaluation, the therapist constructs a 2-by-2 grid similar to the previous one. The next step involves calculating the "expected" frequencies for each cell (by multiplying the column total acts by the row total acts, and then dividing the result by the grand total acts to create Table 13.7). The fourth step involves using the traditional chi-square test formula (Bloom, Fischer, and Orme, 1999) to calculate the chi-square statistic:

1. Subtract each Expected Frequency from the Observed Frequency.
2. Square each Product.
3. Divide each Product by its own Expected Frequency.
4. Sum up all the results.

The resulting chi-square statistic for Sarah's play acts was 25.91. To assess its clinical significance, the therapist next consults a chi-square statistic table (any behavioral science text) and chooses a probability level (conventional social-science probability level is two standard deviations from the mean, or 95 percent accuracy, probability of $p < .05$). Then the clinician calculates the degrees of freedom (df) as (Number of Rows – 1) × (Number of Columns – 1) and finds the table's expected chi-square result that could have occurred just by chance at that probability level. The final step is comparing the calculated chi-square statistic result (25.91) against the expected table chi-square result of 3.84 (df = 1, $p < .05$). Because the observed result in Sarah's case is greater than the table's expected

TABLE 13.7   Cross Tabulation of Sarah's Observed and Expected Frequencies by Treatment

Phases of Treatment	Observed Frequency (−)	Expected Frequency (+)	Observed Frequency (+)	Expected Frequency (+)	Total Acts
Sessions 1–5	20	10	5	15	25
Sessions 6–14	8	18	37	27	45
Total Acts	28		42		70

result, her calculated chi-square result is considered statistically significant at that particular level of probability. In other words, the calculated difference between her observed and expected frequencies could not have happened by chance. The implication of this finding is that there is a statistically significant likelihood that the difference between desired and undesired play acts is significantly different from beginning to end, with about a 5 percent chance of being inaccurate. The therapist is reminded, however, that several technical considerations may limit the use of this test and that reliance only on statistical significance to validate achievement of outcome objectives is unwise.

Two-Standard-Deviation.   The most common way to evaluate a single-subject design is the application of the two-standard-deviation approach to assess the statistical significance of the results for 95 percent accuracy. This approach requires some designation of a baseline period. For demonstration purposes, the therapist examines Sarah's eye-contact data with scaled levels of eye contact (None = 4, A little = 3, Some = 2, A lot = 1).

The two-standard-deviation method requires that the practitioner calculate the mean for the baseline period (Sessions 1–5), standard deviation from the mean, and the mean for the intervention (Sessions 6–14). Ideally, the baseline period has at least three observations and depicts a horizontal wavy pattern. If the recorded data depict an increasing or decreasing pattern, then the clinician can perform a similar procedure, but with a slightly different calculation (for in-depth discussion, see Alter and Evens, 1990; Bloom, Fischer, and Orme, 1999). The basic idea in the two-standard-deviation approach is that scores that occur within the band of + or − 2 standard deviations from the mean have a 95 percent likelihood of happening by chance (based on the principles of normally distributed scores). Consequently, the scores that would be found outside this 2 standard deviation band would be rare, or would have only a 5 percent chance of occurring. Ideally, most of the desired scores of intervention would not only fall into the expected direction, but also the client's average should be found past the 2 standard deviation score to demonstrate that the client in all likelihood was affected by the intervention. Therefore, for Sarah's eye contacts, the therapist first needs to calculate her mean eye contact for the early sessions (3.2). Next, the therapist computes a standard deviation for the beginning mean (for specific procedures, see Bloom, Fischer, and Orme, 1999, p. 590):

- Subtract each baseline score from the baseline mean (s–M).
- Square each product (s–M)^2.
- Sum all the squared products.
- Subtract 1 from the number of scores in the baseline (n–1).
- Divide the sum of the squared products by (n–1).
- Compute a square root of the previous result.

In Sarah's case, the standard deviation equaled 0.83. Third, the therapist computes a two-standard-deviation band around the baseline mean. This computation produced an upper band score of 4.86 (1.66 + 3.2) and a lower band score of 1.54 (3.2–1.66) in the beginning period. These two scores may be graphed to depict a band around the mean. In Sarah's case, however, the therapist is mainly interested in increasing her eye contacts and, therefore, is primarily focused on the scores below the lower band (note that a lower score means more eye contact). Fourth, the therapist calculates the mean for the intervention period—in Sarah's case, an average of 2.2 for the later period. Finally, the therapist compares the intervention mean (2.2) with the desired two-standard-deviation score (1.54). In Sarah's case the intervention mean is not smaller than the two-standard-deviation score. Thus, the result is not statistically significant at the 0.05 level.

Technically, results from this data-analysis approach suggest that the change was not scientifically significant and, therefore, might not be viewed as meaningful. There are, however, several mitigating issues to be considered. The beginning period did not represent a true baseline. Sarah rarely made eye contact before treatment. Theoretical hypotheses supported the fluctuations of her observed progress. Visual inspection yielded improved ability to make eye contact with the therapist. Because the clinical goal was increased eye contact as part of Sarah's ability to demonstrate rapport with the therapist, her clinical progress was not invalidated by these quantitative results from a monitoring design.

Clinical Significance

The clinical significance, or practical clinical importance of achieving client objectives, must be salient to the client's needs and congruent with theoretical hypotheses about the client's functioning. Sarah's eye-contact results and her progress in her play approach by the fourteenth session were judged clinically adequate enough to pursue setting other goals.

To draw reasonable conclusions about recorded client observations, the therapist primarily needs to demonstrate clinical and theoretical utility with as much statistical support as is feasible and possible. When clinical, theoretical, and statistical significance are aligned, it is plausible to interpret the findings as significant. When they are not so aligned and there is no plausible reason, reconsideration of the treatment goals, theoretical framework, and evaluation design is indicated.

Treatment Process and Outcome Summary: Jack
by Elizabeth M. Timberlake, D.S.W., LCSW-C

Biopsychosocial Assessment Highlights

Removed from his parents for abuse and neglect, Jack was placed in foster care at age one. By the time he entered treatment at age seven, Jack had been in three foster homes. Psychosocial developmental history was not available. His current foster parents complained that he was stubborn, did not trust them, seemed afraid of being beaten, episodically dissolved into frightened screams and tears, periodically displayed temper tantrums, and did not get along with other children at home or in the neighborhood. He frequently refused to do his schoolwork and was failing in school. During assessment, Jack did not make eye contact, was generally nonresponsive, and seemed fearful about involving himself in assessment activities.

Targeted Problem for Process Evaluation

Jack's presenting problems, psychosocial history, and initial resistance to becoming involved indicated that the interim or stage-specific goal of creating a therapeutic alliance (Stage II) would be critical to achieving the desired outcomes in developmental play therapy. Therefore, I thought that documenting and assessing the alliance's evolution during the early sessions would be an important way of evaluating his progress through the second stage of treatment. For process-evaluation purposes, the degree and quality of Jack's engagement were defined in terms of:

- nonverbal avoidance behaviors of eye contact, periods of silence lasting five minutes or more, and shrugging responses to comments (avoidance patterns were rated [1] none, [2] some, [3] a lot for each interview or cluster)
- play patterns along a range of no play, solitary play, parallel play, cooperative play
- narrative developmental themes of trust/mistrust (Erikson, 1950) and clinical issue themes of attachment/loss (Bowlby, 1973a)
- clinical assessment of the nature and quality of the therapeutic alliance

Omitting the two assessment sessions in Stage I: Biopsychosocial Assessment, data were collected from Interviews 3–31 using (1) case notes that documented presence of nonverbal avoidance behaviors, play patterns, and clinical assessment of the alliance; and (2) content analysis of the focal developmental theme and clinical issue noted in the process recordings. Interviews were fifty minutes in length.

When the twenty-nine interviews in Stage II: Creating a Therapeutic Alliance were divided in two, the average scores of nonverbal avoidance behaviors of silence decreased from 2.9 to 1.9, shrugs decreased from 2.9 to 1.8, and eye contact increased from 1.1 to 2.1. These clinically significant changes were in the predicted directions of increased engagement with his therapist.

As shown in Table 13.8, there was a marked shift in play patterns from the first to the second half of Stage II. Initially, there were sixteen occasions in which Jack did not play; later, none. Similarly, Jack engaged in solitary play on fifty-four occasions during the first half of Stage II, but on only four occasions in the latter half. This pattern was reversed for the two patterns involving the clinician. Jack engaged in parallel play on five occasions initially, on thirty-three occasions later. He engaged in no cooperative play initially and on thirty-four occasions in the second half of Stage II. These clinically significant changes were also in the predicted direction of increased engagement with his therapist.

As shown in Table 13.9, there was a marked shift in the direction of the trust/mistrust developmental themes expressed in the therapeutic narrative of Stage II. In the early sessions, Jack expressed mistrust in 104 themes and metaphors, and trust in twenty-one themes and metaphors. In the later sessions, he expressed the reverse, with seven themes and metaphors of mistrust and fifty-seven of trust. These clinically significant changes were in the predicted direction of increased trust, and suggested a relational shift from a very high level of mistrust to a moderate level of trust.

Together, these quantitative findings supported the clinical assessment case notes, which contained comments indicating minimal relatedness in the early sessions; for example, "hard to connect with Jack, he avoids contact, Jack excluded me from his play, I might as well be furniture, minimal investment in the play." By contrast, notes for the later sessions suggested a growing therapeutic alliance: "Jack tolerates my being with him, we engaged in parallel play most of the session, included in cooperative play with cars, more inclusive activity, settles into activity quickly, sense of working together purposively, Jack seems more responsive to verbal reflections."

TABLE 13.8 Play Patterns in Stage II: Creation of Therapeutic Alliance*

	Sessions 3–17	Sessions 18–31
No Play	16	0
Solitary Play	54	4
Parallel Play	5	33
Cooperative Play	0	34

*Fifty minutes per session = five ten-minute intervals for noting play patterns

TABLE 13.9   Trust versus Mistrust Themes in Stage II: Creation of Therapeutic Alliance

	Sessions 3–17	Sessions 18–31	Row Totals
Mistrust	104	7	111
Trust	21	57	78
Column Totals	125	64	189

In summary, the findings from behavioral measures, observed play patterns, observed developmental themes, and clinical assessment were congruent. Together, they supported the stage-specific goal of creating a therapeutic alliance by the end of Stage II that would be strong enough to withstand the vicissitudes of growth and change. That this initially very resistant child was able to develop a solid working alliance supported moving forward with the long-term treatment goals established during Stage I: Biopsychosocial Assessment. The slow pace in establishing a therapeutic alliance was not surprising and confirmed the thinking that Jack's therapy would take several years.

Targeted Problems for Outcome Evaluation

Stage I: Biopsychosocial Assessment yielded a case formulation in which the early abuse/neglect and removal from home into caretaking instability were associated with developmental disruption, anxiety, and oppositionality. Long-term developmental play therapy goals, therefore, included remediating developmental disruption and ameliorating anxiety and oppositionality. For evaluative purposes, it was hypothesized that:

Within-session treatment outcomes would evidence:

1. fewer narrative themes and metaphors and less time focused on separation and loss by the end of Stage IV, with an increase/decrease pattern apparent in Stage V
2. less anxiety
3. less oppositionality
4. progression in developmental themes and metaphors such that age-appropriate developmental issues and tasks of the latency stage of industry would be dominant

External treatment outcomes from teacher would evidence:

1. more positive cooperative relationship with his teacher
2. more positive peer relationships

3. passing school grades
4. more adequate psychosocial functioning at school

Measurement.   To measure these internal and external outcomes, the following indicators were used:

■ *Anxiety.* Anxiety was operationally defined as an attitude of being fearful of making mistakes, being nervous, worrying that something bad might happen, and worrying about being hurt. Level of anxiety was assessed on a five-point scale from (1) not anxious to (5) very high level of anxiety.

■ *Oppositionality.* Oppositionality was operationally defined as an attitude of stubbornness, refusal to cooperate, and nonresponsiveness. Level of oppositionality was assessed on a five-point scale from (1) not oppositional to (5) very high level of oppositionality.

■ *Separation/Loss.* Separation and loss was operationalized as play narrative representations and metaphors of leaving, being left, aloneness, grief, searching for someone, and hide and seek. The presence of separation and loss themes was recorded by frequency of occurrence per session or session cluster. It was hypothesized that narrative themes and metaphors of separation/loss would wax, then wane, and then experience renewal during Stage V: Termination, which explicitly deals with the loss of the therapeutic alliance.

■ *Developmental Tasks.* Development was operationalized as narrative themes and metaphors reflecting developmental tasks and desired outcomes of the Eriksonian developmental themes of trust, autonomy, initiative, and industry (Erikson, 1950). It was hypothesized that the developmental themes for each psychosocial stage would wax and then wane during the course of treatment, until Jack reached a balance of developmental themes in which industry would be dominant.

■ *Classroom Psychosocial Functioning Inventory.* This forty-five-item inventory includes nine conceptual dimensions (for item listing, see Table 13.12) that measure the interpersonal, emotional, and task dimensions of the child's psychosocial functioning in the classroom as perceived by the teacher. The presence of these items, as noted on a five-point interval scale (describes child (1) not at all to (5) very well), connotes personal strengths and assets. Their absence connotes personal vulnerabilities and deficits in psychosocial functioning that are likely to interfere with the child's ability to profit from school experiences. Although data furnished by teachers are biased in the direction of their personal experiences with the child, this very bias furnishes information about the social climate of this child's classroom. Scale validity and reliability have been established in several studies (Timberlake, 1979; Timberlake and Verdieck, 1987).

Data Analysis.   Data were collected over Jack's three years of developmental play therapy (i.e., 140 fifty-minute interviews) from case notes of interviews that systematically documented the selected behavior patterns and content analysis of developmental themes and clinical issues found in the process recordings of individual interviews and narrative theme summaries of interview clusters (four interviews per cluster). Process recordings were completed for twenty-nine (of twenty-nine) interviews in Stage II, fourteen (of fifty-four) interviews interspersed throughout Stage III, twelve (of forty-four) interviews interspersed throughout Stage IV, and three (of eleven) interviews interspersed throughout Stage V. Narrative theme summaries were completed for ten interview clusters in Stage III, eight in Stage IV, and two in Stage V.

Taking the conservative route, data analysis was limited to tabular reporting of the frequencies and means across the stages of treatment and at pre- and post-testing. Visual analysis was used to explore the clinical and theoretical significance of the findings.

Results.   As shown in Table 13.10, the mean number of treatment process themes of anxiety and oppositionality steadily decreased. These changes were in the direction predicted and were considered clinically and theoretically significant. As predicted, the mean number of separation and loss themes decreased steadily through Stage IV, increased initially in Stage V, and then decreased below the means of Stages II, III, and the initial period of Stage IV. The changes were in the direction predicted and were considered clinically and theoretically significant.

As shown in Table 13.11, the mean number of developmental growth themes revealed patterns such that:

- Trust themes tripled by the end of Stage II and in the early phase of Stage III. By the end of Stage III, the trust themes were twice as prevalent as they were in the early phase of Stage II but half that of the next two phases. Trust themes were not present in Stages IV and V.
- Autonomy themes revealed a curvilinear pattern with a steady increase that peaked by the end of Stage III and then declined below the early phase of Stage II.
- Initiative themes were not present in Stage II, began in Stage III, peaked in the later phase of Stage IV, and decreased by half in Stage V.
- Industry themes were not present in Stages II and III, began in Stage IV, and steadily increased through Stage V. By Stage V, the dominant developmental theme in the play therapy was industry.

These results were in the predicted direction of progression and shifting over the course of treatment until industry themes became dominant. They support the perspective of developmental theory that developmental tasks, and consequently preoccupying themes, shift as children mature. The changes were in the direction predicted and were considered clinically and theoretically significant.

As shown in Table 13.12, teacher rating of Jack's psychosocial functioning in the classroom revealed a marked increase in the rating of his strengths, albeit

TABLE 13.10   Anxiety, Oppositionality, and Separation/Loss Themes Across Treatment Stages*

	Stage I	Stage II		Stage III		Stage IV		Stage V	
Interviews	(1–2)	(3–17)	(18–31)	(32–59)	(60–85)	(86–108)	(109–129)	(130–135)	(136–140)
Anxiety									
Frequency		73	61	47	38	23	13	5	2
Mean		4.9	4.4	3.9	3.2	2.3	1.3	1.7	1.0
Opposition-ality									
Frequency		75	60	51	33	21	15	3	2
Mean		5.0	4.3	4.3	2.8	2.1	1.5	1.0	1.0
Separation/Loss									
Frequency		71	68	58	53	31	15	13	5
Mean		4.7	4.9	4.8	4.4	3.1	1.5	3.3	2.5

*Interviews by substages and number of process recordings and narrative cluster recordings by substages.

Interviews	(1–2)	(3–17)	(18–31)	(32–59)	(60–85)	(86–108)	(109–129)	(130–135)	(136–140)
Process		(15)	(14)	(7)	(7)	(6)	(6)	(2)	(1)
Cluster		(0)	(0)	(5)	(5)	(4)	(4)	(1)	(1)

TABLE 13.11   Developmental Growth Themes Across Treatment Stages*

	Stage I	Stage II		Stage III		Stage IV		Stage V	
Interviews	(1–2)	(3–17)	(18–31)	(32–59)	(60–85)	(86–108)	(109–129)	(130–135)	(136–140)
Trust									
Frequency		21	57	58	31	0	0	0	0
Mean		1.4	4.1	4.8	2.6	0	0	0	0
Autonomy									
Frequency		42	63	53	57	41	38	7	3
Mean		2.8	4.5	4.4	4.8	4.1	3.8	2.3	1.5
Initiative									
Frequency		0	0	12	25	35	41	7	4
Mean		0	0	1.0	2.1	3.5	4.1	2.3	2.0
Industry									
Frequency		0	0	0	0	10	25	8	7
Mean		0	0	0	0	1.0	2.5	2.7	3.5

*Interviews by substages and number of process recordings and narrative cluster recordings by substages.

Interviews	(1–2)	(3–17)	(18–31)	(32–59)	(60–85)	(86–108)	(109–129)	(130–135)	(136–140)
Process		(15)	(14)	(7)	(7)	(6)	(6)	(2)	(1)
Cluster		(0)	(0)	(5)	(5)	(4)	(4)	(1)	(1)

TABLE 13.12   Classroom Psychosocial Functioning Inventory: Strengths

	Pre-test	Post-test
Academic Performance		
Works at grade level	1	3
Completes homework	1	4
Hands in homework on time	1	5
Comes to school prepared	1	3
Attends school regularly	4	5
Self-Image		
Feels good about self	2	4
Has good sense of humor	2	3
Acts his/her age	2	4
Approaches new experiences confidently	1	4
Is pleased with accomplishments	2	4
Peer-Relationship Skills		
Shares things with others	1	3
Stands up to group pressure	3	4
Works out problems with friends	1	4
Tries to help others	1	2
Has many friends	1	3
Adult-Relationship Skills		
Works well without adult support	1	3
Carries out requests and directions responsibly	1	3
Is polite and courteous	1	3
Is trustworthy	1	3
Volunteers to help	1	3
Self-Control of Actions		
Does well despite distractions	2	5
Thinks before acting	2	5
Follows directions and rules	1	3
Does well in unstructured situations	1	3
Is well behaved	1	3
Motivation		
Shares ideas willingly	3	5
Works for own satisfaction, not just awards	2	4
Works up to potential	1	4
Is energetic	3	5
Asks for help when needed	1	4
Handling Learning Demands		
Can handle things not going own way	1	3
Handles schoolwork well	1	3
Handles school competition well	1	3

TABLE 13.12 Continued

	Pre-test	Post-test
Makes few careless mistakes	2	5
Listens to directions	1	5
Adaptability and Learning Style		
Accepts criticism well	1	3
Adjusts well to changes in routine	1	3
Is generally relaxed	1	3
Is creative	2	5
Has good study habits	1	4
Expression and Handling of Feelings		
Is affectionate toward others	2	4
Anger, when displayed, is justified	1	3
Expresses needs and feelings appropriately	1	3
Is a happy child	1	3
Is easily soothed when upset	1	4

still room for improvement. At the pre-test, Jack evidenced three out of forty-five possible strengths present at moderate levels (rating of 3). At the post-test, by contrast, Jack evidenced forty-four of forty-five possible strengths present at a moderate level or higher. Improvement was evidenced in academic performance, self-image, peer-relationship skills, adult-relationship skills, self-control of actions, motivation, handling learning demands, adaptability, learning style, and expression and handling of feelings. These changes were in the direction predicted and were considered clinically and theoretically significant.

His most recent two report cards indicated B level of performance across the board. No behavior problems were noted. His foster parents reported an improvement in their relationships with Jack and that he was fighting less with his siblings.

In summary, the findings from behavioral measures, observed play patterns, observed developmental themes, and clinical assessment were congruent. Together, they supported the idea that developmental play therapy with Jack had resulted in developmental maturation to the point of age-appropriateness, decreased symptoms of anxiety and oppositionality, increased psychosocial functioning at home, and improved school grades.

Conclusion

Formalized systematic evaluation of treatment process and outcome is clearly useful in documenting practice effectiveness. However, it is usually desirable and feasible to measure only a carefully selected array of the multiple goals and objectives often found in developmental play therapy and concurrent parent work. Thus, it is important that the selected goals and objectives:

- be representative of the clinician's, parents', and child's views of what needs to change
- be meaningful conceptually in relation to the practice model and practically in the day-to-day reality of home and school
- be measurable or observable
- provide a triangulated view of change from multiple perspectives and
- be understood as fixed positions at selected points in time that symbolize the fluid, dynamic developmental process of growth and change

When reported alone, however, even the most carefully selected outcome measures often appear flat, unidimensional, and disconnected from the child and his or her family. To maintain the depth and nuance of the human growth experience in therapy, it is critical to accompany outcome measures with a succinct explanatory narrative that incorporates theoretical reflection about the expected and actual findings in relation to the measured goals and objectives. In addition, a narrative summary of the therapeutic change is needed to provide qualitative professional judgment in relation to both measured and non-measured goals.

EPILOGUE

The principles of developmental play therapy and concurrent parent work are at the heart of clinical social work with children because they correlate directly with the natural endowment and maturation of the child in relation to another person. Indeed, the reciprocity and mutuality in the relationship between child and caregiver is likened to the growing therapeutic alliance between child and clinician.

Whether the child presents with a disruption or delay in development or with conflicts of the mind, he or she is viewed through the lens of developmental theory and play. Within the therapeutic alliance, these responsive and receptive venues for observation, exploration, and treatment help the clinical social worker determine which techniques, play objects, and symbolic metaphor are most useful in returning a particular child to a normal developmental pathway.

Therapeutic change gradually occurs over five identified stages of intervention: Biopsychosocial Assessment, Creation of Therapeutic Alliance, Identification of Narrative Themes, Developmental Growth and Change, and Termination. During these intervention stages, children feel supported as they initiate exploration and gain understanding of their internal and external worlds. As they progress through these intervention stages, children consolidate their therapeutic gains. They learn how to regulate actions that, heretofore, may have resulted in explosive outbursts or inappropriate self-regulation. Their style of relating to others is practiced both in and outside of therapy sessions as they relinquish previous dysfunctional patterns and test out new patterns. Their growing knowledge results from a new found ability to understand both their own mind and the mind of others. There is a more reflective and realistic sense of self and other. Finally, there is a rapprochement as the transition to therapeutic independence takes place.

BIBLIOGRAPHY

Addams, J. (1938). *Twenty years at Hull House*. New York: Macmillan.

Ainsworth, M., Blehar, M., Waters, E., and Wall, S. (1978). *Patterns of attachment: A psychological study of the strange situation*. New York: Basic Books.

Allen, A., Leonard, H., and Swedo, S. (1995). Current knowledge of medications for the treatment of childhood anxiety disorders. *Journal of the American Academy of Child and Adolescent Psychiatry,* 34: 8, 976–986.

Allen, F. (1942). *Psychotherapy with children*. New York: W.W. Norton.

Allen, J., and Berry, P. (1987). Sand play. *Elementary School Guidance and Counseling,* 21, 301–307.

———, and Brown, K. (1993). Jungian play therapy in elementary schools. *Elementary School Guidance and Counseling,* 28, 1, 30–41.

———, and Lawton-Speert, S. (1993). Play psychotherapy of a profoundly incest-abused boy: A Jungian approach. *International Journal of Play Therapy,* 2, 33–48.

Allyon, T., and Azin, N. (1968). *The token economy: A motivational system for therapy and rehabilitation*. New York: Appleton-Century Crofts.

Alter, C., and Evens, W. (1990). *Evaluating your practice: A guide to self assessment*. New York: Springer.

American Academy of Child and Adolescent Psychiatry. (1993). AACAP official action: Practice parameters for the assessment and treatment of anxiety disorders. *Journal of the American Academy of Child and Adolescent Psychiatry,* 32, 1089–1098.

American Psychiatric Association (APA). (1994). *Diagnostic and statistical manual of mental disorders, IV*. Washington, DC.

Anderson, E. (1997). Violence and the inner-city street code. In J. McCord, ed. *Violence and childhood in the inner-city*. New York: Cambridge University Press. pp. 1–30.

Angold, A. (1994). Clinical interviewing with children and adolescents. In M. Rutter, E. Taylor, and L. Hersov, eds. *Child and adolescent psychiatry: Modern approaches*. 3rd ed. Oxford: Blackwell Scientific Publications. pp. 51–63.

Anthony, E. (1964). Communicating therapeutically with the child. *Journal of Child Psychiatry,* 3, 106–125.

———. (1975). Influence of a manic-depressive environment on the child. In E. Anthony and T. Benedek, eds. *Depression and human existence*. Boston: Little, Brown. pp. 93–107.

———. (1986a). Terrorizing attacks on children by psychotic parents. *Journal of the American Academy of Child Psychiatry,* 25, 326–335.

———. (1986b). Contrasting neurotic styles in the analysis of two preschool children. *Journal of the American Academy of Child Psychiatry,* 25, 46–57.

———, and Cohler, B. (1987). *The invulnerable child*. New York: Guilford.

Applegate, J. and Bonovitz, J. (1995). *The facilitating partnership*. Northvale, NJ: Jason Aronson.

Arlow, J., and Kadis, A. (1976). Finger painting with children. In C. Schaefer, ed. *Therapeutic use of child's play*. New York: Jason Aronson. pp. 329–343.

Association for Exceptionality and Learning Disorders. (1988). *Checklist*. Toronto, Ontario, Canada: Association for Exceptionality and Learning Disorders.

Axline, V. (1947). *Play therapy: The inner dynamics of childhood*. Boston: Houghton-Mifflin.

Bandura, A. (1977). *Social learning theory*. Englewood Cliffs, NJ: Prentice-Hall.

Barkley, R. (1990). *Attention-deficit hyperactivity disorder: A handbook for diagnosis and treatment.* New York: Guilford.

———. (1996). Linkages between attention and executive functions. In G. Lyon and N. Krasnegor, eds. *Attention, memory, and executive function.* Baltimore, MD: Paul H. Brookes. pp. 307–325.

Barlow, K., Landreth, G., and Strother, J. (1985). Child-centered play therapy: Nancy from baldness to curls. *The School Counselor,* 34, 347–356.

Baron-Cohen, S. (1995). *Mindblindness.* Cambridge, MA: Massachusetts Institute of Technology.

Barth, R.(1986). *Social and cognitive treatment of children and adolescents.* San Francisco: Jossey-Bass.

———, (1994). Shared family care: Child protection and family preservation. *Social Work,* 39, 515–524.

Baumgaertel, A., Wolraich, M., and Dietrich, M. (1995). Comparison of diagnostic criteria for attention-deficit disorders in a German elementary school sample. *Journal of American Child and Adolescent Psychiatry,* 34, 629–638.

Beck, A. (1979). Cognitive therapy and the emotional disorders. New York: Meridian.

———, Rush, A., Shaw, B., and Emory, B. (1979). *Cognitive therapy of depression.* New York: Guilford.

———, Wright, F., Newman, C., and Leise, B. (1993). *Cognitive therapy of substance abuse.* New York: Guilford.

Bell, C., and Jenkins, E. (1993). Community violence and children on Chicago's Southside. In D. Reiss, J. Richters, M. Radke-Yarrow, and D. Scharff, eds. *Children and violence.* New York: Guilford. pp. 46–54.

Benedek, E. (1985). Children and psychic trauma: A brief review of contemporary thinking. In S. Eth and R. Pynoos, eds. *Post-traumatic stress disorder in children.* Washington, DC: American Psychiatric Association. pp. 3–16.

Benedek, T. (1959). Parenthood as a developmental phase: A contribution to the libido theory. *Journal of the American Psychoanalytic Association,* 7, 389–417.

———. (1970). The family as a psychologic field. In E. Anthony and T. Benedek, eds. *Parenthood: Its psychology and psychopathology.* Boston: Little, Brown. pp. 109–136.

Berlin, S. (1996). Constructivism and the environment: A cognitive-integrative perspective for social work practice. *Families in Society,* 77, 326–335.

Bettelheim, B. (1950). *Love is not enough.* New York: Free Press.

———. (1977). *The uses of enchantment: The importance and meaning of fairy tales.* New York: Vintage Books.

Biederman, J. (1987). Clonazepam in the treatment of prepubertal children with panic-like symptoms. *Journal of Clinical Psychiatry,* 48 (supplement), 38–42.

Biestek, F. (1957). *The casework relationship.* Chicago: Loyola University.

Biringen, Z. (1994). Attachment theory and research: Application to clinical practice. *American Journal of Orthopsychiatry,* 64: 404–420.

Bloom, M. (1984). *Configurations of human behavior: Lifespan development in social environments.* New York: Macmillan.

———, Fischer, J., and Orme, J. (1999). *Evaluating practice.* Boston: Allyn & Bacon.

Bowlby, J. (1969). *Attachment and loss: Attachment.* New York: Basic Books.

———. (1973a). *Attachment and loss: Separation.* New York: Basic Books.

———. (1973b). *Separation: Anxiety and anger.* London: Hogarth and Institute of Psychoanalysis.

———. (1980). *Attachment and loss: Loss.* New York: Basic Books.

————. (1982). Attachment and loss: Retrospect and prospect. *American Journal of Ortho-psychiatry*, 52: 664–678.

————. (1988). *A secure base: Clinical applications of attachment theory*. London: Routledge.

Boyd-Franklin, N. (1989). *Black families in therapy: A multisystems approach*. New York: Guilford.

Brandell, J. (1984). Stories and storytelling in child psychotherapy. *Psychotherapy*, 21, 454–462.

————. (1985). Using children's autogenic stories in dynamic clinical assessment. *Child & Adolescent Social Work Journal*, 2, 181–190.

Braswell, L., and Kendall, P. (1988). Cognitive-behavioral methods with children. In K. Dobson, ed. *Handbook of cognitive-behavioral therapy with ADHD children*. New York: Guilford. pp. 167–213.

Braukmann, C., and Wolf, M. (1987). Behaviorally-based group homes for juvenile offenders. In E. Morris and C. Braukmann, eds. *Behavioral approaches to crime and delinquency: A handbook of application, research, and concepts*. New York: Plenum Press. pp. 135–160.

Briere, J. (1992). *Child abuse trauma*. Newbury Park, CA: Sage.

Bromfield, R. (1995). The use of puppets in play therapy. *Child &Adolescent Social Work Journal*, 12, 435–444.

Bruner, J. (1966). *Toward a theory of instruction*. Cambridge: Harvard University.

————, Jolly, A., and Sylva, K. eds. (1976). *Play—Its role in development and evolution*. New York: Basic Books.

Burch, C. (1980). Puppet play in a thirteen-year-old boy: Remembering, repeating, and working through. *Clinical Social Work Journal*, 8, 79–89.

Burgess, A., Hartman, C., and McCormack, A. (1987). Abused to abuser: Antecedents of socially deviant behaviors. *American Journal of Psychiatry*, 144, 1431–1436.

Burman, S., and Allen-Meares, P. (1994). Neglected victims of murder: Children's witness to parental homicide. *Social Work*, 39, 28–34.

Burns, B. (1970). The use of play techniques in the treatment of children. *Child Welfare*, 49, 37–41.

Burton, C. (1986). "Peek-a-boo" to "All the, all the outs in free:" Hide-and-seek as a creative structure in drama therapy. *The Arts in Psychotherapy*, 13, 129–136.

Caplan, F,. and Caplan, T. (1973). *The power of play*. Garden City, NY: Anchor Books.

Carey, L. (1990). Sand-play therapy with a troubled child. *The Arts in Psychotherapy*, 17, 197–209.

Carter, S. (1987). Use of puppets to treat traumatic grief: A case study. *Elementary School Guidance and Counseling*, 21, 210–245.

Cassidy, J. (1988). Child-mother attachment and the self at age six. *Child Development*, 57, 331–337.

Castellanos, F., (1997a). Approaching a scientific understanding of what happens in the brain in AD/HD. *Attention*, summer, 30–35, 43.

————. (1997b). Neuro-imaging of Attention-Deficit Hyperactivity Disorder. *Child and Adolescent Psychiatric Clinics of North America*, 6, 383–411.

————. (1997c). Toward a psychopathology of Attention-Deficit Hyperactivity Disorder. *Clinical Pediatrics*, July, 381–393.

CHADD. (1999). *Report*. Landover, MD: Children and Adults with Attention-Deficit/Hyperactivity Disorder.

Chazan, S. (1995). *The simultaneous treatment of parent and child*. New York: Basic Books.

Chescheir, M. (1985). Some implications of Winnicott's concepts for clinical practice. *Clinical Social Work Journal*, 13, 218–233.

Chessick, R. (1993). *A dictionary for psychotherapists: Dynamic concepts in psychotherapy.* Northvale, NJ: Jason Aronson.

Chethik, M. (1989). *Techniques of child therapy: Psychodynamic strategies.* New York: Guilford.

Child Abuse Prevention and Treatment Act. (1984). Amended by Public Law 98-457, 98th Congress, 9 October.

Chodorow, N. (1978). *The reproduction of mothering.* Berkeley: University of California.

Chused, J. (1988). The transference neurosis in child analysis. *Psychoanalytic Study of the Child*, 43, 51–81.

Cicchetti, D. (1989). How research on child maltreatment has informed the study of child development: Perspectives from developmental psychopathology. In D. Cicchetti and V. Carlson, eds. *Maltreatment: Theory and research on the causes and consequences of child abuse and neglect.* New York: Cambridge University. pp. 377–431.

Coleman, J. (1976). Learning through games. In J. Bruner, A. Jolly, and K. Sylva, eds. *Play—Its role in development and evolution.* New York: Basic Books. pp. 460–465.

Compton, B., and Galloway, B. (1994). *Social work processes.* Pacific Grove, CA: Brooks/Cole.

Costantino, G. Malgady, R., and Rogler, L. (1986). Cuento therapy: A culturally sensitive modality for Puerto Rican children. *Journal of Consulting Clinical Psychology*, 54, 639–645.

———, and Malgady, R. (1996). Culturally sensitive treatment: Cuento and hero/heroine modeling therapies for Hispanic children and adolescents. In E. Hibbs and P. Jensen, eds. *Psychosocial treatments for child and adolescent disorders: Empirically-based strategies for clinical practice.* Washington, DC: American Psychological Association. pp. 639–669.

Costello, E., and Angold, A. (1995). Epidemiology. In J. March, ed., *Anxiety disorders in children and adolescents.* New York: Guilford. pp. 109–124.

Crittenden, P. (1992). Children's strategies for coping with adverse home environments: An interpretation using attachment theory. *Child Abuse and Neglect*, 16:3, 329–343.

Cummings, E., and Davies, P. (1994). *Children and marital conflict: The impact of family dispute and resolution.* New York: Guilford.

Curry, J., and Murphy, L. (1995). Comorbidity of anxiety disorders. In J. March, ed. *Anxiety disorders in children and adolescents.* New York: Guilford. pp. 301–320.

Daro, D. (1988). *Confronting child abuse: Research for effective program design.* New York: Free Press.

DeJong, P., and Berg, I. (1998). *Interviewing for solutions.* Pacific Grove, CA: Brooks Cole.

DeMulder, E., and Radke-Yarrow, M. (1991). Attachment in affectively ill and well mothers: Concurrent behavioral correlates. *Development and Psychopathology*, 3, 227–242.

Denckla, M. (1989). Executive functioning, the overlap zone between Attention-deficit hyperactivity disorder and learning disabilities. *International Pediatrics*, 4, 155–160.

———. (1996). A theory and model of executive functioning: A neuropsychological perspective. In G. Lyon and N. Krasnegor, eds. *Attention, memory, and executive function.* Baltimore, MD: Paul H. Brooks. pp. 263–278.

Dennison, S. (1989). *Twelve counseling programs for children at risk.* Springfield, IL: Charles C. Thomas.

Despert, J. (1948). Play therapy: Remarks on some of its aspects. *Nervous Child*, 7, 287–295.

de Young, M. (1982). *The sexual victimization of children.* Jefferson, NC: McFarland.

Digest of Educational Statistics. (1977). Washington, DC: National Center for Education Statistics, U.S. Department of Education.

DiLeo, J. (1970). *Young children and their drawings.* New York: Bruner/Mazel.

Dobson, K., and Block, L. (1988). Historical and philosophical bases of the cognitive-behavioral therapies. In K. Dobson, ed. *Handbook of cognitive-behavioral therapies*. New York: Guilford. pp. 3–38.

Donovan, D., and McIntyre, D. (1990). *Healing the hurt child*. New York: Norton.

Dryden, W., and Ellis, A. (1988). Rational emotive therapy. In K. Dobson, ed. *Handbook of cognitive-behavioral therapies*. New York: Guilford. pp. 214–272.

Dubrow, N., and Garbarino, J. (1989). Living in the war zone: Mothers and young children in a public-housing development. *Child Welfare, 68*, 3–19.

Eagle, R. (1994). The separation experience of children in long-term care: Theory, research, and implications for practice. *American Journal of Orthopsychiatry, 64*, 421–434.

Early, B. (1993). The healing magic of myth: Allegorical tales and the treatment of children of divorce. *Child & Adolescent Social Work Journal, 10*, 97–106.

Easterbrooks, A., and Goldberg, W. (1990). Security of toddler-parent attachment: Relation to children's sociopersonality functioning during kindergarten. In M. Greenberg and E. Cummings, eds. *Attachment in the preschool years*. Chicago: University of Chicago Press. pp. 221–244.

Edward, J. and Sanville, J. (1996). *Fostering healing and growth*. Northvale, NJ: Jason-Aronson.

Ehri, L. (1989). The development of spelling knowledge and its role in reading acquisition and reading disability. *Journal of Learning Disabilities, 22*, 356–365.

Eifermann, R. (1987). Children's games, observed and experienced. *Psychoanalytic Study of the Child, 42*, 127–144.

Elliott, D., Wilson, W., Huizinga, D., Sampson, R., Elliott, A., and Rankin, B. (1996). Effects of neighborhood disadvantage on adolescent development. *Journal of Research in Crime and Delinquency, 33*, 389–426.

Ellis, M. (1973). *Why people play*. Englewood Cliffs, NJ: Prentice-Hall.

———. (1979). The complexity of objects and peers. In B. Sutton-Smith, ed. *Play and learning*. New York: Gardner. pp. 157–174.

Erikson, E. (1950). *Childhood and society*. London: Hogarth.

———. (1959). *Identity and the life cycle*. New York: W.W. Norton.

———. (1977). *Toys and reasons*. New York: W.W. Norton.

Ervin, R., Bankert, C., and DuPaul, G. (1996). Treatment of attention-deficit/hyperactivity disorder. In M. Reineke, F. Dattilio, and A. Freeman. *Cognitive therapy with children and adolescents*. New York: Guilford. pp. 38–61.

Estrada, R. (1997). A broken brain. *Washington Post*. October 18, p. A23.

Evans, R., and Borenzweig, S. (1996). Early intervention for ADD. In A. Zelman, ed. *Early intervention for high-risk children*. New Jersey: Jason Aronson. pp. 85–102.

Faller, K. (1988). *Child sexual abuse*. New York: Columbia University.

Famularo, R., Kinscherff, R., and Fenton, T. (1990). Symptom differences in acute and chronic presentation of childhood posttraumatic stress disorder. *Child Abuse and Neglect, 14*, 439–444.

Finkelhor, D. (1984). *Child sexual abuse*. New York: The Free Press.

Fisch, J. (1984). Parenthood and the therapeutic alliance. In R. Cohen, B. Cohler, and S. Weissman, eds. *Parenthood: A psychodynamic perspective*. New York: Guilford. pp. 338–355.

Fischer, J,. and Corcoran, K. (1994). *Measures for clinical practice*. v. I. New York: The Free Press.

Fish, B., Marcus, J., and Hans, S. (1992). Infants at risk for schizophrenia: Sequelae of a generic neurointegrative defect. *Archives of General Psychiatry, 49*, 221–235.

Fleishner, J. (1994). Diagnosis and assessment of mathematics learning disabilities. In G. Lyon, ed. *Frames of reference for the assessment of learning disabilities: New views on measurement issues*. Baltimore, MD: Paul H. Brookes. pp. 441–458.

Fletcher, K. (1996). Childhood post-traumatic stress disorder. In E. Mash and R. Barkley, eds. *Child psychopathology.* New York: Guilford. pp. 242–276.

Fonagy, P. (1993). Psychoanalytic and empirical approaches to developmental psychopathology: An object-relations perspective. *Journal of American Psychoanalytic Association,* 41 (Supplement), 245–260.

———, Edgecumbe, R., Kennedy, H., and Target, M. (1993). The roles of mental representation and mental processes in therapeutic action. *Psychoanalytic Study of the Child, 48,* 9–48.

———. and Target, M. (1996). A contemporary psychoanalytical perspective: Psychodynamic developmental therapy. In E. Hibbs and P. Jensen, eds. *Psychosocial treatments for child and adolescent disorders: Empirically-based strategies for clinical practice.* Washington, DC: American Psychological Association. pp. 619–638.

Fraiberg, S. (1951). Clinical notes on the nature of transference in child analysis. *Psychoanalytic Study of the Child, 6,* 286–306.

———. (1954a). Counseling for the parents of the very young child. *Social Casework, 35,* 47–57.

———. (1954b). *Psychoanalytic principles in casework with children.* New York: Family Service Association of America.

———. (1954c). Tales of the discovery of the secret treasure. *Psychoanalytic Study of the Child, 9,* 218–241.

———. (1959). *The magic years.* New York: Scribner and Sons.

———. (1961). Case consultation with E. Timberlake.

———. (1962). A therapeutic approach to reactive ego disturbances in children in placement. *American Journal of Orthopsychiatry, 32,* 18–31.

———. (1966). Further considerations of the role of transference in latency. *Psychoanalytic Study of the Child, 21,* 213–236.

———. (1980). *Child studies in infant mental health: The first year of life.* New York: Basic Books.

———, Adelson, E., and Shapiro, V. (1975). Ghosts in the Nursery. *Journal of the American Academy of Child Psychiatry, 14,* 387–421.

Franzke, E. (1989). *Fairy tales in psychotherapy.* Toronto: Hogrefe and Huber.

Fraser, M. ed. (1997). *Risk and resilience in childhood.* Washington, DC: National Association of Social Workers.

Freedman, J., and Combs, G. (1996). *Narrative therapy: The social construction of preferred realities.* New York: Norton.

Freud, A. (1946). The role of transference in the analysis of children. *Psychoanalytic treatment of children.* London: Imago. pp. 79–93.

———. (1963). Concept of developmental lines. *Psychoanalytic Study of the Child, 18,* 245–265.

———. (1965). *Normality and pathology in childhood.* New York: International Universities.

———. (1966). *The ego and the mechanisms of defense.* New York: International Universities.

———. (1970). *The writings of A. Freud: The infantile neurosis.* Vol. VII. New York: International Universities.

Freud, S. (1908). Creative writers and daydreaming. In J. Strachey, ed. *Standard edition of the complete works of Sigmund Freud.* Vol. IX. London: Hogarth and the Institute of Psychoanalysis, 1953. pp. 171–181.

———. (1914). Remembering, repeating, and working through. In J. Strachey, ed. *Standard edition of the complete works of Sigmund Freud.* Vol. XII. London: Hogarth and the Institute of Psychoanalysis, 1953. pp. 143–153.

————. (1933). New introductory lectures on psycho-analysis. In J. Strachey, ed. *Standard edition of the complete works of Sigmund Freud.* Vol. XXII. London: Hogarth and the Institute of Psychoanalysis, 1953.

Furman, E. (1986). On trauma: When is the death of a parent traumatic? *Psychoanalytic Study of the Child,* 41, 191–209.

————. (1996). Bereavement of the grade-school child. In M. Lewis. *Childhood and adolescent psychiatry.* Baltimore, MD: Williams & Wilkins. pp. 1066–1073.

Gabor, P., and Grinnell, R. (1994). *Evaluation and quality improvement in the human services.* Boston: Allyn & Bacon.

Gambrill, E. (1994). Concepts and methods of behavioral treatment. In D. Granvold, ed. *Cognitive and behavioral treatment.* Pacific Grove, CA: Brooks Cole. pp. 32–62.

————. (1995). Behavioral social work: Past, present and future. *Research on Social Work Practice,* 5, 460–484.

Gardner, R. (1971). *Therapeutic communications with children.* New York: Science.

————. (1976). Mutual storytelling technique. In C. Schaefer, ed. *Therapeutic use of child's play.* New York: Jason Aronson. pp. 313–322.

Garot, P. (1986). Therapeutic play: Work of both child and nurse. *Journal of Pediatric Nursing,* 1, 111–115.

Gaston, L. (1990). The concept of the alliance and its role in psychotherapy: Theoretical and empirical consideration. *Psychotherapy,* 27, 143–153.

————. (1991). Reliability and criterion-related validity of the California Psychotherapy Alliance Scales—patient version. *Psychological Assessment,* 3, 68–74.

Geddes, M., and Pajik, A. (1990). A multidimensional typology of countertransference responses. *Clinical Social Work Journal,* 18, 257–272.

Gelso, C., and Carter, J. (1985). The relationship in counseling and psychotherapy: Components, consequences, and theoretical antecedents. *Counseling Psychologist,* 2, 155–243.

George, H. (1988). Child therapy and animals. In C. Schaefer, ed. *Innovative interventions in child and adolescent therapy.* New York: John Wiley & Sons. pp. 400–418.

Gil, E. (1991). *The healing power of play.* New York: Guilford.

Gilligan, C. (1982). *In a different voice: Psychological theory and women's development.* Cambridge, MA: Harvard University.

Gold, E. (1986). Long-term effects of sexual victimization in childhood: An attributional approach. *Journal of Consulting and Clinical Psychology,* 54, 471–475.

Goldberg, S. (1993). Early attachment: A passing fancy or a long-term affair? *Canadian Psychology,* 34, 307–314.

Goldstein, H. (1990). Strength or pathology: Ethical and rhetorical contrasts in approaches to practice. *Families in Society,* 7, 267–275.

Gonick, R. and Gold, M. (1992). Fragile attachments: Expressive arts therapy with children in foster care. *Arts in Psychotherapy,* 18, 433–440.

————. (1996). Constructivist psychotherapy. *Families in Society,* 77, 345–359.

Granvold, D. (1996). Constructivist psychotherapy. *Families in Society,* 77, 345–359.

Grayer, E. and Sax, P. (1986). A model for the diagnostic and therapeutic use of countertransference. *Clinical Social Work Journal,* 14, 295–309.

Green, A. (1985). Children traumatized by physical abuse. In S. Eth and R. Pynoos, eds. *Post-traumatic stress disorder in children.* Washington, DC: American Psychiatric Association. pp. 135–154.

Greenacre, P. (1959). Play in relation to creative imagination. *Psychoanalytic Study of the Child,* 14, 61–80.

Greenberg, L., and Horvath, A. (1991). The role of the therapeutic alliance in psychotherapy research. Paper presented at the annual meeting of the Society for Psychotherapy Research. Lyon, France.

Greenson, R. (1965). The working alliance and the transference neurosis. *Psychoanalytic Quarterly*, 34, 155–181.

Hales, R., and Yudofsky, S. (1987). *The American psychiatric press textbook of neuropsychiatry.* Washington, DC: American Psychiatric Association.

Hamilton, G. (1947). *Psychotherapy in child guidance.* New York: Columbia University.

Hartley, R., and Goldenson, R. (1963). *Children's play.* New York: Thomas Crowell.

————, Frank, L., and Goldenson, R. (1964). The benefits of water play. In M. Haworth, ed. *Child psychotherapy: Practice and theory.* New York: Basic Books. pp. 364–368.

Hartmann, H. (1939). *Ego psychology and the problem of adaptation.* New York: International Universities. 1958 translation.

Haworth, M., and Keller, M. (1964). The use of food in therapy. In M. Haworth, ed. *Child psychotherapy: Practice and theory. New York: Basic Books.* pp. 330–338.

Herman, J. (1992). *Trauma and recovery.* New York: Basic Books.

Hibbs, E., and Jensen, P. (1996). *Psychosocial treatments for child and adolescent disorders: Empirically-based strategies for clinical practice.* Washington, DC: American Psychological Association.

Hollis, F. (1939). *Social casework in practice: Six case studies.* New York: Family Welfare Association of America.

Hooper, S., Montgomery, J., Swartz, C., Reed, M. Sandler, A., Levine, M., Watson, T., and Wasileski, T. (1994). Measurement of written language. In G. Lyon, ed. *Frames of reference for the assessment of learning disabilities: New views on measurement issues.* Baltimore, MD: Paul H. Brookes. pp. 375–418.

Hortacsu, N., Cesur, S., and Oral, A. (1993). Relationship between depression and attachment styles in parent- and institution-reared Turkish children. *Journal of Genetic Psychology*, 154, 329–337.

Horvath, A., and Symonds, B. (1991). Relations between working alliance and outcome in psychotherapy: A meta-analysis. *Journal of Clinical and Consulting Psychology*, 38, 139–149.

Institute of Medicine. (1989). *Research on children and adolescents with mental, behavioral, and developmental disorders.* Washington, DC: National Academy of Science.

Jacobson, E. (1964). *The self and the object world.* New York: International Universities.

James, B. (1989). *Treating traumatized children.* Lexington, MA: Lexington Books.

Johnson, K. (1989). *Trauma in the lives of children.* Claremont, CA: Hunter House.

Johnson-Powell, G., and Yamamoto, J. (1997). *Transcultural child development.* New York: John Wiley & Sons.

Jordan, C., and Franklin, C. (1995). *Clinical assessment for social workers: Quantitative and qualitative methods.* Chicago: Lyceum Books.

Kagan, R., and Schlossberg, S. (1989). *Families in perpetual crisis.* New York: W.W. Norton.

Kashani, J., and Orvaschel, H. (1990). A community study of anxiety in children and adolescents. *American Journal of Psychiatry*, 147, 313–318.

Keith, C. and Chansky, T. (1991). Considering cognition in anxiety-disordered children. *Journal of Anxiety Disorders*, 5, 167–185.

————, (1995). Psychodynamic psychotherapy. In J. March, ed. *Anxiety disorders in children and adolescents.* New York: Guilford Press. pp. 386–400.

Kendall-Tackett, K. Meyer-Williams, L., and Finkelhor, D. (1993). Impact of sexual abuse in children: A review and synthesis of recent empirical studies. *Psychological Bulletin*, 113, 164–180.

Khan, M. (1963). The concept of cumulative trauma. *Psychoanalytic Study of the Child*, 18, 286–306.

Kiresuk, T., Smith, A., and Cardillo, J. (1993). *Goal attainment scaling: Application, theory, and measurement*. New York: Erlbaum.

Kirk, S. and Kirk, W. (1971). *Prolinguistic learning disabilities: Diagnosis and remediation*. Chicago, IL: University of Chicago Press.

———, and Chalfant, J. (1984). *Academic and developmental learning disabilities*. Columbus, OH: Love Publishing.

———, (1999). *Social work research methods*. Washington, DC: NASW.

Klein, M. (1950). *Symposium on child analysis: Contributions to psychoanalysis, 1921–1945, of Melanie Klein*. London: Hogarth.

Klein, R., and Last, C. (1989). Anxiety disorders in children. *Developmental Clinical Psychology and Psychiatry*, 20, 76–83.

Klem, P. (1992). The use of the dollhouse as an effective disclosure technique. *International Journal of Play Therapy*, 1, 69–73.

Kluckhohn, F., and Strodtbeck, F. (1961). *Variations in value orientation*. Evanston, IL: Rowe, Peterson.

Kluft, R. (1985). Childhood multiple personality disorder: Predictors, clinical findings, and treatment results. In R. Kluft, ed. *Childhood antecedents of multiple personality disorder*. Washington, DC: American Psychiatric Association.

Knell, S. and Moore, D. (1990). Cognitive-behavioral play therapy in the treatment of encopresis. *Journal of Clinical Child Psychology*, 19, 55–60.

———, (1996). *Cognitive-behavioral play therapy*. Northvale, NJ: Jason Aronson.

Kramer, E. (1971). *Art as therapy with children*. New York: Schocken.

Kuhli, L. (1983). Use of two houses in play therapy. In C. Schaefer and K. O'Connor, eds. *Handbook of play therapy*. New York: John Wiley and Sons. pp. 274–280.

Kutcher, S., Reiter, S., and Gardner, D. (1995). Pharmacotherapy: Approaches and applications. In J. March, ed. *Anxiety disorders in children and adolescents*. New York: Guilford. pp. 341–385.

Laird, J. (1994). Thick description revisited: Family therapist as anthropologist-constructivist. In E. Sherman and W. Reid, eds. *Qualitative research in social work*. New York: Columbia. pp. 71–88.

Lambert, M., Shapiro, D., and Bergin, A. (1986). The effectiveness of psychotherapy. In S. Garfield and A. Bergin, eds. *Handbook of psychotherapy and behavior change*. New York: John Wiley and Sons. pp. 157–212.

Last, C., Hersen, M., Kazdin, A., Finkelstein, R., and Strauss, C. (1987). Comparison of *DSM III* separation anxiety and overanxious disorders: Demographic characteristics and patterns of comorbidity. *Journal of the American Academy of Child Psychiatry*, 26, 527–531.

———, Perrin, S., and Hersen, M. (1992). *DSM III-R* anxiety disorders in children: Sociodemographic and clinical characteristics. *Journal of the American Academy of Child and Adolescent Psychiatry*, 31, 1070–1076.

Lazarus, R., and Folkman, S. (1984). *Stress, appraisal, and coping*. New York: Springer.

LeVieux, J. (1994). Terminal illness and death of father: Case of Celeste, age 5 1/2. In N. Webb, *Helping bereaved children: A handbook for practitioners*. New York: Guilford. pp. 81–95.

Levin, M., Ashmore-Callahan, S., Kendall, P., and Ichii, M. (1996). Treatment of separation anxiety disorder. In M. Reinecke, F. Dattilio, and A. Freeman. *Cognitive therapy with children and adolescents*. New York: Guilford. pp. 153–174.

Lewin, K. (1964). *Field theory in social science*. New York: Harper Torchbook.

Lewis, M. (1982). *Clinical aspects of child development*. Philadelphia: Lea & Febinger.

———. (1991). *Child and adolescent psychiatry*. Baltimore, MD: Williams & Wilkins.

———, Lewis, D., and Schonfeld, D. (1996). Dying and death in childhood and adolescence. In M. Lewis. *Childhood and adolescent psychiatry*. Baltimore, MD: Williams & Wilkins. pp. 1066–1073.

Lieberman, A. and Pawl, J. (1990). Disorders of attachment and secure base behavior in the second year of life: Conceptual issues and clinical intervention. In M. Greenberg, M. Cicchetti, and E. Cummings. *Attachment in the preschool years: Theory, research, and intervention*. Chicago: University of Chicago.

———, and Zeanah, C. (1995). Disorders of attachment. In K. Minde, ed. *Infant psychiatry: Child and adolescent clinics of North America*. Philadelphia: Lippincott. pp. 571–588.

Lieberman, F. (1979). *Social work with children*. New York: Human Sciences.

Litoff, S. (1959). The use of food in the treatment of children. *Smith College Studies in Social Work*, 9, 189–203.

Littner, N. (1956). *Some traumatic effects of separation and placement*. New York: Child Welfare League of America.

———. (1969). The caseworker's self-observation and the child's interpersonal defenses. *Smith College Studies in Social Work*, 39, 95–117.

Livingston, R. (1991). Anxiety disorders. In M. Lewis, ed. *Child and adolescent psychiatry*. Baltimore, MD: Williams & Wilkins. pp. 673–685.

Lloyd, K. (1978). A treatment framework for use of food as a therapeutic tool. In E. Timberlake, *Social work treatment of children*. Washington, DC: National Catholic School of Social Service, The Catholic University of America.

Loewald, E. (1987). Therapeutic play in space and time. *Psychoanalytic Study of the Child*, 42, 173–192.

Loomis, E. (1964). Use of checkers in handling certain resistances in child therapy and child analysis. In M. Haworth, ed. *Child psychotherapy: Practice and theory*. New York: Basic Books. pp. 407–414.

Lorion, R., and Saltzman, W. (1993). Children's exposure to community violence: Following a path from concern to research to action. In D. Reiss, J. Richters, M. Radke-Yarrow, and D. Scharff. *Children and violence*. New York: Guilford. pp. 55–65.

Lowenfeld, M. (1935). *Play in childhood*. London: Victor Gollancz.

Lynn, S., and Rhue, J. (1994). *Dissociation: Clinical and theoretical perspectives*. New York: Guilford.

Lyon, G. (1995). Toward a definition of dyslexia. *Annals of Dyslexia*, 45, 3–27.

———, Connell, D., Grunebaum, H., and Botein, S. (1990). Infants at social risk: Maternal depression and family support services as mediators of infant development and security of attachment. *Child Development*, 61, 85–98.

———, Repacholi, B., McLeod, S., and Silva, E. (1991). Disorganized attachment behavior in infancy: Short-term stability, maternal and infant correlates, and risk-related subtypes. *Development and Psychopathology*, 3, 377–396.

Lyons-Ruth, K. (1996). Attachment relationships among children with aggressive behavior problems: The role of disorganized early attachment patterns. *Journal of Consulting and Clinical Psychology*, 64,: 64–73.

Machler, T. (1965). Pinocchio in the treatment of school phobia. *Bulletin of the Menninger Clinic*, 29, 212–219.

Mahler, M., Pine, F., and Bergman, A. (1975). *The psychological birth of the human infant*. New York: Basic Books.

Main, M., and George, C. (1985). Responses of abused and disadvantaged toddlers to distress in agemates: A study in the daycare setting. *Developmental Psychology,* 21, 407–412.

———, and Solomon, J. (1990). Procedures for identifying infants as disorganized/disoriented during the Ainsworth Strange Situation. In M. Greenberg, D. Cicchetti, and E. Cummings, eds. *Attachment in the preschool years.* Chicago: University of Chicago. pp. 121–160.

Malmquist, C. (1986). Children who witness parental murder: Post-traumatic aspects. *Journal of the American Academy of Child Psychiatry,* 25, 320–325.

March, J., Johnston, H., and Jefferson, J. (1990). Do subtle neurological impairments predict treatment resistance in children and adolescents with obsessive-compulsive disorder? *Journal of Child and Adolescent Psychopharmacology,* 1, 133–140.

———. (1995). ed. *Anxiety disorders in children and adolescents.* New York: Guilford.

Marks, I. (1987). *Fears, phobias, and rituals.* New York: Oxford University.

Martinez, P., and Richters, J. (1993). The NIMH Community Violence Project: II. Children's distress symptoms associated with violence exposure. In D. Reiss, J. Richters, M. Radke-Yarrow, and D. Scharff. *Children and violence.* New York: Guilford. pp. 22–35.

Maughan, B., and Yule, W. (1994). Reading and other learning disabilities. In M. Rutter, E. Taylor, and L. Hersov, eds. *Child and adolescent psychiatry: Modern approaches.* Oxford, England: Blackwell. pp. 647–665.

Mayes, L., and Cohen, D. (1994). Experiencing self and others: Autism and psychoanalytic social development theory. *Journal of the American Psychoanalytic Association,* 42, 191–218.

McCall, R. (1979). Stages in play development between zero and two years of age. In B. Sutton-Smith, ed. *Play and learning.* New York: Gardiner. pp. 35–44.

McCord, J. (1997). Placing American urban violence in context. In J. McCord, ed. *Violence and childhood in the inner city.* Cambridge, UK: Cambridge University. pp. 78–115.

Meeks, J. (1970). Children who cheat at games. *Journal of the American Academy of Child Psychiatry,* 9, 157–170.

Meichenbaum, D. (1971). Examination of model characteristics in reducing avoidance behavior. *Journal of Personality and Social Psychology,* 17, 298–307.

———. (1979). Teaching children self control. In B. Lahey and A. Kazdin, eds. *Advances in child clinical psychology,* v. 2. New York: Plenum. pp. 1–33.

Meyer, W. (1993). In defense of long-term treatment: On the vanishing holding environment. *Social Work,* 38, 571–578.

Miles, M., and Huberman, A. (1994). *Qualitative data analysis.* Newbury Park, CA: Sage Publications.

Miller, A. (1981). *Prisoners of childhood.* New York: Basic Books.

Miller, J. (1976). *Toward a new psychology of women.* Boston: Beacon.

———. (1991). The development of women's sense of self. In V. Jordan, A. Kaplan, J. Miller, I. Stiver, and J. Surrey, eds. *Women's growth in connection.* New York: Guilford. pp. 11–26.

Milos, M. and Reiss, S. (1982). Effects of three play conditions on separation and anxiety in young children. *Journal of Counseling and Consulting Psychology,* 50, 389–395.

Mishne, J. (1983). *Clinical work with children.* New York: Free Press.

Morrissette, P. (1999). Post-traumatic stress disorder in childhood sexual abuse: A synthesis and analysis of theoretical models. *Child & Adolescent Social Work Journal,* 16, 77–99.

Moustakas, C. (1953). *Children in play therapy.* New York: McGraw-Hill.

National Association of Social Workers (NASW). (1996). *Code of ethics.* Washington, DC: National Association of Social Workers.

National Center on Child Abuse and Neglect. (1988). *U.S. 1986 National incidence and prevalence study.* Washington, DC: US Department of Health and Human Services.

————, (1995). *Current trends in child abuse reporting and fatalities: 1994 survey.* Washington, DC: National Center on Child Abuse and Neglect.

National Center on Child Abuse Prevention. (1998). Research of the National Committee to Prevent Child Abuse. *Current trends in child abuse reporting and fatalities: The results of the 1997 annual fifty state survey.* Chicago, IL: National Committee to Prevent Child Abuse.

National Research Council (1993). *Understanding child abuse and neglect.* Washington, DC: National Academy of Science.

Neuwirth, S. (1993). *Learning disabilities.* Washington, DC: U.S. Department of Health and Human Services, Public Health Service, National Institute of Health, National Institute of Mental Health, NIH Publication NO. 93–3611.

————. (1994). *Attention-deficit hyperactivity disorder.* Washington, DC: U.S. Department of Health and Human Services, Public Health Service, National Institute of Health, National Institute of Mental Health, NIH Publication No. 93–3572.

Nickerson, E. and Inhelder, B. (1969). *The psychology of the child.* New York: Basic Books.

————. (1973). Psychology of play and play therapy in classroom activities. *Educating Children,* 1, 1–6.

————. (1983). Art as a play therapeutic medium. In C. Schaefer and K. O'Connor, eds. *Handbook of play therapy.* New York: John Wiley & Sons. pp. 234–250.

————. and O'Laughlin, K. (1983). Therapeutic use of games. In C. Schaefer and K. O'Connor, eds. *Handbook of play therapy.* New York: John Wiley & Sons. pp. 174–188.

Noshpitz, J. and King, R. eds. (1991). *Pathways of growth: Normal development.* New York: John Wiley & Sons.

———— (1993). Personal communication with M. Cutler.

Nurius, P., and Berlin, S. (1994). Treatment of negative self-concept and depression. In G. Granvold, ed. *Cognitive and behavioral treatment.* Pacific Grove, CA: Brooks Cole.

Oaklander, V. (1988). *Windows to our children.* Highland, NY: Center for Gestalt Development.

Oster, G., and Gould, P. (1987). *Using drawings in assessment and therapy: A guide for mental health professionals.* New York: Brunner/Mazel.

Oxley, G. (1971). A life model approach to change. *Social Casework,* 2, 627–633.

Par, M. (1990). Sand and water play: A case study. *Association for Play Therapy Newsletter,* 9, 4–6.

Pavlov, I. (1927). *Conditioned reflexes.* New York: Liveright.

Peccora, P., Fraser, M., and Haapala, D. (1992). Intensive home-based family preservation services: Update from the FIT Project. *Child Welfare,* LXXI, 2, 177–188.

Peirce, K. and Edwards, E. (1988). Children's construction of fantasy stories: Gender differences in conflict resolution strategies. *Sex Roles,* 18, 393–404.

Perlman, H. (1957). *Social casework: A problem-solving process.* Chicago: University of Chicago.

————. (1979). *Relationship: The heart of helping people.* Chicago: University of Chicago.

Persons, J. (1989). *Cognitive therapy in practice.* New York: Norton.

Phillips, E. (1968). Achievement place: Token reinforcement procedures in home-style rehabilitation setting for "predelinquent" boys. *Journal of Applied Behavior Analysis,* 3, 213–223.

Piaget, J. (1952). *The origins of intelligence in children.* New York: International Universities.

————. (1954). *The construction of reality in the child.* New York: Basic Books.

————. (1969). *The mechanisms of perception.* New York: Basic Books.

———. (1976). Rules of the game of marbles. In J. Bruner, A. Jolly, and K. Sylva, eds. *Play— Its role in development and evolution*. New York: Basic Books. pp. 413–441.

Pine, F. (1980). On phase-characteristic pathology of the school-age child: Disturbances of personality development and organization (borderline conditions) of learning and behavior. In S. Greenspan and G. Pollack, eds. *The course of life, vol. II: Latency, adolescence, and youth*. Washington, DC: U.S. Department of Health and Human Services Publication No. (AOM) 80–999. pp. 165–204.

Polansky, N., Hally, C., and Polansky, N. (1975). *A profile of neglect: A survey of the state of knowledge of child neglect*. Washington, DC: Community Services Administration, Department of Health, Education, and Welfare.

———, Chalmers, M., Buttenweiser, F., and Williams, D. (1981). *Damaged parents*. Chicago: University of Chicago.

Pynoos, R., and Eth, S. (1985a). Developmental perspective in psychic trauma in childhood. In C. Figley, ed. *Trauma and its wake*, v. 1. New York: Brunner/Mazel. pp. 36–52.

———, and Eth, S. (1985b). Children traumatized by witnessing acts of personal violence: Homicide, rape, or suicide behavior. In S. Eth and R. Pynoos, eds. *Post-traumatic stress disorder in children*. Washington, DC: American Psychiatric Association. pp. 19–43.

———, Frederick, C., Nader, K., Arroyo, W., Steinberg, A., Eth, S., Nunez, F., and Fairbanks, L. (1987). Life threat and posttraumatic stress in school-age children. *Archives of General Psychiatry*, 44, 1057–1062.

Rapoport, J. (1989). *The boy who couldn't stop washing*. Washington, DC: American Psychiatric Association.

Reeves, J., and Boyett, N. (1983). What does children's art work tell us about gender? *Qualitative Sociology*, 6, 322–333.

Reinecke, M., Dattilio, F., and Freeman, A. (1996). *Cognitive therapy with children and adolescents*. New York: Guilford.

Richmond, M. (1917). *Social diagnosis*. New York: Russell Sage Foundation.

Richters, J. (1993). Community violence and children's development: Toward a research agenda for the 1990s. In D. Reiss, J. Richters, M. Radkke-Yarrow, and D. Scharff. *Children and violence*. New York: Guilford Press. pp. 3–6.

———, and Martinez, P. (1993). The NIMH Community Violence Project: I. Children as victims of and witnesses to violence. In D. Reiss, J. Richters, M. Radke-Yarrow, and D. Scharff. *Children and violence*. New York: Guilford. pp. 7–21.

Robinson, V. (1936). *Supervision in social casework*. Chapel Hill, NC: University of North Carolina.

Rogers, C. (1951). *Client-centered therapy*. Boston: Houghton Mifflin.

Ronen, T., Wozner, Y., and Rahav, G. (1992). Cognitive intervention in enuresis. *Child and Family Behavior Therapy*, 14, 1–14.

Rossman, B. (1992). School-age children's perceptions of coping with distress: Strategies for emotion regulation and the moderation of adjustment. *Journal of Child Psychology and Psychiatry*, 33, 1373–1397.

Rubin, A., and Babbie, E. (1997). *Research methods for social work*. Belmont, CA: Brooks Cole.

Saari, C. (1986). The use of metaphor in therapeutic communication with young adolescents. *Child & Adolescent Social Work Journal*, 3, 15–25.

Safran, J., Crocker, P., McMain, S., and Murray, P. (1990). Therapeutic alliance rupture as a therapy event for empirical investigation. *Psychotherapy*, 27, 154–165.

Saleebey, D. (1996). The strengths perspective in social work practice: Extensions and cautions. *Social Work*, 41, 296–305.

———. (1997). *Strengths perspective in social work practice*. New York: Longman.

Salladin, L., and Timberlake, E. (1995). Assessing clinical progress: A case study of Daryl. *Child & Adolescent Social Work Journal*, 12, 289–316.

Sampson, R., and Groves, W. (1989). Community structure and crime: Testing social-disorganization theory. *American Journal of Sociology*, 94, 774–802.

———. (1997). The embeddedness of child and adolescent development: A community-level perspective on urban violence. In J. McCord, ed. *Violence and childhood in the inner city*. Cambridge, UK: Cambridge University. pp. 31–77.

Samuels, S. (1995). Helping foster children to mourn past relationships. *Psychoanalytic Study of the Child*, 50, 308–325.

Sandler, J., and Rosenblatt, B. (1962). The concept of the representational world. *Psychoanalytic Study of the Child*, 17, 128–145.

———, Holder, A., and Meers, D. (1963). The ego ideal and the ideal self. *Psychoanalytic Study of the Child*, 18, 139–158.

———, Kennedy, H., and Tyson, R. (1975). Discussions on transference. *Psychoanalytic Study of the Child*, 30, 409–441.

———. (1980). *The technique of child psychoanalysis: Discussions with Anna Freud*. Boston: Harvard University.

———; with Freud, A. (1985). *The analysis of defense: The ego and mechanisms of defense revisited*. New York: International Universities.

Sanville, J. (1991). *The playground of psychoanalytic therapy*. Hillsdale, NJ: Analytic Press.

Schaefer, C. (1980). Play therapy. In G. Sholevar, R. Benson, and B. Blinder, eds. *Emotional disorders in children and adolescents*. New York: Spectrum. pp. 95–105.

Schwab-Stone, M., Ayers, T., Kasprow, W., Voyce, W., Barone, C., Shriver, T., and Weissberg, R. (1995). No safe haven: A study of school violence exposure in an urban community. *Journal of the American Academy of Child and Adolescent Psychiatry*, 34, 1343–1352.

Seligman, M., and Darling, R. (1989). *Ordinary families, special children*. New York: Guilford Press.

Shakoor, B., and Chalmers, D. (1991). Co-victimization of African-American children who witness violence: Effects on cognitive, emotional, and behavioral development. *Journal of the National Medical Association*, 83, 233–238.

Shanahan, J., and Morgan, M. (1989). Television as a diagnostic indicator in child therapy: An exploratory study. *Child & Adolescent Social Work Journal*, 6, 175–192.

Shapiro, V., and Gisynski, M. (1989). Ghosts in the nursery revisited. *Child & Adolescent Social Work Journal*, 6, 18–37.

Silver, L. (1976). The playroom diagnostic evaluation of children with neurologically-based learning disabilities. *Journal of Child Psychiatry*, 15, 240–256.

Simcha-Fagan, O., and Schwartz, J. (1986). Neighborhood and delinquency: An assessment of contextual effects. *Criminology*, 24, 667–704.

Simeon, J., Ferguson, H., and Knott, V. (1992). Clinical, cognitive, and neurophysiological effects of alprazolam in children and adolescents with overanxious and avoidant disorders. *Journal of the American Academy of Child and Adolescent Psychiatry*, 31, 29–33.

Simon, B. (1960). *Relationship between theory and practice in social work*. New York: National Association of Social Workers.

Singer, D., and Singer, J. (1990). *The house of make-believe: Children's play and developmental imagination*. Cambridge, MA: Harvard University.

Skinner, B. (1953). *Science and human behavior*. New York: McMillan.

Smith, C. (1991). *Learning disabilities: The interaction of learner, task, and setting*. Boston, MA: Allyn & Bacon.

Solnit, A. (1987). A psychoanalytic view of play. *Psychoanalytic Study of the Child*, 42, 205–219.

Speece, M., and Brent, S. (1984). Children's understanding of death: A review of three components of a death concept. *Child Development*, 55, 1671–1686.

Spitz, R., and Wolff, P. (1946). The smiling response: A contribution to the ontogenesis of social relations. *Genetic Psychology Monographs*, 34, 57–125.

Stallings, P., and March, J. (1995). Assessment. In J. March, ed. *Anxiety disorders in children and adolescents*. New York: Guilford. pp. 125–149.

Stern, D. (1995). *The motherhood constellation*. New York: Basic Books.

Strauss, C., Lease, C., and Last, C. (1988). Overanxious disorder: An examination of developmental differences. *Journal of Abnormal Child Psychology*, 16, 433–443.

Strub, R., and Black, F. (1980). *The Mental Status Exam in neurology*. Philadelphia: F. A. Davis.

Strupp, H. (1960). *Psychotherapists in action: Explorations of the therapist's contribution to the treatment process*. New York: Grune & Stratton.

Stuart, R. (1996). Behavior modification: A technology of social change. In F. Turner, ed. *Social work treatment: Interlocking theoretical approaches*. New York: Free Press. pp. 400–419.

Surrey, J. (1991). The "self-in-relation:" A theory of women's development. In V. Jordan, A. Kaplan, J. Miller, I. Stiver, and J. Surrey, eds. *Women's growth in connection*. New York: Guilford. pp. 51–66.

Sutton-Smith, B. (1979). Ed. *Play and learning*. New York: Gardiner.

———. (1986). *Toys as culture*. New York: Gardiner.

Szatmari, P. (1992). The epidemiology of attention-deficit hyperactivity disorder. *Child and Adolescent Psychiatric Clinics of North America*, 1, 361–371.

Taft, J. (1933). *The dynamics of therapy in a controlled relationship*. New York: Macmillan.

Tait, D., and Depta, J. (1994). Play therapy group for bereaved children. In N. Webb. *Helping bereaved children: A handbook for practitioners*. New York: Guilford. pp. 169–185.

Target, M., and Fonagy, P. (1994). The efficacy of psychoanalysis for children with emotional disorders. *Journal of the American Academy of Child and Adolescent Psychiatry*, 33, 361–371.

Taylor, E. (1994). Syndromes of attention deficit and overactivity. In M. Rutter, E. Taylor, and L. Hersov, eds. *Child and adolescent psychiatry: Modern approachess*. Oxford: Blackwell Scientific Publications. pp. 285–307.

Taylor, R., Gottfredson, S., and Brower, S. (1984). Block crime and fear: Defensible space, local social ties, and territorial functioning. *Journal of Research in Crime and Delinquency*, 21, 303–331.

Terr, L. (1985). Psychic trauma in children and adolescents. *Psychiatric Clinics of North America*, 8, 815–835.

———. (1991a). Forbidden games: Post-traumatic children's play. *Journal of the American Academy of Child Psychiatry*, 20, 741–759.

———. (1991b). Childhood trauma: An outline and overview. *American Journal of Psychiatry*, 148, 10–20.

———. (1991c). Acute responses to external events and posttraumatic stress disorders. In M. Lewis. *Childhood and adolescent psychiatry*. Baltimore, MD: Williams & Wilkins. pp. 755–766.

Tharinger, D. (1990). Impact of child sexual abuse on developing sexuality. *Professional Psychology: Research and Practice*, 21, 331–337.

The Economist. (October 3, 1998). Crime in America, 35–38.

Thomas, A., and Chess, S. (1977). *Temperament and development*. New York: Brunner/Mazel.

———. (1986). *Temperament in clinical practice*. New York: Guilford.

Thorndike, E. (1933). *An experimental study of rewards*. New York: Teachers College.

Thyer, B. (1989). *Behavioral family therapy.* Springfield, IL: Charles C. Thomas.

———, and Wodarski, J. (1990). Social learning theory: Toward a comprehensive conceptual framework for social work education. *Social Service Review,* 37, 144–152.

Timberlake, E. (1978a). *Social work treatment of children.* Washington, DC: National Catholic School of Social Service, The Catholic University of America.

———. (1978b). After abuse: Child coping and clinical approaches. *Social Thought,* 4, 33–45.

———. (1979). Aggression and depression among abused and non-abused children in foster care. *Children and Youth Services Review,* 1, 279–292.

———. (1979). Child social functioning: A data base for planning, *School Social Work Quarterly,* 1, 229–240.

———. (1981). Child abuse and externalized aggression: Preventing a delinquent lifestyle. In R. Hunner and Y. Walker, eds. *Exploring the relationship between child abuse and delinquency.* Montclair, NJ: Allenheld-Osmun. pp. 43–51.

———, and Truitt, A. (1981). *Social work treatment of parents.* Washington, DC: National Catholic School of Social Service, The Catholic University of America and Child Welfare Training Program, Region III, Department of Health and Human Services.

———, and Verdieck, M. (1987). Psychosocial functioning of adolescents in foster care, *Social Casework,* 68, 214–222.

Tower, C. (1999). *Child abuse and neglect.* Boston: Allyn & Bacon.

Towle, C. (1945, reprint 1965). *Common human needs.* New York: National Association of Social Workers.

Trickett, P., and Putnam, F. (1993). Impact of child sexual abuse on females. *Psychological Science,* 4, 81–87.

Tripodi, T. (1995). *A primer on single subject design for clinical social workers.* Washington, DC: NASW.

Troy, M., and Sroufe, L. (1987). Victimization among preschoolers: Role of attachment relationship history. *Journal of the American Academy of Child and Adolescent Psychiatry,* 26, 166–172.

Urban, E. (1990). The eye of the beholder: Work with a ten-year-old. *Journal of Child Psychotherapy,* 16, 63–81.

Vaillant, G. (1992). *Ego mechanisms of defense.* Washington, DC: American Psychiatric Association.

Van Ijzendoorn, M. (1995). Adult attachment representations, parental responsiveness, and infant attachment: A meta-analysis on the predictive validity of the Adult Attachment Interview. *Psychological Bulletin,* 117, 387–403.

Wang, C., and Daro, D. (1997). *Current trends in child abuse reporting and fatalities: The results of the 1996 Annual Fifty-State Survey.* Chicago: National Committee to Prevent Child Abuse.

Wasserman, S., and Rosenfeld, A. (1986). Decision-making in child abuse and neglect. *Child Welfare,* 65, 515–529.

Webb, N. (1991). *Play therapy with children in crisis.* New York: Guilford.

———. (1994). *Helping bereaved children.* New York: Guilford.

———. (1996). *Social work practice with children.* New York: Guilford.

Weber, G., and Timberlake, E. (1986). Engaging parents at intake. *School Social Work Journal,* X, 54–63.

Weick, A., and Saleebey, D. (1998). Postmodern perspectives for social work. *Social Thought,* 18, 21–40.

Weisz, J., Weiss, B., and Donenberg, G. (1992). The lab versus the clinic: Effects of child and adolescent psychotherapy. *American Psychologist,* 47, 1578–1585.

Wellman, H. (1992). *The child's theory of mind.* Cambridge, MA: Massachusetts Institute of Technology.

Werner, E., and Smith, R. (1982). *Vulnerable but invincible: A longitudinal study of resilient children and youth.* New York: McGraw-Hill.

West, J. (1983). Play therapy with Rosy. *British Journal of Social Work,* 13, 645–661.

White, R. (1966). *Lives in progress.* New York: Holt, Rinehart, & Winston.

Whiting, B., and Whiting, J., with Longabaugh, R. (1975). *Children of six cultures: A psychocultural analysis.* Cambridge, MA: Harvard University.

Wilens, T., Biederman, J., and Baldessarini, R. (1992). Developmental changes in serum concentrations of desipramine and 2–hydroxydesipramine during treatment with desipramine. *Journal of the American Academy of Child and Adolescent Psychiatry,* 31, 691–698.

Winnicott, D. (1945). Primitive emotional development. In D. Winnicott. *Through paediatrics to psychoanalysis.* New York: Basic Books, 1975 reproduction. pp. 145–165.

———. (1949). Mind and its relation to psyche-soma. In D. Winnicott. *Through paediatrics to psychoanalysis.* New York: Basic Books, 1975 reproduction. pp. 243–254.

———. (1953). Transitional objects and transitional phenomena. *International Journal of Psychoanalysis.* 34, 89–97.

———. (1965a). *The maturational processes and the facilitating environment: Studies in the theory of emotional development.* Madison, CT: International Universities.

———. (1965b). *The family and individual development.* London: Tavistock.

———. (1971). *Playing and reality.* New York: Basic Books.

Woltmann, A. (1964). Mud and clay, their functions as developmental aids and as media of projection. In M. Haworth, ed. *Child psychotherapy: Practice and theory.* New York: Basic Books. pp. 349–363.

Yates, T. (1996). Theories of cognitive development. In M. Lewis, ed. *Child and adolescent psychiatry.* Baltimore, MD: Williams & Wilkins. pp. 134–155.

Yin, R. (1993). *Applications of case study research.* v. 34. Newbury Park, CA: Sage Publications.

Young, L. (1981). *Physical child neglect.* Chicago: National Committee for Prevention of Child Abuse.

Zeanah, C., Mammen, O., and Lieberman, A. (1993). In C. Zeanah, ed. *Handbook of infant mental health.* New York: Guilford. pp. 332–349.

———, and Emde, R. (1994). Attachment disorders in infancy. In M. Rutter, E. Taylor, and L. Hersov, eds. *Child and adolescent psychiatry: Modern approaches.* Oxford, England: Blackwell. pp. 490–504.

———. (1996). Beyond insecurity: A reconceptualization of attachment disorders of infancy. *Journal of Consulting and Clinical Psychology,* 64, 42–52.

Zelman, A. (1996). *Early intervention for high-risk children.* New Jersey: Jason Aronson.

INDEX